VSAM

The Macmillan Database/Data Communications Series

Shaku Atre, Consulting Editor

Available
Cave/Maymon *Software Lifecycle Management*
Fadok *Effective Design of CODASYL Data Base*
Ranade/Ranade *VSAM: Concepts, Programming, and Design*
Singer *Written Communication for MIS/DP Professionals*

In Press
Ha *Digital Satellite Communications*
St. Amand *A Guide to Packet-Switched, Value-Added Networks*
Towner *The ADS/OnLine Cookbook*

Forthcoming
Brown/Geelen *Data Modeling in a Business Environment*
Bubley *Data Communications Systems*
Callender *An Introduction to PSL/PSA*
Cohen *A Guide to DBMs for Microcomputers*
Crout *Designing Better Systems for Endusers*
Fields *The DP/User Interface Conflict*
Johnson *Implementing the Information Center Concept; A Strategic View*
Myer *Global Communications: A Computer-Based Message System Approach*
Potter *Local Area Networks: Applications and Design*
Wipfler *CICS Application Development and Programming*

VSAM Concepts, Programming, and Design

Jay Ranade
Assistant Vice President
Merrill Lynch, Pierce, Fenner & Smith Inc.

Hirday Ranade
Senior Systems Analyst
American International Group

Macmillan Publishing Company
NEW YORK
Collier Macmillan Publishers
LONDON

Macmillan Publishing Company
866 Third Avenue, New York, NY 10022

Collier Macmillan Canada, Inc.

Printed in the United States of America

printing number
2 3 4 5 6 7 8 9 10

Library of Congress Cataloging-in-Publication Data

Ranade, Jay.
VSAM, concepts, programming, and design.

(The Macmillan database/data communications series)
Includes index.
1. Virtual computer systems. 2. Virtual storage (Computer science) I. Ranade, Hirday. II. Title. III. Series.
QA76.9.V5R36 1985 005.4′3 85-18921
ISBN 0-02-948630-0

To our maternal grandparents

the late Mr. Karam Chand Joshi
and
the late Mrs. Lajwanti Joshi

CONTENTS

PREFACE

VSAM is IBM's most widely used access method for batch as well as on-line applications in **MVS, DOS/VSE, OS/VS1,** and **VM/CMS** systems. If you are working in any one of these environments, you probably require some knowledge of VSAM to perform your job. The information on VSAM in IBM's publications is scattered over more than two dozen manuals, constituting approximately 10,000 pages of reading material. They are designed primarily for reference purposes, not for learning VSAM in a systematic way. Although the significance of these manuals should not be underestimated, they are not meant for the first-time user. They provide excellent reference material once you *already* know the subject well. It has been the authors' experience that programmers learn VSAM in bits and pieces, gathering scattered information from their peers when they run into trouble. Even experienced CICS/VS programmers, data-base administrators, and systems designers lack the thorough knowledge of this access method so necessary to perform these functions well.

Who This Book Is For

This book can be used by batch application programmers, on-line application (CICS/VS) programmers, data-base designers and administrators, technical support personnel, and others who work in IBM mainframe environments. The *prerequisite* for reading this book is a basic understanding of Job Control Language (JCL) and the Cobol language. Even if you are not a Cobol programmer, you will learn about the architecture of VSAM and about Access Method Services, which are the subject matter of 13 out of a total of 17 chapters.

This book has been structured in such a way that it may be used as a *self-teaching guide* without additional guidance. It may also be used as a textbook for a 3- to 5-day in-house or public seminar on VSAM. The basic style is similar to that of a textbook, but once you have finished it, the numerous tables and practical examples may be used for guidelines and reference purposes.

This book was written primarily for **OS/MVS** (and **MVS/XA**) environments, but since most of the concepts are similar, **DOS/VS, DOS/VSE,** and **OS/VS1** users should also be able to benefit from it. A separate book for the **DOS/VSE** environment is forthcoming.

If You Already Know VSAM

Even if you already know VSAM, you may still learn a lot from reading this book. Its completeness and thorough coverage of the lesser used features (alternate indexes, ESDS, RRDS, ALTER, AIXBLD, etc.) will make it interesting reading for experienced users. Some of the techniques and style described here, which have evolved from the authors' extensive experience, should give you some insight into alternatives of which you were not aware.

A Word on the Style Used

The style of this book has purposely been kept simple. The authors understand the complexity of the data processing environment and the limited amount of time one can spare to learn new things in a constantly changing environment. The lack of availability of good books and good teachers make it even more difficult to keep up-to-date. The authors have worked hard to make reading the contents of this book a pleasant experience rather than a strenuous mental exercise. VSAM is presented with the ample use of diagrams, illustrations, and examples.

Why This Book Is Complete

Specific discussions of various IBM software are dependent on the different releases and versions, so an effort has been made to keep the material up-to-date with the latest releases. The book includes both VSAM as well as ICF catalogs. Wherever applicable, the DF/EF differences have been covered. A separate section is devoted to VSAM differences for the VS Cobol II compiler, the latest IBM Cobol compiler that supports MVS/XA architecture.

VSAM Knowledge Gap

This book is highly recommended for programmers and analysts who moved directly from batch programming to CICS/VS and/or IMS/DB/DC environments, thus missing the essential VSAM link. It will fill in the "VSAM knowledge gap." This will improve productivity considerably and will enhance the file design capabilities that are so vital to an overall view of the whole-system concept.

What Is Included

Part 1 discusses the basic concepts and the internal architecture of VSAM. It describes alternate indexes and VSAM and ICF catalogs. The use of examples and graphics help to make the text easier to understand.

Part 2 provides extensive coverage of Access Method Services and its utility program IDCAMS. Detailed examples include sample JCL and command formats. The major AMS commands are described in detail, as are some of the less frequently used, more advanced commands.

Part 3 is for Cobol programmers. It discusses coding techniques and syntax for all types of VSAM files.

Finally, Part 4 is a collection of miscellaneous subjects including performance and fine-tuning, JCL restrictions, the VS Cobol II compiler, ISAM, TSO/SPF, and other useful topics.

After reading this book you will not only know how to use VSAM but also how it works internally. The latter will help you become a better designer and trouble-shooter. Knowledge of all the different aspects and techniques will be helpful when managing a project involving VSAM files. You will be able to incorporate various techniques and styles to suit your own environment. The authors expect that, after finishing this book, you will be able to use VSAM with a high degree of confidence and competence.

Acknowledgments

First and foremost we are grateful to Carol Lehn for her enthusiasm and cooperation in evaluating this book. She spent countless hours reading, reviewing, and criticizing all the chapters. Her suggestions on style and language have made this book what it is today. We are indeed indebted to her, and it is a pleasure to acknowledge this debt.

We would like to express our appreciation to Shaku Atre for her suggestions and criticism. It is an honor to have had this book reviewed by a data processing professional of the highest caliber. Thanks are also due to George O. Wise who checked for technical completeness and accuracy. We are especially grateful to Peter J. DeFilippis for spending valuable time reading the manuscript and providing many useful suggestions. We gratefully acknowledge the assistance of our sister, Chander Ranade, and brother Jagmohan Ranade, who reviewed, proofread, and compared the different versions of the manuscript. Jack Schreibman deserves our thanks for his encouragement, and we are also indebted to Mr. Charles Vamossy, Vice President of Merrill Lynch and Company for granting permission to use his department's computer facilities to produce various listings. Our thanks are also due to Sunita Engira for all of her assistance.

We especially want to thank our senior editor, Jerry Papke, for his constant encouragement and Sheila Gillams, production editor at Macmillan, for taking care of so many minute details during production. We express our sincerest thanks to the hundreds of students at Women in Data Processing, Inc., New York, and other schools, who were patient enough to review and criticize the contents of this book when it was tested on them. Finally Jay would like to express his deepest gratitude to his lovely wife Ranjna for providing the necessary understanding when countless weekends were spent in writing this book rather than with her.

Jay Ranade
Hirday Ranade

VSAM

one

INTRODUCTION AND CONCEPTS

In Part 1 you will be introduced to some of the basic concepts of the Virtual Storage Access Method (VSAM). In order to fully understand its strengths and weaknesses, you must understand its internal architecture, which will be discussed in Chap. 2. Chapter 3 introduces a powerful feature of VSAM, its ability to have alternate indexes. Chapter 4 discusses VSAM and Integrated Catalog Facility (ICF) catalogs, which are the hub of the MVS cataloging structure. Although Part 1 only introduces the concepts, obtaining a knowledge of them is essential and will be rewarding in the long run. You will find VSAM to be an interesting, versatile, powerful software product. Just how powerful it is will become more evident as you become more familiar with it.

chapter 1

Basic Concepts of VSAM

1.1 INTRODUCTION

The data management services of an operating system help in the storing, cataloging, organizing, and retrieving of data on magnetic media. The different modes of such storage organizations in OS/VS are (1) physical sequential, (2) partitioned, (3) indexed sequential, and (4) direct. Different access methods are used in the storage and retrieval of information from these storage organizations. Examples of such access methods are the Basic Sequential Access Method (BSAM), Queued Sequential Access Method (QSAM), Partitioned Access Method (PAM), Basic Direct Access Method (BDAM), and Queued Indexed Sequential Access Method (QISAM).

There are other highly evolved and sophisticated organizations which are managed by Access Method Services (AMS) of OS/VS and DOS/VS. The access method used to manipulate information in these organizations is called the *Virtual Storage Access Method* or, as it is most commonly known, VSAM.

VSAM is IBM's latest and most advanced access method. It makes efficient use of the virtual storage of OS/VS and DOS/VS, hence the name "Virtual Storage Access Method." In the initial releases, it appeared to be only a replacement for the Indexed Sequential Access Method, but as a result of continuing enhancements it has proven to be more than just an access method. The system catalog of the MVS operating system is a VSAM catalog (called the *master catalog*). VSAM catalogs support not only VSAM data sets, but also non-VSAM data sets and generation data groups. Paging data sets in the MVS system are also VSAM data sets. The Virtual Telecommunication Access Method (VTAM) uses some of the VSAM macros. If you have a thorough understanding of VSAM, you won't have to use sequential, indexed sequential, or direct files because the different organizations of VSAM data sets can serve as a superior replacement. VSAM is also used as an access method for database management systems such as IMS/VS, DL/I DOS/VS, and DB2. In a nutshell, it appears that IBM is totally committed to VSAM and that this software will be with us for a long time.

As you will see later, learning VSAM consists of the following: (1) how to use the Access Method Services utility called IDCAMS and (2) how to access and use VSAM data sets through a language like Cobol, PL/I, or assembler. However, this book will only discuss access through the Cobol language.

1.1.1 What Is VSAM?

VSAM is a high-performance access method used in OS/VS and DOS/VS operating systems. VSAM software resides in virtual storage along with the program that needs its services for the manipulation of data on a direct access storage device (DASD).

1.1.2 What Is Access Method Services?

Access Method Services is a service program that helps you to allocate, maintain, and delete catalogs and data sets. It currently consists of one utility program called IDCAMS. This utility program is used in a job step just like any other utility program of OS/VS (e.g., IEBGENER, IEHPROGM, or IEBPTPCH).

IDCAMS is a multipurpose utility that can be used for the following functions.

1. Allocating, maintaining, and deleting catalogs
2. Allocating, maintaining, and deleting VSAM data sets
3. Reorganizing and printing data sets
4. Cataloging non-VSAM data sets and generation data groups
5. Defining page space for the MVS operating system

The above list of the capabilities of IDCAMS is not exhaustive, and we will learn more about its capabilities as we go further.

The allocation and deletion of non-VSAM data sets is accomplished by the data management services of the operating system. In OS/VS, these functions are carried out through the DISPOSITION parameter of the DD statement in the job control language (JCL). This is not so for VSAM data sets, which must be preallocated by using IDCAMS before you can load or update them. Deletion is also effected with the IDCAMS utility and not with the DISPOSITION parameter of JCL.

In Part 2, you will learn Access Method Services (which basically involves learning the IDCAMS utility program) for an OS/VS environment. In Part 3, the methods of manipulating data in VSAM data sets with the Cobol language will be discussed.

Once again it must be stressed that learning the utility IDCAMS involves learning Access Method Services.

1.1.3 Advantages and Drawbacks Compared to Other Access Methods

VSAM is superior to other access methods in the following respects.

1. The retrieval of records is faster because of an efficiently organized index. The index is small because of a key compression algorithm used to store and retrieve its records.
2. Imbedded free space makes the insertion of records easy, and data sets therefore require less reorganization. However, when this feature is used, data sets require more disk space.
3. The deletion of records in VSAM, unlike that in ISAM, means that they are physically deleted, thus allowing the reclaiming of free space within the data set.
4. Records can be accessed randomly by key or by address and can also be accessed sequentially at the same time.
5. VSAM data sets can be shared concurrently by partitions, regions, address spaces, and systems. The type and level of sharing can be controlled through AMS and JCL.
6. In MVS, Access Method Services commands can be executed as time-sharing option (TSO) commands.
7. In Customer Information Control System (CICS), the VSAM pool of buffers, control blocks, and channel programs can be shared by many VSAM data sets.
8. JCL for VSAM data sets is much simpler than for other file structures.
9. VSAM provides data security through password protection of a data set at different levels such as read and update.
10. VSAM provides the ability to physically distribute data sets over various volumes based on key ranges.
11. VSAM catalogs and data sets are portable between operating systems (OS/VS to DOS/VS and vice versa).
12. VSAM data sets are device-independent.

The above advantages will become apparent as we go into further detail. It is worthwhile repeating that, if you get to know VSAM thoroughly, you probably won't have to use any other access method.

Some of the major drawbacks of VSAM are as follows:

1. To take advantage of the partial self-reorganization capabilities of VSAM data sets, free space must deliberately be left. This results in increased disk space requirements. However, free space is left only for data sets requiring record adds, deletes, and changes. For data sets that are used for read-only purposes, no free space is required.
2. Except for read-only data sets, the integrity of VSAM data sets in cross-system and cross-region sharing must be controlled by the user. Data integrity must be a prime consideration in the initial design of applications that will be shared across systems or regions.

1.1.4 Operating Systems Supporting VSAM

IBM provides three major operating systems for its mainframes. VSAM is supported by all three. However, there are significant differences in their implementation of VSAM.

1. DOS/VS: VSAM is supported on DOS/VS and DOS/VS(E) systems. VSE/VSAM is much more powerful than its DOS/VS versions and has simplified JCL statements.
2. OS/VS: VSAM is supported on OS/VS1 and OS/VS2 operating systems. An enhanced version of VSAM, called Data Facility/Extended Functions (DF/EF), is now being used at many MVS installations. This book gives it due coverage.
3. VM/370: In a VM environment, CMS/VSAM support is based on DOS/VSAM.

1.2 THREE TYPES OF VSAM DATA SETS

VSAM data sets may have one of three possible types of organization. They are *key sequenced data set* (KSDS), *entry-sequenced data set* (ESDS), and *relative record data set* (RRDS). Functionally, they can not only replace indexed sequential, physical sequential, and direct files, but they also provide more advanced and powerful features not available with the other access methods. Many people consider VSAM a logical replacement of ISAM. It is true that one of the three types of VSAM data sets (KSDS) seems to fulfill the same functional requirements as ISAM, but that is not the extent of VSAM's capabilities.

1.2.1 Key-Sequenced Data Set

As the name implies, a key-sequenced data set has a data set organization in which records are sequenced on a key field. Knowing the value of a key field, you can randomly access the logical record. A KSDS consists of

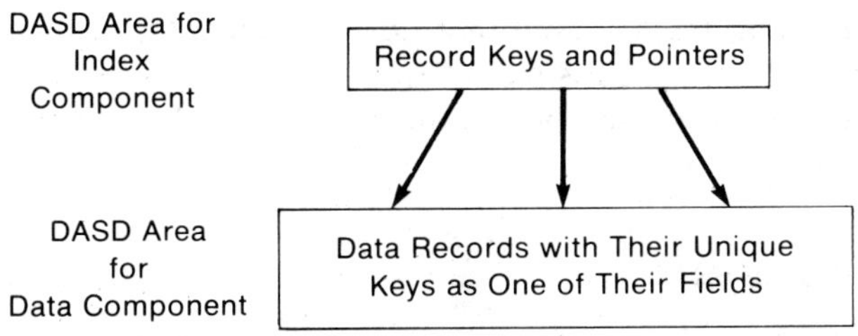

Figure 1.1 Symbolic representation of a KSDS file. The index component has the keys and pointers to the data component which contains the data records and their respective embedded keys.

two physical components on the DASD. The first one, called the *data component,* contains the records that hold the user data, including the key field. The second component is called the *index component* and contains the key fields and pointers to the location of the record (or records) to which that key field belongs (Fig. 1.1).

Usually the key field is small when compared to the whole record. Therefore, the index component is a small, compact entity. It is analogous to the index of a book. It is short and can be searched quickly to find the physical location (in this case the page number) of a particular topic. The index and data components of a KSDS organized file are jointly called a *base cluster.*

In a KSDS, records are stored in ascending collating sequence of the *prime key* field. Records can be retrieved and inserted, both randomly and sequentially. Free space for additional records is provided by the initial allocation of a KSDS. This space is allocated at regular intervals and is left free at the time of the initial loading of the data set. To some extent, depending on the circumstances, this helps to keep the data component in physical sequence in spite of many subsequent random insertions. But, as a result of excessive random insertions and deletions, they eventually become physically out of sequence, although they are still in logical sequence when accessed through the index of the cluster. Keeping records in physical sequence permits more efficient sequential retrieval of records. Therefore, key-sequenced data sets require occasional reorganization to put the records back into physical key sequence, although they always remain in logical key sequence. Unlike ISAM, VSAM data sets do not have an overflow component. Records can be updated in place. Also, records can be physically deleted, thus freeing space to be reused for other insertions. Records in a KSDS may be of variable length.

Remember that the key field of a KSDS *must* be unique and that, while updating a KSDS record, its key field cannot be modified. Examples of unique key fields are Social Security Number or Employee-Number in a payroll system, Part-Number in an inventory control system, and Invoice Number in an accounts payable system.

Records of a KSDS can be accessed in a key sequence other than that of the prime key field. Such a key is called an *alternate key* and need not be unique. An example of a nonunique alternate key is Employee-Name in a payroll system.

1.2.2 Entry-Sequenced Data Set

As the name suggests, the records in an ESDS are sequenced in the order in which they are entered in the data set. An ESDS is analogous to a physical sequential file. As in a physical sequential file, new insertions in an ESDS are always added to the end of the data set (Fig. 1.2).

An ESDS has greater update and access flexibility than a physical sequential data set. Records in an ESDS can be updated in place, although you cannot change the record length. Records can be accessed randomly as well as sequentially. They cannot, however, be physically deleted.

Since records in an ESDS are not sequenced on any key field, there is no prime key index component. However, as in a KSDS, you may have an alternate index on an ESDS. Imbedded free space is not allocated at the time of allocation of an ESDS, since records are not added to the middle of the file. Records in an ESDS may be of variable length.

An ESDS is usually used as an audit-trail file or a data-entry file for on-line systems. Such a file can later be used for report generation or batch update of master files. Since CICS does not support physical sequential data sets in a simple manner, any such design requirements can be satisfied by an ESDS. ESDS's are heavily used in IMS/VS and DL/1 DOS/VS data bases.

1.2.3 Relative Record Data Set

In an RRDS, the entire data set is a string of fixed-length slots. Each slot occupies a fixed position and is identified by its position relative to the first slot of the data set. The relative position of each slot is called the *rela-*

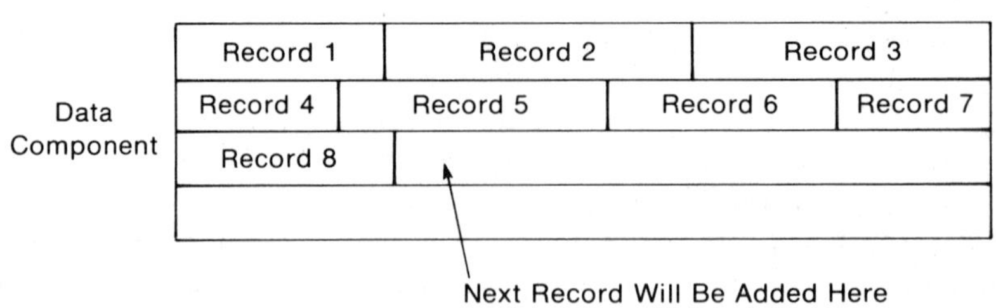

Figure 1.2 Symbolic representation of an ESDS. New records are always added at the end of the data set. An ESDS has only a data component.

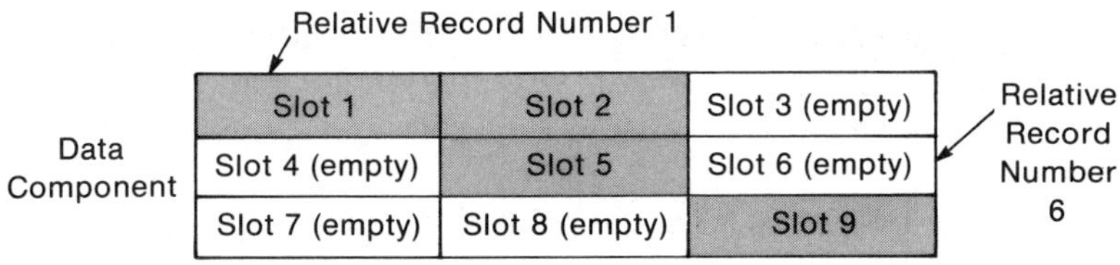

Figure 1.3 Symbolic representation of an RRDS with fixed-length slots for records. Shaded slots have records, while slots with no records are marked "Empty." An RRDS has only a data component.

tive record number (RRN) (Fig. 1.3). An RRN is an integer that identifies the position of the slot, not the value of a particular field within the slot. Each slot of an RRDS may or may not contain a record.

Records in an RRDS may be inserted, retrieved, updated, and deleted both sequentially and randomly. The most difficult problem in using an RRDS is designing an algorithm that can develop a relationship between a record and an RRN slot where the record can be stored. When such a relationship can be established, an RRDS is the fastest random access method. For example, if a company has 100,000 employees whose employee numbers range from 1 to 100,000, each employee number can be used as an RRN.

Records in an RRDS are always fixed in length. Like an ESDS, an RRDS has only a data component. Alternate indexes are not supported on RRDS files. When a record is deleted from a particular slot, the slot remains in the same physical location although a record does not exist in that slot anymore. RRDS is ill-suited for applications that leave a high percentage of empty slots in the data set. Relative record data sets are maintenance-free and do not require any reorganization.

Unlike direct files and OS relative record files, an RRDS is not dependent on the physical device on which it is stored. This makes it device-independent.

1.3 COMPARISON WITH OTHER ACCESS METHODS

In many ways, VSAM data set types are superior to conventional data set organizations. The following comparisons will help in deciding where VSAM data set organizations will be a better choice.

1.3.1 KSDS vs Indexed Sequential

Indexed sequential organization is the predecessor of the KSDS. Both have keyed access, and both have almost equal performance after the initial loading of the data sets. But as more and more insertions are made, access becomes slow in ISAM. Because of partial self-reorganization, random access in a KSDS still gives a comparable performance. For random insertions, records are reorganized in virtual storage and are written back to a KSDS. In the case of indexed sequential files, they are written into overflow areas.

In a KSDS, a deleted record is physically deleted and its space is reclaimed as free space. This free space can be used to insert another record at a later time. In ISAM, deleted records stay in the file and are physically deleted only during reorganization. Therefore, as a result of its self-reorganization capabilities, KSDS may require less frequent reorganization than indexed sequential files, depending on the kind of operations being performed.

With indexed sequential files, in order to process the records both randomly and sequentially in the same program, you must have two data control blocks (DCB's). In Cobol, this means having two SELECT statements, one with ACCESS IS SEQUENTIAL and the other with ACCESS IS RANDOM. In the case of KSDS, the same thing can be done with one SELECT statement that specifies ACCESS IS DYNAMIC.

While an alternate index may be developed for a KSDS, it is not possible to do so for an indexed sequential data set. An alternate index gives you an inverted view of the data set, as if its records were sequenced on the alternate index key field itself.

Of course a price must be paid for having all the powerful features of a KSDS—more disk space is required. Additional space is needed for the free space intentionally left in the data set to provide for random updates. But, the requirement for additional storage space is more than offset by the efficient storage and retrieval provided by the use of a KSDS. Figure 1.4 lists these comparisons in tabular form.

1.3.2 ESDS vs Physical Sequential

Records in both these file organizations are stored in the order in which they are written. The records are contiguous to each other and can be fixed or variable in length. Once the records are written, they can be replaced in a physical sequential (PS) data set. In an ESDS too, they can be read, modified, and written back in the same space, provided that the record length has not been changed. Additionally, up to 253 alternate indexes can be supported on an ESDS. Physical sequential data sets are supported in CICS/VS for a limited purpose, while an ESDS is extensively supported in such an environment. Figure 1.5 lists these and other comparisons in tabular form.

1.3.3 RRDS vs Direct Organization

Direct organization data sets [accessible through the Direct Access Method (DAM) or BDAM] are complex and mostly device-dependent.

Characteristic	Indexed sequential/ISAM	KSDS/VSAM
Data set allocation	JCL parameters with DISPOSITION of NEW	Access Method Services (IDCAMS utility)
Data set deletion	DISPOSITION parameter of DD statement	Access Method Services (IDCAMS utility)
Alternate index support	No	Yes
Deleting records	Records logically deleted	Records physically deleted and space reclaimed
Reorganization of data set	Needed more often	Needed less often
Disk space requirement	Less	Greater because of imbedded free space and control fields in the data set
Concurrent sequential and random access	Not supported unless two data control blocks are created	Supported in one access control block (ACB)

Figure 1.4 Comparison of an indexed sequential data set and a KSDS.

Characteristic	Physical sequential	ESDS
Data set allocation	JCL parameters with DISPOSITION of NEW	Access Method Services (IDCAMS utility)
Data set deletion	JCL parameters with DISPOSITION of DELETE	Access Method Services (IDCAMS utility)
Can records be altered and replaced?	Yes (but record length cannot be changed)	Yes (but record length cannot be changed)
Alternate index supported	No	Yes (up to 253)
Random access of records	No	Yes (through relative byte address)
Supported in CICS	Yes*	Yes
Non-DASD (magnetic tape) support	Yes	No

*Physical sequential data sets are supported in CICS for a different purpose (e.g., CICS journals and extra partition transient data queues are, in fact, PS in structure).

Figure 1.5 Comparison of a physical sequential (PS) data set and an ESDS.

Characteristic	Direct organization file	RRDS
Allocation and deletion of data set	DISPOSITION parameter of JCL	Access Method Services (IDCAMS)
Device-independent	Mostly no	Yes
Variable-length records supported	Yes	No

Figure 1.6 Comparison of a direct organization file and an RRDS.

Relative record data sets are easy to understand, access, and maintain, and they are device-independent. One of the major drawbacks of an RRDS is that variable-length records are not supported. However, both data set types are supported in CICS. Figure 1.6 illustrates these comparisons.

chapter 2

Internal Organization

In physical sequential data sets, records are clustered in blocks, and a block can have one or more records. VSAM does not use blocks in the traditional sense. It has another, similar, unit of record storage called a *control interval* (CI).[1] A control interval may contain one or more records. If a record's length is greater than the length of the CI, it may span multiple control intervals. A control interval is the smallest unit of information storage transferred between the buffers and a direct access storage device.

Control intervals are part of a larger storage structure called a *control area* (CA). A control area may consist of many control intervals. An example of a control area is one cylinder of an IBM 3380 disk pack. Leaving free control intervals within a control area allows for partial self-reorganization of a KSDS that may require it as a result of random record additions.

Figure 2.1 illustrates the data component of a typical KSDS with fixed-length records.

The storage organization of a VSAM data set can be summarized as follows:

- A *data set* consists of a *data component* and, additionally, an *index component* for a KSDS.

[1]Internally a control interval consists of one or more physical blocks, but it is transparent to applications.

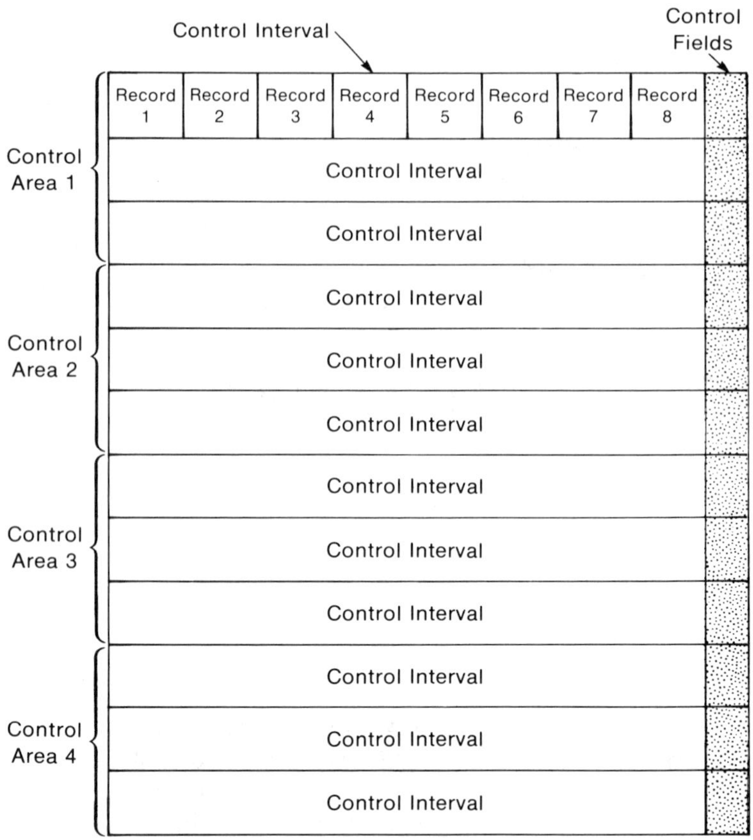

Figure 2.1 Storage organization of the data component of a VSAM data set. The data set in this example has four control areas. Each control area has three control intervals. Each control interval has a maximum of eight fixed-length records. Control fields, as shown, are used by VSAM for internal housekeeping information for the control interval.

- Each component consists of one or more *control areas.*
- A control area may consist of many *control intervals.*
- A control interval may have one or more *records.*
- For a data component, a record may span *many* control intervals.

2.1 CONTROL INTERVAL, CIDF, AND RDF

We have already seen that a control interval is the smallest unit of information transferred between I/O buffers and the data set. A control interval may vary in size from 512 to 32,768 bytes (with some restrictions).

There are four components within the physical space owned by a control interval (Fig. 2.2). The first component consists of the records

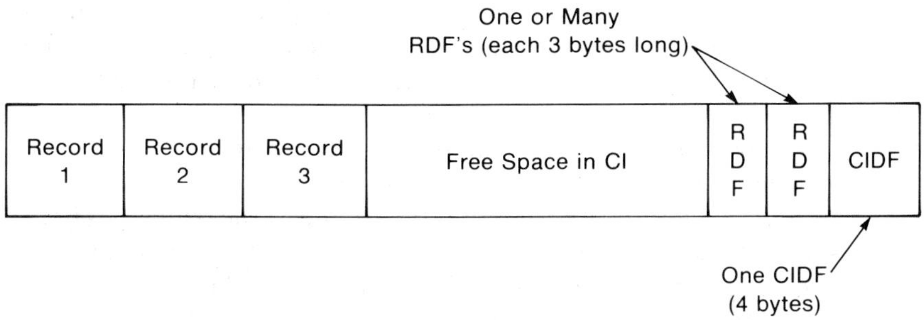

Figure 2.2 Data records, free space, RDF's, and a CIDF within a control interval.

that your program is interested in processing. The second one is called the *control interval description field* (CIDF). It is 4 bytes long and occupies the last 4 bytes of the CI. It contains information about the free space available within the CI. The third component is called the *record description field* (RDF). It is 3 bytes long. A CI may have one or more RDF's, depending on whether it contains fixed-length, variable-length, or spanned records. RDF's are contained in a space just before the CIDF. The fourth component is free space. Free space is used for in-place reorganization of a KSDS in case of record additions, updates, or deletions within a CI.

It may be noted that the CIDF, RDF's, and free space are transparent to the application program. A Cobol application program processes records without a knowledge of the CIDF, RDF's, or free space. Figure 2.2 gives a pictorial view of these four components.

2.2 CONTROL AREA

A control area consists of a minimum of two control intervals. The minimum size of a control area is one track, while the maximum size is one cylinder.

When defining and initially loading a KSDS, not only may free space be intentionally left within CI's, but also free CI's may be left within a control area.

2.3 FREE SPACE

Free space may be left within a KSDS at the time of initial loading of the data set. This free space falls into three categories:

1. Free space left within a CI that is used when new records are added to the CI
2. Free CI's left within a CA that are used when new record additions cannot fit into a particular CI because there is not enough free space in the CI where the record being inserted belongs

3. Free CA's left within a data set that are utilized after all the free CI's in a particular CA have been used up and none of the CI's in that CA can accommodate the record being inserted.

It is the free space management within a KSDS that makes it superior to ISAM for the random accessing of records.

Free space is left in an ESDS only at the end of the data set. There is no imbedded free space within a CI or CA in this type of file organization, because records can be added only to the end of the data set.

An RRDS has neither imbedded free space, as in a KSDS, nor free space at the end of the data set, as in an ESDS. The whole data set consists of fixed-length slots. These slots may have records or they may be empty, and empty slots may be used to add new records.

Free space management is handled by the VSAM software and is transparent to the application program.

2.4 SPANNED RECORDS

When a record size is larger than the CI size (minus 7 bytes), the record must be contained in more than one CI. Such a record is called a *spanned record.* A spanned record may span two or more control intervals, however, it may not span more than one control area. Free space left by a spanned record in a control interval cannot be used by any other record (Fig. 2.3).

2.5 REUSABLE FILES

In OS/VS, temporary files can be allocated, used, and deleted within a job or a job step. Such files have data set names prefixed with "&&". There are no such files in VSAM, however, a VSAM file can be allocated with a reusable attribute. In OS/VS, although such a file is preallocated by Access Method Services, anytime you open such a file as output (as

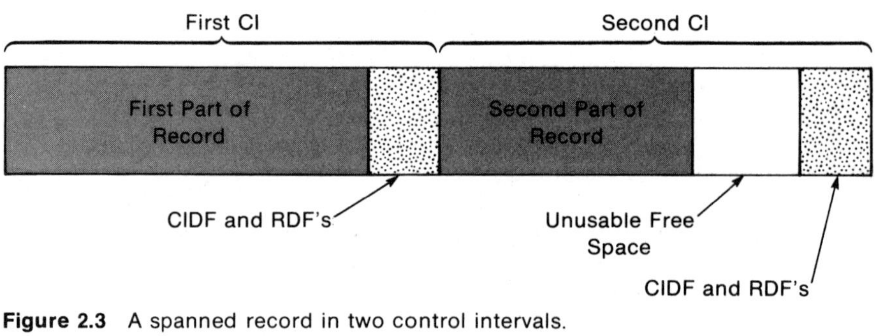

Figure 2.3 A spanned record in two control intervals.

OPEN OUTPUT in Cobol), all preexisting records are logically deleted. This type of file must be deleted through Access Method Services when it is no longer needed.

2.6 CONTROL INTERVAL AND CONTROL AREA SPLITS

Now that you understand the concepts of CI, CA, and free space, let's see how record insertions can cause CI splits and CA splits. *Such splits occur only in a KSDS*. In an ESDS no insertions are made between records, and in an RRDS the slots are preallocated. Thus, neither ESDS's nor RRDS's are subject to CI or CA splits.

Let's assume that our KSDS has the structure outlined in Fig. 2.4 to begin with. For simplicity, let's also suppose that it consists of only fixed-length records. In our example, we are representing a record by its key value. As you can see, there are many records scattered over different control intervals in the data set.

All the horizontal boxes in Fig. 2.4 represent control intervals of the index component, while the vertical boxes represent control intervals within their respective control areas of the data component. The index component is further subdivided into two parts called the *index set* and the *sequence set*. These are different hierarchical levels of the index component. The sequence set is always at the lowermost level of the index and points to control intervals in the data component. The index set may consist of one to three levels, each pointing to the next lower level until you reach the sequence set. The number of index set levels depends on the size of the file and other factors such as CI size, CA size, and free space allocation.

In our example, the data component consists of three control areas. Each CA contains three control intervals, each of which can contain five fixed-length records. The shaded portions within the CI contain CIDF's and RDF's. *There is always only one sequence set record for each data CA*. As shown in Fig. 2.4, three sequence set records point to their respective CA's. The different entries in a sequence set record point to the highest key record in the data component control intervals. Further up in the index hierarchy, different entries in the index set record point to the highest key record in the sequence set control interval.

To understand these concepts better, let's return to Fig. 2.4 and retrieve a record with key 52. VSAM begins its search at the highest level of the index component. It starts the comparison from the left and compares the key (52) with the leftmost key value in the index set (25). If the key is not less than or equal to the value in the index set, it makes a comparison with the next key. In the example, our key (52) is less than 95, so VSAM follows the pointer for key 95 and reaches the appropriate sequence set record (the sequence set in the middle in our example).

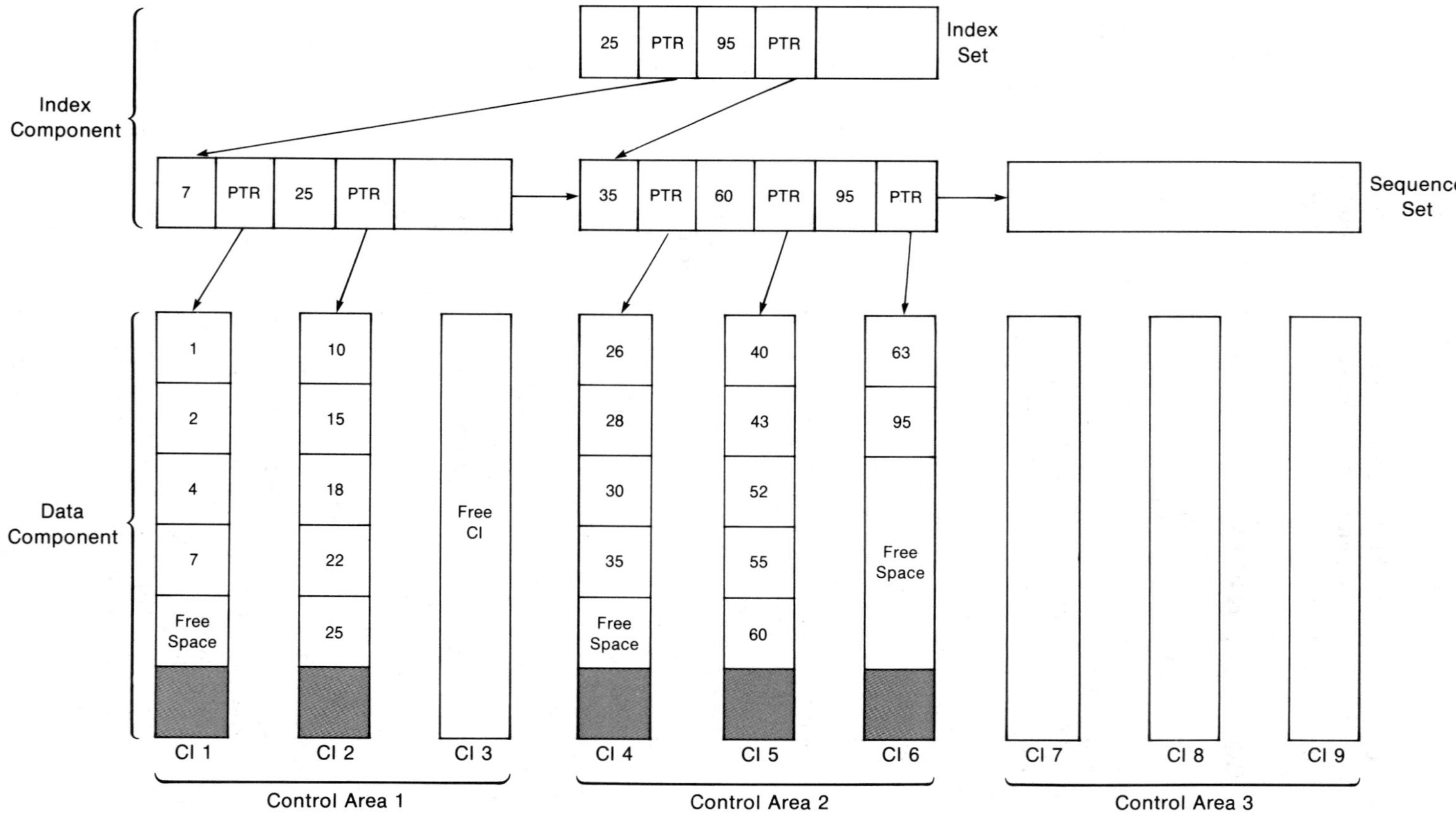

Figure 2.4 Composition of a typical key-sequenced data set.

VSAM makes the same kind of comparisons within the sequence set until it finds the field in the sequence set that is greater than or equal to the key we are looking for. In this case, the sequence set field that fulfills the search is 60. VSAM follows the pointer (PTR) downward to find the control interval of the data component (the middle CI of control area 2) where the record with key 52 can be found. Once it locates the record within the CI, the record is moved to your program.

You may have noticed that there is free space within the control intervals. This may be used for the addition of records. There is also a free CI in control area 1. This will be used if a CI split takes place in that CA. The last control area (CA 3) is completely empty. It will be used if any of the other CA's are split.

Now, let's say that we want to add a record whose key is 5. VSAM will try to find the appropriate data component CI where this record should be placed. Traversing the hierarchical chain, as we did in the last example, we find that a record with a key value of 5 logically belongs to the first control interval of the first control area. VSAM will determine that there is enough free space to insert another record. Record 5 logically fits between records 4 and 7, so VSAM will push record 7 down to free space and place record 5 in the location previously occupied by record 7. It will then update the RDF and CIDF information to indicate that there is no free space left in that CI.

Control Interval Split Let's find out how a CI split occurs. Suppose you want to add a record whose key is 20 to the data set illustrated in Fig. 2.4. VSAM determines that this record belongs to CI 2 between records 18 and 22. It also determines that there is not enough free space in that CI in which to place the record. So VSAM locates a free CI (CI 3) within that control area. It then moves approximately half of the records from CI 2 to the newly acquired free CI. This process is called a CI split. VSAM also updates the information in sequence set 1 to reflect the new key-pointer pairs that point to the highest key in each control interval. After records 5 and 20 are added, the KSDS looks like Fig. 2.5. Note that sequence set 1 has been updated so that it points to the highest key record in the control intervals after the split.

Control Area Split We will start with the data set configuration in Fig. 2.5. Suppose you want to add a record with key 45. It should logically be inserted between record keys 43 and 52 in CI 5. However, there is not enough free space in that CI. VSAM tries to find a free CI within CA 2. Since there is no free CI in that CA as well, VSAM performs a *CA split*. First, it acquires a free CA within the data set. If there is no free CA available, VSAM makes a secondary space allocation of the data set, if possible, and acquires a CA from the secondary allocation. If you did not

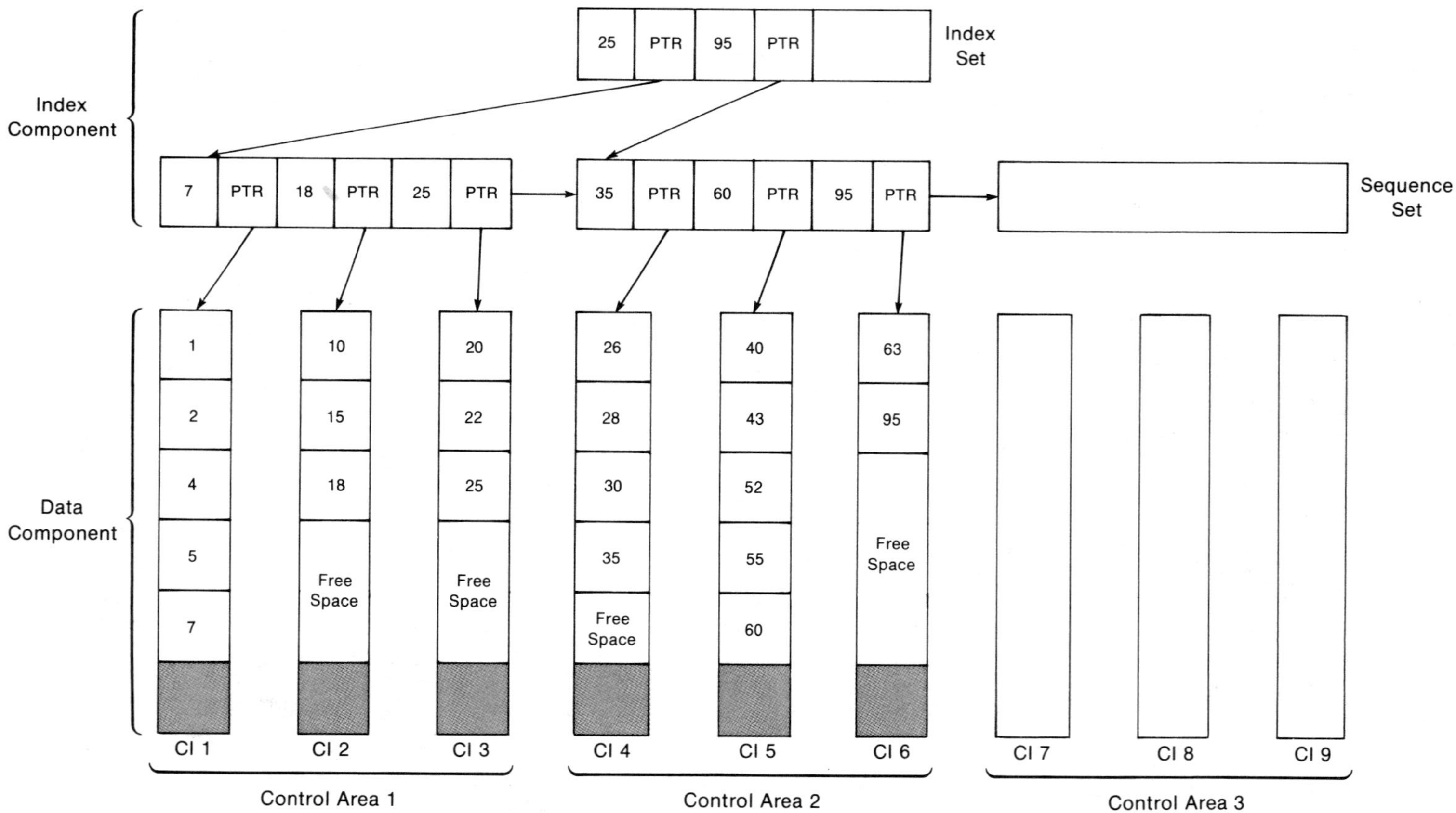

Figure 2.5 Records with keys 5 and 20 were added to the data set illustrated in Fig. 2.4. This diagram illustrates what the data set looks like after a control interval split.

provide for secondary allocation when you defined your VSAM data set, or if a secondary allocation cannot be made because there is insufficient space, VSAM will inform your program of the problem. In such a case, you will probably want to terminate your processing and then reorganize the data set and/or provide more space. In our hypothetical example, however, a free CA is available. VSAM acquires it and moves approximately half of the records from the problem CA to the acquired CA, spreading them evenly over the new CI's. It also updates information at the different levels of the index component, so that each key-pointer pair points to the highest key element at the next lower level in the hierarchy. The process just described is called a CA Split. Figure 2.6 illustrates the data set after a CA split caused by the addition of a record with key 45. Note the increased amount of free space available in the control intervals of control areas 2 and 3 as a result of CA split.

CI and CA splits cause a lot of I/O's on a data set while the splits are taking place. Since I/O operations take a proportionately large amount of time, the processing time of a batch program may be increased. For on-line systems (e.g., CICS), response time may increase during split activity. Particularly for on-line systems, efforts should be made to minimize CI and CA splits so that response time remains acceptable. We will see later how this can be accomplished.

2.7 RELATIVE BYTE ADDRESS

Some of the non-VSAM file structures used in OS and DOS are device-dependent. With such file organizations, you have to know the cylinder, track, and block within the track where your logical record exists. Direct access files are classic examples of such organizations. When moving from one direct access storage device (say an IBM 3350) to another (an IBM 3380), you have to change the programs to make more efficient utilization of disk space. However, all VSAM data set organizations are device-independent. The transfer of data sets from one DASD to another is relatively simple. All addresses in VSAM data sets are counted relative to the beginning of the data set. To understand this concept better, let's imagine that all the control intervals of a VSAM data set are strung together one after the other with no gaps in between (Fig. 2.7).

Let's also say that each control interval is 4096 bytes long. The first byte of the first CI will have a relative byte address (RBA) of 0. Counting ahead, the first byte of the second CI will have an RBA of 4096, and so on. It should be remembered that the relative byte address is always relative to the beginning of the data set, which is byte 0, not byte 1. By programming an access routine in assembler language, you can access a record randomly in a KSDS or an ESDS if you know the RBA of the record. In such a case, you will bypass the index component of the KSDS and the access will be faster. However, RBA access to KSDS should be

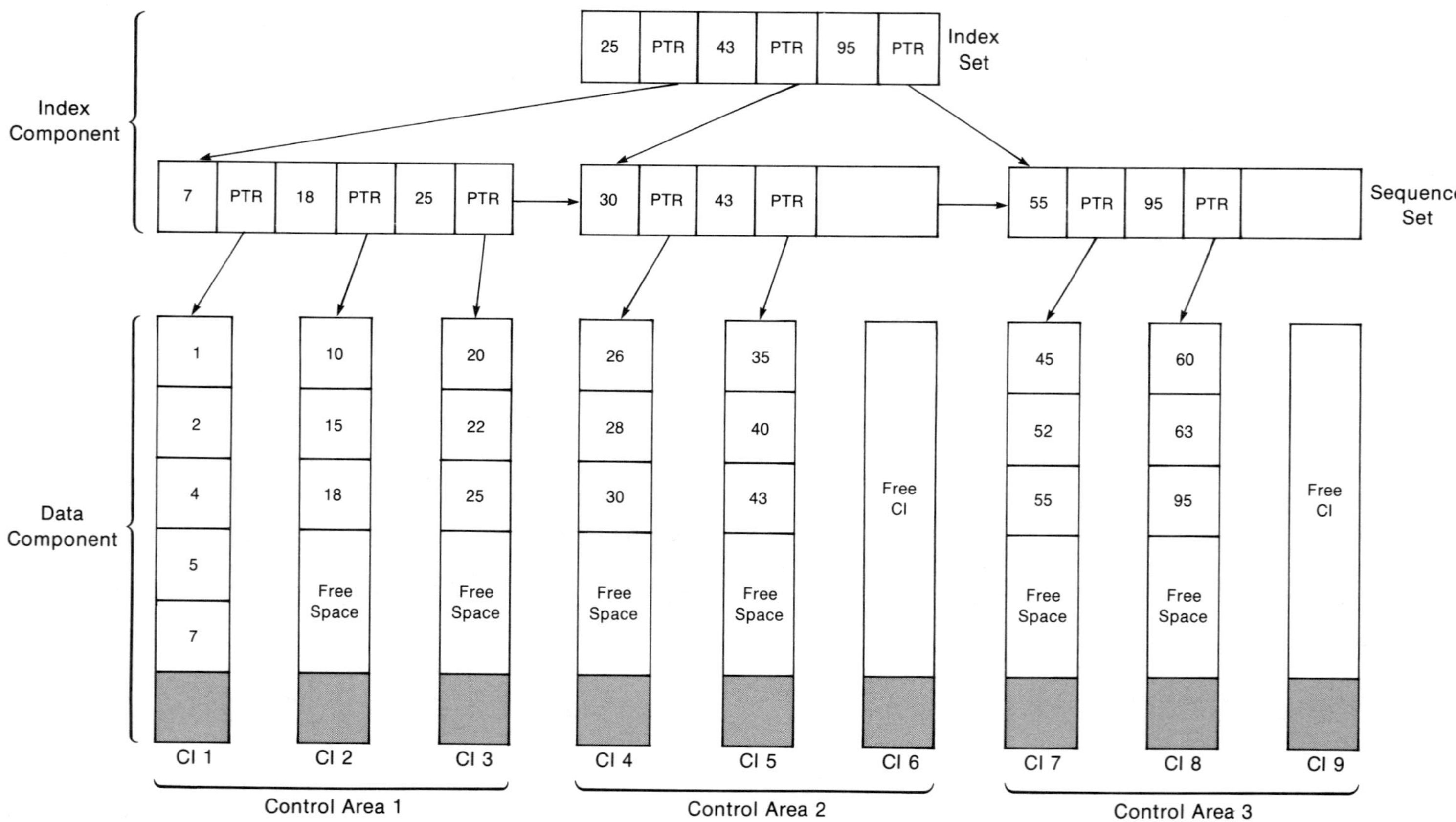

Figure 2.6 A record with key 45 was added to the data set illustrated in Fig. 2.5. This diagram shows the data set after a control area split.

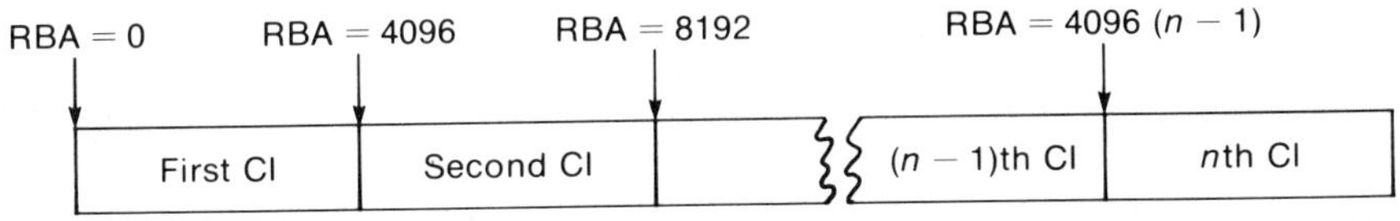

Figure 2.7 Each CI in this figure is 4096 bytes long. Note that the beginning RBA of the first CI is 0 and not 1.

avoided, since record additions/updates and CI/CA splits can invalidate a previously valid RBA address.

2.8 ACCESS OF VSAM RECORDS

Depending on the data set type (KSDS, ESDS, or RRDS), records in a VSAM data set can be accessed in different ways. Each has its own limitations and performance characteristics.

2.8.1 Keyed Access

Keyed access involves searching the index component and then the corresponding control interval in the data component. Hence, keyed access takes longer than access by RBA or RRN. However, because of its ease of use, it is the most popular access technique.

It can be accomplished in the following ways.

- In a KSDS, if you know the prime key or one of the alternate keys
- In an ESDS, if you know the alternate key. It bears repeating that present-day Cobol compilers do not support alternate index clusters for ESDS's in a batch environment. However, CICS permits the access of records in an ESDS through alternate keys (or paths).

2.8.2 Access by Relative Byte Address

Records in KSDS's and ESDS's can be accessed through an RBA. This is quicker than keyed access because it does not involve an index search. Since the RBA of records can be changed in a KSDS—because of reorganization, CI splits, or CA splits—caution must be observed when designing such a system. The RBA in an ESDS never changes, therefore a need for caution does not exist.

Access through an RBA has limited application in real life because it is difficult to establish a relationship between an RBA and a key field. Present-day Cobol compilers do not support RBA access in a batch environment, although it is supported by CICS.

2.8.3 Access by Relative Record Number

Records in an RRDS cannot be accessed by RBA; they can only be accessed by relative record number. Access by RRN is very fast because no index search is involved and the RRN is always fixed for each slot. Records in an RRDS cannot be accessed by key because there is no concept of key or alternate key in an RRDS.

2.9 COMPARISON OF KSDS, ESDS, AND RRDS

The three data set types of VSAM each have unique attributes of their own. Based on their various features, they are used for different application purposes. The following comparisons will help you to understand them better.

Access through key fields: Only KSDS has a prime key field. A unique alternate key can be used as a kind of key field on an ESDS, but Cobol compilers do not support this feature in a batch environment. An RRDS does not have a key, but if a relationship can be established between a unique field of an RRDS record and the relative record number, the functions of a KSDS can be simulated.

Alternate keys: KSDS's and ESDS's can have up to 253 unique and nonunique alternate keys. RRDS's do not support alternate keys.

Space requirements: Space is best utilized in an ESDS because there is no free space. A KSDS needs additional space for the index component, and free space is purposely left within the data component for random insertions.

Deletions: Records can be physically deleted from KSDS and RRDS files. An ESDS does not have this feature.

CI and CA splits: Only KSDS files are subject to CI and CA splits. ESDS's and RRDS's do not have them.

Reorganization: KSDS files may need frequent reorganization because records become physically out of sequence as a result of CI and CA splits. It should be noted that records remain in logical sequence in a KSDS despite the fact that they may be physically out of sequence. ESDS's and RRDS's do not require reorganization.

Access through RBA: Records in KSDS's and ESDS's may be accessed through the relative byte address in a CICS environment. However, relative byte address access is not supported for any of the VSAM data set types in a batch Cobol environment.

Record length: Records can be of variable length in KSDS's and ESDS's. RRDS's may have only fixed-length records.

Spanned records: A KSDS or an ESDS may have spanned records; an RRDS cannot.

Application use: A KSDS should be used in applications that require access to records based on a particular key field such as Social Security Number, Part Number, or Employee-Number. An ESDS is usually used when records can be processed sequentially, as in an audit-trail for an on-line system. An RRDS is used if a relationship can be developed between a unique field of the record and a relative record number of the RRDS.

Thorough knowledge of the characteristics and limitations of the different data set organizations is required for optimum and efficient design of files for batch and on-line systems. Figure 2.8 provides a comparison of the different data set organizations in tabular form.

Characteristics	KSDS	ESDS	RRDS
Mode of record access	Key and/or RBA	RBA	RRN
Alternate index supported	Yes	Yes	No
Reorganization required	Yes	No	No
Variable-length records	Yes	Yes	No
Spanned records	Yes	Yes	No
Index component present	Yes	No	No
CI and CA splits upon updates	Yes	No	No
Record insertion to existing data set	Yes	Yes, at the end of data set	Yes, in empty slot
Record deletions possible	Yes	No	Yes
Record length may be changed during update	Yes	No	No
Sequential and random processing supported	Yes	Yes	Yes
Physical I/O's needed to randomly access a nonspanned record	Max. 4, min. 2	1	1
Sequence of records	Sequenced on key field	Order in which they were entered	RRN sequence

Figure 2.8 Comparison of the features of a KSDS, an ESDS, and an RRDS.

chapter 3

Alternate Index

To explain the concept of an alternate index (AIX), we will use a hypothetical KSDS/VSAM data set that contains fixed-length records of a personnel/payroll system. Among many fields within each record, three are Social Security Number (SSN), Employee-Number, and Employee-Name. Social Security Number is the prime key of the KSDS. Thus, if you know the SSN, you can access the record belonging to a particular employee. What happens if you don't know the key field? Suppose a different user group in our system wants to access the records knowing only the employee's number, and yet another wants to access the records with the employee's name. In the latter case, there could be many records in the data set having a particular employee's name, because more than one employee having the same name can work for a company.

If we were working with ISAM file organization, we would probably create a second data set whose key would be the employee's number. Of course, we would not be able to have a third data set with the employee's name as the key, because in ISAM the key of the record must be a unique field. Although we may have found a way of getting around the problem, this technique creates data redundancy. We will have to create more than one data set using ISAM, each having the same data in it but defined with different access keys. Such data redundancy not only creates the need for more disk space but also adds complexity to any file-update programs.

ISAM file-update programs, in such cases, have to make sure that redundant data in all the files is kept in synchronization at all times.

We can create redundant data files in VSAM too, but then we will have to cope with the same problems we would have had with ISAM. In VSAM, however, we have an easier, better, more sophisticated way of dealing with our problem. We are able to create an alternate index over the data set. An alternate index alleviates the problem of data redundancy and maintenance. We can build an alternate index over a KSDS and an ESDS, but *not* over an RRDS.

3.1 WHAT IS AN ALTERNATE INDEX?

We have already seen how record retrieval and insertion are accomplished in a base cluster of a KSDS. We also know that only if the record key (or RBA) is known can we randomly retrieve the data record. In the example above, what happens if it is necessary to retrieve a record by Employee-Number rather than Social Security Number?

Suppose we have a second KSDS and each record in this data set has only two useful fields. One of the fields is Employee-Number, and the other one is Social Security Number. Let's further suppose that the record key in our second data set is Employee-Number. We will have as many records in our second data set as we have in our base cluster, because for each record in the base cluster there is a record in the second KSDS.

Let's return to the problem of accessing a record in the base cluster using Employee-Number. This will be a two-step procedure:

> *Step 1:* The second data set is a KSDS. We will access the record in this data set whose key is Employee-Number. Once the record has been read into the I/O buffer (in the Cobol DATA DIVISION), you will have access to the Social Security Number, which is the other field in that record.
>
> *Step 2:* Read the employee record in the base cluster with the Social Security Number from step 1.

The second data set in the above example is called an *alternate index cluster,* and the Employee-Number is called an *alternate key.* Figure 3.1 is a pictorial representation of this base cluster, the alternate index, and their relationship.

You may wonder why we still have two data sets, thus keeping redundant information. The second data set (the alternate index cluster) is a small subset of the base cluster, has only two fields in it, and doesn't occupy much space on the disk. It is, nevertheless, a KSDS and has an index and a data component. As far as maintenance of data in the alternate index is concerned, VSAM does it for you. You don't have to worry

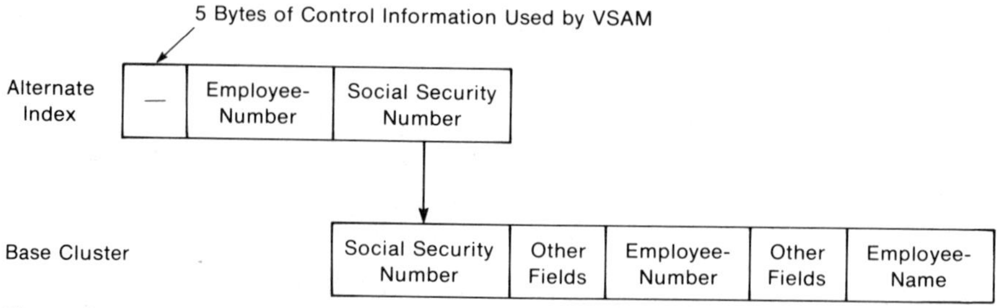

Figure 3.1 Employee-Number is the key field in the alternate index, while Social Security Number is the key field in the base cluster. The Social Security Number field in the alternate index record points to the record in the base cluster that has the same value in the prime key.

about writing programs to maintain the alternate index. However, when defining the alternate index (you will learn how to do this later), you have to tell Access Method Services that VSAM should do the necessary maintenance. After that, it is all transparent to you.

Referring to Fig. 3.1, you will notice that accessing a record in the base cluster through an alternate index involves reading two KSDS files, each having its own index and data component. Retrieval through alternate indexes takes about twice as long as if retrieval is effected through the prime key of the base cluster.

We can have up to 253 alternate index data sets per base cluster. Although this is a powerful feature of VSAM, it is not advisable to have more than 5 alternate indexes per base cluster because of the additional overhead generated during updates and retrievals.

3.2 ALTERNATE INDEX OVER A KSDS

We saw in the previous section how an alternate index functions when built over a KSDS. To gain a better understanding of alternate indexing, let's look at Fig. 3.2.

Five records are shown in our sample of a personnel/payroll system file, which is a KSDS. As you can see, the records are sequenced on the prime key, Social Security Number. The data set has two alternate keys, namely, Employee-Number and Employee-Name. Since there are two alternate keys, we must define two alternate index clusters for this data set. The first alternate index cluster will be based on Employee-Number, which is a unique alternate key itself (there is a one-to-one relationship between Social Security Number and Employee-Number). The second alternate index cluster will be based on Employee-Name, which is a nonunique alternate key (there can be many employees with the same name).

	Social Security Number		Employee-Number		Employee-Name
Record 1	111111111	—	10	—	RANADE
Record 2	222222222	—	63	—	TANAKA
Record 3	333333333	—	28	—	KRANTZ
Record 4	444444444	—	05	—	BUTLER
Record 5	555555555	—	52	—	RANADE
	Prime Key		Alternate Key 1		Alternate Key 2

Figure 3.2 Five records in the personnel/payroll file. Social Security Number is the prime key, Employee-Number is the first alternate key, and Employee-Name is the second alternate key. To keep things simple, the index component is not shown for this KSDS.

3.2.1 Unique Alternate Key

Figure 3.3 outlines how an alternate index cluster built using Employee-Number will look.

There are five records in the data set. The first 5 bytes of an alternate index record contain information which will not be of much concern to an application programmer, as it is used only by VSAM software. The next 2 bytes in our example are the Employee-Number, and the following 9 bytes are the Social Security Number. Note that Employee-Number is the alternate key in the base cluster, while it acts like the prime key if you consider the alternate index cluster a KSDS.

Let's say that you want to retrieve a record from the personnel/payroll file with Employee-Number 28. You first read the record in the alternate index cluster, shown in Fig. 3.3, whose key is 28. This will give you record 3. You now know that the SSN associated with Employee-Number 28 is 333333333. Since the SSN is the prime key in the base cluster (Fig. 3.2), you can randomly retrieve the record whose key is 333333333. This will give you the record you wanted, record 3 in the base cluster. Note that if you want to add a sixth record to the personnel/payroll file, a new entry will automatically be added to the alternate index cluster by the VSAM software, provided it has been defined with the proper parameter to do so. Chapter 9 will discuss such parameters in detail.

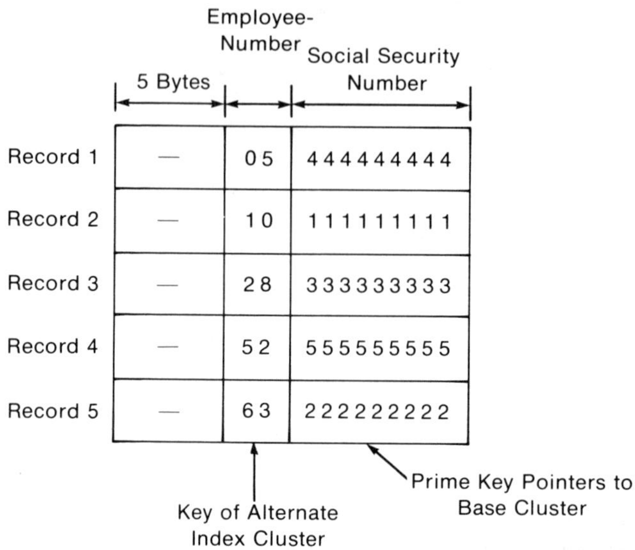

Figure 3.3 Records of this alternate index cluster are sequenced on Employee-Number. The first 5 bytes are used by VSAM for internal housekeeping functions.

3.2.2 Nonunique Alternate Key

Now we will see how the alternate index cluster, using Employee-Name as its alternate key, is structured. The base cluster over which the alternate index will be created is the same as the one shown in Fig. 3.2. Records in the Employee-Name alternate index cluster will be as shown in Fig. 3.4.

Instead of five, we have only four records in the alternate index cluster. This is because only one record was created in the alternate index for the two records in the personnel/payroll file having the Employee-Name "RANADE". Employee-Name, being a nonunique alternate key, can have many records with the same name but, of course, different SSN's. Note that the employee name "RANADE" points to two different SSN's in the alternate index cluster. For this reason, records in a nonunique alternate index cluster are always *variable-length records*. The 5-byte prefix in the alternate index record again is used by VSAM only for internal housekeeping. Remember that the records in the alternate index cluster are sequenced on Employee-Name.

As a typical example, suppose we want to access records with the employee name "RANADE". We read the Employee-Name alternate index cluster randomly with a key value of "RANADE" and get record 3. Record 3 has two SSN's associated with it. We can then read each of the records (one at a time) in the personnel/payroll file whose keys are 111111111 and 555555555 and do the necessary processing. Again, it

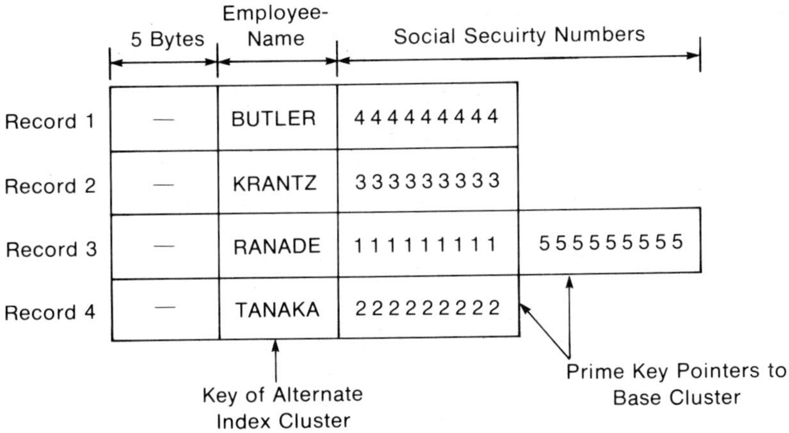

Figure 3.4 Records of this alternate index are sequenced on Employee-Name. The first 5 bytes are used by VSAM for internal housekeeping functions.

should be noted that, if you add a new record to the personnel/payroll file, VSAM will automatically update the Employee-Name alternate index cluster, depending on the options specified at the time of its allocation.

When you define an alternate index cluster with the help of Access Method Services, you have a choice of defining it as having a unique or a nonunique key.

3.3 ALTERNATE INDEX ON ESDS

The records of an ESDS do not have a prime key. However, you can define one or more alternate key clusters over them. A unique key alternate index on an ESDS simulates the same functions as that of a KSDS. To understand this concept, we will use the same personnel/payroll file as in our KSDS base cluster example. Since no prime key is involved, records in an ESDS are identified by their relative byte address. We already know, from a previous section, that an RBA is a conceptual address relative to the beginning of the data set. An RBA does not occupy any space in the record; it is just an address. So, we will identify each record in the ESDS base cluster by its RBA. Figure 3.5 shows the same five records as in our KSDS example, but now they are in an ESDS.

Note that the first record is identified by an RBA of 0, the second by an RBA of 50, and so on. The length of the records is 50 bytes each. This file was created sequentially (ESDS files are always created sequentially), with the records in no particular sequence. It is only a coincidence that the records are in an ascending sequence of Social Security Number. As a matter of fact, they don't have to be, because ESDS records are written in

	Social Security Number	Other Fields	Employee-Number	Other Fields	Employee-Name
RBA = 0	111111111	—	10	—	RANADE
RBA = 50	222222222	—	63	—	TANAKA
RBA = 100	333333333	—	28	—	KRANTZ
RBA = 150	444444444	—	05	—	BUTLER
RBA = 200	555555555	—	52	—	RANADE
	↑ Alternate Key 1		↑ Alternate Key 2		↑ Alternate Key 3

Figure 3.5 Records in an ESDS base cluster. The record length is 50 bytes. There are three alternate keys—Social Security Number, Employee-Number, and Employee-Name. Each record can be identified with its relative byte address.

entry sequence order, not by key field (there is no prime key field in an ESDS).

Since our application needs to access the records in the personnel/payroll file randomly, by three different fields, we will have three alternate index clusters defined over the base cluster.

3.3.1 Unique Key Alternate Index

The first alternate index is on Social Security Number, which is a unique field. The alternate index cluster will look like the one in Fig. 3.6.

The alternate index cluster is always a KSDS, regardless of whether it belongs to a KSDS or an ESDS base cluster. Suppose we want to access a record with the SSN 333333333. First, we read the alternate index cluster randomly with the key value 333333333. It will give us record 3. We now know that the corresponding base cluster record of the ESDS has an RBA of 0100. Since we know the RBA in the ESDS, we can retrieve the record which exists at the RBA of 100. In reality, the RBA is stored in the alternate index cluster of an ESDS as a 4-byte binary field. It is shown in display format in Fig. 3.6 only to make it more readable.

The alternate index cluster in the second alternate key, Employee-Number will be as shown in Fig. 3.7.

Since you already know about the different components and the

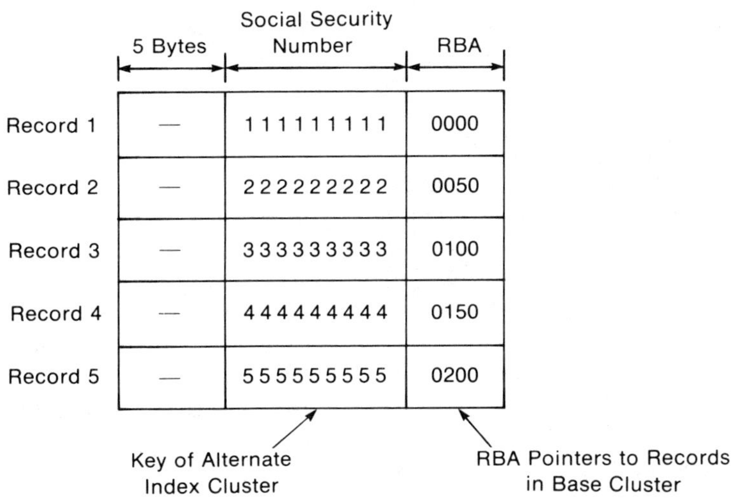

Figure 3.6 Alternate index using Social Security Number as its alternate key. The data set is sequenced on Social Security Number and the RBA's of the corresponding records of the base cluster are stored in the alternate index records themselves. The RBA is a 4-byte binary field. The first 5 bytes are used by VSAM for internal housekeeping functions.

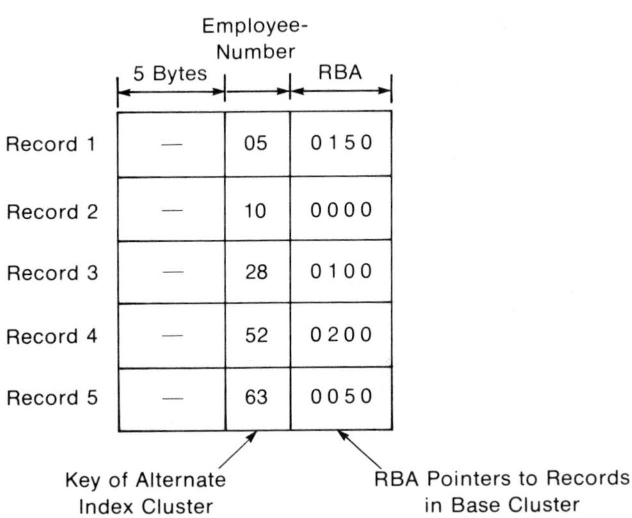

Figure 3.7 Alternate index cluster using Employee-Number as its alternate key. This data set is sequenced on Employee-Number. The RBA's of the corresponding records of the base cluster are stored in the alternate index records themselves. The RBA is a 4-byte binary field. The first 5 bytes in each record are used by VSAM for internal housekeeping functions.

structure of an alternate index, we will not go into the details of record retrievals using Employee-Number as an alternate key.

3.3.2 Nonunique Key Alternate Index

The third alternate index uses Employee-Name as the alternate key. We already know that the name is a nonunique key field, so, we can expect to see more than one base cluster record RBA associated with a particular name. The alternate index cluster will be as shown in Fig. 3.8.

Note that the Employee-Name "RANADE" has more than one 4-byte RBA field. Each RBA field gives the address of the corresponding record in the base cluster. Record retrieval is accomplished as discussed in the previous examples. However, if more than one RBA is associated with a name, we may retrieve more than one record in the ESDS base cluster one after another.

Cobol Compiler/CICS Support Present-day Cobol compilers do not support access of an ESDS through alternate indexes in a batch environment. However, such access is supported in CICS.

3.4 PATH AND ALTERNATE INDEX

So far, we have seen that accessing a record in the base cluster of a KSDS or an ESDS can be done in one of two ways: (1) The record can be accessed directly from the base cluster if you know the prime key value in a

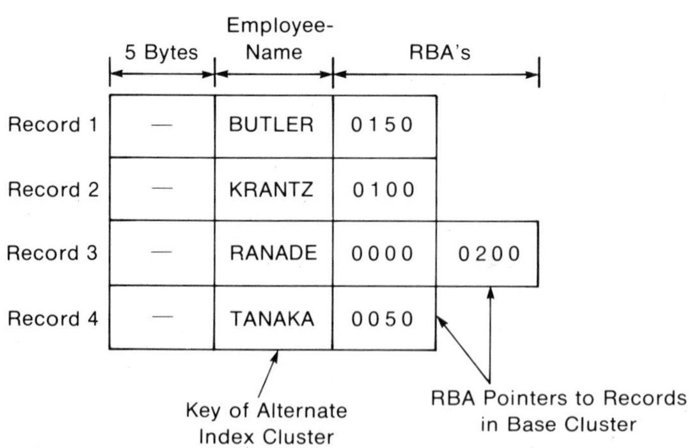

Figure 3.8 Alternate index cluster using Employee-Name as the alternate key. This data set is sequenced on Employee-Name. The RBA's of the corresponding records of the base cluster are stored in the alternate index records themselves. The RBA is a 4-byte binary field. The first 5 bytes are used by VSAM for internal housekeeping functions.

KSDS, or with the RBA in an ESDS, or (2) the record can be accessed through an alternate index if you know the alternate key value. In the second case, as we have already seen in many examples, two distinct elements are involved: first, finding the record in the alternate index cluster through the alternate key, thus getting the corresponding prime key or RBA; second, accessing the record in the base cluster once you know the prime key or RBA.

It is clear that accessing a record through an alternate key involves more coding on the part of the programmer. It also requires two I/O areas defined in the DATA DIVISION of a Cobol program, one for accessing the alternate index cluster record and the other for accessing base cluster records. The way to avoid all this extra coding is to use Access Method Services to define a PATH between the base cluster and the associated alternate index cluster. A *PATH* is an entry in the VSAM catalog that establishes a logical link between an alternate index cluster and a base cluster. It doesn't contain any records; it justs establishes a relationship. PATH has a name like any other OS/VS data set name.

Opening a data set with the path name opens both the alternate index and its associated base cluster. Then, if you want to read a record in the base cluster by using an alternate key value, it *automatically* finds the corresponding prime key in the alternate index. You do not have to do any coding in your program to search for the corresponding prime key—VSAM does all the searching for you. It will appear to your program as if the base cluster is sequenced on many different alternate key fields. You can have as many different paths as you have alternate index clusters. Figure 3.9 is a pictorial representation of the path concept.

Things will become more clear when we reach the programming part of this book. For the moment, suffice it to say that a path helps you avoid extra coding and programming complexity when dealing with alternate indexes.

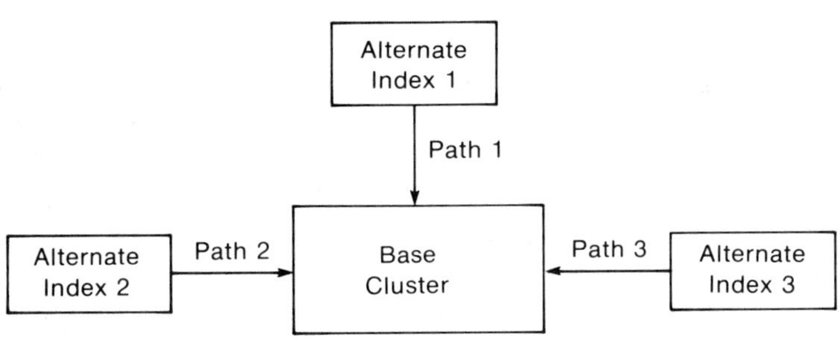

Figure 3.9 This diagram shows three different alternate index clusters defined over a base cluster. Between each alternate index and base cluster pair there is a path which links them logically.

chapter 4

VSAM/ICF Catalog Management and Security

4.1 VSAM CATALOGS AND VSAM SPACE

All VSAM data sets must be cataloged. It is not possible to have an uncataloged VSAM data set. In an OS/VS2 MVS operating system, you have a choice of two catalogs for cataloging VSAM data sets. The first one is the VSAM catalog which, at the time of the writing of this book, is being used at most MVS installations. The second one is the ICF (Integrated Catalog Facility) catalog, which is an enhancement of the VSAM catalog structure.

An improved catalog structure like the ICF catalog was badly needed because of some of the inherent limitations of traditional VSAM catalogs. A disk volume can be owned by one, and only one, VSAM catalog, while there is no such limitation for ICF catalogs. ICF catalogs also have enhanced recovery facilities for data sets and the catalogs themselves. To use the ICF catalog, you must have Data Facility/Extended Function software installed on the system.

The difference between VSAM and ICF catalogs should not be of much concern to an application programmer. Whenever necessary, both types of catalogs have been given due coverage. With the passage of time and with user acceptance, ICF catalogs might gain popularity at MVS installations. We will learn both of them in this chapter.

4.1.1 Master Catalog and User Catalogs

There is always one *master catalog* in a system. VSAM and non-VSAM data sets can be cataloged in the VSAM master catalog. Since the master catalog is an important element in the proper running of a computer, few entries should be cataloged in it. Another entity, called a *user catalog,* is cataloged in a master catalog. Usually, user data sets are cataloged in VSAM user catalogs. There can be many user catalogs in a system, and this helps maintain the proper running of the system if a user catalog becomes damaged. However, if the master catalog is damaged, things become more difficult.

Defining the master and user catalogs is the responsibility and function of a systems programmer. The usual practice is to give a user catalog to each application development group at an installation. This way, if one user catalog becomes inaccessible, the rest of the systems can still run smoothly. Figure 4.1 shows the relationships of different catalogs and data sets in an OS/VS2 MVS environment.

We can see that the primary catalog of an MVS system is the VSAM master catalog or the ICF master catalog. It further points to non-VSAM data sets, OS catalogs (called control volumes or CVOL's in MVS), VSAM data sets, VSAM user catalogs, and ICF user catalogs. Remember that, while VSAM data sets can be cataloged only in VSAM catalogs or ICF catalogs (master or user), non-VSAM data sets can be cataloged in OS catalogs (CVOL's), VSAM catalogs (master or user), or ICF catalogs (master or user). Figure 4.2 summarizes the different cataloging combinations.

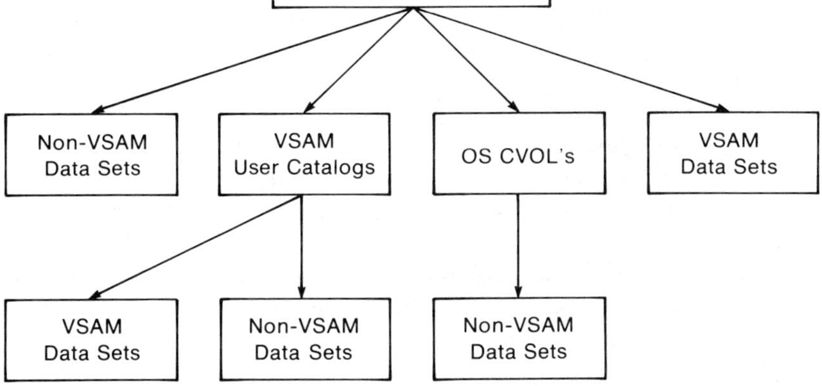

Figure 4.1 The hierarchy of VSAM catalogs, CVOL's, VSAM data sets, and non-VSAM data sets in an MVS system.

Catalog structure	Can a VSAM data set be cataloged?	Can a non-VSAM data set be cataloged?
VSAM master catalog	Yes	Yes
VSAM user catalog	Yes	Yes
ICF master catalog	Yes	Yes
ICF user catalog	Yes	Yes
OS catalog (CVOL)	No	Yes

Figure 4.2 Different combinations in which VSAM and non-VSAM data sets can be cataloged in VSAM and ICF catalogs.

It goes without saying that the master catalog in a system is a critical element. It should be kept as small as possible. It is preferable that all VSAM and non-VSAM data sets be cataloged in user catalogs and CVOL's (OS catalogs), respectively. Only user catalogs, CVOL's (MVS only), and critical system files should be cataloged in the master catalog. If the master catalog is small and manageable, a quick and easy system recovery will be assured if it becomes damaged.

4.1.2 VSAM SPACE: UNIQUE vs SUBALLOCATED Data Sets

VSAM data sets can be defined only within VSAM space. VSAM space can be allocated on one disk or on a multiple number of disks. Non-VSAM data sets may be defined only in non-VSAM space. Either part of a disk can be defined as VSAM space, or the whole disk can have nothing but VSAM space. In the latter case, non-VSAM data sets cannot exist on the disk.

Management of data sets within VSAM space is accomplished by VSAM management modules and not by the operating system. VSAM catalogs, which are also VSAM objects, exist within VSAM space only.

In summary, a VSAM space can have two types of objects within it: (1) VSAM catalogs and (2) VSAM data sets including base clusters and alternate indexes.

SUBALLOCATED Data Sets VSAM space on a disk can be defined by using Access Method Services. Normally, it is done by a systems programmer. Such VSAM space can have one or more VSAM data sets in it (Fig. 4.3).

Since such data sets are suballocated within a preallocated VSAM space, they are called *SUBALLOCATED VSAM data sets*. If you are using ICF catalogs (MVS only), there is *no* concept of suballocated data sets.

UNIQUE Data Sets It is also possible that VSAM space does not preexist on a pack, or that we do not want to define data sets in preexist-

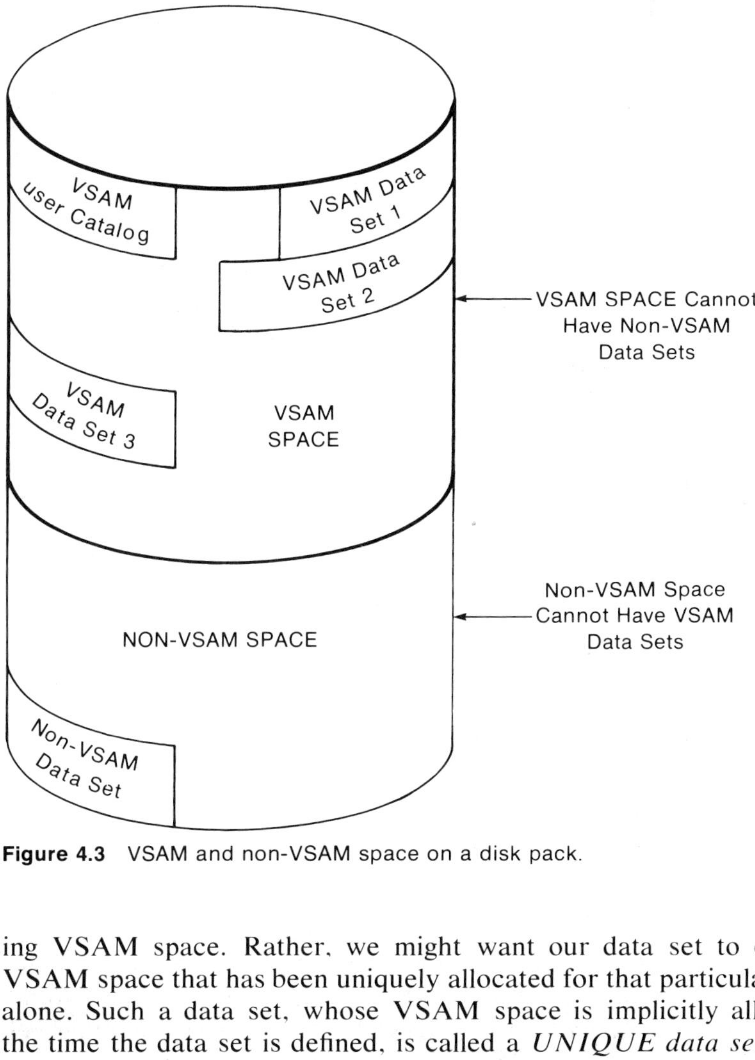

Figure 4.3 VSAM and non-VSAM space on a disk pack.

ing VSAM space. Rather, we might want our data set to exist in a VSAM space that has been uniquely allocated for that particular data set alone. Such a data set, whose VSAM space is implicitly allocated at the time the data set is defined, is called a *UNIQUE data set*. We will see later that each data set type (suballocated vs unique) has its own advantages and disadvantages. Figure 4.4 shows data sets in their own unique VSAM space and in a preexisting VSAM space. However, both unique and suballocated VSAM data sets are cataloged in a VSAM catalog. If you are using ICF catalogs (MVS only), *all data sets are UNIQUE* in their own VSAM space.

4.1.3 Volume Ownership by a VSAM Catalog

A disk volume on which a VSAM catalog (user or master) has been defined is said to be *owned* by that catalog—no other VSAM catalog may be defined on that volume. All VSAM data sets allocated on that volume

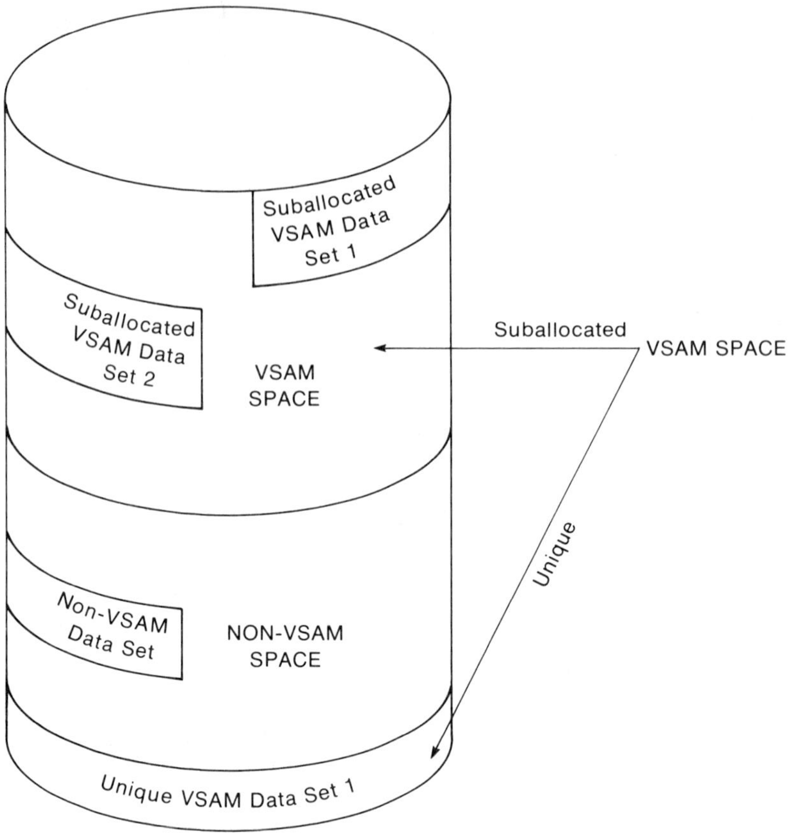

Figure 4.4 VSAM data sets in suballocated and unique VSAM space.

must be cataloged in that catalog alone. A VSAM catalog can also own more than one disk volume. But VSAM data sets allocated on the other volumes can be cataloged only in the catalog which owns the other volumes. Figure 4.5 shows a VSAM user catalog that owns additional disk volumes apart from the one on which it itself exists.

A *candidate volume,* as shown, is a volume that is owned by the catalog but does not have any VSAM space on it yet. This volume may have VSAM space created on it in the future and thus provide additional room for VSAM data sets.

Non-VSAM data sets allocated on *any* volume can be cataloged in *any* VSAM catalog—not only in the one that owns the volumes.

If your installation uses ICF catalogs (MVS only), there is no concept of volume ownership. As we will see later in this chapter, a volume can be owned by up to 36 ICF catalogs.

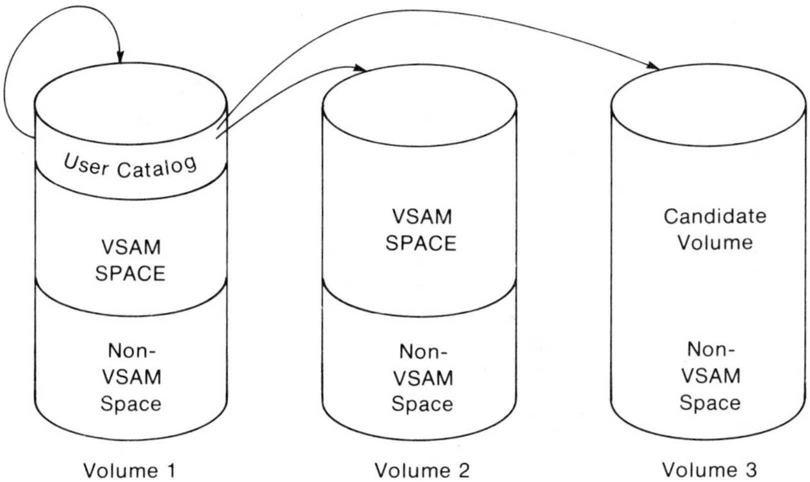

Figure 4.5 A user catalog owning multiple disk volumes.

4.1.4 Non-VSAM Data Sets in a VSAM Catalog

In OS/VS2 MVS, non-VSAM data sets can be cataloged in a CVOL catalog, a VSAM catalog (user or master), or an ICF catalog (user or master). Non-VSAM data sets are cataloged in VSAM catalogs through Access Method Services. If there are multiple user catalogs in a system, you can catalog your non-VSAM data sets in any one of them. Tape data sets can also be cataloged in a VSAM catalog.

4.1.5 Generation Data Groups in a VSAM Catalog (MVS Only)

In OS/VS2 MVS, a generation data group (GDG) index may be defined in a VSAM catalog (user of master) using Access Method Services. If you are using ICF catalogs, you can define it in an ICF catalog too.

4.2 DATA INTEGRITY AND DATA PROTECTION

Data integrity includes the protection of data from accidental destruction due to system or software errors. There is no element of malevolence in such cases. Data protection pertains to theft or intentional destruction of data by unauthorized use.

4.2.1 Data Integrity in VSAM

When a VSAM set can be accessed only by a single program or address space, it exists in a *nonshared environment*. VSAM ensures complete data integrity in this type of environment. Even if an update is being made in a CICS system, VSAM locks the control interval for the duration of the update so that it cannot be updated concurrently by someone else. In a shared environment, where a data set is shared concurrently by many address spaces (MVS) or systems (multiple CPU's) data integrity is ensured only if you use ENQ, DEQ, RESERVE, and RELEASE macros. The Cobol language has no provision for using these macros.

VSAM data set share characteristics are defined at the time of data set allocation through Access Method Services. They can, of course, be modified later if there is a need. The shared environment can be set at *read-only* or at *update* levels.

4.2.2 Password Protection

A VSAM data set can have different levels of protection for the various functions to be performed on it. Up to four passwords may be defined at the time of data set allocation. Their meanings are as follows.

1. Read password: This password allows you to read the data set, but you cannot perform any updates.
2. Update password: You may perform reads, updates, changes, and deletions on a data set.
3. Control password: In addition to giving you the capabilities of the read and update passwords, this password lets you access the control intervals themselves. You cannot access a CI as data in a Cobol program, so you will probably not need this password. Through the Cobol language, you can access only logical records.
4. Master password: The master password lets you do anything, including deleting the data set itself.

Passwords are defined for a particular data set when it is being allocated using Access Method Services. Subsequently, they are supplied in the program to enable it to open the data sets correctly. For example, if your program supplies the read password, you cannot open a data set as input/output. If you do not password-protect your data sets, any program can access them for any purpose. Note that, if the VSAM catalog is not password-protected, data set passwords will be ignored.

Different passwords can be defined for different components. That is, the cluster, data component, and index component can each have its own set of four passwords. Similarly, an alternate index and a path can have different passwords for their protection.

In MVS only, Resource Access Control Facility (RACF) protection may be used as an alternative to or in addition to VSAM passwords. VSAM also provides you with additional protection through User Security Verification Routines (USVR). Such routines are assigned to a data set at the time of its allocation.

4.3 SHARING VSAM DATA SETS

VSAM data sets can be shared by different jobs at different levels. Cross-region sharing occurs when many programs running in different regions/address spaces of the *same CPU* access a data set. Cross-system sharing takes place when different programs running under *different CPU's* access a data set on a shared disk pack. Such share options are defined at the time of allocation of the data set through Access Method Services. Once defined, the options can be changed later to suit the changed environment.

Share options will be discussed in more detail in the Access Method Services portion of this book.

4.4 DATA FACILITY/EXTENDED FUNCTION (MVS ONLY)

Data Facility/Extended Function is the latest IBM program product in the field of VSAM data sets and catalog management. It provides more control over shared data, along with some improved features of data set processing. The DF/EF program must be installed if you want to use ICF catalogs.

4.4.1 ICF Catalogs (MVS Only)

DF/EF provides the means to build a new catalog structure called an Integrated Catalog Facility catalog. It has advantages over VSAM catalogs in performance, space utilization, the volume ownership concept, and catalog recovery. ICF catalogs can replace both VSAM catalogs and OS control volumes. Both VSAM and non-VSAM data sets can be cataloged in an ICF catalog.

As discussed previously, there is no concept of volume ownership in an ICF catalog. In MVS systems, the VSAM master catalog can be replaced by an ICF master catalog. OS control volumes, VSAM catalogs, and ICF catalogs can all coexist in a system. An ICF catalog can own data sets on more than one volume. While each volume can be owned by up to 36 ICF catalogs, each data set on the volume may belong to *only one* catalog. All VSAM data sets cataloged in an ICF catalog have their own unique VSAM space.

two

ACCESS METHOD SERVICES

In Part 1 you learned all the background information you need to understand the concepts of VSAM. In Part 2 you will learn to actually use the powerful utility product of VSAM, Access Method Services.

Chapter 6 shows you how to allocate a KSDS, an ESDS, and an RRDS. Chapter 7 describes the facilities for loading records into them. Chapter 8 discusses the printing of their contents, and Chap. 9 gives the details of allocating and building alternate indexes. In Chap. 10 we will discuss the commands used to purge, modify, and close an improperly closed VSAM file. Chapter 11 will give you the techniques for looking at the characteristics of an existing data set and interpreting their meaning. In Chap. 12, you will be introduced to some of the advanced commands usually used by the systems programmer. At the end of this part, you will be able to use AMS not only for VSAM data sets but also for non-VSAM files. AMS is a powerful program. The more you use it, the more uses you find for it.

chapter 5

AMS Commands: An Overview

Access Method Services (AMS) is used to perform various functions on VSAM data sets and catalogs. AMS has a utility program, called IDCAMS, that is invoked in a standard operating system job step just like any other OS utility. The functions of AMS are performed by using the different functional commands of IDCAMS.

5.1 INTRODUCTION TO AMS COMMANDS

There are 28 AMS functional commands. Some of them are used by systems programmers, others by application programmers. Before we go into the nuts and bolts of these commands in the subsequent chapters, let's get an overview of the ones most commonly used.

5.1.1 DEFINE USERCATALOG/MASTERCATALOG

This command is used by systems programmers to allocate an ICF or a VSAM catalog. A user catalog is always allocated, whether or not you mention USERCATALOG or MASTERCATALOG. However, a catalog is established as a master catalog only at the time of the initial program load (IPL) of the system. A user catalog must be successfully allocated and cataloged in the master catalog before you can define VSAM data sets in it.

5.1.2 DEFINE SPACE

This command allocates VSAM space on a particular disk pack. This VSAM space is subsequently used to define suballocated VSAM data sets within it. By using this command, you can also set aside a disk pack as a CANDIDATE volume for the future allocation of VSAM space. If you are using ICF catalogs at your installation, you won't have any occasion to use this command because the concept of suballocated data sets does not exist for ICF catalogs.

5.1.3 DEFINE CLUSTER

This command allocates and catalogs a VSAM data set (KSDS, ESDS, or RRDS). This command allocates primary space (suballocated or unique) according to the command parameters. If the cluster is a KSDS, it allocates the index as well as the data component.

5.1.4 REPRO

This command is very versatile and can be used to load records into a VSAM data set. It may be used to load records from an ISAM to a VSAM cluster, as well as to load records from or to a physical sequential (PS) or a partitioned data set (PDS) member. Thus, in some respects, it performs some of the functions of the IEBGENER utility.

5.1.5 DEFINE ALTERNATEINDEX

This command is used to allocate space for an alternate index cluster. Such an alternate index can be on a KSDS or an ESDS. This command only allocates space; it does not load records into the alternate index, a function which is performed by the BLDINDEX command. The base cluster must exist before you can define an alternate index on it.

5.1.6 BLDINDEX

This command loads alternate key-pointer pair records into the alternate index cluster after extracting them from the base cluster. Therefore, the base cluster must contain records and the alternate index must already be defined before you initiate this command.

5.1.7 DEFINE PATH

This command establishes a path between an alternate index and the base cluster. Before this command is used, the base cluster and alternate index must exist.

5.1.8 PRINT

This command can be used to get a character and/or hex dump of a VSAM data set. It can also be useful in printing ISAM files, physical sequential files, or partitioned data set members. This command has a wide range of variations, including the ability to print only a selected portion of the data set.

5.1.9 VERIFY

If your batch job ended abnormally or the CICS system went down for some reason, any VSAM files open at the time will be left open. It is also possible that, as a result, the index and data components may not be in synchronization. The VERIFY command closes the files, brings the index component up to date with the data component, and records the necessary changes in the catalog.

5.1.10 DELETE

VSAM files cannot be deleted with the DELETE option of the DISPOSITION parameter of JCL. The AMS DELETE command is used for this purpose. However, it can also be used to delete non-VSAM files cataloged in a VSAM or ICF catalog or in a CVOL (OS catalog).

5.1.11 ALTER

Under certain circumstances, you may want to change the characteristics of a VSAM data set or a catalog without having to delete and redefine it. These might include the changing of passwords, renaming of data sets, changing of free space in a KSDS, etc. The ALTER command is used for such purposes.

5.1.12 DEFINE NONVSAM

This command is used to catalog a non-VSAM data set in a VSAM catalog. The non-VSAM data set must already exist, because this command will not allocate space for a data set.

5.1.13 DEFINE GDG

Instead of using IEHPROGM to define an index for a generation data group you can use this AMS command. A GDG index defined through AMS has the same capabilities as those defined through IEHPROGM.

5.1.14 DEFINE ALIAS

This command defines an alias for a user catalog (VSAM or ICF). Such an alias, when used as the first qualifier of a data set name, eliminates the need for coding catalog parameters or coding JOBCAT or STEPCAT cards in JCL. If you use an alias as the high-end (first) qualifier of a data set name, you do not need to know the name of the VSAM or ICF catalog where the data set is cataloged or accessed from.

5.1.15 DEFINE PAGESPACE

This is strictly a systems programming function that defines page data sets for an MVS system. Such data sets are ESDS's in organization.

5.1.16 LISTCAT

The different attributes and characteristics of a VSAM data set or catalog are listed with this command. A listing produced by the LISTCAT command shows not only the attributes with which a data set was defined but also other characteristics such as secondary allocations, the number of records, the number of index levels, and the number of CI and CA splits.

5.1.17 DIAGNOSE

This command is used only for ICF catalogs and is useful for detecting faults in the ICF catalog structure. After diagnosis of these faults, you can use various techniques to repair the damage.

5.1.18 EXPORT

This command can be used for transporting catalogs and data sets across systems. This comes in handy when converting from DOS/VS to OS/VS2 MVS. It can also be used for creating backup copies of a VSAM data set.

5.1.19 IMPORT

This command is used to recreate VSAM data sets or catalogs from backup copies created with the EXPORT command.

5.2 JCL FOR INVOKING ACCESS METHOD SERVICES

Access Method Services is invoked by executing a utility program called IDCAMS in a regular job step. The different functions of AMS (as outlined in the previous section) are performed through functional commands. A functional command can have one or more parameters that can be *positional* or *keyword*. A positional parameter is identified by its position in relation to other parameters; a keyword parameter can be used in any place in relation to other keyword parameters because it is identified by the particular keyword used. A keyword parameter may also have subparameters which can also be positional or keyword. Figure 5.1 gives the skeleton JCL for invoking Access Method Services.

All functional commands and their parameters are contained in a data set listed in the **SYSIN DD** statement. This data set can also be an in-stream file and, in such a case, must have the delimiter "/*" in columns 1 and 2 of the last card. All messages from the execution of AMS commands, whether successful or not, go to the **SYSPRINT** data set. Usually, such a data set is assigned to a print device. Additional DD statements may be required for some specific commands. Since we will consider AMS commands in depth in subsequent chapters, a discussion of those features is deferred until then.

If a functional command cannot be fully contained on one line, it may be continued on the next line, provided you enter a continuation character on the previous line. In AMS, the continuation character is a hyphen. The absence of a hyphen as the last character in a line indicates the end of a functional command. All functional commands and their parameters must start in or after the second column and cannot extend beyond the seventy-second column.

Multiple functional commands can be executed in the same AMS job step, but each new functional command must begin on a new line. You can also have as many AMS job steps in a job as needed.

Comments may be inserted between functional commands and parameters. They must be preceded by "/*" and followed by "*/".

```
//JOBNAME JOB (ACCTINFO),'PROG NAME'        (job card)
//STEPNAME EXEC PGM=IDCAMS                  (step card)
//SYSPRINT DD SYSOUT=A                      (AMS messages go here)
//SYSIN     DD *
         Functional commands
         Positional parameters
         Keyword parameters
         Subparameters
         Comments, etc.
/*
//
```

Figure 5.1 Skeleton JCL for invoking Access Method Services.

Access Method Services can be invoked in TSO. Almost all the functional commands can be executed interactively under TSO or option 6 of System Productivity Facility (SPF). This capability provides real-time execution of AMS commands without ever having to write JCL.

5.3 COMMON ERRORS IN CODING AND EXECUTING AMS COMMANDS

Starting with the next chapter, you will learn the AMS commands in detail. You might like to execute these commands on your system while you are learning them, but you may make some mistakes in coding. The messages printed on the SYSPRINT-assigned device will give you some idea of what these errors are. They fall into two categories: (1) errors caused by incorrect syntax and (2) errors caused by missing prerequisites.

All error messages printed on a SYSPRINT device are preceded by an 8-character identifier. Most of them will have a prefix of "**IDC**", indicating that they are AMS or VSAM messages. If the printed error message does not make much sense, IBM's *OS/VS2 Messages and Codes* manual will come in handy. It is best to refer to the manual for a detailed explanation of an error.

5.3.1 Syntax Errors

Although it is impossible to enumerate all the syntax errors that one can make, some of the most common ones are:

1. Omitting the continuation character (hyphen) at the end of a line when continuing the functional command on the next line.
2. Putting a continuation character (hyphen) on the last line of a functional command
3. Misspelling a command name, positional parameter, or keyword parameter
4. Improperly using delimiters by omitting or mismatching parentheses
5. Using one or more mutually exclusive parameters
6. Omitting essential parameters of a command
7. Starting or continuing a command in column 1

5.3.2 Missing Prerequisite Requirements

Sometimes an AMS command cannot be successfully executed because one or more of the prerequisites needed do not exist. Examples of such errors are as follows.

1. Attempting to allocate space on a disk which is either not owned by the user catalog or is owned by a different user catalog

2. Finding there is not enough VSAM space on a disk to define a suballocated data set
3. Defining an alternate index on a base cluster that does not exist
4. Defining a path before an alternate index is allocated

There are numerous other causes of such errors. It is advisable to refer to IBM's *OS/VS2 Messages and Codes* manual for details on any AMS command failure.

chapter **6**

VSAM Data Set Allocation

Non-VSAM data sets are allocated and deleted with the usual JCL parameters SPACE, DCB, DISP, UNIT, VOLUME, etc. They may be cataloged or uncataloged and, when allocated with the disposition (DISP) of NEW, may be used in the same job step. VSAM data sets, on the other hand, must be allocated with the AMS utility program IDCAMS. They must always be cataloged in either a VSAM or an ICF catalog before they can be used by a program. In most cases, a VSAM data set is defined in one job step and used in subsequent separate job steps.

6.1 PREREQUISITES OF DATA SET ALLOCATION

In order to define a VSAM data set (also called a *cluster*), you must know the VSAM or ICF catalog in which the data set will be cataloged. If you use VSAM catalogs in your installation, you must also know the volumes owned by the particular VSAM catalog you are using. Your VSAM data sets can be defined only on these volumes. However, if your installation uses ICF catalogs, you can define your VSAM data sets on any volume that has been specified as a VSAM volume[1] (ICF catalogs do not own

[1]Under ICF catalogs, a DASD volume may become eligible to contain VSAM data sets when a VSAM Volume Data Set (VVDS) is allocated on it.

volumes the way VSAM catalogs do). Since it is not unusual to have 20 to 30 catalogs in a single- or twin-CPU data center installation, you should ask your systems programmer for the VSAM of ICF catalog's name and the volumes that you may use to define your cluster.

6.2 BASIC NEEDS FOR DEFINING A CLUSTER

Some of the basic information you must have to define a VSAM data set includes

- The volume(s) on which the data set will be allocated
- The name of the catalog owning these volumes, if you have VSAM catalogs
- The type of data set (KSDS, ESDS, or an RRDS)
- The amount of space needed for the data set
- For a KSDS, the length of the prime key and its offset from the beginning of the record
- The record size and whether it is fixed or variable in length
- The control interval size you want for the data set
- For a KSDS, the amount of free space you would like to keep within a CI and a CA
- The name you are giving to the cluster [*this cluster name will be your data set name* (DSN)]

After you determine this information, you will be ready to write JCL for invoking Access Method Services and allocate a VSAM data set.

6.3 DEFINING A KSDS

To begin with, let's say that you want to define a key-sequenced data set for a personnel system. You can include many fields in the record layout for such a file, but to keep our example simple we will use only six. The record layout appears in Fig. 6.1.

The first 9 bytes of the record contain the Social Security Number of the employee, which is also the prime key of the record.[2] The other fields in the record are Employee-Address, Employee-Number, Employee-Sex (male or female), Employee-Date-of-Birth, and Employee-Name. For the time being, we will concentrate on allocating space for the cluster. Figure 6.2 gives an example of the JCL used to invoke Access Method Services and to allocate the VSAM cluster.

Note the use of a hyphen (-) as the continuation character on each

[2] Bear in mind that the prime key of a KSDS *does not have to be* the first field in the record. The SSN could just as well have started in the second, twentieth, or any other byte of the record.

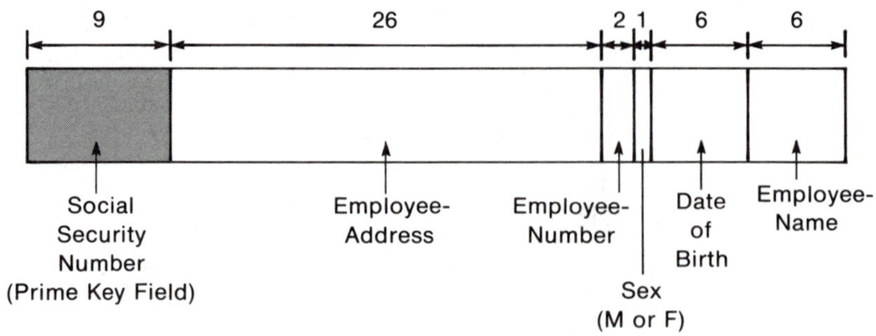

Figure 6.1 The record layout of our KSDS. Social Security Number is the prime key of the record and is in the first nine positions. The other fields have lengths as shown. The record length is 50 bytes.

line of the command and its parameters. This indicates that the AMS command is not complete yet and that the following line should be treated as a continuation of the command parameters. On the last line, however, there is no continuation character. This indicates the end of a particular AMS command. If the continuation character were missing on any line

```
//AMSJOB    JOB (ACCTNO),'JAY RANADE'
//DEFKSDS   EXEC PGM=IDCAMS
//SYSPRINT DD SYSOUT=A
//SYSIN     DD *
 DEFINE CLUSTER                       -
 (NAME(EMPLOYEE.KSDS.CLUSTER)         -
 VOLUMES(VSAM02)                      -
 CYLINDERS(2,1)                       -
 CONTROLINTERVALSIZE(4096)            -
 FREESPACE(10,20)                     -
 KEYS(9,0)                            -
 RECORDSIZE(50,50)          )         -
 DATA                                 -
 (NAME(EMPLOYEE.KSDS.DATA))           -
 INDEX                                -
 (NAME(EMPLOYEE.KSDS.INDEX)           -
 CONTROLINTERVALSIZE(1024))           -
 CATALOG(VSAM.USERCAT.TWO)
/*
//
```

Figure 6.2 Sample JCL for invoking Access Method Services for defining a KSDS. Matching parentheses and usage of the continuation character (-) should be carefully noted.

between lines 5 and 17, the AMS command would terminate unsuccessfully with an error message.

Let's analyze the JCL line by line:

Line 1: The JOB card may be different, depending on your installation standards.

Line 2: The EXEC card invokes Access Method Services (program IDCAMS).

Line 3: SYSPRINT is assigned to a printer device. Your installation may have a different SYSOUT assignment for the printer.

Line 4: The SYSIN card indicates that in-stream data containing functional commands and their parameters follows.

Line 5: DEFINE CLUSTER is the functional command used to allocate a VSAM data set.

Line 6: NAME is a positional parameter and must follow the functional command DEFINE CLUSTER. When the data set is successfully allocated, the cluster name will be used as the data set name when accessing this KSDS. Notice that one of the left parentheses is not yet matched by a corresponding right one.

Line 7: The VOLUMES parameter gives the name of the volume serial number where space for the cluster will be allocated.

Line 8: The CYLINDERS parameter indicates that two cylinders of primary space will now be allocated. When all this space has been utilized, secondary allocations will be made in increments of one cylinder each.

Line 9: The CONTROLINTERVALSIZE (abbreviated CISZ) for the cluster will be 4096 bytes.

Line 10: FREESPACE (10,20) means that, at the time of the initial loading of records into this cluster, each control interval will have 10 percent of its space left free and that 20 percent of the control intervals in each control area will be left unused. This free space will minimize CI and CA splits later when random updates are made to the data set.

Line 11: The KEYS parameter indicates that the prime key is 9 bytes long and starts in position 0 of the record. Don't forget that in VSAM the first byte is called byte 0, the second is called byte 1, etc. So, when giving the offset of the beginning of the key, you should subtract 1 from the actual position of the key.

Line 12: RECORDSIZE has two values. The first value gives the average record length, and the second gives the maximum record length. In our example, we are dealing with fixed-length records, so the average and the maximum are equal. Also, notice one additional right parenthesis which closes the open left parenthesis of the NAME parameter in line 6.

Line 13: DATA indicates the beginning of the data component parameters.

Line 14: The NAME parameter under DATA gives a separate name to the data component of the cluster. Note the extra set of parentheses.

Line 15: INDEX indicates the beginning of the index component parameters.

Line 16: The NAME parameter under INDEX gives a separate name to the index component of the cluster. Note the extra set of parentheses.

Line 17: A CONTROLINTERVALSIZE value of 1024 specifies the index component control interval size. If this parameter is omitted, AMS will determine the appropriate index CI size for the index component.

Line 18: The CATALOG parameter specifies the name of the VSAM or ICF catalog in which the cluster will be cataloged. If you are using a VSAM catalog, then it must own the volume specified in the VOLUMES parameter on line 7.

Line 19: A "/*" delimiter indicates the end of the in-stream SYSIN data set.

It is good practice to give separate names to the data and index components of the cluster. If we had omitted the DATA and INDEX parameters altogether, Access Method Services would have generated a name for each of the data and index components. However, generated names contain date and time stamps and are difficult to relate to the cluster to which they belong. Although you will rarely ever have to refer to data or index components by their individual names (normally, you refer to the cluster name which points to both of the components), for recovery purposes this is sometimes necessary. Therefore, it is strongly recommended that you give separate, meaningful names to the data and index components for those few occasions and also to improve readability.

If the allocation of a KSDS is completed successfully by AMS, you will get a condition code of 0 and a message on the SYSPRINT device as shown in Fig. 6.3.

Successful allocation of this cluster means that (1) two cylinders have been allocated for the data set named EMPLOYEE.KSDS.CLUSTER and (2) the data set has been cataloged in the catalog named VSAM.USERCAT.TWO. You can now use the data set in any way you like. The status of the data set is "unloaded" at this time. You can write a Cobol program to load records into the cluster or use the REPRO command to perform the same function.

```
IDCAMS  SYSTEM SERVICES

 DEFINE CLUSTER                          -
 (NAME(EMPLOYEE.KSDS.CLUSTER)            -
 VOLUMES(VSAM02)                         -
 CYLINDERS(2,1)                          -
 CONTROLINTERVALSIZE(4096)               -
 FREESPACE(10,20)                        -
 KEYS(9,0)                               -
 RECORDSIZE(50,50)           )           -
 DATA                                    -
 (NAME(EMPLOYEE.KSDS.DATA))              -
 INDEX                                   -
 (NAME(EMPLOYEE.KSDS.INDEX)              -
 CONTROLINTERVALSIZE(1024))              -
 CATALOG(VSAM.USERCAT.TWO)

IDC0508I DATA ALLOCATION STATUS FOR VOLUME VSAM02 IS 0

IDC0509I INDEX ALLOCATION STATUS FOR VOLUME VSAM02 IS 0

IDC0520I CATALOG RECOVERY VOLUME IS VSAM02

IDC0001I FUNCTION COMPLETED, HIGHEST CONDITION CODE WAS 0


IDC0002I IDCAMS PROCESSING COMPLETE. MAXIMUM CONDITION CODE WAS 0
```

Figure 6.3 Message indicating successful allocation of a KSDS named EMPLOYEE.KSDS.CLUSTER.

It should be noted that the parameters of DEFINE CLUSTER shown in Fig. 6.2 are not the only parameters. There are many more that can be used to customize the allocation of a cluster according to your needs. In a subsequent section of this chapter, a brief explanation of these parameters will be given. However, to understand the meanings and interrelationships of the different parameters in detail, you should refer to IBM's manual on Access Method Services. A list of all such manuals is given at the end of this book.

If you want to use the JCL in Fig. 6.2 to allocate a KSDS cluster on your system, you will have to

1. Change the JOB card to suit your installation standards.
2. Get a VSAM or an ICF catalog name from your systems programmer and substitute it for the one listed.
3. Get a valid volume serial number on which you can define (allocate) a VSAM data set.

6.4 DEFINING AN ESDS

In the previous section, we defined a KSDS. Defining an ESDS is similar, but with the following differences.

- Since the ESDS does not have embedded free space, the FREESPACE parameter is not used.
- The KEYS parameter has no meaning in ESDS, so it is not used either.

```
//AMSJOB    JOB (ACCTNO),'JAY RANADE'
//DEFESDS   EXEC PGM=IDCAMS
//SYSPRINT  DD SYSOUT=A
//SYSIN     DD *
 DEFINE CLUSTER                          -
 (NAME(EMPLOYEE.ESDS.CLUSTER)            -
 VOLUMES(VSAM02)                         -
 CYLINDERS(2,1)                          -
 CONTROLINTERVALSIZE(4096)               -
 RECORDSIZE(50,50)                       -
 NONINDEXED                      )       -
 DATA                                    -
 (NAME(EMPLOYEE.ESDS.DATA))              -
 CATALOG(VSAM.USERCAT.TWO)
/*
//
```

Figure 6.4 Sample JCL for invoking Access Method Services for defining an ESDS.

- Since an ESDS has only a data component, a parameter related to INDEX cannot be used.
- An additional parameter, NONINDEXED, is added to the command to tell AMS that an ESDS is to be defined.

Sample JCL for defining an ESDS cluster is shown in Fig. 6.4.

Notice that the keyword parameter NONINDEXED has been added to the command. If this had not been done, AMS would have defined a KSDS with default values for FREESPACE, KEYS, etc. This is because the keyword parameter INDEXED, which is used to define a KSDS, is also the default parameter if nothing is coded.

Upon successful execution of this JCL, space will be allocated for an ESDS cluster named EMPLOYEE.ESDS.CLUSTER. This cluster will have only a data component named EMPLOYEE.ESDS.DATA. It will have a CI size of 4096 bytes, a record size of 50 bytes, and a primary space allocation of two cylinders on volume VSAM02.

As explained at the end of Sec. 6.3, you can make the necessary modifications in the JCL in Fig. 6.4 to run it on your system and allocate an ESDS.

6.5 DEFINING AN RRDS

Since an RRDS also has only a data component, the syntax of the command is similar to that for an ESDS. The following points must be considered when coding a DEFINE CLUSTER command for an RRDS.

- No FREESPACE parameter is used in an RRDS.

- Since an RRDS does not have a key, the KEYS parameter must not be coded.
- There is no coding for the INDEX component because it has only a data component.
- Since an RRDS does not support variable-length records, the average and maximum record length values of the RECORDSIZE parameter must be the same.
- The keyword parameter NUMBERED must be coded to have AMS define an RRDS.

Sample JCL for defining an RRDS is shown in Fig. 6.5.

Note the use of the parameter NUMBERED in the command. This parameter indicates that an RRDS is being requested. Again, if you don't code this parameter, the default is INDEXED, which will define a KSDS.

Upon successful execution of the JCL, an RRDS cluster named EMPLOYEE.RRDS.CLUSTER will be allocated. The name of the data component for this cluster will be EMPLOYEE.RRDS.DATA. It will have a CI size of 4096 bytes, fixed-length records of 50 bytes each, and a primary space allocation of two cylinders on volume VSAM02. Notice that the CYLINDERS parameter has values of (2,0). This means that, once the primary space allocation of two cylinders is used up, there will not be any allocation of secondary space. The second value of the parameter, 0, indicates that there is to be no secondary allocation. We could have coded this parameter the same way when defining a KSDS or an ESDS if we did not want to provide for secondary space allocations.

```
//AMSJOB    JOB (ACCTNO),'JAY RANADE'
//DEFRRDS   EXEC PGM=IDCAMS
//SYSPRINT DD SYSOUT=A
//SYSIN     DD *
 DEFINE CLUSTER                          -
 (NAME(EMPLOYEE.RRDS.CLUSTER)            -
 VOLUMES(VSAM02)                         -
 CYLINDERS(2,0)                          -
 CONTROLINTERVALSIZE(4096)               -
 RECORDSIZE(50,50)                       -
 NUMBERED                       )        -
 DATA                                    -
 (NAME(EMPLOYEE.RRDS.DATA))              -
 CATALOG(VSAM.USERCAT.TWO)
/*
//
```

Figure 6.5 Sample JCL for invoking Access Method Services for defining an RRDS.

As explained at the end of Sec. 6.3, with slight modifications, the JCL given in Fig. 6.5 can be made suitable for your own installation and may be used to allocate an RRDS.

6.6 MOST COMMONLY USED PARAMETERS OF DEFINE CLUSTER

We have used only a few of the parameters of the DEFINE CLUSTER command in the previous examples. AMS uses default values for any parameters that are not coded. Since the defaults will not always suit us, we will have to learn some of the major parameters, their default values, and their effect on subsequent processing so that we can customize a cluster based on our needs. Some of these parameters are used in the cluster, while others are used to give the characteristics of the data or index component. A brief overview of these parameters is as follows.

6.6.1 NAME

The names of the cluster, data, and index components can each be up to 44 characters long. Restrictions on naming are the same as those imposed for other OS/VS non-VSAM data sets.

6.6.2 CYLINDERS, RECORDS, and TRACKS

The space allocation parameter can be coded using any of the three options. For example, the following are valid parameters.

```
CYLINDERS(25,5)
TRACKS(3,2)
RECORDS(500,250)
```

It is advisable to use CYLINDERS because it ensures a CA size of one cylinder. A CA size of one cylinder will be helpful for fine-tuning and proper use of the IMBED parameter which is discussed later.

6.6.3 SUBALLOCATION and UNIQUE

If a cluster is defined with the SUBALLOCATION parameter (which is the default if you are using VSAM rather than ICF catalogs) you may have a total of 122 secondary extents. A secondary extent of space is allocated only if

1. Primary allocation of space has been used up by inserts and updates of data records.

2. At the time of data set allocation (DEFINE CLUSTER), provision was made for secondary space allocation. For example, CYLINDERS(2,0) means that, once the primary space of two cylinders has been used up, no secondary allocation of extents should be made.

With the UNIQUE parameter, the maximum number of secondary extents is 15. Recall that suballocated data sets are defined within preallocated VSAM space, while UNIQUE data sets have VSAM space of their own. In an ICF catalog environment, the SUBALLOCATION parameter is ignored because you can only have UNIQUE data sets. Your data sets may have up to 122 secondary extents under these circumstances.

6.6.4 VOLUMES

You may code multiple values in the VOLUMES parameter, e.g., VOLUMES(VSAM02, VSAM03, VSAM04). This allows you to get secondary allocations on additional disk packs if the currently used volume has no space left on it. But the volumes must be *owned* by the VSAM catalog if you are using VSAM catalogs, or must be allocated as VSAM volumes if you are using ICF catalogs.

6.6.5 INDEXED, NONINDEXED, and NUMBERED

These indicate whether a KSDS, an ESDS, or an RRDS (in that order) is being defined. INDEXED is the default.

6.6.6 CONTROLINTERVALSIZE

The internal architecture of VSAM requires that the data CI size be a multiple of 512 up to a maximum of 8192, and thereafter a multiple of 2048 with a maximum of 32,768. In other words,

$$\text{CI size} = N \times 512 \qquad \text{or} \qquad N \times 2048$$

where N can have a value from 1 to 16. The index component in a KSDS may have a different CI size than the data component. The only values allowed for the index component are 512, 1024, 2048, and 4096. Selecting the appropriate CI size is a factor of record size, free space allocated, type of disk device, amount of buffer storage available, etc.[3]

[3]For a detailed discussion on CONTROLINTERVALSIZE and the optimization of other parameters, refer to Jay Ranade, *VSAM: Performance, Design, and Fine Tuning.*

6.6.7 ERASE and NOERASE

Files containing sensitive information (e.g., payroll, security information) should be defined with the ERASE parameter so that, when such a file is deleted, its data component is physically erased. Thus, subsequent dumping of the disk pack with IEHDASDR or similar software does not reveal any information. A file defined with NOERASE (which is the default) is not erased on deletion; only its entry is removed from the catalog.

6.6.8 FREESPACE

The syntax of this parameter is:

```
FREESPACE(CI percent,CA percent)
```

This parameter is coded only for a KSDS. It is coded at the time of data set allocation but is, in fact, used when the data set is being loaded sequentially. The values of freespace are coded as percentages. The first value indicates what percentage of space within each CI should remain as free space at the time of the sequential loading of the data set. The second value indicates what percentage of free CI's within a CA will be left totally unused at the same time. The first value helps reduce CI splits, while the second helps minimize CA splits. The default values of free space are (0,0). While this may be the right choice for a read-only KSDS, the optimum values for free space depend on each application's characteristics, such as insert activity, delete activity, and the effect of CI and CA splits on CICS response time. As a general rule, if you want to reduce the number of CI splits, increase the CI percent free space figure. In order to reduce the number of CA splits, increase the CA percent free space figure. On the other hand, to conserve DASD space, reduce these figures.

Suppose you define a KSDS cluster with FREESPACE values of (25,50). After the initial sequential loading of this cluster, the free space distribution within a CA will appear as in Fig. 6.6.

6.6.9 KEYS

The syntax of this parameter is as follows:

```
KEYS(key length,offset)
```

This parameter gives the length of the KSDS key and its offset from the beginning of the record. If this parameter is not coded, the default value is (64,0). Unless your key begins at the first character and is 64 bytes long, you must code this parameter. The key length can be from 1 through 255 bytes.

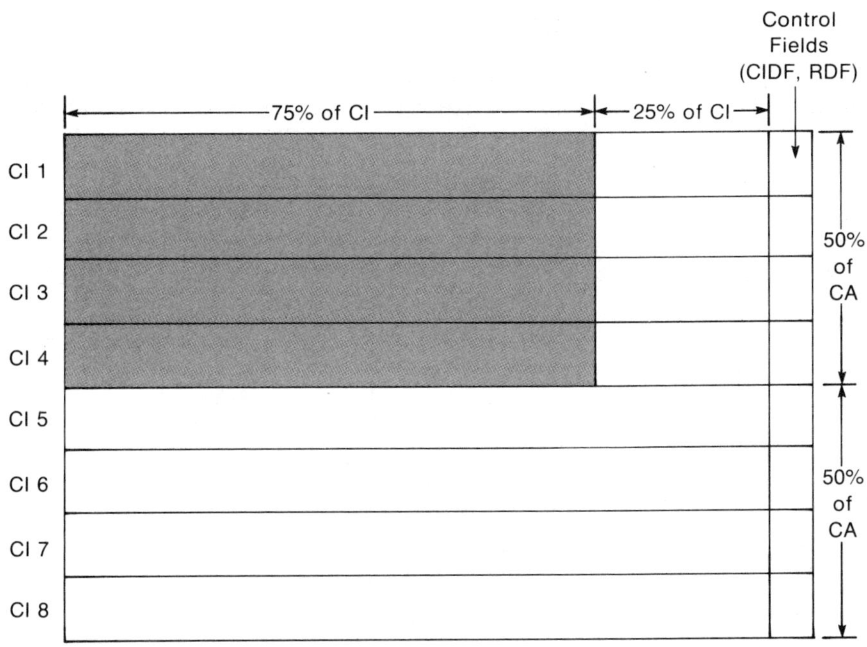

Figure 6.6 Free space distribution within a CA of a KSDS after the initial sequential load. The data set was defined with a parameter of FREESPACE(25,50). The shaded area within a CI indicates space in use, while unshaded areas are free space.

6.6.10 RECORDSIZE

The syntax of this parameter is as follows:

```
RECORDSIZE(average,maximum)
```

This provides AMS with average and maximum record lengths for a data set. For a fixed-length record data set, both values will be the same. Don't forget that an RRDS supports fixed-length records only. In VSAM, a record can vary in length from a minimum of 1 byte to a maximum nonspanned size of 32,761 bytes.

6.6.11 SPANNED and NONSPANNED

If the maximum record length is more than the CI size specified, allocation will fail unless you specify the SPANNED parameter. Records that cannot be contained in one CI will span over more than one CI. Remember that CICS/VS does not support spanned records in its releases prior to CICS/VS 1.7.

6.6.12 SPEED and RECOVERY

RECOVERY, which is the default, preformats a VSAM data set at the time of an initial load or a resume load. It takes longer to perform the load operation through RECOVERY than through SPEED, which does not preformat the data set. However, if the load operation is aborted in the middle, RECOVERY enables you to resume immediately after the last record loaded. If SPEED is specified, the load will have to be restarted from the beginning. SPEED is, nevertheless, highly recommended, because it does not pay to cause preformat overhead every time just to take care of a few scattered instances of load failure. Once again, SPEED must be coded in the command, because RECOVERY is the default.

6.6.13 TO and FOR

The syntax for this parameter is as follows:

```
TO(date)     or     FOR(days)
```

These mutually exclusive parameters specify the retention period for the cluster being defined. The format of the TO parameter is yyddd, where yy is the year and ddd is the Julian day (1 to 365). The format of the FOR parameter is the number of days for which the data set should be retained. The number of days can vary from 1 to 9999. Any number between 1831 and 9999 results in the data set being retained through the year 1999. The DELETE command of AMS cannot delete a data set whose retention period has not expired unless you force it to with the PURGE option of the DELETE command. If TO or FOR is not specified, the data set can be deleted at any time. Valid examples of these parameters are

```
TO(87365)
FOR(60)
```

In the first case, the data set will be retained through the last day of the year 1987. In the second case, the data set will be retained for 60 days from the date it was defined.

A detailed discussion is needed to understand certain other important parameters of DEFINE CLUSTER such as REUSE, IMBED, REPLICATE, SHAREOPTIONS, and password protection parameters. They are covered in subsequent sections. Almost all the parameters of DEFINE CLUSTER are also used in the DEFINE ALTERNATEINDEX command.

This review of the different parameters is not meant to replace the Access Method Services reference manual. In order to understand the complete details of the function of each parameter, refer to IBM's manuals.

6.7 ALIAS OF A USERCATALOG

In a twin-CPU IBM environment, there are frequently more than 20 VSAM or ICF user catalogs. There may be one catalog for each application system (payroll, accounts payable, etc.) or one catalog for each disk volume. You have already seen in the DEFINE CLUSTER command that through the CATALOG parameter you supply the catalog name in which your cluster will be defined. You will also see that, when coding JCL for VSAM data sets, the catalog name is given in the STEPCAT or JOBCAT statements. Briefly, a VSAM data set can be associated with a user catalog in one of two ways: (1) coding the CATALOG parameter in AMS commands, or (2) coding the STEPCAT and JOBCAT statements in execution JCL.

Remembering and coding those long catalog names would not be pleasant. But there is an easy way out—the ALIAS of a user catalog.

An alias is the "other name" of a VSAM object. A systems programmer, through the DEFINE ALIAS command, can define an alias for a user catalog. This alias can be up to 8 characters long. When the alias is used as the first qualifier of a VSAM or non-VSAM data set, the system can determine which catalog is being referred to. In the previous examples, EMPLOYEE had already been defined as the alias of the user catalog VSAM.USERCAT.TWO. So, by making EMPLOYEE the first qualifier of the cluster name, there was no need to code the CATALOG parameter. Similarly, when this data set is referred to in the execution JCL, there will be no need to code STEPCAT or JOBCAT cards. Each user catalog may have more than one alias. However, an alias cannot be associated with more than one user catalog. If you are a TSO user, your logon ID is an alias for a VSAM, ICF, or OS catalog (CVOL). That's why, when you use your TSO ID as the first qualifier of a data set name, the data set is automatically cataloged in the proper catalog.

6.8 REUSABLE CLUSTERS

In OS/VS, if the name of the physical sequential data set starts with "&&", it becomes a temporary data set and is deleted at the end of the job. There is no facility for defining a temporary VSAM data set. However, there is one way in which you can simulate a similar function. A VSAM data set may be defined with the REUSE parameter. Whenever such a data set is opened as OUTPUT, all the existing records within it are deleted logically and become inaccessible. Thus, the processing program can start writing new records from the beginning of the data set. Such a data set can be reused as many times as it is opened for output. It should be noted that a VSAM data set is opened as OUTPUT at the time of sequential load processing only. For random updates it is opened as INPUT-OUTPUT. Reusable VSAM data sets are defined and deleted using Access Method Services commands. A major drawback of a reusable cluster is that it cannot have alternate indexes.

6.9 IMBED AND REPLICATE

The IMBED parameter implies that the sequence set (lowermost level) of the index component of a KSDS will be placed on the first track of a data component control area and will be replicated as many times as possible on that track. For example, let's say that we have a KSDS whose entire space allocation is in cylinders on an IBM 3380 disk device. Thus, each CA in this data set will be equal in size to one cylinder of an IBM 3380 disk. Each cylinder of an IBM 3380 disk has 15 tracks. So, if the KSDS is defined with the IMBED option, the first of the 15 tracks will be used for the sequence set of the index component, and the other 14 tracks will be used to contain the data component. The sequence set CI on the first track will also be replicated as many times on the track as space permits (Fig. 6.7). The IMBED option reduces the seek time[4] it takes the read-write head to move from the index to the data component, and the replication factor reduces the rotational delay[5] of the revolving disk. This option should be considered a performance parameter for heavy random-access-oriented files in CICS/VS systems. The price paid for this performance is that you lose one track in each data CA for storing sequence set index data.

What IMBED does for a sequence set, REPLICATE does for an index set. The REPLICATE parameter forces each CI of the index set of the index component to be written on a separate track and replicated as many times as possible. This parameter reduces rotational delay when VSAM is accessing high-level index CI's. Note that both these options are used only for a KSDS.

6.10 PASSWORD PROTECTION

VSAM data sets can be password-protected at four different levels. Each level gives a different access capability to the data set. The levels are

1. READPW: Provides read-only capability.
2. UPDATEPW: Records may be read, updated, added, or deleted at this level.

[4]The *seek time* is the length of time the read-write arm of the DASD takes to move from its current position to the appropriate cylinder where the record is expected to be found.

[5]The *rotational delay* is the length of time it takes for data on the revolving disk to come to the read-write arm after the seek has been completed.

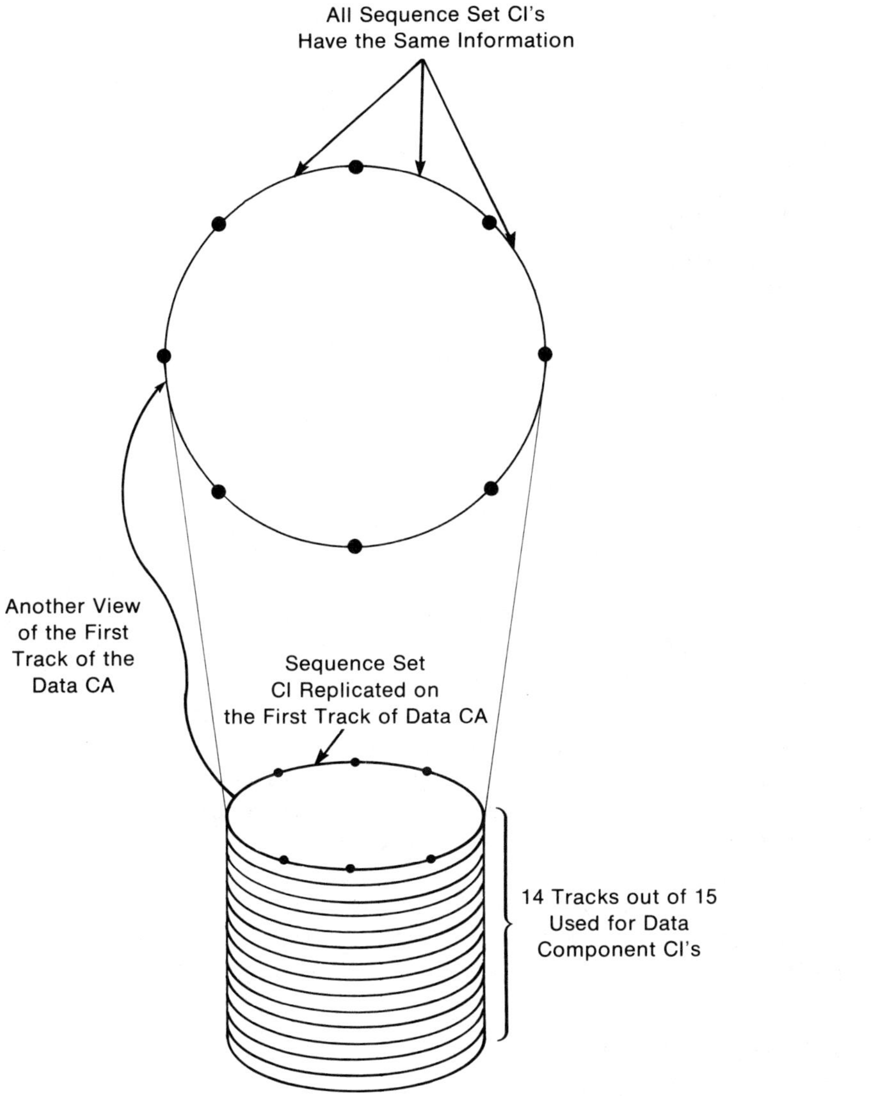

Figure 6.7 Sequence set track and data component tracks on a KSDS, where a CA is one cylinder in size and the data set was defined on an IBM 3380 disk with the IMBED option.

3. CONTROLPW: Allows you the access capabilities provided by READPW and UPDATEPW and also lets you access a CI as a record. As a Cobol programmer you may never need to do this because you can't access a CI as data through a Cobol program.
4. MASTERPW: With MASTERPW you may perform all the

above operations. In addition, it is also required for deletion of a data set.

Examples of coding password-protection parameters using the passwords ALPHA, BETA, GAMMA, and OMEGA are

```
READPW(ALPHA) -
UPDATEPW(BETA) -
CONTROLPW(GAMMA) -
MASTERPW(OMEGA) -
```

In this example, ALPHA is a read-only-level password, BETA is a read-plus-update-level password, GAMMA is a read-plus-update plus a control interval access password, and OMEGA is a password that permits you to perform any operation on the data set including its deletion.

If password parameters are not coded, there is no protection and anyone can perform any operation on the data set. Each password can be up to 8 characters long. If you are a Cobol programmer, passwords assigned to a data set have to be specified within the SELECT clause of the program as required by the type of operation being performed. For example, you can not perform updates on the data set if only the read-only level password is supplied in the program.

Passwords at the cluster level protect only if access requires using the cluster's name as the data set name. If only the cluster is password-protected, someone could access the data and index components by name without having to specify a password. So, it is advisable to password-protect the different components also. Remember that, if the user catalog is not password-protected (a function performed by systems programmers), passwords assigned to a cluster will not have any significance.

Another feature of MVS, called Resource Access Control Facility, can be used instead of or in addition to VSAM password protection.

6.11 SHAREOPTIONS

The syntax for this parameter is

```
SHAREOPTIONS(cross region,cross system)
```

This is a powerful feature of VSAM which permits you to access a data set from different programs running concurrently (multiple address spaces/regions). Such programs running in different regions can be running in the same CPU (*cross-region sharing*) or different CPU's (*cross-system sharing*). In the latter case, the VSAM data set must be on a shared disk pack.

The value of the cross-region sharing parameter can be 1, 2, 3, or 4, while the cross-system sharing parameter may be 3 or 4. The different values offer different levels of data set sharing.

Shareoption 1 means that either one user can update *or* many users can read the data set. This option ensures complete read and write integrity.

Shareoption 2 allows multiple users to read a data set at the same time that one user is updating it. This option gives complete write integrity but does not ensure read integrity.

Shareoption 3 allows any number of users to read the data set and also allows multiple users to update at the same time. This shareoption does not ensure read or write integrity, so it should be used with great caution. However, when it is necessary to use this option, responsibility for read and write data integrity lies with the user's application.

Shareoption 4 has the same problems associated with it as shareoption 3. However, buffers used for direct processing are refreshed each time an I/O is performed on the data set. This increases I/O's on the data set, causing response time problems in on-line systems (CICS/VS).

For cross-region sharing (within the same CPU), shareoptions 1 and 2 are recommended. Cross-system sharing should be avoided altogether unless an application issues RESERVE and RELEASE macros for taking exclusive control of the shared disk pack. The Cobol language does not support these macros. Cross-region sharing is possible only if all the users use **DISPOSITION=SHR** (not OLD) on a **DD** card for the data set. Anyone using DISPOSITION=OLD could obtain exclusive control of the data set and the shareoptions would lose their meaning for the duration of the program's execution. If this parameter is not coded, the default is SHAREOPTIONS(1,3), i.e., 1 for cross-region and 3 for cross-system.

Note that a CICS/VS region is considered one user as far as the shareoption is concerned. So, no matter what you code as the cross-region value, any number of tasks within the CICS/VS region can read or update a data set concurrently. Under these circumstances, CICS/VS ensures its own internal data integrity by putting a lock on a CI during an update.

6.12 A COMPREHENSIVE EXAMPLE

All the parameters discussed so far may not be used in every data set being allocated. However, a knowledge and understanding of them will help in optimizing VSAM file design for various applications. Let's wrap up this topic by defining a KSDS using most of these parameters.

This hypothetical KSDS has the same features as EMPLOYEE.KSDS.CLUSTER but, in addition, we will imbed its sequence set on the first track of a data component CA, its index set will be replicated, password protection will be required at all four levels for the cluster as well as the data component (but not for the index component), and we will require shareoptions of (2,3). The data set is to be erased when deleted, defined with the SPEED option, and retained for 60 days. When it is *initially loaded*, we will leave 25 percent of the CI's in each CA free, and 15 percent of the space in the used CI's will also be left free. Figure 6.8 gives sample JCL for allocating this KSDS cluster.

Notice that the CATALOG parameter has been omitted altogether. EMPLOYEE, which is being used as the first qualifier of the cluster name, also happens to be the alias of the user catalog named

```
//AMSJOB     JOB (ACCTNO),'JAY RANADE'
//DEFKSDS    EXEC PGM=IDCAMS
//SYSPRINT   DD SYSOUT=A
//SYSIN      DD *
  DEFINE CLUSTER                            -
  (NAME(EMPLOYEE.KSDS.CLUSTER)              -
  VOLUMES(VSAM02)                           -
  CYLINDERS(2,1)                            -
  CONTROLINTERVALSIZE(4096)                 -
  FREESPACE(15,25)                          -
  KEYS(9,0)                                 -
  RECORDSIZE(50,50)                         -
  IMBED                                     -
  REPLICATE                                 -
  ERASE                                     -
  SPEED                                     -
  FOR(60)                                   -
  SHAREOPTIONS(2,3)                         -
  READPW(PASS1)                             -
  UPDATEPW(PASS2)                           -
  CONTROLPW(PASS3)                          -
  MASTERPW(PASS4)                   )       -
  DATA                                      -
  (NAME(EMPLOYEE.KSDS.DATA)                 -
  READPW(PASS5)                             -
  UPDATEPW(PASS6)                           -
  CONTROLPW(PASS7)                          -
  MASTERPW(PASS8)                   )       -
  INDEX                                     -
  (NAME(EMPLOYEE.KSDS.INDEX))
/*
//
```

Figure 6.8 A comprehensive example of defining a KSDS.

VSAM.USERCAT.TWO. Hence, the CATALOG parameter may be omitted without causing any problems.

Simple passwords have been used in this example to facilitate your understanding. This is not intended to encourage you to develop a naming convention for passwords. They should always be a random combination of characters that would be difficult to guess.

6.13 AMS COMMANDS IN PDS MEMBERS

So far we have been using AMS commands and their parameters as in-stream data sets. They start after the **SYSIN DD** * card and end with a "/*" card. In a real working environment, you might prefer to store them as members of partitioned data sets (PDS) for the following reasons.

1. The commands will be used by multiple jobs or different job steps within the same job. By using in-stream data sets, you will create redundancy by coding the same commands a number of times. Redundancy will also create the problem of maintaining the sychronization of different in-stream data sets if changes are required.
2. In production environments, cataloged procedures (PROC's) are used extensively. In-stream data sets are not supported in them, so you must store AMS commands in PDS members.
3. Keeping commands in a PDS provides central control and a known source of documentation to all users.

Let's suppose that the AMS command in Fig. 6.8 is stored as PDS member KSDSDEF in SAMPLE.PDS.LIBRARY. The in-stream data set DD statement and all its associated records can be replaced with the one statement:

```
//SYSIN DD DSN=SAMPLE.PDS.LIBRARY(KSDSDEF),DISP=SHR
```

Bear in mind that, while you are coding the AMS commands in a PDS member, the same AMS rules for coding in in-stream data sets still apply. The record length of the PDS must be 80 bytes, and commands must start in or after the second column.

chapter 7

Loading Data Sets

In the last chapter, we learned how to define VSAM data sets. The DEFINE CLUSTER command allocates space and catalogs data sets with given or default attributes. After allocation of a data set, the next task is to load records into it. This can be done in one of two ways: (1) Use the REPRO command of Access Method Services to read an input data set and load records into an output data set; or (2) write a program in Cobol, PL/I, or assembler to perform the same function.

In this chapter, we will learn about the use of the REPRO command. In Part 3, the same function will be accomplished using a Cobol program. REPRO can be used not only for VSAM data sets but for non-VSAM data sets as well.

7.1 PREREQUISITES OF THE LOAD FUNCTION

In order to use the REPRO command, you must have the following information available.

1. The name of the input data set from which the records are to be copied. Is it an indexed sequential file, a physical sequential data set, a partitioned data set member, a KSDS, an ESDS, or an RRDS?
2. The name of the data set that will receive the records. Is the out-

put data set a PS data set, a PDS member, a KSDS, an ESDS, or an RRDS?

3. Which records from the input data set are to be copied and which ones are to be skipped?

In order to maintain consistency throughout the remainder of the book, we will consider a physical sequential data set of a personnel system as our input. It has nine fixed-length records of 50 bytes each. The records are illustrated in Fig. 7.1.

Each record has six fields defined as follows.

1. EMPLOYEE-SSN is the social security number of the employee. It is 9 bytes long and occupies positions 1 to 9. It is also the prime key of our KSDS. This field is always unique.
2. EMPLOYEE-ADDRESS is 26 bytes long and occupies positions 10 to 35.
3. EMPLOYEE-NUMBER is assigned by the company and is unique for each employee. It is 2 bytes long and occupies positions 36 to 37.
4. EMPLOYEE-SEX is 1 byte long and has a value of M or F. It occupies position 38 in the record.
5. EMPLOYEE-DOB is the employee's date of birth in the format YYMMDD. It is 6 bytes long and occupies positions 39 to 44.
6. EMPLOYEE-NAME is the last name of the employee. It is 6 bytes long and occupies positions 45 to 50.

Employee-SSN	Employee-Address	Employee-Number	Employee-Sex	Employee-Dob	Employee-Name
111111111	WORLD PLAZA, N.Y., N.Y.	10	M	092150	RANADE
222222222	25 OAKWOODS, N.Y.	19	M	022536	TANAKA
333333333	18 MARSH AVE, S.I., N.Y.	16	F	030942	KRANTZ
444444444	2-52 FOREST HILLS, QUEENS	05	M	090252	BUTLER
555555555	7 PARK AVE, JERSEY CITY	17	M	092057	RANADE
666666666	15 GREENWICH, CT	12	M	030511	ADLER
777777777	8 BROAD ST., S.I., N.Y.	07	F	082913	JOSHI
888888888	KENNER TOWERS, N.Y., N.Y.	04	F	111855	LEHN
999999999	23 SOUTH ST., BRONX. N.Y.	13	F	100846	RAMSEY

Employee-SSN
Employee-Address
Employee-Number
Employee-Sex
Employee-Dob
Employee-Name

Figure 7.1 A physical sequential data set having nine fixed-length records of 50 bytes each. Each record has six fields as shown. The data set name is SAMPLE.INPUT.DATA.

The name of our data set is SAMPLE.INPUT.DATA. In real life, a personnel system would not be as simple as this record layout indicates. Since the purpose of this book is to learn the intricacies of VSAM and not systems analysis, this record layout will satisfy our needs in the subsequent examples.

7.2 LOADING VSAM DATA SETS

The process of loading records into a VSAM data set involves opening an input file, reading its records one by one, and writing them into the target VSAM data set. All these functions are accomplished by REPRO. In the following examples, our input file will be SAMPLE.INPUT.DATA and the target VSAM files will be the ones created in the last chapter. To refresh your memory, their names are

EMPLOYEE.KSDS.CLUSTER
EMPLOYEE.ESDS.CLUSTER
EMPLOYEE.RRDS.CLUSTER

7.2.1 Loading a KSDS

Figure 7.2 gives the sample JCL for loading records into a KSDS.

In the command syntax, INFILE has the value of SOURCE and OUTFILE has the value of TARGET, which correspond to the DD names of the input and output files coded in the JCL. These DD names could have been given any value, but they must be identical to the values of the INFILE and OUTFILE parameters. After the successful execution of this REPRO command, the nine records in SAMPLE.INPUT.DATA will be copied into EMPLOYEE.KSDS.CLUSTER.

```
//AMSJOB    JOB (ACCTNO),'JAY RANADE'
//LOADKSDS  EXEC PGM=IDCAMS
//SYSPRINT  DD SYSOUT=A
//SOURCE    DD DSN=SAMPLE.INPUT.DATA,
//             DISP=OLD
//TARGET    DD DSN=EMPLOYEE.KSDS.CLUSTER,
//             DISP=OLD
//SYSIN     DD *
  REPRO                                   -
  INFILE(SOURCE)                          -
  OUTFILE(TARGET)
/*
//
```

Figure 7.2 Sample JCL for copying records into a KSDS.

Sorting Input Records The input file in the last example is in ascending collating sequence on Social Security Number, which is the prime key (Fig. 7.1). If this weren't so, REPRO would give an error message whenever it found an out-of-sequence record in the input data set. After four such error messages, the load operation is aborted. An out-of-sequence record is one whose key is equal to or less than the key of the last loaded record. Since in real-life applications you may not always have an input file in ascending order by the prime key, you must perform an external sort on the input file before you execute REPRO. In such cases, loading a KSDS will be a two-step procedure:

1. Execute an external sort on the prime key field using the SORT utility and put the sorted records into a new data set.
2. Use the same JCL as in Fig. 7.2 with INFILE and SOURCE DD pointing to the new, sorted data set.

Figure 7.3 gives the complete two-step procedure (SORT and REPRO) for loading a KSDS.

```
//AMSJOB    JOB (ACCTNO),'JAY RANADE'
//**************************************************
//******  SORT  INPUT PS  FILE  ***************
//**************************************************
//SORT      EXEC PGM=SORT
//SORTLIB   DD DSN=SYS1.SORTLIB,DISP=SHR
//SORTIN    DD DSN=SAMPLE.INPUT.DATA,
//             DISP=OLD
//SORTOUT   DD DSN=&&TEMP,DISP=(NEW,PASS,DELETE),
//             DCB=(RECFM=FB,LRECL=50,BLKSIZE=5000),
//             SPACE=(TRK,(5,1)),UNIT=SYSDA
//SYSIN     DD *
  SORT FIELDS=(1,9,CH,A)
/*
//**************************************************
//******  REPRO FROM SORTED FILE  *************
//**************************************************
//LOADKSDS EXEC PGM=IDCAMS
//SYSPRINT DD SYSOUT=A
//SOURCE    DD DSN=&&TEMP,DISP=(OLD,DELETE,DELETE)
//TARGET    DD DSN=EMPLOYEE.KSDS.CLUSTER,
//             DISP=OLD
//SYSIN     DD *
  REPRO                          -
  INFILE(SOURCE)                 -
  OUTFILE(TARGET)
/*
//
```

Figure 7.3 Use of external SORT and REPRO command to load a KSDS.

Since we know that our input file is small (it has only nine records), the sort will be performed in virtual memory. If you are dealing with large input files, you must code SORTWK01, SORTWK02, SORTWK03, etc., as work files in the SORT step.

Dynamic Allocation of Files As you look at the sample JCL in Fig. 7.4, notice the different syntax of both the required DD statements and the REPRO parameters. This demonstrates how we load a KSDS using the dynamic allocation feature.

Notice that we are using the INDATASET and OUTDATASET parameters instead of the INFILE and OUTFILE parameters. We have also not coded DD statements for allocating the data sets. In this syntax format, AMS performs a dynamic allocation of the data sets for you. This format is simpler to use than the previous one. Using either of these syntax formats is a matter of personal preference. However, you must be careful, since dynamic allocation can be performed only for data sets that are cataloged. To keep JCL simple, we will use the dynamic allocation feature of AMS wherever possible.

Mixed Format Different formats may be mixed within a REPRO command. For example, the following two combinations are valid.

```
REPRO                                  -
INFILE(SOURCE)                         -
OUTDATASET(EMPLOYEE.KSDS.CLUSTER)
```

and

```
REPRO                              -
INDATASET(SAMPLE.INPUT.DATA) -
OUTFILE(TARGET)
```

```
//AMSJOB    JOB (ACCTNO),'JAY RANADE'
//LOADKSDS  EXEC PGM=IDCAMS
//SYSPRINT  DD SYSOUT=A
//SYSIN     DD *
  REPRO                                  -
  INDATASET(SAMPLE.INPUT.DATA)           -
  OUTDATASET(EMPLOYEE.KSDS.CLUSTER)
/*
//
```

Figure 7.4 Loading a KSDS from a PS data set using the dynamic allocation feature.

```
//AMSJOB    JOB (ACCTNO),'JAY RANADE'
//LOADESDS  EXEC PGM=IDCAMS
//SYSPRINT  DD SYSOUT=A
//SYSIN     DD *
  REPRO                                       -
  INDATASET(SAMPLE.INPUT.DATA)                -
  OUTDATASET(EMPLOYEE.ESDS.CLUSTER)
/*
//
```

Figure 7.5 JCL for loading an ESDS.

7.2.2 Loading an ESDS

Loading records into an ESDS is no different than loading records into a KSDS. Since an ESDS doesn't have a prime key, sorting of the input file is not required. However, if the application requires that the records be loaded in sequence based on a particular field, the sorting should be taken care of as a separate task. REPRO writes records to an ESDS in the same sequence in which it reads them from the input data set. Figure 7.5 gives the JCL for loading records from SAMPLE.INPUT.DATA to EMPLOYEE.ESDS.CLUSTER.

7.2.3 Loading an RRDS

Loading an RRDS using REPRO is the same as loading a KSDS or an ESDS. Figure 7.6 gives the JCL for loading EMPLOYEE.RRDS.CLUSTER. Records will be loaded from the input file into the RRDS beginning with RRN 1. The few applications where records loaded into an RRDS *this way* would be useful are those where a field needed for access is sequenced from 1 to the end consecutively, as in consecutively numbered airplane flights, part numbers, employee numbers, etc. Most ap-

```
//AMSJOB    JOB (ACCTNO),'JAY RANADE'
//LOADRRDS  EXEC PGM=IDCAMS
//SYSPRINT  DD SYSOUT=A
//SYSIN     DD *
  REPRO                                       -
  INDATASET(SAMPLE.INPUT.DATA)                -
  OUTDATASET(EMPLOYEE.RRDS.CLUSTER)
/*
//
```

Figure 7.6 JCL for loading an RRDS.

plications use a particular field and relate it to an RRN. This, of course, can be accomplished if you first develop an algorithm that can generate a relationship between the RRN and a particular record field in the RRDS and then use a program (Cobol, PL/I, or assembler) to load the records into the file. The same algorithm, when used in reverse order, could retrieve the records from an RRDS. However, the purpose of this example was to show you what you can do with REPRO. Incorporating the various features of VSAM and AMS into an application will be a separate design task.

7.3 VERSATILITY OF THE REPRO COMMAND

REPRO can be used not only for loading VSAM data sets but also for performing backups and restores on non-VSAM data sets. Figure 7.7 gives the possible combinations of INFILE (or INDATASET) and OUTFILE (or OUTDATASET) parameters supporting the different file organizations.

An indexed sequential output file is not supported by REPRO. All the powerful features of REPRO can be used to perform backup and restore functions of different data set organizations. When used for only non-VSAM files, it can be helpful as a backup and recovery utility in place of IEBGENER.

7.4 OTHER PARAMETERS OF REPRO

So far, we have seen that REPRO will copy all the records of an input file into an output file. In some cases, however, you may need to copy only a

	Output file					
Input file	**Indexed sequential**	**Physical sequential**	**Partitioned data set member**	**KSDS**	**ESDS**	**RRDS**
Indexed sequential	No	Yes	Yes	Yes	Yes	Yes
Physical sequential	No	Yes	Yes	Yes	Yes	Yes
Partitioned data set member	No	Yes	Yes	Yes	Yes	Yes
KSDS	No	Yes	Yes	Yes	Yes	Yes
ESDS	No	Yes	Yes	Yes	Yes	Yes
RRDS	No	Yes	Yes	Yes	Yes	Yes

It is assumed that the output file is empty to start with. "Yes" indicates the combination is supported; "No" indicates that it is not.

Figure 7.7 Possible combinations of file organizations supported by REPRO.

selected group of records into the output file. We will discuss some of the other parameters of REPRO which make this possible.

7.4.1 REPLACE

This optional parameter is used to merge records into a VSAM file. It has meaning only when the target data set already has records and is either a KSDS or an RRDS. Let's look at these situations one at a time.

Target Data Set Is a NonEmpty KSDS All the records in the source file whose keys do not match the keys of the target data set are added to the target data set. All the records in the source file whose keys match keys of the target data set replace those records in the target data set. All the records which exist in the target data set but not in the source data set remain untouched. The source data set can be of any organization such as PS, ESDS, RRDS, KSDS, or PDS member. In the following example, records from SAMPLE.NEWINPUT.DATA will be merged with the records of EMPLOYEE.KSDS.CLUSTER (as loaded through the JCL in Fig. 7.2).

```
REPRO                                   -
INDATASET(SAMPLE.NEWINPUT.DATA)         -
OUTDATASET(EMPLOYEE.KSDS.CLUSTER) -
REPLACE
```

Figure 7.8 gives an example of the execution of the above command. Remember that, if the REPLACE option is not coded, records from the source data set that have matching key records in the target data set will not be replaced and you will get *duplicate record* messages.

Target Data Set Is a NonEmpty RRDS *If the target data set is a nonempty RRDS, the source data set must be an RRDS too.* You cannot merge records from a non-RRDS source data set with a nonempty target RRDS data set. The reason for this restriction is that only a source RRDS has relative record numbers which identify where the source records should be placed in the target data set. Consider the following example.

```
REPRO                                   -
INDATASET(EMPLOYEE.RRDS1.CLUSTER)       -
OUTDATASET(EMPLOYEE.RRDS2.CLUSTER) -
REPLACE
```

In this example, records in the source data set that have the same RRN's as records in the target data set will replace those in the target data set. If the RRN of a record in the source data set points to an empty slot in the target data set, it will be added to the target RRDS. Other records

```
SAMPLE.NEWINPUT.DATA
|222222222|65 DOWN ST., N.Y. N.Y.    |19|M|022536|TANAKA|
|333000000|31 RICHARD LANE, QUEENS   |11|F|032054|CHENG |
|777777777|8 BROWN ST., S.I., N.Y.   |07|F|082913|JOSHI |
|888000000|81 GREEN ST., SCARSDALE   |15|F|020242|MURPHY|
```

```
EMPLOYEE.KSDS.CLUSTER (BEFORE)
|111111111|WORLD PLAZA, N.Y.,N.Y.       |10|M|092150|RANADE|
|222222222|25 OAKWOODS, N.Y.            |19|M|022536|TANAKA|
|333333333|18 MARSH AVE., S.I., N.Y.    |16|F|030942|KRANTZ|
|444444444|2-52, FOREST HILLS, QUEENS   |05|M|090252|BUTLER|
|555555555|7 PARK AVE, JERSEY CITY      |17|M|092057|RANADE|
|666666666|15 GREENWICH, CT.            |12|M|030511|ADLER |
|777777777|8 BROAD ST, S.I.  N.Y.       |07|F|082913|JOSHI |
|888888888|KENNER TOWERS, N.Y., N.Y.    |04|F|111855|LEHN  |
|999999999|23 SOUTH ST., BRONX, N.Y.    |13|F|100846|RAMSEY|
```

```
| REPRO                               - |
| INDATASET(SAMPLE.NEWINPUT.DATA)     - |
| OUTDATASET(EMPLOYEE.KSDS.CLUSTER)   - |
| REPLACE                               |
```

```
EMPLOYEE.KSDS.CLUSTER (AFTER EXECUTION OF COMMAND)
|111111111|WORLD PLAZA, N.Y., N.Y.      |10|M|092150|RANADE|  SAME
|222222222|65 DOWN ST, N.Y., N.Y.       |19|M|022536|TANAKA|  REPLACED
|333000000|31 RICHARD LANE, QUEENS      |11|F|032054|CHENG |  ADDED
|333333333|18 MARSH AVE, S.I., N.Y.     |16|F|030942|KRANTZ|  SAME
|444444444|2-52, FOREST HILLS, QUEENS   |05|M|090252|BUTLER|  SAME
|555555555|7 PARK AVE, JERSEY CITY      |17|M|092057|RANADE|  SAME
|666666666|15 GREENWICH, CT             |12|M|030511|ADLER |  SAME
|777777777|8 BROWN ST, S.I., N.Y.       |07|F|082913|JOSHI |  REPLACED
|888000000|81 GREEN ST., SCARSDALE      |15|F|020242|MURPHY|  ADDED
|888888888|KENNER TOWERS, N.Y., N.Y.    |04|F|111855|LEHN  |  SAME
|999999999|23 SOUTH ST, BRONX, N.Y.     |13|F|100846|RAMSEY|  SAME
```

Figure 7.8 SAMPLE.NEWINPUT.DATA, with 4 records, is merged with EMPLOYEE.KSDS.CLUSTER (9 records) by executing a REPRO command with the REPLACE option. RECORDS with keys 222222222 and 777777777 replace existing records, while records with keys 333000000 and 888000000 are added to the merged VSAM file. At the end, EMPLOYEE.KSDS.CLUSTER will have 11 records.

in the target RRDS will remain unchanged. Figure 7.9 gives an example of the execution of the above command. The REPRO default for this option is NOREPLACE.

7.4.2 REUSE

In the previous chapter, we discussed the use of the REUSE option when allocating a cluster. We also noted that, when a VSAM data set defined with the REUSE option is opened as OUTPUT in a Cobol program, all the existing records are logically deleted and new records are added from the beginning of the data set. The same function can be performed through REPRO. The REUSE option of REPRO will logically delete the records of a target KSDS, ESDS, or RRDS and add new records from

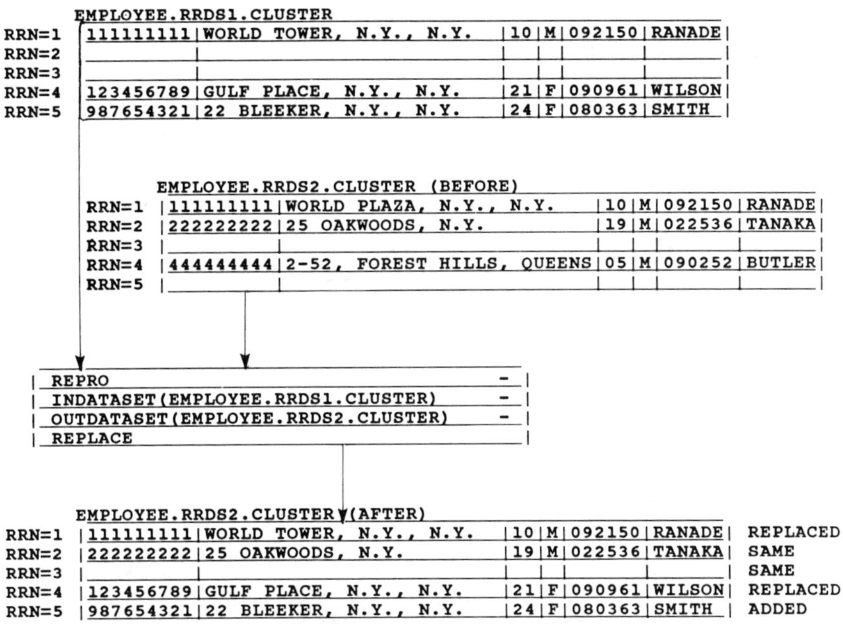

Figure 7.9 EMPLOYEE.RRDS1.CLUSTER, with three records, is merged with EMPLOYEE.RRDS2.CLUSTER, which also has three records, by executing a REPRO command with the REPLACE option. Records with RRN's of 1 and 4 are replaced, while the record with an RRN of 5 is added to the target data set. The record with an RRN of 2 remains untouched, and the RRN 3 slot stays empty.

the source data set as if the target data set were empty. The following is the syntax for the use of the REUSE option.

```
REPRO                                  -
INDATASET(SAMPLE.NEWINPUT.DATA)        -
OUTDATASET(EMPLOYEE.KSDS.CLUSTER)      -
REUSE
```

With the above command, records from INDATASET will be loaded into outdataset as if OUTDATASET never had any records. Figure 7.10 shows how the command is executed.

In order to use the REUSE option of REPRO, the target data set *must* have been defined with the REUSE option in the DEFINE CLUSTER command. Otherwise, the REPRO command will terminate with an error message. A data set defined with the REUSE option will probably never have to be deleted and redefined, because the purpose of deleting and redefining is to eliminate the existing records and to allocate a new, empty cluster. REUSE empties out the cluster logically rather than having to delete and define it again.

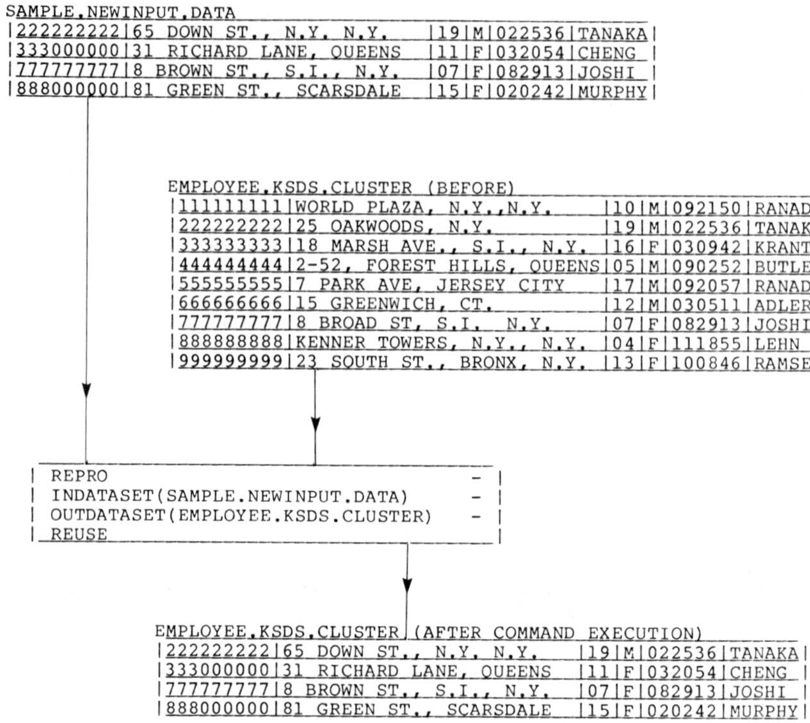

Figure 7.10 The REUSE option of REPRO will delete all records from the target data set before loading it with records of the source data set. The nine records in the target data set that existed before the execution of the command cannot be accessed anymore.

7.4.3 SKIP and COUNT

So far, we have dealt with examples in which all the records from the source data set were copied into the target data set. You might have applications in which only a selected group of records are to be copied into the output file. Figure 7.11 provides sample JCL for using the SKIP and COUNT options to achieve this goal.

In this example, the first two records in the source file (physical sequential) will be skipped, and the next four records (starting from the third record) will be read and loaded into the target file. Any additional records will not be read or copied. After successful execution of the command, EMPLOYEE.KSDS.CLUSTER will contain four records, assuming that the file was empty to start with.

The SKIP and COUNT parameters refer only to records in the source file. If SKIP is not coded, the default is SKIP(0). If COUNT is not coded, the default is to read and load records until the end of the source

```
//AMSJOB    JOB (ACCTNO),'JAY RANADE'
//REPRO     EXEC PGM=IDCAMS
//SYSPRINT DD SYSOUT=A
//SYSIN     DD *
  REPRO                                    -
  INDATASET(SAMPLE.INPUT.DATA)             -
  OUTDATASET(EMPLOYEE.KSDS.CLUSTER)        -
  SKIP(2)                                  -
  COUNT(4)
/*
//
```

Figure 7.11 Use of the SKIP and COUNT options of REPRO to copy selected records into the output file.

file is reached. SKIP and COUNT can be mixed with optional parameters such as REPLACE and REUSE.

7.4.4 FROMKEY and TOKEY

It is likely that the source data set in some applications will be a KSDS or indexed sequential file from which you only want to copy records beginning with a particular key value and ending with another key value. For example, you might want to copy records from EMPLOYEE.KSDS.CLUSTER, beginning with key value 333333333 and ending with 777777777, into a physical sequential data set named SAMPLE.SOME.RECORDS.DATA. The JCL in Fig. 7.12 will accomplish this.

```
//AMSJOB    JOB (ACCTNO),'JAY RANADE'
//REPRO     EXEC PGM=IDCAMS
//SYSPRINT DD SYSOUT=A
//OUTPS     DD DSN=SAMPLE.SOME.RECORDS.DATA,
//             DISP=NEW,UNIT=SYSDA,VOL=SER=VSAM02,
//             DCB=(RECFM=FB,LRECL=50,BLKSIZE=5000),
//             SPACE=(TRK,(5,1))
//SYSIN     DD *
  REPRO                                -
  INDATASET(EMPLOYEE.KSDS.CLUSTER)     -
  OUTFILE(OUTPS)                       -
  FROMKEY(333333333)                   -
  TOKEY(777777777)
/*
//
```

Figure 7.12 Sample JCL with the use of FROMKEY and TOKEY options.

You can also use a generic key instead of the full key with these options. A generic key is a left-justified (starting with the first byte of the key) subset of the full key. For example, 567 is one of the generic keys of the full key 567123489. In our example, we could have used the following REPRO command syntax in Fig. 7.12.

```
REPRO                                 -
INDATASET(EMPLOYEE.KSDS.CLUSTER) -
OUTFILE(OUTPS)                        -
FROMKEY(33)                           -
TOKEY(77)
```

The above command will copy all records from the source data set having 33 as the first two characters of their keys through the records having 77 as the first two characters of their keys.

In order to copy only one record from the source data set, the values in the FROMKEY and TOKEY parameters should be the same. For example, we could use the following command syntax to copy the record with key 555555555 from the KSDS into the physical sequential file.

```
REPRO                                 -
INDATASET(EMPLOYEE.KSDS.CLUSTER) -
OUTFILE(OUTPS)                        -
FROMKEY(555555555)                    -
TOKEY(555555555)
```

If the source file is an ESDS, one can use the FROMADDRESS and TOADDRESS options. These options give the starting and ending relative byte addresses of the records to be copied. If the source file is an RRDS, you can use the FROMNUMBER and TONUMBER options. These give the starting and ending RRN's of the records to be copied. Details of the use of these parameters can be found in IBM's *Access Method Services* manual.

7.4.5 ENVIRONMENT(DUMMY)

This parameter applies only to a *source file* that is indexed sequential. If the source file is indexed sequential and this parameter is *not* coded, dummy ISAM records (records having high values, i.e., hexadecimal **FF** in the first byte) will *not* be copied into the target file. This is usually what you want. However, if you *do* want to copy dummy ISAM records from an indexed sequential source file to a target file, you must code the ENVIRONMENT(DUMMY) parameter. The following command syntax gives an example of the use of this parameter.

```
REPRO                                    -
INDATASET(SAMPLE.ISAM.FILE               -
ENVIRONMENT(DUMMY)         )             -
OUTDATASET(EMPLOYEE.KSDS.CLUSTER)
```

Note the use of parentheses in the above example. You can use the REPRO command with different variations of this parameter when converting an indexed sequential file to a KSDS.

7.5 REPRO AS BACKUP AND RESTORE FACILITY

For any computer application in a production environment, backup and restore procedures are designed and implemented as a normal requirement. Backups of VSAM data sets are made so that they can be used to restore the original files in case any of the following circumstances occur:

1. The batch update jobs abend or the system comes down in the middle of a batch update of a VSAM file. A backup made with the help of REPRO command before the batch update job was started will allow you to restore the file and reapply the updates.
2. The on-line system (e.g., CICS) comes down in the middle of a transaction update which caused a CI or CA split of the KSDS. Such an incomplete CI or CA split will normally render the file unusable. Under these circumstances, you will have to restore the file from the most current backup and reapply all the on-line changes from the journal file to bring the file up to date as of the time of the CI/CA split.
3. You need to reorganize a KSDS. This function will be discussed in detail in a subsequent section.
4. A VSAM or ICF catalog becomes unusable, preventing access to some or all of the VSAM data sets cataloged in it. You will then need backup copies to re-create the data sets.

We have already mentioned that REPRO can be used to make copies of both non-VSAM and VSAM files. Therefore, this command can be used as a backup and restore facility for non-VSAM data sets as well as for the VSAM data sets we've already discussed.

7.5.1 Backup

Making a backup of a VSAM file is a one-step procedure. Figure 7.13 shows how a backup of a KSDS to a physical sequential data set can be accomplished.

```
//AMSJOB     JOB (ACCTNO),'JAY RANADE'
//BACKUP     EXEC PGM=IDCAMS
//SYSPRINT DD SYSOUT=A
//TARGET     DD DSN=SAMPLE.BACKUP.FILE(+1),
//              DISP=(NEW,CATLG,DELETE),UNIT=TAPE,
//              LABEL=(1,SL),
//              DCB=(MOD.DSCB,RECFM=FB,LRECL=50,BLKSIZE=5000)
//SYSIN      DD *
  REPRO                                        -
  INDATASET(EMPLOYEE.KSDS.CLUSTER)             -
  OFILE(TARGET)
/*
//
```

Figure 7.13 Sample JCL for making a backup of a VSAM (KSDS) file.

As you can see from the JCL, a generation data set[1] is being used to make a backup of the VSAM file. It is a fairly common practice to create multiple generations of backups so that in case of disaster you can re-create data sets from as far back as 5, 10, or more generations if necessary.

7.5.2 RESTORE

Restoring the VSAM file from its backup is usually a three-step procedure:

1. Delete the VSAM file with the DELETE command.
2. Reallocate the file with the DEFINE CLUSTER command.
3. Load records from the backup file into the VSAM file using the REPRO command.

We have not discussed the DELETE command yet. However, to get an idea of what the JCL for carrying out the above sequence would be, look at Fig. 7.14.

In Fig. 7.14, three commands of Access Method Services have been coded to delete, define, and restore a VSAM data set. Note that there is no continuation character (hyphen) at the end of each command. Recall from our previous discussions that omission of the continuation character denotes the end of a functional command. The use of "/*" and "*/" as the delimiters of comments should also be noted. Any characters or remarks between such delimiters are ignored by IDCAMS and are used for documentation purposes only. Each line of a comment must be surrounded by the "/*" and "*/" combination.

[1]Using generation data sets is a way of creating and accessing multiple copies of a data set by referring to them by relative numbers. For example, + 1 is the new generation that will be created, +0 is the current (latest) generation to be accessed, − 1 is the one prior to the current one, and so on. For further details, refer to the *OS/VS2 MVS JCL* manual.

```
//AMSJOB    JOB (ACCTNO),'JAY RANADE'
//RESTORE   EXEC PGM=IDCAMS
//SYSPRINT DD SYSOUT=A
//SOURCE    DD DSN=SAMPLE.BACKUP.FILE(0),
//             DISP=OLD,UNIT=TAPE,LABEL=(1,SL)
//SYSIN     DD *
  /*****************************************************/
  /*** FOLLOWING COMMAND DELETES VSAM DATASET ***/
  /*****************************************************/
   DELETE    EMPLOYEE.KSDS.CLUSTER
  /*****************************************************/
  /*** FOLLOWING COMMAND ALLOCATES VSAM DATASET */
  /*****************************************************/
   DEFINE CLUSTER                                  -
     (NAME(EMPLOYEE.KSDS.CLUSTER)                  -
     VOLUMES(VSAM02)                               -
     CYLINDERS(2,1)                                -
     KEYS(9,0)                                     -
     RECORDSIZE(50,50)                             -
     CONTROLINTERVALSIZE(4096)    )                -
     DATA  (NAME(EMPLOYEE.KSDS.DATA))              -
     INDEX  (NAME(EMPLOYEE.KSDS.INDEX))            -
     CATALOG(VSAM.CATALOG.TWO)
  /*****************************************************/
  /*** FOLLOWING COMMAND RESTORES VSAM DATASET **/
  /*****************************************************/
     REPRO                                         -
     IFILE(SOURCE)                                 -
     OUTDATASET(EMPLOYEE.KSDS.CLUSTER)
/*
//
```

Figure 7.14 JCL for restoring a VSAM file (a KSDS in this example) from its backup.

Restoring Reusable Clusters In the example in Fig. 7.14, the purpose of the DELETE and DEFINE commands was to create an empty data set so that records could be loaded from scratch. If you recall the characteristics of a reusable cluster (defined with the REUSE parameter), you will realize that it is not necessary to delete and define a data set defined with the REUSE option. Records within such a data set are logically deleted whenever it is opened for OUTPUT or records are loaded into it using REPRO with the REUSE option. So the format of the REPRO command for restoring such a data set will be as follows.

```
REPRO                                -
IFILE(SOURCE)                        -
OUTDATASET(EMPLOYEE.KSDS.CLUSTER) -
REUSE
```

The following points must be kept in mind when considering the use of reusable data sets.

- When defined with DEFINE CLUSTER, such data sets must include the REUSE parameter.
- When restored with REPRO, such data sets must have the REUSE parameter specified again.
- Reusable data sets cannot have alternate indexes.

Reusable VSAM data sets are recommended for use in CICS/VS unless you want to have alternate indexes on the cluster. The reason for doing this is that, if a VSAM data set which is part of the CICS initialization JCL does not exist (because it was deleted and never allocated again), CICS will not come up. Batch jobs usually involve the deletion and redefinition of VSAM clusters. The redefinition of a data set after deletion may not always be possible, because the disk space can be claimed by another job before redefinition begins. The next time an attempt is made to bring the CICS/VS system up, a missing data set may prevent it, causing unnecessary delays for all the users. If reusable data sets are used, this problem will not occur because there is no need to delete data sets.

7.5.3 Reorganization of a KSDS

Frequent adds and updates to a KSDS in batch and on-line (CICS) environments can cause CI and CA splits. Although the data set is still logically in collating sequence on the prime key after such splits, the records are physically out of sequence. While you can still access these records randomly and sequentially, access time increases. These I/O delays can cause response time problems in CICS/VS and other on-line systems and also increase the run time of batch jobs. In order to put the KSDS records back into physical sequence, it is necessary to reorganize the data set. Reorganization is a four-step procedure:

1. Make a backup of the KSDS into a physical sequential data set using the REPRO command.
2. Delete the KSDS with the DELETE command.
3. Define the KSDS using the DEFINE CLUSTER command.
4. Reload the KSDS from the backup file using the REPRO command.

If you are using reusable data sets, steps 2 and 3 will not be necessary.

Notice that there is no difference between the backup and restore procedures and the reorganization procedures of a KSDS. Remember that a reorganization of records is necessary only for a KSDS and *not* for an ESDS or an RRDS. Determining when it is necessary to reorganize a KSDS depends upon the application. Usually, if the total number of CA splits exceeds 15 percent of the total number of CA's in the data set, it is best to reorganize it. The LISTCAT command, which is covered later, can be used to determine the number of CI and CA splits in a data set.

7.6 REPRO FOR MERGING FILES

REPRO can be used to merge two files into one. The first file to be merged is called the *source file*, while the second one is called the *target file*. Merging two files involves copying the records of a source file into a nonempty target file. Before the merge takes place, make sure that the target file has enough space to contain the records of the source file. If you are merging a source KSDS with a target KSDS, the following command syntax can be used.

```
REPRO              -
INFILE(SOURCE)     -
OUTFILE(TARGET)
```

Where SOURCE and TARGET are the DD names of the files to be merged.

If the target file is a KSDS, the source file should not have any records with the same key values as the target file. If there are duplicate records, you must specify the REPLACE option of the REPRO command. Remember, however, that the REPLACE option will replace records in the target file with records from the source file having the same keys. The source file can have any organization (PS, ESDS, RRDS, KSDS, or indexed sequential) if the target file is a KSDS.

If the target file is an RRDS, the source file to be merged *must* be an RRDS. During the merge process, records from the source file are merged into the target file using the relative record numbers of the source file. If the target file already has records in these slots, a duplicate record condition will occur and the records in the slots in the target file will remain unchanged. Again, if the REPLACE option is used, records in these slots in the target file will be replaced by source file records with the same relative record numbers.

Remember that, whether you get a duplicate record error condition on a target KSDS or a target RRDS (if you are not using the REPLACE option), the command will be terminated the fourth time the condition occurs and you will receive a non-zero condition code on termination. Testing for such a condition code (using the COND parameter of JCL) is very important. If you do not test for a condition code of zero and you have had three or fewer duplicate record error messages, you will probably never know such a condition exists and the results might be other than what you wanted. Also, if you have had four or more duplicate record error messages and the command is terminated, you could potentially lose many records if the error is undetected.

If the target file of a merge is an ESDS, the records from the source file are added to the end of the file. In such cases the source file can have any organization.

chapter 8

Printing Data Sets

The PRINT command of Access Method Services is used to print the contents of both VSAM and non-VSAM data sets. The command syntax is similar to that of REPRO. While REPRO copies an input data set into another output data set, PRINT dumps an input data set to a printer. This command is versatile and can be used to print a complete data set or only a selected part of it. Other utilities of MVS, such as IEBPTPCH and IEBGENER, can be used to print only non-VSAM data sets.

The contents of a data set may be printed in one of the following formats.

Character Format When this format is specified, the data set contents are printed in EBCDIC characters. Any combination of bits that does not correspond to a printable character will be printed as a period. A maximum of 120 characters are printed on each line. If the record length is greater than 120 characters, it is printed in blocks of 120 characters per line.

Hex Format This format prints each character in the data set as 2 hexadecimal digits. A maximum of 120 hexadecimal digits are printed on each line, the equivalent of 60 characters. If the record length is greater than 120 hex digits (60 characters), the record is printed in blocks of 120 hex digits per line. A file printed in hex format will take up about twice as much paper as one in character format because each character is printed as 2 hex digits.

Dump Format The dump format is a combination of the character and hex formats. Each character is printed both as a character and as the corresponding hex representation. Each print line contains 64 hex digits and the 32 related characters. If the record length is more than 32 characters, the rest of the record is printed in blocks of 64 hex digits and 32 corresponding characters per line. A file printed in this format takes about four times as much space as one printed in character format.

8.1 PRINTING A VSAM DATA SET

The syntax of the PRINT command in its simplest form (for printing both VSAM and non-VSAM files) is

```
PRINT              -
INFILE(INPUT)
```

where input is the DD name of the file to be printed. **DUMP**, the keyword parameter which corresponds to the dump format printout (hex and character) is also the default parameter if nothing is coded in the command. To print in character format, the keyword **CHAR** must be coded in the command. To get a hex format print, the keyword **HEX** should be coded in the command. You can also code INDATASET instead of INFILE in this command. However, when using the INDATASET parameter, the value of the parameter must be the data set name rather than the DD name.

8.1.1 Printing a KSDS

Let's say you want to print the contents of the KSDS EMPLOYEE.KSDS.CLUSTER which was defined in Chap. 6 (using the JCL in Fig. 6.2) and loaded in Chap. 7 (with the JCL in Fig. 7.2) with the records as they appear in Fig. 7.1. The JCL for printing EMPLOYEE.KSDS.CLUSTER in the dump format is given in Fig. 8.1.

If the JCL in Fig. 8.1 is executed successfully, the printout of the data set in dump format will look like Fig. 8.2.

Notice that the records are printed in Social Security Number sequence because it is the prime key of this KSDS. On the left side the records are printed in hex format, while on the right the corresponding characters are printed. The key of the record is given on a separate line before the record itself is printed. The end of the printout indicates that nine records were processed and that the highest condition code was zero.

```
//AMSJOB    JOB (ACCTNO),'JAY RANADE'
//KSDSPRNT  EXEC PGM=IDCAMS
//SYSPRINT  DD SYSOUT=A
//SYSIN     DD *
  PRINT                                  -
  INDATASET(EMPLOYEE.KSDS.CLUSTER)       -
  DUMP
/*
//
```

Figure 8.1 JCL for printing EMPLOYEE.KSDS.CLUSTER in character as well as hex format.

If the data set is to be printed in character format, the command syntax will be

```
PRINT                              -
INDATASET(EMPLOYEE.KSDS.CLUSTER) -
CHAR
```

The printout of the data set produced by the successful execution of the command with the CHAR parameter appears in Fig. 8.3.

Similarly, to print the data set in hex format only, the following command syntax can be used.

```
PRINT                              -
INDATASET(EMPLOYEE.KSDS.CLUSTER) -
HEX
```

The printout produced from the successful execution of the above command appears in Fig. 8.4.

In subsequent examples of the PRINT command, we will use the character format wherever possible to keep the printouts more readable.

Printing Individual Components So far, in all the examples for printing a KSDS shown, the name of the cluster was used. Records were read and printed from the data component in key sequence, which was determined from the index component. For all practical purposes, you will print the records by giving the cluster name in the INFILE (or INDATASET) parameter. However, to understand the internal organization of each of the individual components of the KSDS cluster, let's print them separately.

In order to print the data component, you have to use its name as the value of the INDATASET parameter. The following JCL can be used to print the data component of EMPLOYEE.KSDS.CLUSTER in character format.

```
LISTING OF DATA SET -EMPLOYEE.KSDS.CLUSTER

KEY OF RECORD - F1F1F1F1F1F1F1F1F1
000000  F1F1F1F1 F1F1F1F1 F140E6D6 D9D3C440   D7D3C1E9 C16BD54B E86BD54B E8404040   *111111111 WORLD PLAZA,N.Y,N.Y   *
000020  404040F1 F0D4F0F9 F2F1F5F0 D9C1D5C1   C4C5                                  *    10M092150RANADE              *

KEY OF RECORD - F2F2F2F2F2F2F2F2F2
000000  F2F2F2F2 F2F2F2F2 F240F2F5 6BD6C1D2   E6D6D6C4 E26BD54B E8404040 40404040   *222222222 25,OAKWOODS,N.Y       *
000020  404040F1 F9D4F0F2 F2F5F3F6 E3C1D5C1   D2C1                                  *    19M022536TANAKA              *

KEY OF RECORD - F3F3F3F3F3F3F3F3F3
000000  F3F3F3F3 F3F3F3F3 F340F1F8 6BD4C1D9   E2C840C1 E56BE24B C96BD54B E8404040   *333333333 18,MARSH AV,S.I,N.Y   *
000020  404040F1 F6C6F0F3 F0F9F4F2 D2D9C1D5   E3E9                                  *    16F030942KRANTZ              *

KEY OF RECORD - F4F4F4F4F4F4F4F4F4
000000  F4F4F4F4 F4F4F4F4 F440F260 F5F26BC6   D6D9C5E2 E340C8C9 D3D3E26B D8E4C5C5   *444444444 2-52,FOREST HILLS,QUEE*
000020  D5E240F0 F5D4F0F9 F0F2F5F2 C2E4E3D3   C5D9                                  *NS 05M090252BUTLER               *

KEY OF RECORD - F5F5F5F5F5F5F5F5F5
000000  F5F5F5F5 F5F5F5F5 F540F76B D7C1D9D2   40C1E56B D1C5D9E2 C5E840C3 C9E3E840   *555555555 7,PARK AV,JERSEY CITY *
000020  404040F1 F7D4F0F9 F2F0F5F7 D9C1D5C1   C4C5                                  *    17M092057RANADE              *

KEY OF RECORD - F6F6F6F6F6F6F6F6F6
000000  F6F6F6F6 F6F6F6F6 F640F1F5 6BC7D9C5   C5D5E6C9 C3C8406B C3E34040 40404040   *666666666 15,GREENWICH ,CT      *
000020  404040F1 F2D4F0F3 F0F5F1F1 C1C4D3C5   D940                                  *    12M030511ADLER               *

KEY OF RECORD - F7F7F7F7F7F7F7F7F7
000000  F7F7F7F7 F7F7F7F7 F740F86B C2D9D6C1   C440E2E3 6BE24BC9 6BD54BE8 40404040   *777777777 8,BROAD ST,S.I,N.Y    *
000020  404040F0 F7C6F0F8 F2F9F1F3 D1D6E2C8   C940                                  *    07F082913JOSHI               *

KEY OF RECORD - F8F8F8F8F8F8F8F8F8
000000  F8F8F8F8 F8F8F8F8 F840D2C5 D5D5C5D9   40E3D6E6 C5D9E26B D54BE86B D54BE840   *888888888 KENNER TOWERS,N.Y,N.Y *
000020  404040F0 F4C6F1F1 F1F8F5F5 D3C5C8D5   4040                                  *    04F111855LEHN                *

KEY OF RECORD - F9F9F9F9F9F9F9F9F9
000000  F9F9F9F9 F9F9F9F9 F940F2F3 6BE2D6E4   E3C840E2 E36BC2D9 D6D5E76B D54BE840   *999999999 23,SOUTH ST,BRONX,N.Y *
000020  404040F1 F3C6F1F0 F0F8F4F6 D9C1D4E2   C5E8                                  *    13F100846RAMSEY              *

IDC0005I NUMBER OF RECORDS PROCESSED WAS 9

IDC0001I FUNCTION COMPLETED, HIGHEST CONDITION CODE WAS 0
```

Figure 8.2 Printout of EMPLOYEE.KSDS.CLUSTER produced by the execution of the JCL in Fig. 8.1.

```
IDCAMS  SYSTEM SERVICES


LISTING OF DATA SET -EMPLOYEE.KSDS.CLUSTER

KEY OF RECORD - 111111111
111111111 WORLD PLAZA,N.Y,N.Y          10M092150RANADE

KEY OF RECORD - 222222222
222222222 25,OAKWOODS,N.Y              19M022536TANAKA

KEY OF RECORD - 333333333
333333333 18,MARSH AV,S.I,N.Y          16F030942KRANTZ

KEY OF RECORD - 444444444
444444444 2-52,FOREST HILLS,QUEENS 05M090252BUTLER

KEY OF RECORD - 555555555
555555555 7,PARK AV,JERSEY CITY        17M092057RANADE

KEY OF RECORD - 666666666
666666666 15,GREENWICH ,CT             12M030511ADLER

KEY OF RECORD - 777777777
777777777 8,BROAD ST,S.I,N.Y           07F082913JOSHI

KEY OF RECORD - 888888888
888888888 KENNER TOWERS,N.Y,N.Y        04F111855LEHN

KEY OF RECORD - 999999999
999999999 23,SOUTH ST,BRONX,N.Y        13F100846RAMSEY

IDC0005I NUMBER OF RECORDS PROCESSED WAS 9

IDC0001I FUNCTION COMPLETED, HIGHEST CONDITION CODE WAS 0
```

Figure 8.3 Character format printout of EMPLOYEE.KSDS.CLUSTER.

```
PRINT                                -
INDATASET(EMPLOYEE.KSDS.DATA) -
CHAR
```

The printout of the data component appears in Fig. 8.5. Note that no key is involved when accessing the data component separately, so each record is printed by its relative byte address. Also note that the RBA of the first record is 0, not 1. Although the records are printed in RBA sequence, they are in the same order as that of the key sequence (Fig. 8.3). This means that records in *this* data component are physically loaded in the ascending sequence of the prime key. If you add records to this file (using a Cobol program), it may not remain in ascending key sequence within the data component. As soon as the first CI or CA split takes place, some of the records will be out of key sequence. If the data

```
LISTING OF DATA SET -EMPLOYEE.KSDS.CLUSTER

KEY OF RECORD - F1F1F1F1F1F1F1F1F1
F1F1F1F1F1F1F1F1F140E6D6D9D3C440D7D3C1E9C16BD54BE86BD54BE8404040404040F1F0D4F0F9F2F1F5F0D9C1D5C1C4C5

KEY OF RECORD - F2F2F2F2F2F2F2F2F2
F2F2F2F2F2F2F2F2F240F2F56BD6C1D2E6D6D6C4E26BD54BE8404040404040404040F1F9D4F0F2F2F5F3F6E3C1D5C1D2C1

KEY OF RECORD - F3F3F3F3F3F3F3F3F3
F3F3F3F3F3F3F3F3F340F1F86BD4C1D9E2C840C1E56BE24BC96BD54BE8404040404040F1F6C6F0F3F0F9F4F2D2D9C1D5E3E9

KEY OF RECORD - F4F4F4F4F4F4F4F4F4
F4F4F4F4F4F4F4F4F440F260F5F26BC6D6D9C5E2E340C8C9D3D3E26BD3E4C5C5D5E240F0F5D4F0F9F0F2F5F2C2E4E3D3C5D9

KEY OF RECORD - F5F5F5F5F5F5F5F5F5
F5F5F5F5F5F5F5F5F540F76BD7C1D9D240C1E56BD1C5D9E2C5E840C3C9E3E8404040F1F7D4F0F9F2F0F5F7D9C1D5C1C4C5

KEY OF RECORD - F6F6F6F6F6F6F6F6F6
F6F6F6F6F6F6F6F6F640F1F56BC7D9C5C5D5E6C9C3C8406BC3E34040404040404040F1F2D4F0F3F0F5F1F1C1C4D3C5D940

KEY OF RECORD - F7F7F7F7F7F7F7F7F7
F7F7F7F7F7F7F7F7F740F86BC2D9D6C1C440E2E36BE24BC96BD54BE84040404040404040F0F7C6F0F8F2F9F1F3D1D6E2C8C940

KEY OF RECORD - F8F8F8F8F8F8F8F8F8
F8F8F8F8F8F8F8F8F840D2C5D5D5C5D940E3D6E6C5D9E26BD54BE86BD54BE8404040F0F4C6F1F1F1F8F5F5D3C5C8D54040

KEY OF RECORD - F9F9F9F9F9F9F9F9F9
F9F9F9F9F9F9F9F9F940F2F36BE2D6E4E3C840E2E36BC2D9D6D5E76BD54BE8404040F1F3C6F1F0F0F8F4F6D9C1D4E2C5E8

IDC0005I NUMBER OF RECORDS PROCESSED WAS 9

IDC0001I FUNCTION COMPLETED, HIGHEST CONDITION CODE WAS 0
```

Figure 8.4 Hex format dump of EMPLOYEE.KSDS.CLUSTER.

```
LISTING OF DATA SET -EMPLOYEE.KSDS.DATA

RBA OF RECORD - 0
111111111 WORLD PLAZA,N.Y,N.Y           10M092150RANADE

RBA OF RECORD - 50
222222222 25,OAKWOODS,N.Y               19M022536TANAKA

RBA OF RECORD - 100
333333333 18,MARSH AV,S.I,N.Y           16F030942KRANTZ

RBA OF RECORD - 150
444444444 2-52,FOREST HILLS,QUEENS 05M090252BUTLER

RBA OF RECORD - 200
555555555 7,PARK AV,JERSEY CITY         17M092057RANADE

RBA OF RECORD - 250
666666666 15,GREENWICH ,CT              12M030511ADLER

RBA OF RECORD - 300
777777777 8,BROAD ST,S.I,N.Y            07F082913JOSHI

RBA OF RECORD - 350
888888888 KENNER TOWERS,N.Y,N.Y         04F111855LEHN

RBA OF RECORD - 400
999999999 23,SOUTH ST,BRONX,N.Y         13F100846RAMSEY

IDC0005I NUMBER OF RECORDS PROCESSED WAS 9

IDC0001I FUNCTION COMPLETED, HIGHEST CONDITION CODE WAS 0
```

Figure 8.5 Character format dump of EMPLOYEE.KSDS.DATA.

component is printed at that time, it will be printed in a different sequence, beginning with the location of the first CI split.

The following JCL can be used to print the contents of the index component in dump format.

```
PRINT                                -
INDATASET(EMPLOYEE.KSDS.INDEX) -
DUMP
```

The printout of the index component will look like Fig. 8.6.

Reading either a character or hexadecimal dump of the index component is not easy. This is because VSAM uses an algorithm that causes front and rear key compression on the keys when storing them in the index component. This helps to keep the index component as small as possible. Also, if key compression did not take place, too much space would be required to store key-pointer pairs in the index sequence set CI for each

```
LISTING OF DATA SET -EMPLOYEE.KSDS.INDEX

RBA OF RECORD - 0
000000  07F90301 00000000 00000000 00000000  010000AD 07F607F6 95949392 91908F8E  *.9...................6.6........*
000020  8D8C8B8A 89888786 85848382 81807F7E  7D7C7B7A 79787776 75747372 71706F6E  *.............."='@#:..........?>*
000040  6D6C6B6A 69686766 65646362 61605F5E  5D5C5B5A 59585756 55545352 51504F4E  *_%,.........../-¬;)*$........&|+*
000060  4D4C4B4A 49484746 45444342 41403F3E  3D3C3B3A 39383736 35343332 31302F2E  *(<........... ..................*
000080  2D2C2B2A 29282726 25242322 21201F1E  1D1C1B1A 19181716 15141312 11100F0E  *................................*
0000A0  0D0C0B0A 09080706 05040302 01000000  00000000 00000000 00000000 00000000  *................................*
0000C0  00000000 00000000 00000000 00000000  00000000 00000000 00000000 00000000  *................................*
0000E0  00000000 00000000 00000000 00000000  00000000 00000000 00000000 00000000  *................................*
000100  00000000 00000000 00000000 00000000  00000000 00000000 00000000 00000000  *................................*
000120  00000000 00000000 00000000 00000000  00000000 00000000 00000000 00000000  *................................*
000140  00000000 00000000 00000000 00000000  00000000 00000000 00000000 00000000  *................................*
000160  00000000 00000000 00000000 00000000  00000000 00000000 00000000 00000000  *................................*
000180  00000000 00000000 00000000 00000000  00000000 00000000 00000000 00000000  *................................*
0001A0  00000000 00000000 00000000 00000000  00000000 00000000 00000000 00000000  *................................*
0001C0  00000000 00000000 00000000 00000000  00000000 00000000 00000000 00000000  *................................*
0001E0  00000000 00000000 00000000 00000000  00000000 00000000 00000000 00000000  *................................*
000200  00000000 00000000 00000000 00000000  00000000 00000000 00000000 00000000  *................................*
000220  00000000 00000000 00000000 00000000  00000000 00000000 00000000 00000000  *................................*
000240  00000000 00000000 00000000 00000000  00000000 00000000 00000000 00000000  *................................*
000260  00000000 00000000 00000000 00000000  00000000 00000000 00000000 00000000  *................................*
000280  00000000 00000000 00000000 00000000  00000000 00000000 00000000 00000000  *................................*
0002A0  00000000 00000000 00000000 00000000  00000000 00000000 00000000 00000000  *................................*
0002C0  00000000 00000000 00000000 00000000  00000000 00000000 00000000 00000000  *................................*
0002E0  00000000 00000000 00000000 00000000  00000000 00000000 00000000 00000000  *................................*
000300  00000000 00000000 00000000 00000000  00000000 00000000 00000000 00000000  *................................*
000320  00000000 00000000 00000000 00000000  00000000 00000000 00000000 00000000  *................................*
000340  00000000 00000000 00000000 00000000  00000000 00000000 00000000 00000000  *................................*
000360  00000000 00000000 00000000 00000000  00000000 00000000 00000000 00000000  *................................*
000380  00000000 00000000 00000000 00000000  00000000 00000000 00000000 00000000  *................................*
0003A0  00000000 00000000 00000000 00000000  00000000 00000000 00000000 00000000  *................................*
0003C0  00000000 00000000 00000000 00000000  00000000 00000000 00000000 00000000  *................................*
0003E0  00000000 00000000 00000000 00000000  00000000 00000000 00000000 00000000  *................................*
000400  00000000 00000000 00000000 00000000  00000000 00000000 00000000 00000000  *................................*
000420  00000000 00000000 00000000 00000000  00000000 00000000 00000000 00000000  *................................*
000440  00000000 00000000 00000000 00000000  00000000 00000000 00000000 00000000  *................................*
000460  00000000 00000000 00000000 00000000  00000000 00000000 00000000 00000000  *................................*
000480  00000000 00000000 00000000 00000000  00000000 00000000 00000000 00000000  *................................*
0004A0  00000000 00000000 00000000 00000000  00000000 00000000 00000000 00000000  *................................*
0004C0  00000000 00000000 00000000 00000000  00000000 00000000 00000000 00000000  *................................*
0004E0  00000000 00000000 00000000 00000000  00000000 00000000 00000000 00000000  *................................*
000500  00000000 00000000 00000000 00000000  00000000 00000000 00000000 00000000  *................................*
000520  00000000 00000000 00000000 00000000  00000000 00000000 00000000 00000000  *................................*
```

```
000540  00000000 00000000 00000000 00000000  00000000 00000000 00000000 00000000  *................................*
000560  00000000 00000000 00000000 00000000  00000000 00000000 00000000 00000000  *................................*
000580  00000000 00000000 00000000 00000000  00000000 00000000 00000000 00000000  *................................*
0005A0  00000000 00000000 00000000 00000000  00000000 00000000 00000000 00000000  *................................*
0005C0  00000000 00000000 00000000 00000000  00000000 00000000 00000000 00000000  *................................*
0005E0  00000000 00000000 00000000 00000000  00000000 00000000 00000000 00000000  *................................*
000600  00000000 00000000 00000000 00000000  00000000 00000000 00000000 00000000  *................................*
000620  00000000 00000000 00000000 00000000  00000000 00000000 00000000 00000000  *................................*
000640  00000000 00000000 00000000 00000000  00000000 00000000 00000000 00000000  *................................*
000660  00000000 00000000 00000000 00000000  00000000 00000000 00000000 00000000  *................................*
000680  00000000 00000000 00000000 00000000  00000000 00000000 00000000 00000000  *................................*
0006A0  00000000 00000000 00000000 00000000  00000000 00000000 00000000 00000000  *................................*
0006C0  00000000 00000000 00000000 00000000  00000000 00000000 00000000 00000000  *................................*
0006E0  00000000 00000000 00000000 00000000  00000000 00000000 00000000 00000000  *................................*
000700  00000000 00000000 00000000 00000000  00000000 00000000 00000000 00000000  *................................*
000720  00000000 00000000 00000000 00000000  00000000 00000000 00000000 00000000  *................................*
000740  00000000 00000000 00000000 00000000  00000000 00000000 00000000 00000000  *................................*
000760  00000000 00000000 00000000 00000000  00000000 00000000 00000000 00000000  *................................*
000780  00000000 00000000 00000000 00000000  00000000 00000000 00000000 00000000  *................................*
0007A0  00000000 00000000 00000000 00000000  00000000 00000000 00000000 00000000  *................................*
0007C0  00000000 00000000 00000000 00000000  00000000 00000000 00000000 00000000  *................................*
0007E0  00000000 00000000 00000000 00000000  00000000 00000000 00                 *.........................       *

IDC0005I NUMBER OF RECORDS PROCESSED WAS 1

IDC0001I FUNCTION COMPLETED, HIGHEST CONDITION CODE WAS 0
```

Figure 8.6 Character and hex format dump of EMPLOYEE.KSDS.INDEX.

of the data component CI's, particularly when the key is large (a key can be up to 255 bytes long). While this compression technique makes efficient use of storage, it renders the index component unreadable. You should never have to read an index component dump except, perhaps, for academic reasons.

8.1.2 Printing an ESDS

Printing an ESDS is no different than printing a KSDS. Since an ESDS has only a data component, the dumps produced for the cluster and the data component are the same. The following command statement can be used to print the ESDS defined in Chap. 6 using the JCL in Fig. 6.4 and loaded with the JCL in Fig. 7.5.

```
PRINT                                -
INDATASET(EMPLOYEE.ESDS.CLUSTER) -
CHAR
```

The printout of the data set appears in Fig. 8.7.

Note that records are printed in order of their relative byte address. The RBA of the first record is 0, that of the second is 50, that of the third is 100, and so on. Each successive RBA is offset 50 bytes from the last one because the data set has fixed-length records of 50 bytes each. Since there are only 9 records in the data set, only the first 450 bytes of the first CI are being used. If there were more than 40 of these 50-byte records, enough records to use the second (or higher) CI, the RBA of the first record in the second CI would be 2048. This is because the CI size of this ESDS is 2048 bytes and, with 0 being the first byte, the ending RBA of the first CI will be 2047. Note that you cannot simply calculate the RBA of a record by multiplying the record number minus 1 by the record length. This is because, once a CI is filled with as many *complete* records as possible, there may be some additional unused free space bytes in each CI that must be taken into consideration in your calculations.

8.1.3 Printing an RRDS

The syntax used for printing a KSDS and an ESDS is also used for printing an RRDS. The following command can be used to print EMPLOYEE.RRDS.CLUSTER which was allocated using the JCL in Fig. 6.5 and loading using the JCL in Fig. 7.6.

```
PRINT                                -
INDATASET(EMPLOYEE.RRDS.CLUSTER) -
CHAR
```

```
LISTING OF DATA SET -EMPLOYEE.ESDS.CLUSTER

RBA OF RECORD - 0
111111111 WORLD PLAZA,N.Y,N.Y           10M092150RANADE

RBA OF RECORD - 50
222222222 25,OAKWOODS,N.Y               19M022536TANAKA

RBA OF RECORD - 100
333333333 18,MARSH AV,S.I,N.Y           16F030942KRANTZ

RBA OF RECORD - 150
444444444 2-52,FOREST HILLS,QUEENS 05M090252BUTLER

RBA OF RECORD - 200
555555555 7,PARK AV,JERSEY CITY         17M092057RANADE

RBA OF RECORD - 250
666666666 15,GREENWICH ,CT              12M030511ADLER

RBA OF RECORD - 300
777777777 8,BROAD ST,S.I,N.Y            07F082913JOSHI

RBA OF RECORD - 350
888888888 KENNER TOWERS,N.Y,N.Y         04F111855LEHN

RBA OF RECORD - 400
999999999 23,SOUTH ST,BRONX,N.Y         13F100846RAMSEY

IDC0005I NUMBER OF RECORDS PROCESSED WAS 9

IDC0001I FUNCTION COMPLETED, HIGHEST CONDITION CODE WAS 0
```

Figure 8.7 Character format printout of EMPLOYEE.ESDS.CLUSTER.

A printout of the records from the successful execution of the above command will look like Fig. 8.8.

Notice that the nine records are printed in relative record number sequence. If the records with RRN's of 3, 5, and 7 had been deleted and the data set printed afterward, the records with the RRN's 1, 2, 4, 6, 8, and 9 would be printed. The records are printed with the RRN of their respective slots even though there may be empty slots in between.

8.2 PRINTING NON-VSAM DATA SETS

As already discussed, Access Method Services can be used to print non-VSAM data sets also. Recall that a physical sequential data set,

```
LISTING OF DATA SET -EMPLOYEE.RRDS.CLUSTER

RELATIVE RECORD NUMBER - 1
111111111 WORLD PLAZA,N.Y,N.Y        10M092150RANADE

RELATIVE RECORD NUMBER - 2
222222222 25,OAKWOODS,N.Y            19M022536TANAKA

RELATIVE RECORD NUMBER - 3
333333333 18,MARSH AV,S.I,N.Y        16F030942KRANTZ

RELATIVE RECORD NUMBER - 4
444444444 2-52,FOREST HILLS,QUEENS 05M090252BUTLER

RELATIVE RECORD NUMBER - 5
555555555 7,PARK AV,JERSEY CITY      17M092057RANADE

RELATIVE RECORD NUMBER - 6
666666666 15,GREENWICH ,CT           12M030511ADLER

RELATIVE RECORD NUMBER - 7
777777777 8,BROAD ST,S.I,N.Y         07F082913JOSHI

RELATIVE RECORD NUMBER - 8
888888888 KENNER TOWERS,N.Y,N.Y      04F111855LEHN

RELATIVE RECORD NUMBER - 9
999999999 23,SOUTH ST,BRONX,N.Y      13F100846RAMSEY

IDC0005I NUMBER OF RECORDS PROCESSED WAS 9

IDC0001I FUNCTION COMPLETED, HIGHEST CONDITION CODE WAS 0
```

Figure 8.8 Character format printout of EMPLOYEE.RRDS.CLUSTER.

SAMPLE.INPUT.DATA, was used in Chap. 7 to load records into different clusters. The following command can be used to print its contents.

```
PRINT                               -
INDATASET(SAMPLE.INPUT.DATA) -
CHAR
```

Upon successful execution of the command, the records will be printed as in Fig. 8.9.

Records of a non-VSAM data set are printed in record number sequence starting with 1. The sequence numbers are always consecutive because a non-VSAM data set cannot have records missing in the middle.

The contents of an indexed sequential data set and partitioned data set members can be printed using the same command syntax. Records of indexed sequential data sets are printed in key sequence, just like a KSDS. Since a generation data set cannot be dynamically allocated with its relative generation number, you cannot use the INDATASET

```
LISTING OF DATA SET -SAMPLE.INPUT.DATA

RECORD SEQUENCE NUMBER - 1
111111111 WORLD PLAZA,N.Y,N.Y        10M092150RANADE

RECORD SEQUENCE NUMBER - 2
222222222 25,OAKWOODS,N.Y            19M022536TANAKA

RECORD SEQUENCE NUMBER - 3
333333333 18,MARSH AV,S.I,N.Y        16F030942KRANTZ

RECORD SEQUENCE NUMBER - 4
444444444 2-52,FOREST HILLS,QUEENS 05M090252BUTLER

RECORD SEQUENCE NUMBER - 5
555555555 7,PARK AV,JERSEY CITY      17M092057RANADE

RECORD SEQUENCE NUMBER - 6
666666666 15,GREENWICH ,CT           12M030511ADLER

RECORD SEQUENCE NUMBER - 7
777777777 8,BROAD ST,S.I,N.Y         07F082913JOSHI

RECORD SEQUENCE NUMBER - 8
888888888 KENNER TOWERS,N.Y,N.Y      04F111855LEHN

RECORD SEQUENCE NUMBER - 9
999999999 23,SOUTH ST,BRONX,N.Y      13F100846RAMSEY

IDC0005I NUMBER OF RECORDS PROCESSED WAS 9

IDC0001I FUNCTION COMPLETED, HIGHEST CONDITION CODE WAS 0
```

Figure 8.9 Character format printout of SAMPLE.INPUT.DATA.

parameter with it. You must use the IFILE parameter to allocate the data set. Figure 8.10 gives the sample JCL for printing a generation data set.

```
//AMSJOB    JOB (ACCTNO),'JAY RANADE'
//GDGPRINT EXEC PGM=IDCAMS
//SYSPRINT DD SYSOUT=A
//GDGIN     DD DSN=SAMPLE.BACKUP.FILE(0),
//             DISP=OLD,UNIT=TAPE,LABEL=(1,SL)
//SYSIN     DD *
  PRINT                               -
  IFILE(GDGIN)                        -
  CHAR
/*
//
```

Figure 8.10 Sample JCL for printing contents of a generation data set.

8.3 SELECTIVE PRINTING

So far, we have been dealing with cases where the data set is printed from the first to the last record. Often you may want to print only a selected subset of the data set. The various optional parameters of the PRINT command can be used to do this. These parameters are the same as those discussed in the last chapter in the context of the REPRO command.

SKIP can be used to skip a specific number of records before starting the printing. The default is to skip no records. COUNT can be used to print a specific number of records. Both these parameters can be used for KSDS's, ESDS's, RRDS's, and non-VSAM data sets. The FROMKEY and TOKEY parameters can be used to print records of a KSDS beginning with a particular key field and ending with another. These parameters may be generic and can also be used for indexed sequential data sets. FROMADDRESS and TOADDRESS can be used to print records of an ESDS between two addresses. The value of these parameters are the relative byte addresses of the records. FROMNUMBER and TONUMBER can be used to print records of an RRDS between two relative record numbers. The proper use of these optional parameters will be clearer when you look at the following examples.

Example 1: SAMPLE.INPUT.DATA is a physical sequential data set. Records 4 through 7 will be printed in character format. The command syntax is as follows:

```
PRINT                               -
INDATASET(SAMPLE.INPUT.DATA) -
SKIP(3) COUNT(4)                    -
CHAR
```

The printout appears in Fig. 8.11.

Example 2: EMPLOYEE.KSDS.CLUSTER is a KSDS. Three of its records are to be printed starting from the key value 444444444. The command syntax is

```
PRINT                                    -
INDATASET(EMPLOYEE.KSDS.CLUSTER) -
FROMKEY(444444444)                       -
COUNT(3)                                 -
CHAR
```

The results of the above command appear in Fig. 8.12.

Example 3: SAMPLE.ISAM.FILE is an indexed sequential file with a key in the first nine positions of the record. It has the same records as

```
LISTING OF DATA SET -SAMPLE.INPUT.DATA

RECORD SEQUENCE NUMBER - 4
444444444 2-52,FOREST HILLS,QUEENS 05M090252BUTLER

RECORD SEQUENCE NUMBER - 5
555555555 7,PARK AV,JERSEY CITY     17M092057RANADE

RECORD SEQUENCE NUMBER - 6
666666666 15,GREENWICH ,CT          12M030511ADLER

RECORD SEQUENCE NUMBER - 7
777777777 8,BROAD ST,S.I,N.Y        07F082913JOSHI

IDC0005I NUMBER OF RECORDS PROCESSED WAS 4

IDC0001I FUNCTION COMPLETED, HIGHEST CONDITION CODE WAS 0
```

Figure 8.11 Printout from Example 1.

EMPLOYEE.KSDS.CLUSTER. The following command will print from generic key 33 through 666.

```
PRINT                            -
INDATASET(SAMPLE.ISAM.FILE)      -
FROMKEY(33)                      -
TOKEY(666)                       -
CHAR
```

The printout appears in Fig. 8.13.

Example 4: EMPLOYEE.KSDS.CLUSTER is a KSDS. Records 3 through generic key 8888 will be printed when the following syntax is used.

```
LISTING OF DATA SET -EMPLOYEE.KSDS.CLUSTER

KEY OF RECORD - 444444444
444444444 2-52,FOREST HILLS,QUEENS 05M090252BUTLER

KEY OF RECORD - 555555555
555555555 7,PARK AV,JERSEY CITY     17M092057RANADE

KEY OF RECORD - 666666666
666666666 15,GREENWICH ,CT          12M030511ADLER

IDC0005I NUMBER OF RECORDS PROCESSED WAS 3

IDC0001I FUNCTION COMPLETED, HIGHEST CONDITION CODE WAS 0
```

Figure 8.12 Printout from Example 2.

```
LISTING OF DATA SET -SAMPLE.ISAM.FILE

KEY OF RECORD - 333333333
333333333 18,MARSH AV,S.I,N.Y        16F030942KRANTZ

KEY OF RECORD - 444444444
444444444 2-52,FOREST HILLS,QUEENS 05M090252BUTLER

KEY OF RECORD - 555555555
555555555 7,PARK AV,JERSEY CITY     17M092057RANADE

KEY OF RECORD - 666666666
666666666 15,GREENWICH ,CT          12M030511ADLER

IDC0005I NUMBER OF RECORDS PROCESSED WAS 4

IDC0001I FUNCTION COMPLETED, HIGHEST CONDITION CODE WAS 0
```

Figure 8.13 Printout from Example 3.

```
PRINT                               -
INDATASET(EMPLOYEE.KSDS.CLUSTER) -
SKIP(2)                             -
TOKEY(8888)                         -
CHAR
```

The resulting printout appears in Fig. 8.14.

Example 5: EMPLOYEE.ESDS.CLUSTER is an ESDS. The records located at relative byte addresses 200 through 350 will be printed with the following command syntax.

```
PRINT                               -
INDATASET(EMPLOYEE.ESDS.CLUSTER) -
FROMADDRESS(200)                    -
TOADDRESS(350)                      -
CHAR
```

The printout from this command appears in Fig. 8.15.

Example 6: EMPLOYEE.RRDS.CLUSTER is an RRDS. Its records are to be printed starting with relative record number 5 and ending with RRN 8. The command syntax is

```
PRINT                               -
INDATASET(EMPLOYEE.RRDS.CLUSTER) -
FROMNUMBER(5)                       -
TONUMBER(8)                         -
CHAR
```

```
LISTING OF DATA SET -EMPLOYEE.KSDS.CLUSTER

KEY OF RECORD - 333333333
333333333 18,MARSH AV,S.I,N.Y          16F030942KRANTZ

KEY OF RECORD - 444444444
444444444 2-52,FOREST HILLS,QUEENS 05M090252BUTLER

KEY OF RECORD - 555555555
555555555 7,PARK AV,JERSEY CITY       17M092057RANADE

KEY OF RECORD - 666666666
666666666 15,GREENWICH ,CT             12M030511ADLER

KEY OF RECORD - 777777777
777777777 8,BROAD ST,S.I,N.Y           07F082913JOSHI

KEY OF RECORD - 888888888
888888888 KENNER TOWERS,N.Y,N.Y       04F111855LEHN

IDC0005I NUMBER OF RECORDS PROCESSED WAS 6

IDC0001I FUNCTION COMPLETED, HIGHEST CONDITION CODE WAS 0
```

Figure 8.14 Printout from Example 4.

The printout generated from this command appears in Fig. 8.16.

PRINT vs IEBISAM To print an indexed sequential file, you can use the utility program IEBISAM instead of the PRINT command of Access Method Services. However, since there is no provision for record selec-

```
LISTING OF DATA SET -EMPLOYEE.ESDS.CLUSTER

RBA OF RECORD - 200
555555555 7,PARK AV,JERSEY CITY       17M092057RANADE

RBA OF RECORD - 250
666666666 15,GREENWICH ,CT             12M030511ADLER

RBA OF RECORD - 300
777777777 8,BROAD ST,S.I,N.Y           07F082913JOSHI

RBA OF RECORD - 350
888888888 KENNER TOWERS,N.Y,N.Y       04F111855LEHN

IDC0005I NUMBER OF RECORDS PROCESSED WAS 4

IDC0001I FUNCTION COMPLETED, HIGHEST CONDITION CODE WAS 0
```

Figure 8.15 Printout from Example 5.

```
IDCAMS  SYSTEM SERVICES

LISTING OF DATA SET -EMPLOYEE.RRDS.CLUSTER

RELATIVE RECORD NUMBER - 5
555555555 7,PARK AV,JERSEY CITY     17M092057RANADE

RELATIVE RECORD NUMBER - 6
666666666 15,GREENWICH ,CT          12M030511ADLER

RELATIVE RECORD NUMBER - 7
777777777 8,BROAD ST,S.I,N.Y        07F082913JOSHI

RELATIVE RECORD NUMBER - 8
888888888 KENNER TOWERS,N.Y,N.Y     04F111855LEHN

IDC0005I NUMBER OF RECORDS PROCESSED WAS 4

IDC0001I FUNCTION COMPLETED, HIGHEST CONDITION CODE WAS 0
```

Figure 8.16 Printout from Example 6.

tion in IEBISAM, you must print *all* the records in the file. With the PRINT command, you can be selective by using the SKIP, COUNT, FROMKEY, and TOKEY options.

chapter 9

Alternate Index Allocation

We discussed the theory and internal architecture of an alternate index in Chap. 3. Before you start this chapter, make sure you thoroughly understand the alternate index concepts that have already been explained. The following is a summary of the key points.

1. An alternate index enables you to look at the base cluster as if it were sequenced on a field other than the prime key field.
2. An alternate index cluster is a different data set physically. It is always a KSDS, having its own data and index components.
3. An alternate index can be created on an ESDS or a KSDS base cluster but not on an RRDS. A base cluster defined with the REUSE option cannot have an alternate index.
4. A record in the base cluster accessed through the alternate index (rather than directly) requires approximately twice the number of I/O's required if it were accessed through the prime key.
5. You can have up to 253 different alternate indexes on a base cluster.
6. An alternate key and the prime key fields may overlap, but they cannot start at the same location.
7. An alternate index is called a unique key alternate index if, for each alternate key value, there is only one prime key value. For

example, an alternate index on the Employee-Number field in EMPLOYEE.KSDS.CLUSTER will always be unique.

8. An alternate index is called a nonunique key alternate index if, for any alternate key value, there can be more than one prime key value. For example, an alternate index on the Employee-Name field in EMPLOYEE.KSDS.CLUSTER will be nonunique. However, there may not be more than 32,767 prime key values associated with one nonunique alternate key value. A nonunique alternate key cluster always has variable-length records in it.
9. An alternate index cluster must be defined in the same VSAM or ICF catalog as the base cluster.

Three distinct Access Method Services commands are used to create an alternate index:

DEFINE ALTERNATEINDEX (abbreviated DEFINE AIX) is used to allocate space for the alternate index cluster.

BLDINDEX is used to load an alternate index with alternate key-pointer pair records. Such pointers are the prime key values of the base cluster in a KSDS, while in an ESDS they are the relative byte addresses of the records.

DEFINE PATH is used to develop a bridge (or path) between the alternate index cluster and the base cluster.

Before we go into the details of each of the commands, you must understand an important concept called the *upgrade set* of the base cluster.

9.1 WHAT IS AN UPGRADE SET?

Basically there are three update functions that may be performed on a VSAM data set: (1) add a new record, (2) delete an existing record (except in an ESDS), and (3) change the contents of an existing record.

These functions are related to the base cluster which is, of course, the real storehouse of the logical records. An alternate index contains only the alternate key-pointer pair records. Let's suppose that there is a KSDS base cluster that has several alternate indexes defined on it. A number of questions should arise in the application system designer's mind when dealing with such a situation.

- When a record is added to the base cluster, will the corresponding change be reflected in the alternate index clusters so that you can access the record immediately through an alternate key?
- When you delete a record in the base cluster, will the corresponding alternate key-pointer pairs be deleted in the alternate index clusters?

- When you update an existing record in the base cluster, thus also modifying the alternate key fields in it, will the corresponding changes be reflected in the alternate index cluster?
- Once the initial loading of the alternate index cluster with alternate key-pointer records is completed, is an application program then responsible for ensuring that all alternate indexes are in synchronization with the base cluster? If they are not synchronized, any records accessed through an alternate key might provide erroneous information.

The underlying question is, Will changes made in the base cluster *automatically* be made in the alternate index clusters or not? Normally, an application program should not be responsible for the complex task of keeping the alternate index(es) synchronized with the base cluster. It should instead be the responsibility of the access method, VSAM. However, at the time the alternate index is allocated, you have to specify whether or not you want VSAM to do this automatically. Ideally, you can divide the alternate index(es) on a base cluster into two categories:

1. Alternate index(es) that should automatically be updated when records are added, deleted, or updated in the base cluster. Such alternate indexes are said to belong to the *upgrade set* of the base cluster.
2. Alternate indexes that do not have to be updated automatically. These will not reflect any changes made in the base cluster. However, synchronization with the base cluster can be achieved if you delete them, reallocate them with DEFINE AIX, and then reload them with alternate key-pointer pairs using the BLDINDEX command.

You may ask, Why not make all the alternate indexes members of the upgrade set? The answer is that you want to minimize I/O's to maintain an acceptable response time in an on-line (CICS/VS) system. Each alternate index that is a member of the upgrade set incurs additional I/O's to update its alternate key-pointer pair records. High I/O activity is one of the main reasons for poor response time in on-line systems. If the needs of the application design require a particular alternate index to always be in synchronization with the base cluster, make it a member of the upgrade set of the base cluster. When allocating an alternate index with the DEFINE AIX command, the coding of an optional parameter, UPGRADE, makes the alternate index a member of the upgrade set.

9.2 AIX ON A KSDS

An alternate index is defined using the DEFINE AIX command. Just as DEFINE CLUSTER allocates space for a base cluster, DEFINE AIX allocates space for an alternate index cluster. A separate DEFINE AIX command is coded for each alternate index (you can have up to 253). The following points must be noted before an alternate index can be defined.

- The base cluster to which that alternate index will be related must already exist (through DEFINE CLUSTER).
- The base cluster does not have to have records loaded into it. (e.g., through REPRO).

9.2.1 Unique AIX on a KSDS

In Chap. 6, we defined a KSDS called EMPLOYEE.KSDS.CLUSTER (refer to Fig. 6.1 for the record layout). Its prime key is Employee-SSN, which is in the first 9 bytes of the record. In byte positions 36 and 37, there is a field called Employee-Number. This field is always unique because you cannot have more than one employee with the same employee number. In other words, there will always be a one-to-one correspondence between Employee-Number and Employee-SSN. We will develop an alternate index on this field to understand the concepts better. Remember that the DEFINE AIX command only allocates space for the alternate index. It does not load any records into it. Figure 9.1 gives the sample JCL for defining an alternate index on the Employee-Number field for our personnel system.

Let's discuss the function of each parameter in the JCL.

DEFINE AIX is the Access Method Services command used to define an alternate index.

The NAME parameter identifies the name of the alternate index cluster. It is better to have a naming convention so that an alternate index can easily be related to the base cluster to which it belongs. In this case, the third qualifier, AIX1, identifies this as the first alternate index.

RELATE gives the name of the base cluster to which the alternate index is related.

The VOLUMES parameter indicates the disk pack on which space for the alternate index will be allocated. It *does not* have to be the volume on which the base cluster was allocated.

CISZ (the abbreviation for CONTROLINTERVALSIZE) gives the size of the control interval for the alternate index cluster. This size does not have to be the same as the CISZ of the base cluster.

CYLINDERS identifies the primary space to be allocated (the first value before the comma) on execution of this command. The second value (after the comma) identifies the secondary space that will be allocated if all the primary space is used up.

The KEYS parameter has two values. The first indicates the length of the alternate key, which in this case is 2 bytes. The second value indicates the offset of this key from the beginning of the record. Since the

```
//AMSJOB    JOB (ACCTNO),'JAY RANADE'
//DEFAIX1   EXEC PGM=IDCAMS
//SYSPRINT DD SYSOUT=A
//SYSIN     DD *
 DEFINE AIX                                    -
 (NAME(EMPLOYEE.KSDS.AIX1.CLUSTER)             -
 RELATE(EMPLOYEE.KSDS.CLUSTER)                 -
 VOLUMES(VSAM02)                               -
 CISZ(2048)                                    -
 CYLINDERS(1,1)                                -
 KEYS(2,35)                                    -
 UNIQUEKEY                                     -
 UPGRADE                                       -
 RECORDSIZE(16,16)                             -
 FREESPACE(20,20)                              -
 SHAREOPTIONS(2,3)                      )      -
 DATA                                          -
 (NAME(EMPLOYEE.KSDS.AIX1.DATA)  )             -
 INDEX                                         -
 (NAME(EMPLOYEE.KSDS.AIX1.INDEX))
/*
//
```

Figure 9.1 JCL for defining a unique key alternate index named EMPLOYEE.KSDS.AIX1.CLUSTER on a KSDS named EMPLOYEE.KSDS.CLUSTER.

key starts from the thirty-sixth byte, this value is 35 (remember, in VSAM, the first byte is counted as byte 0).

UNIQUEKEY specifies that the alternate index will have only unique keys. The opposite of this option is the NONUNIQUEKEY parameter, which is also the default value. With the UNIQUEKEY parameter, if you try to add an employee record with an already existing employee number, you will get an error condition. You must code UNIQUEKEY if the design considerations dictate a one-to-one correspondence between the alternate key and the prime key.

The UPGRADE option makes the alternate index a member of the upgrade set of the base cluster. In the future, any updates made on base cluster records will make the corresponding changes in the alternate index cluster. Whenever you open a base cluster for update purposes, its upgrade set is also opened.

The RECORDSIZE parameter has two values of 16 bytes each, which means that the alternate index will have fixed-length records of 16 bytes. How did we arrive at this figure? If you recall the record structure of a unique key alternate index from Chap. 3, you will remember that it consists of three fields. The first field is 5 bytes long and has information about the record. The second field is equal to the length of the alternate key, which is 2 bytes in this case. The third field is the length of the pointer, which in a KSDS is a prime key and in this case is 9 bytes long. The sum of these three fields is 16 bytes. The following formula summarizes this discussion for a unique key alternate index on a KSDS.

Record length of unique key alternate index
= 5 + length of alternate key + length of prime key

FREESPACE indicates the percentage of CI's and CA's left as free space. Since any records added to the base cluster will also result in additions to the alternate index, this free space will be needed to minimize CI and CA splits of the alternate index cluster.

SHAREOPTIONS provides the values for cross-region and cross-system sharing for the alternate index cluster. It has already been discussed in detail in Chap. 6.

The rest of the parameters give separate names to the data and index components of the alternate index cluster. The CATALOG parameter is not being coded, because EMPLOYEE is an alias of the VSAM catalog called VSAM.USERCAT.TWO and is being used as the first qualifier of the data set name.

Depending on your requirements, you could have also used the password protection parameters, IMBED, REPLICATE, REUSE, SPEED, TO/FOR, UNIQUE, etc. Bear in mind that, although you cannot define an alternate index on a base cluster defined with the REUSE option, you *can* define an alternate index itself with the REUSE parameter.

After successful execution of this JCL, an alternate index cluster named EMPLOYEE.KSDS.AIX1.CLUSTER will be allocated with a primary space allocation of one cylinder on volume VSAM02 and will be cataloged in catalog VSAM.USERCAT.TWO. It does not have any records yet. Later, we will use the BLDINDEX command to load it with alternate key-pointer records.

9.2.2 Nonunique AIX on a KSDS

In the record layout for EMPLOYEE.KSDS.CLUSTER (refer to Fig. 6.1), character positions 45 to 50 contain the field Employee-Name. There may be applications where you need to access employee records randomly—not by Social Security Number or Employee-Number, but by Employee-Name. If so, an alternate index must be defined on this field, too. However, such an alternate index will have nonunique keys because there can be more than one employee with the same name. This alternate index will be different from the one defined previously. It will have its own data and index components and its own records containing alternate key-pointer pairs. In conformity with our naming conventions, it will be

```
//AMSJOB    JOB (ACCTNO),'JAY RANADE'
//DEFAIX2   EXEC PGM=IDCAMS
//SYSPRINT DD SYSOUT=A
//SYSIN     DD *
 DEFINE AIX                                    -
 (NAME(EMPLOYEE.KSDS.AIX2.CLUSTER)             -
 RELATE(EMPLOYEE.KSDS.CLUSTER)                 -
 VOLUMES(VSAM02)                               -
 CISZ(2048)                                    -
 CYLINDERS(1,1)                                -
 KEYS(6,44)                                    -
 NONUNIQUEKEY                                  -
 UPGRADE                                       -
 RECORDSIZE(29,56)                             -
 FREESPACE(20,20)                              -
 SHAREOPTIONS(2,3)                       )     -
 DATA                                          -
 (NAME(EMPLOYEE.KSDS.AIX2.DATA)  )             -
 INDEX                                         -
 (NAME(EMPLOYEE.KSDS.AIX2.INDEX))
/*
//
```

Figure 9.2 JCL for defining a nonunique key alternate index named EMPLOYEE.KSDS.AIX2.CLUSTER on a KSDS named EMPLOYEE.KSDS.CLUSTER.

called EMPLOYEE.KSDS.AIX2.CLUSTER. Figure 9.2 gives sample JCL for allocating this alternate index.

The command syntax and the parameters are used in the same way as those for the unique key alternate index. Those that require a detailed discussion are explained here.

The KEYS parameter has the two values 6 and 44. The first value is the length of the alternate key, while the second is the offset of the key field from the beginning of the record,

NONUNIQUEKEY identifies the alternate index as having nonunique keys. Future updates on the base cluster that add records with an existing employee name will not result in an error condition. This parameter could have been omitted, since NONUNIQUEKEY is the default value.

The UPGRADE option makes the alternate index a member of the upgrade set. This, too, could have been omitted, because UPGRADE is the default value.

RECORDSIZE has the two values 29 and 56. The first value gives the average record length, while the second gives the maximum record length of the records in the alternate index cluster. How did we arrive at these figures? Before we calculate these record lengths, you must understand the requirements of the personnel system. We must determine how many employees with the same name can exist in the base cluster. The answer will no doubt differ depending on the size of the company. The number of same-named employees will be larger if the system is being designed for a company with 100,000 employees than if it will be used by one with 100 employees. To keep our system simple, we will assume that there cannot be more than 5 employees with the same name. Also, we are assuming that the average number of such occurrences will be 2. You can use the following formula to calculate the average and the maximum record lengths.

Record length = 5 (for housekeeping) + length of alternate key
+ *n* × length of prime key

where n is the number of occurrences of the nonunique alternate key.

By plugging in 2 and 5 as values of n, we arrive at figures of 29 and 56, respectively. It is also evident that the records of a nonunique key alternate index are always variable-length records. In our hypothetical system, if we tried to add a sixth employee with the same name, an error condition would occur. So, caution must be observed when estimating the maximum number of nonunique key occurrences.

The other parameters have been discussed previously and are self-explanatory. To customize this alternate index according to your needs, you could also use IMBED, REPLICATE, REUSE, SPEED, TO/FOR, UNIQUE, password protection parameters, etc. Upon successful execution of the JCL, a second alternate index will be allocated. EMPLOYEE.KSDS.CLUSTER will now have two alternate indexes, and both will be members of its upgrade set. None of these alternate indexes has any records yet, however.

9.3 AIX ON AN ESDS

Before you read this section, it is important to remember that the Cobol compiler *does not* support alternate indexes on ESDS files. You might want to define an alternate index on an ESDS for the following reasons.

1. The programming language used is the one which supports them on an ESDS, e.g., assembler language.
2. The services of CICS/VS are being used to access an ESDS through an alternate index.
3. The services of AMS commands alone are being used to access an ESDS through an alternate index. For example, the REPRO or PRINT command is being used to view the base cluster (an ESDS) sequenced on an alternate key field.

Whatever the reason, defining an alternate index on an ESDS is not much different than defining one on a KSDS.

9.3.1 Unique AIX on an ESDS

In Chaps. 6 and 7, an ESDS named EMPLOYEE.ESDS.CLUSTER was defined and loaded with records from SAMPLE.INPUT.DATA. We can develop an alternate index on the Employee-Number field which occupies character positions 36 and 37. The sample JCL for performing this function is coded in Fig. 9.3.

All the parameters listed have been discussed previously. The RECORDSIZE parameter, however, is calculated with a different formula. We already know that an ESDS does not have a prime key. Only the relative byte address can be used to identify a record in an ESDS. The RBA of an ESDS record never changes because, once a record is written, it is fixed forever at a given location. While developing an alternate index on a KSDS, the only link between an alternate key and the base cluster is the prime key of the base cluster records. In an ESDS, this link is the

```
//AMSJOB    JOB (ACCTNO),'JAY RANADE'
//ESDSAIX1  EXEC PGM=IDCAMS
//SYSPRINT  DD SYSOUT=A
//SYSIN     DD *
 DEFINE AIX                                         -
 (NAME(EMPLOYEE.ESDS.AIX1.CLUSTER)                  -
 RELATE(EMPLOYEE.ESDS.CLUSTER)                      -
 VOLUMES(VSAM02)                                    -
 CISZ(2048)                                         -
 CYLINDERS(1,1)                                     -
 KEYS(2,35)                                         -
 UNIQUEKEY                                          -
 UPGRADE                                            -
 RECORDSIZE(11,11)                                  -
 FREESPACE(20,20)                                   -
 SHAREOPTIONS(2,3)                          )       -
 DATA                                               -
 (NAME(EMPLOYEE.ESDS.AIX1.DATA)  )                  -
 INDEX                                              -
 (NAME(EMPLOYEE.ESDS.AIX1.INDEX))
/*
//
```

Figure 9.3 JCL for defining a unique key alternate index named EMPLOYEE.ESDS.AIX1.CLUSTER on an ESDS named EMPLOYEE.ESDS.CLUSTER.

RBA of the records. The RBA, as we already know, is a 4-byte binary field. So, we can use the following formula to calculate the average and the maximum record lengths (they are the same) of a unique key alternate index on an ESDS:

Record length = 5 (for housekeeping)
+ length of alternate key + 4 (for the RBA)

When 2 is substituted as the value of the length of the alternate key (Employee-Number), the record length comes out to be 11. Upon successful execution of this JCL, an alternate index will be defined for the ESDS. If you like, you can also define another unique key alternate index on the Employee-SSN field for this ESDS.

9.3.2 Nonunique AIX on ESDS

A nonunique key alternate index can be defined on an ESDS if, for a particular alternate key value, it is possible to have more than one record in the base cluster. We will define an alternate index on the Employee-Name field for the cluster named EMPLOYEE.ESDS.CLUSTER. According to our naming convention, the name of the alternate index will be EMPLOYEE.ESDS.AIX2.CLUSTER. Since an employee's name may not be unique for any personnel/payroll system, this alternate index will have nonunique keys. Figure 9.4 gives the sample of JCL for defining it.

Most of the parameters have been discussed before and have the same meaning. The UPGRADE parameter makes this alternate index a member of the upgrade set of the base cluster. NONUNIQUEKEY, even though not coded explicitly, is the default. The RECORDSIZE parameter has average and maximum record length values of 19 and 31, respectively. This is based on the assumption that there will be an average of two employees and a maximum of five employees with the same employee name. The following formula can be used to find the record length for a nonunique key alternate index.

Record length = 5 (for control bytes)
+ length of alternate key + $n \times 4$

where n is the average or maximum occurrences of a nonunique alternate key. By plugging in 2 and 5 for the values of n, we get average and maximum record lengths of 19 and 31, respectively. It is appropriate to repeat that the average and maximum occurrences of an employee name are purely an application design consideration. In our application, if we try to add a record which creates a sixth occurrence of a particular employee name, an error condition will be generated. If such a file is being designed for a large company, the number of employees with the same name could be much higher than 5.

```
//AMSJOB    JOB (ACCTNO),'JAY RANADE'
//ESDSAIX2  EXEC PGM=IDCAMS
//SYSPRINT  DD SYSOUT=A
//SYSIN     DD *
 DEFINE AIX                                        -
 (NAME(EMPLOYEE.ESDS.AIX2.CLUSTER)                 -
 RELATE(EMPLOYEE.ESDS.CLUSTER)                     -
 VOLUMES(VSAM02)                                   -
 CISZ(2048)                                        -
 CYLINDERS(1,1)                                    -
 KEYS(6,44)                                        -
 NONUNIQUEKEY                                      -
 UPGRADE                                           -
 RECORDSIZE(19,31)                                 -
 FREESPACE(20,20)                                  -
 SHAREOPTIONS(2,3)                        )        -
 DATA                                              -
 (NAME(EMPLOYEE.ESDS.AIX2.DATA)  )                 -
 INDEX                                             -
 (NAME(EMPLOYEE.ESDS.AIX2.INDEX))
/*
//
```

Figure 9.4 JCL for defining a nonunique key alternate index named EMPLOYEE.ESDS.AIX2.CLUSTER on an ESDS named EMPLOYEE.ESDS.CLUSTER.

Upon successful execution of the JCL, a nonunique-key alternate index named EMPLOYEE.ESDS.AIX2.CLUSTER will be allocated, and it will be related to the base cluster named EMPLOYEE.ESDS.CLUSTER.

9.4 BLDINDEX: THE LOAD FUNCTION

The DEFINE AIX command allocates space for an alternate index, just as the DEFINE CLUSTER command allocates space for a base cluster. After successful execution of these commands, only the space allocation function has been completed. Loading data records into a base cluster and loading key-pointer records into an alternate index are separate functions. Just as the REPRO command can be used to load records into a base cluster, BLDINDEX can be used to load records (key-pointer) into an alternate index. Although a user-written application program could be used to load an alternate index, this function is usually performed with the BLDINDEX command because it is simple to use. The following functions must be finished before this command can be executed: (1) The base cluster must be allocated, (2) the base cluster must be loaded with records, and (3) the alternate index cluster must be allocated.

Bear in mind that the base cluster must be loaded with records, because the alternate key-pointer records are extracted from the base cluster records by this command. Even if the base cluster has only one record, this command will be executed successfully. When the BLDINDEX command is executed, three distinct functions will occur in the following order (transparent to you, of course).

- Records of a KSDS or an ESDS are read sequentially, and key-pointer pairs are extracted. One key-pointer pair is extracted from each record read. For our Employee-Number alternate index, the pairs will consist of the Employee-Number and Employee-SSN fields.
- All key-pointer pairs are sorted into ascending order on the alternate key field. The sort routine is a built-in function of Access Method Services. If the number of records is small, an internal sort will be performed, while for a large number of records, an external sort will be necessary. In the latter case, two sort work files must be allocated. They have the organization of an *ESDS*. Remember, the BLDINDEX command cannot use non-ESDS files as sort work files.
- Upon successful execution of the sort, records of the sorted file are read sequentially. If it is a unique key alternate index, one alternate index record will be created from each sorted input record. If it is a nonunique key alternate index, one alternate index record will be created for each set of multiple input records containing the same alternate key in the key-pointer pairs. After all the output records are loaded into the alternate index cluster, the alternate index is ready for use.

Figure 9.5 gives the sample JCL for coding BLDINDEX for EMPLOYEE.KSDS.AIX1.CLUSTER.

BASE describes the base cluster, while AIX1 describes the alternate index cluster. You can, of course, choose other names. *In both these statements, a DISP of OLD has been specified to ensure that while BLDINDEX is being executed no other program will be able to open the base cluster for an update.* The DD names BASE and AIX1 have been used in the INFILE and OUTFILE parameters of the command. If we used the INDATASET and OUTDATASET parameters with the data set names instead of the DD names, you wouldn't have to code the BASE and AIX1 DD statements and a DISPOSITION of OLD would be ensured for the base cluster.

IDCUT1 and IDCUT2 describe the two sort work files. These are the default DD names in the BLDINDEX command. However, if you

```
//AMSJOB     JOB (ACCTNO),'JAY RANADE'
//KSDSBLD1   EXEC PGM=IDCAMS
//SYSPRINT   DD SYSOUT=A
//BASE       DD DSN=EMPLOYEE.KSDS.CLUSTER,
//              DISP=OLD
//AIX1       DD DSN=EMPLOYEE.KSDS.AIX1.CLUSTER,
//              DISP=OLD
//IDCUT1     DD DSN=SORT.WORK.FILE.ONE,DISP=OLD,
//              AMP='AMORG',VOL=SER=VSAM02,UNIT=3380
//IDCUT2     DD DSN=SORT.WORK.FILE.TWO,DISP=OLD,
//              AMP='AMORG',VOL=SER=VSAM02,UNIT=3380
//SYSIN      DD *
  BLDINDEX                                  -
       INFILE(BASE)                         -
       OUTFILE(AIX1)                        -
       INTERNALSORT                         -
       CATALOG(VSAM.USERCAT.TWO)
/*
//
```

Figue 9.5 JCL for loading alternate index records into EMPLOYEE.KSDS.AIX1.CLUSTER.

prefer to use other DD names, you must code an additional parameter in this command:

WORKFILES(ddname1,ddname2)

where ddname1 and ddname2 are the DD names you prefer for the sort work files. Note the use of the AMP parameter on the DD statements. Its subparameter, AMORG, specifies that this is a VSAM file. The sort work files used in BLDINDEX have the organization of an ESDS.

INTERNALSORT,which is also the default parameter, indicates that AMS will perform an internal sort if there is enough user-provided virtual storage. Otherwise, it will perform an external sort by allocating and using the sort work files. If you code EXTERNALSORT instead, it will only perform an external sort regardless of whether or not enough virtual storage is available for an internal sort. An internal sort performed in virtual storage is always faster than an external sort.

The CATALOG parameter gives the name of the VSAM or ICF catalog in which the sort work files are defined. *This catalog does not have to be the one in which the base cluster and alternate index have been defined.* In our case, however, it is the same for both the sort work files and the clusters. Upon termination of BLDINDEX, the sort work files are deleted automatically by Access Method Services.

We've just used BLDINDEX to create an example of an alternate index. Let's take a look at a few other examples so that the variety of the syntax will become clearer. The following can be used to build an alternate index for EMPLOYEE.KSDS.AIX2.CLUSTER.

```
BLDINDEX                                    -
INDATASET(EMPLOYEE.KSDS.CLUSTER)            -
OUTDATASET(EMPLOYEE.KSDS.AIX2.CLUSTER)
```

Note the INDATASET and OUTDATASET parameters used for the dynamic allocation of data sets. Since we know that there are only nine records in the base cluster, we don't have to allocate sort work files. INTERNALSORT, the default, does not have to be stated explicitly either. The CATALOG parameter has been omitted, because no sort work files are involved. If enough virtual storage is not available, the internal sort will fail with an error message. However, this problem will not occur in the sorting of only nine records.

There is absolutely no difference in the command syntax for building an alternate index on a KSDS or on an ESDS. The following command can be used for building one on EMPLOYEE.ESDS.AIX1.CLUSTER.

```
BLDINDEX                                    -
INFILE(BASE)                                -
OUTDATASET(EMPLOYEE.ESDS.AIX1.CLUSTER)
```

Note that BASE is the DD name of the JCL statement which defines the ESDS base cluster of EMPLOYEE.ESDS.CLUSTER. Similarly, the following command can be used to build an alternate index on EMPLOYEE.ESDS.AIX2.CLUSTER.

```
BLDINDEX                                    -
INDATASET(EMPLOYEE.ESDS.CLUSTER) -
OUTFILE(AIX2)
```

AIX2 is the DD name of the JCL statement which defines the alternate index cluster named EMPLOYEE.ESDS.AIX2.CLUSTER. You can see from these examples that INFILE, OUTFILE, INDATASET, and OUTDATASET can be used in *any* combination.

9.5 PRINTING AIX RECORDS

Printing alternate index cluster records will help us to understand the whole concept better. The PRINT command can be used to print the records of an alternate index just as it was used to print the records of a base cluster. The following command can be used for EMPLOYEE.KSDS.AIX1.CLUSTER.

```
PRINT                                      -
INDATASET(EMPLOYEE.KSDS.AIX1.CLUSTER) -
DUMP
```

The printout produced from successful execution of the above command appears in Fig. 9.6.

Note that the records are being printed in the alternate key sequence. It looks as if it is not an alternate index, but rather a KSDS with a 2-byte-long key starting in position 6. As a matter of fact, an alternate index is a real KSDS. The first 5 bytes, appearing in character format as dots, are in fact the record control bytes we have been talking about throughout the book. The meaning of their contents in hexadecimal is as follows.

1. The first byte has a value of hex 01. This means that the alternate index is on a KSDS. A hex value of 00 indicates that it is on an ESDS.
2. The second byte contains the key length of the base cluster's prime key. Its value is printed as hex 09.
3. The third and fourth bytes together indicate the number of pointers (prime keys, in this case) contained in the alternate index record. For a unique key alternate index, this value is always 1, while for a nonunique key it may be more than 1.
4. The fifth byte has the alternate index key length, which in our case is hex 02.

Since the hex values are not printable characters, they appear as dots in the character format on the printout. Since this is a unique key alternate index, all records are fixed in length (16 bytes long in this case). The last 9 bytes of each alternate index record are the pointers to the base cluster. Note that for a KSDS they are its prime keys.

Records of the nonunique-key alternate index on a KSDS (EMPLOYEE.KSDS.AIX2.CLUSTER) can be printed using the following command syntax.

```
PRINT                                      -
INDATASET(EMPLOYEE.KSDS.AIX2.CLUSTER) -
CHAR
```

The printout will appear as in Fig. 9.7.

Note that the first 5 bytes are still the control bytes for the record and that records appear in Employee-Name sequence. In our base clus-

```
LISTING OF DATA SET -EMPLOYEE.KSDS.AIX1.CLUSTER

KEY OF RECORD - F0F4
000000  01090001 02F0F4F8 F8F8F8F8 F8F8F8F8        *.....04888888888        *

KEY OF RECORD - F0F5
000000  01090001 02F0F5F4 F4F4F4F4 F4F4F4F4        *.....05444444444        *

KEY OF RECORD - F0F7
000000  01090001 02F0F7F7 F7F7F7F7 F7F7F7F7        *.....07777777777        *

KEY OF RECORD - F1F0
000000  01090001 02F1F0F1 F1F1F1F1 F1F1F1F1        *.....10111111111        *

KEY OF RECORD - F1F2
000000  01090001 02F1F2F6 F6F6F6F6 F5F6F6F6        *.....12666666666        *

KEY OF RECORD - F1F3
000000  01090001 02F1F3F9 F9F9F9F9 F9F9F9F9        *.....13999999999        *

KEY OF RECORD - F1F6
000000  01090001 02F1F6F3 F3F3F3F3 F3F3F3F3        *.....16333333333        *

KEY OF RECORD - F1F7
000000  01090001 02F1F7F5 F5F5F5F5 F5F5F5F5        *.....17555555555        *

KEY OF RECORD - F1F9
000000  01090001 02F1F9F2 F2F2F2F2 F2F2F2F2        *.....19222222222        *

IDC0005I NUMBER OF RECORDS PROCESSED WAS 9

IDC0001I FUNCTION COMPLETED, HIGHEST CONDITION CODE WAS 0
```

Figure 9.6 Printout of the contents of EMPLOYEE.KSDS.AIX1.CLUSTER in character as well as hexadecimal format.

```
LISTING OF DATA SET -EMPLOYEE.KSDS.AIX2.CLUSTER

KEY OF RECORD - ADLER
.....ADLER 666666666

KEY OF RECORD - BUTLER
.....BUTLER444444444

KEY OF RECORD - JOSHI
.....JOSHI 777777777

KEY OF RECORD - KRANTZ
.....KRANTZ333333333

KEY OF RECORD - LEHN
.....LEHN   888888888

KEY OF RECORD - RAMSEY
.....RAMSEY999999999

KEY OF RECORD - RANADE
.....RANADE111111111555555555

KEY OF RECORD - TANAKA
.....TANAKA222222222

IDC0005I NUMBER OF RECORDS PROCESSED WAS 8

IDC0001I FUNCTION COMPLETED, HIGHEST CONDITION CODE WAS 0
```

Figure 9.7 Printout of the contents of EMPLOYEE.KSDS.AIX2.CLUSTER in character format.

ter, loaded as in Fig. 7.1, there were two employees with the name "RANADE". Hence, this alternate index gives two pointers (KSDS prime keys) of 111111111 and 555555555 associated with the Employee-Name "RANADE". As you can see, records for a nonunique key alternate index cluster are always variable in length.

Records of the unique key alternate index on an ESDS can be printed using the same syntax. Since the RBA's of an ESDS are stored in the alternate index in binary format, a character printout will not be very helpful. A printout in dump format can be obtained using the following command syntax.

```
PRINT                                        -
INDATASET(EMPLOYEE.ESDS.AIX1.CLUSTER)        -
DUMP
```

The printed contents will be as in Fig. 9.8.

Except for the pointers, which are the RBA's of the ESDS records rather than the prime keys of a KSDS, the contents of the records are the

```
LISTING OF DATA SET -EMPLOYEE.ESDS.AIX1.CLUSTER

KEY OF RECORD - F0F4
000000  00040001 02F0F400 00015E                                *.....04...;          *

KEY OF RECORD - F0F5
000000  00040001 02F0F500 000096                                *.....05....          *

KEY OF RECORD - F0F7
000000  00040001 02F0F700 00012C                                *.....07....          *

KEY OF RECORD - F1F0
000000  00040001 02F1F000 000000                                *.....10....          *

KEY OF RECORD - F1F2
000000  00040001 02F1F200 0000FA                                *.....12....          *

KEY OF RECORD - F1F3
000000  00040001 02F1F300 000190                                *.....13....          *

KEY OF RECORD - F1F6
000000  00040001 02F1F600 000064                                *.....16....          *

KEY OF RECORD - F1F7
000000  00040001 02F1F700 0000C8                                *.....17...H          *

KEY OF RECORD - F1F9
000000  00040001 02F1F900 000032                                *.....19....          *

IDC0005I NUMBER OF RECORDS PROCESSED WAS 9

IDC0001I FUNCTION COMPLETED, HIGHEST CONDITION CODE WAS 0
```

Figure 9.8 Printout of the records of EMPLOYEE.ESDS.AIX1.CLUSTER in dump format.

same. An RBA is a 4-byte binary field. If you convert the last eight hex digits into decimal format, you will find that they are the RBA's of the different records in the ESDS base cluster.

The following command syntax can be used to print the contents of EMPLOYEE.ESDS.AIX2.CLUSTER, a nonunique key alternate index on an ESDS.

```
PRINT                                     -
INDATASET(EMPLOYEE.ESDS.AIX2.CLUSTER) -
DUMP
```

The printout will appear as shown in Fig. 9.9.
Notice that there are two RBA pointers associated with the name "RANADE" because there are two records with the Employee-Name "RANADE" in our ESDS base cluster. Also note that, for this index entry, the "pointer count" field has a value of hex 0002.

9.6 DEFINE PATH

The DEFINE PATH command establishes a bridge between the base cluster and an alternate index. It is named in the same way as a base cluster and an alternate index. However, a path is not a data set. It does not occupy any data space and does not have any records. It is just an entry in the catalog which establishes a link between an alternate index and a base cluster. Figure 9.10 gives the JCL for defining a path between EMPLOYEE.KSDS.AIX1.CLUSTER and EMPLOYEE.KSDS.CLUSTER.

The naming convention used in this book to name a path should be noted. The qualifier AIX1 has been replaced by PATH1. Such a naming convention helps to identify which paths and alternate index clusters are related. The PATHENTRY parameter identifies the alternate index cluster to which the path is related. This command does not have any space allocation or device parameters, because a path is *not* a data set and does not have any data or index components. A path may, however, have its own set of passwords. Since the high-end qualifier of this path name is EMPLOYEE, which is also the alias of a VSAM catalog, it is not necessary to code the CATALOG parameter.

9.6.1 UPDATE Option

The UPGRADE parameter of the DEFINE AIX command is used to make an alternate index a member of the upgrade set of the base cluster. The UPDATE parameter of the DEFINE PATH command, which is also the default, is used to give specific characteristics to a path name. When a path defined with the UPDATE parameter is opened for

```
LISTING OF DATA SET -EMPLOYEE.ESDS.AIX2.CLUSTER

KEY OF RECORD - C1C4D3C5D940
000000  00040001 06C1C4D3 C5D94000 0000FA                    *.....ADLER ....          *

KEY OF RECORD - C2E4E3D3C5D9
000000  00040001 06C2E4E3 D3C5D900 000096                    *.....BUTLER....          *

KEY OF RECORD - D1D6E2C8C940
000000  00040001 06D1D6E2 C8C94000 00012C                    *.....JOSHI ....          *

KEY OF RECORD - D2D9C1D5E3E9
000000  00040001 06D2D9C1 D5E3E900 000064                    *.....KRANTZ....          *

KEY OF RECORD - D3C5C8D54040
000000  00040001 06D3C5C8 D5404000 00015E                    *.....LEHN  ...;          *

KEY OF RECORD - D9C1D4E2C5E8
000000  00040001 06D9C1D4 E2C5E800 000190                    *.....RAMSEY....          *

KEY OF RECORD - D9C1D5C1C4C5
000000  00040002 06D9C1D5 C1C4C500 00000000   0000C8         *.....RANADE.......H      *

KEY OF RECORD - E3C1D5C1D2C1
000000  00040001 06E3C1D5 C1D2C100 000032                    *.....TANAKA....          *

IDC0005I NUMBER OF RECORDS PROCESSED WAS 8

IDC0001I FUNCTION COMPLETED, HIGHEST CONDITION CODE WAS 0
```

Figure 9.9 Printout of the records of EMPLOYEE.ESDS.AIX2.CLUSTER in dump format.

```
//AMSJOB    JOB (ACCTNO),'JAY RANADE'
//KSDSPTH1  EXEC PGM=IDCAMS
//SYSPRINT  DD SYSOUT=A
//SYSIN     DD *
  DEFINE PATH                                  -
      (NAME(EMPLOYEE.KSDS.PATH1)               -
      PATHENTRY(EMPLOYEE.KSDS.AIX1.CLUSTER)    -
      UPDATE     )
/*
//
```

Figure 9.10 JCL for defining a path between an alternate index named EMPLOYEE.KSDS.AIX1.CLUSTER and a base cluster named EMPLOYEE.KSDS.CLUSTER.

processing, the base cluster *and* its upgrade set are opened automatically. When a path defined with the NOUPDATE parameter is opened for processing, the base cluster is opened but the base cluster's upgrade set is *not*.

The path between Employee-Name alternate index and its KSDS cluster can be defined as follows.

```
DEFINE PATH                                  -
(NAME(EMPLOYEE.KSDS.PATH2)                   -
PATHENTRY(EMPLOYEE.KSDS.AIX2.CLUSTER))
```

The UPDATE parameter does not have to be coded explicitly, because it is the default.

With the same syntax, paths between the alternate indexes and their corresponding ESDS clusters can be defined. The names of these paths will be as follows:

```
EMPLOYEE.ESDS.PATH1
EMPLOYEE.ESDS.PATH2
```

9.7 PRINTING RECORDS THROUGH PATH

It is difficult to understand the concept of a path unless some practical examples are discussed. The execution of the PRINT command using the path name, as in the following command syntax, will shed some light on the subject.

```
PRINT                                -
INDATASET(EMPLOYEE.KSDS.PATH1)       -
CHAR
```

```
LISTING OF DATA SET -EMPLOYEE.KSDS.PATH1

KEY OF RECORD - 04
888888888 KENNER TOWERS,N.Y,N.Y     04F111855LEHN

KEY OF RECORD - 05
444444444 2-52,FOREST HILLS,QUEENS 05M090252BUTLER

KEY OF RECORD - 07
777777777 8,BROAD ST,S.I,N.Y        07F082913JOSHI

KEY OF RECORD - 10
111111111 WORLD PLAZA,N.Y,N.Y       10M092150RANADE

KEY OF RECORD - 12
666666666 15,GREENWICH ,CT          12M030511ADLER

KEY OF RECORD - 13
999999999 23,SOUTH ST,BRONX,N.Y     13F100846RAMSEY

KEY OF RECORD - 16
333333333 18,MARSH AV,S.I,N.Y       16F030942KRANTZ

KEY OF RECORD - 17
555555555 7,PARK AV,JERSEY CITY     17M092057RANADE

KEY OF RECORD - 19
222222222 25,OAKWOODS,N.Y           19M022536TANAKA

IDC0005I NUMBER OF RECORDS PROCESSED WAS 9

IDC0001I FUNCTION COMPLETED, HIGHEST CONDITION CODE WAS 0
```

Figure 9.11 Printout of EMPLOYEE.KSDS.CLUSTER generated using the path name EMPLOYEE.KSDS.PATH1.

The printout generated from successful execution appears in Fig. 9.11.. This printout provides the records of the base cluster in the alternate key sequence of the index over which the path has been defined. The following summarizes the difference between an alternate index and a path:

> An alternate index cluster is a data set with alternate key-pointer pair records loaded into it. Accessing it by its name gives us only these key-pointer records. A path, while named like any data set, does not occupy any data space, because it is not a physical entity. Accessing it by its name gives us the records of the base cluster (not the alternate index cluster) in the alternate key sequence.

For most applications, you will be interested in accessing records of the base cluster. To do this you must use the base cluster and/or path names, depending on your access key (prime or alternate). For those rare applications where you need access only to the actual key-pointer pairs themselves, you must refer to the alternate index by name. *Remember, accessing records with the base cluster or path name gives you a base cluster record; using the alternate index name gives you only the alternate index record.*

The following command syntax will print the records of the KSDS base cluster in Employee-Name key sequence.

```
PRINT                                -
INDATASET(EMPLOYEE.KSDS.PATH2) -
CHAR
```

The printout appears in Fig. 9.12.

Notice that the two records with the Employee-Name "RANADE" are printed one after the other. This is an example of an alternate index having nonunique alternate keys pointing to more than one base cluster record.

```
LISTING OF DATA SET -EMPLOYEE.KSDS.PATH2

KEY OF RECORD - ADLER
666666666 15,GREENWICH ,CT             12M030511ADLER

KEY OF RECORD - BUTLER
444444444 2-52,FOREST HILLS,QUEENS 05M090252BUTLER

KEY OF RECORD - JOSHI
777777777 8,BROAD ST,S.I,N.Y           07F082913JOSHI

KEY OF RECORD - KRANTZ
333333333 18,MARSH AV,S.I,N.Y          16F030942KRANTZ

KEY OF RECORD - LEHN
888888888 KENNER TOWERS,N.Y,N.Y        04F111855LEHN

KEY OF RECORD - RAMSEY
999999999 23,SOUTH ST,BRONX,N.Y        13F100846RAMSEY

KEY OF RECORD - RANADE
111111111 WORLD PLAZA,N.Y,N.Y          10M092150RANADE

KEY OF RECORD - RANADE
555555555 7,PARK AV,JERSEY CITY        17M092057RANADE

KEY OF RECORD - TANAKA
222222222 25,OAKWOODS,N.Y              19M022536TANAKA

IDC0005I NUMBER OF RECORDS PROCESSED WAS 9

IDC0001I FUNCTION COMPLETED, HIGHEST CONDITION CODE WAS 0
```

Figure 9.12 Printout of EMPLOYEE.KSDS.CLUSTER generated using the path name EMPLOYEE.KSDS.PATH2.

9.8 ADVANTAGES AND DISADVANTAGES OF AIX

The greatest advantage of an alternate index is that it gives an alternative view of the records of the base cluster on a nonprime key field. This kind of random access on an alternate key field is required for many on-line applications. However, alternate index clusters that are members of the upgrade set of the base cluster create additional overhead when updates are made on the base cluster. Suppose a base cluster has four alternate indexes in its upgrade set. When you add a record to the base cluster, you are updating five data sets, not one. This generates additional I/O overhead on a system. Heavy I/O activity usually becomes one of the major causes of poor response time in on-line (CICS/VS) systems. Unless it is absolutely necessary, an alternate index should not be made a member of the upgrade set in on-line systems. In batch systems, alternatives to alternate indexes should be carefully evaluated. If all you need is a report sequenced on a particular field of a KSDS, an external sort can be performed and a report generated from the sorted file. Developing an alternate index for such a purpose is an inefficient way of solving the problem.

chapter **10**

Use of DELETE, ALTER, and VERIFY

We will deal with the DELETE, ALTER, and VERIFY commands together, although there is no logical relationship or interdependence among them. DELETE is used to delete both VSAM and non-VSAM files, ALTER changes the characteristics of an existing VSAM object, and VERIFY can close an improperly closed VSAM data set. They have been grouped together here because the simplicity of their use does not warrant a separate chapter for each one.

10.1 DELETE COMMAND

Non-VSAM files can be deleted by using the DISPOSITION parameter of JCL. This method cannot be used for VSAM data sets. Instead, the DELETE command of Access Method Services must be used. In fact, this command can also be used for deleting non-VSAM objects. The following is a list of the VSAM and non-VSAM objects that can be deleted with this command.

1. A KSDS, an ESDS, or an RRDS base cluster
2. An alternate index
3. A path
4. A non-VSAM data set
5. A generation data group
6. VSAM space

7. A VSAM catalog
8. A page data set
9. An alias

There are a variety of reasons for which it may be necessary to delete a VSAM data set. Among them are the following.

1. It is not needed anymore
2. The ALTER command cannot be used to change certain of its attributes, so it must be deleted and reallocated with the desired attributes.
3. It has become inaccessible because of hardware or software errors, so it must be deleted, redefined, and restored from the most recent backup.
4. A KSDS needs reorganization because access has become inefficient as a result of multiple CI and CA splits. To do this, the data set must be backed up, deleted, reallocated, and restored from the backup.

10.1.1 Deleting a Base Cluster

Suppose you would like to delete the base cluster EMPLOYEE.KSDS.CLUSTER. Figure 10.1 provides the JCL for doing this. Upon executing this JCL, the following objects will be deleted: (1) the data and index components of the base cluster, (2) all the alternate indexes related to this base cluster, and (3) all the related paths. Hence, you must be careful when deleting a base cluster with alternate indexes on it. Once such a base cluster has been reallocated and loaded, its alternate indexes must also be reallocated and rebuilt and its paths redefined. The execution of the JCL in Fig. 10.1 will result in the AMS messages in Fig. 10.2. As you can see, the clusters, data components, index components, and paths that have been deleted are all listed. Remember, you cannot delete KSDS data and index components separately.

```
//AMSJOB    JOB (ACCTNO),'JAY RANADE'
//DELKSDS   EXEC PGM=IDCAMS
//SYSPRINT DD SYSOUT=A
//SYSIN     DD *
 DELETE                                    -
     EMPLOYEE.KSDS.CLUSTER                 -
     CLUSTER
/*
//
```

Figure 10.1 JCL for deleting EMPLOYEE.KSDS.CLUSTER.

```
DELETE                                  -
    EMPLOYEE.KSDS.CLUSTER               -
    CLUSTER

IDC0550I ENTRY (R) EMPLOYEE.KSDS.PATH1 DELETED

IDC0550I ENTRY (D) EMPLOYEE.KSDS.AIX1.DATA DELETED

IDC0550I ENTRY (I) EMPLOYEE.KSDS.AIX1.INDEX DELETED

IDC0550I ENTRY (G) EMPLOYEE.KSDS.AIX1.CLUSTER DELETED

IDC0550I ENTRY (R) EMPLOYEE.KSDS.PATH2 DELETED

IDC0550I ENTRY (D) EMPLOYEE.KSDS.AIX2.DATA DELETED

IDC0550I ENTRY (I) EMPLOYEE.KSDS.AIX2.INDEX DELETED

IDC0550I ENTRY (G) EMPLOYEE.KSDS.AIX2.CLUSTER DELETED

IDC0550I ENTRY (D) EMPLOYEE.KSDS.DATA DELETED

IDC0550I ENTRY (I) EMPLOYEE.KSDS.INDEX DELETED

IDC0550I ENTRY (C) EMPLOYEE.KSDS.CLUSTER DELETED

IDC0001I FUNCTION COMPLETED, HIGHEST CONDITION CODE WAS 0


IDC0002I IDCAMS PROCESSING COMPLETE. MAXIMUM CONDITION CODE WAS 0
```

Figure 10.2 The AMS messages from successful execution of the DELETE command in Fig. 10.1.

If the DELETE command is issued when the file is open for processing by an on-going process (e.g., a batch job or CICS), the command will fail and the user will get an appropriate message. However, this is true only if the job processing the VSAM file and the job issuing the DELETE command are running in the *same CPU*. In twin-CPU or multiple-CPU environments, if the VSAM file is on a shared DASD (a DASD which can be accessed by more than one system), caution is required. If the job (or TSO user) issues a DELETE command from one system to a file that is open for processing on another system, the deletion process will be successful. One must be careful in such multi-CPU configurations and take precautionary procedural measures to avoid such a situation.

10.1.2 Deleting an Alternate Index

Deleting an alternate index cluster deletes not only its own data and index components but also all the paths that have been defined over it. The JCL given in Fig. 10.3 (*a*) can be used to delete the Employee-Name alternate index. Upon successful execution, it will produce the messages in Fig. 10.3(*b*).

Suppose there is a base cluster with an alternate index that was not defined with the UPGRADE option. Since this alternate index will not be

(*a*)

```
//AMSJOB    JOB (ACCTNO),'JAY RANADE'
//DELAIX1   EXEC PGM=IDCAMS
//SYSPRINT DD SYSOUT=A
//SYSIN     DD *
 DELETE                              -
     EMPLOYEE.KSDS.AIX1.CLUSTER -
     ALTERNATEINDEX
/*
//
```

(*b*)

```
 DELETE                              -
     EMPLOYEE.KSDS.AIX1.CLUSTER -
     ALTERNATEINDEX

IDC0550I ENTRY (R) EMPLOYEE.KSDS.PATH1 DELETED

IDC0550I ENTRY (D) EMPLOYEE.KSDS.AIX1.DATA DELETED

IDC0550I ENTRY (I) EMPLOYEE.KSDS.AIX1.INDEX DELETED

IDC0550I ENTRY (G) EMPLOYEE.KSDS.AIX1.CLUSTER DELETED

IDC0001I FUNCTION COMPLETED, HIGHEST CONDITION CODE WAS 0
```

Figure 10.3 (*a*) JCL for deleting EMPLOYEE.KSDS.AIX1.CLUSTER. (*b*) Messages after successful execution of the DELETE command.

a member of the base cluster's upgrade set, any changes or updates made on the base cluster will not be reflected in it. The only way to bring it into synchronization with the base cluster is to

1. Delete the alternate index, thus also deleting any paths over it (DELETE command)
2. Define the alternate index (DEFINE AIX command)
3. Load key-pointer records (BLDINDEX command)
4. Establish the paths (DEFINE PATH command)

10.1.3 Deleting a PATH

Using DELETE with the path name deletes only the path entry. It *does not* affect the base cluster or its alternate indexes. Remember, though, if the path does not exist, you cannot directly access the records of the base cluster in the alternate key sequence.[1] The following command syntax can be used if, for example, you wish to delete the path on our Employee-Name alternate index.

[1]Indirectly, you could read the AIX as one file and then read the base cluster as a second file.

```
DELETE               -
EMPLOYEE.KSDS.PATH1 -
PATH
```

10.1.4 Generic DELETE

When an asterisk is substituted for *one* of the qualifiers of a data set name (e.g., EMPLOYEE.KSDS.CLUSTER can be written as EMPLOYEE.KSDS.* or EMPLOYEE.*.CLUSTER), execution of this command will cause a generic delete. All entries in the catalog that have the same qualifiers as those given, except the missing one, will be deleted. The asterisk becomes a "wild card" character and is substituted for any valid qualifier name. Let's suppose that the following command is executed.

```
DELETE               -
EMPLOYEE.*.CLUSTER -
CLUSTER
```

Successful execution means that the following clusters and their associated alternate indexes and paths, if any, will be deleted.

```
EMPLOYEE.KSDS.CLUSTER
EMPLOYEE.ESDS.CLUSTER
EMPLOYEE.RRDS.CLUSTER
```

In this case, any data set having three qualifiers (no more, no less), where the first qualifier is EMPLOYEE and the last one is CLUSTER, will be included in the deletion process. Remember that an asterisk cannot be used as the first qualifier, so, for example, *.KSDS.CLUSTER is an invalid generic name. Also, you cannot use an asterisk to replace more than one qualifier. EMPLOYEE.*.* is an invalid generic name, too.

You must be extra cautious when using the generic delete feature, because you could trigger a chain reaction of deletes. However, this feature does save you extra coding that might otherwise be necessary to delete multiple data sets.

10.1.5 Optional Parameters

Some of the optional parameters of DELETE can be used to cater to specific needs.

ERASE Execution of the DELETE command does not physically delete a data set. Only its ICF or VSAM catalog entry is removed, making this space available for future use. The data component remains on the disk until another data set is allocated on the same spot. This poses a serious data security issue for sensitive data such as payroll files. A simple utility could be used to dump the disk pack, including the sensitive data. When the DELETE command is executed with the ERASE option, not only will the entry be removed from the catalog, but also the data component will immediately be overwritten with binary zeros. The following example shows the use of this option to delete a password file.

```
DELETE                      -
EMPLOYEE.PASSWORD.CLUSTER -
CLUSTER                     -
ERASE
```

PURGE As you already know, a data set can be allocated by AMS and given a retention period by using the TO and FOR parameters. You cannot delete such a data set before the expiration date unless the optional PURGE parameter is coded. Caution must be observed because this option will delete the entry regardless of the retention period specified.

10.1.6 Entry-Type Parameters

Entry-type parameters are used by AMS to verify that the item to be deleted is of the *same type* as that specified in the command. To make this a little clearer, consider the following example.

```
DELETE                  -
EMPLOYEE.ESDS.CLUSTER -
ALTERNATEINDEX
```

We already know, based on the naming convention we've been using, that EMPLOYEE.ESDS.CLUSTER is an ESDS data set. The above command specifies that the file to be deleted is an alternate index. Since the actual file specified and the entry type listed do not match, AMS will issue an error message and the entry will not be deleted. If an entry type is not provided, AMS will delete the item specified in the command regardless of its type.

Although optional, the use of entry types is highly recommended as a precautionary measure. CLUSTER, ALTERNATEINDEX, PATH, etc., may be specified in the command.

10.1.7 DELETE Command vs DISPOSITION Parameter

Consider the following JCL.

```
//FILE1 DD DSN=NON.VSAM.DATASET,
//         DISP=(OLD,DELETE,DELETE)
```

The DISPOSITION parameter directs the system to delete the non-VSAM data set at the end of processing. There may be applications where the data set to be deleted may not physically exist at that moment. The above code will result in a JCL error, and the job will fail at that job step. If the delete is executed through the DELETE command of Access Method Services, there will not be any JCL error.

```
DELETE                   -
NON.VSAM.DATASET
```

The above command will successfully delete the data set if it exists. It will give a return code of 8 if it does not exist, instead of producing a JCL error. The return code can be tested through the COND parameter of JCL in subsequent job steps.

10.2 ALTER COMMAND

The ALTER command of AMS is used to change many of the attributes of an existing VSAM data set. It is far easier to use than the alternative, which is to delete the old data set and redefine it with the new attributes. If the second method is used, the data set will have to be backed up before deletion to preserve the records in it, and restored after reallocation.

It is important to understand that not all attributes can be changed with ALTER—there are many restrictions. Only IBM's AMS manual can provide an exhaustive list. However, the following examples will give you some idea of the kinds of limitations this command has.

1. You cannot change the key length and/or its offset for a KSDS through ALTER if it already has records loaded into it.
2. You cannot change the record size attribute (average or maximum) of a data set if it already contains records.
3. If an alternate index was allocated with the NONUNIQUEKEY parameter and then loaded with key-pointer records, you cannot change the attribute to UNIQUEKEY.

ALTER, despite its limitations, is very powerful. It has a wide variety of uses, each one changing the format of the command somewhat. Let's take a look at several examples so that you can see the variety of its use.

Example 1—Renaming a PDS Member: SAMPLE.TEST.LOAD is a partitioned data set load library which has a member named UPDTPGM. In this example, we will change its name to UPDTPROG. The command syntax is as follows:

```
ALTER                                   -
SAMPLE.TEST.LOAD(UPDTPGM)               -
NEWNAME(SAMPLE.TEST.LOAD(UPDTPROG))
```

Example 2—Adding candidate volumes: In this example, let's suppose that in the middle of the day CICS users start getting a NOSPACE condition when trying to add records to the personnel/payroll VSAM file. At the time of data set allocation, provision was made for secondary allocation, but there is no VSAM space left on the disk pack. You also determine that another volume, VSAM03, is owned by the same VSAM catalog. So, to correct the problem, you close and deallocate the data set to CICS and run the following command.

```
ALTER                 -
EMPLOYEE.KSDS.DATA    -
ADDVOLUMES(VSAM03)
ALTER                 -
EMPLOYEE.KSDS.INDEX   -
ADDVOLUMES(VSAM03)
```

After successful execution of these commands and the opening and reallocation of the data set to CICS, you are back in business. Volume VSAM03 will accommodate any additional allocations for the data set. Note that the names of the data and index components have been used in this command. You cannot use the cluster name when adding candidate volumes to a data set's attributes. If you are using a VSAM user catalog (not an ICF user catalog), make sure that the volume you mention is owned by the same VSAM catalog in which the problem data set is cataloged.

Example 3—Altering free space: Now let's imagine that through analysis you've discovered that most of the new employee record additions to the personnel/payroll file fall between social security numbers 089000000 and 116000000. As a result, most of the CI and CA splits have been caused by activity in this key range, and record insertions in the ranges before and after it have been rare. Thus, you decide that it is not desirable to leave uniform free space throughout the data set because of the variance in activity. While the less active key ranges require a moderate free space allocation of (5,5), the active one needs (25,25). This can be accomplished during the initial loading of the cluster using the JCL in Fig. 10.4.

Note that the FREESPACE parameter of this command requires the name of the data component and *not* the cluster name. Also, make sure that the input data set in REPRO is a KSDS (or indexed sequential), because the FROMKEY and TOKEY parameters have no meaning for other data set organizations.

```
//AMSJOB    JOB (ACCTNO),'JAY RANADE'
//ALTFSPC   EXEC PGM=IDCAMS
//SYSPRINT DD SYSOUT=A
//SYSIN     DD *
 /***************************************************************/
 /******* LOAD RECORDS UPTO KEY RANGE 088 ******/
 /***************************************************************/
     REPRO                                                    -
       IDS(EMPLOYEE.BACKUP.KSDS.CLUSTER)                      -
       ODS(EMPLOYEE.KSDS.CLUSTER)                             -
       FROMKEY(000)                                           -
       TOKEY(088)
 /***************************************************************/
 /******* CHANGE FREE SPACE TO (25,25)        ******/
 /***************************************************************/
     ALTER                                                    -
       EMPLOYEE.KSDS.DATA                                     -
       FREESPACE(25,25)
 /***************************************************************/
 /******* LOAD RECORDS FROM 089 TO 116        ******/
 /***************************************************************/
     REPRO                                                    -
       IDS(EMPLOYEE.BACKUP.KSDS.CLUSTER)                      -
       ODS(EMPLOYEE.KSDS.CLUSTER)                             -
       FROMKEY(089)                                           -
       TOKEY(116)
 /***************************************************************/
 /******* CHANGE FREESPACE BACK TO (5,5)  ******/
 /***************************************************************/
     ALTER                                                    -
       EMPLOYEE.KSDS.DATA                                     -
       FREESPACE(5,5)
 /***************************************************************/
 /*******     LOAD REST OF THE RECORDS        ******/
 /***************************************************************/
     REPRO                                                    -
       IDS(EMPLOYEE.BACKUP.KSDS.CLUSTER)                      -
       ODS(EMPLOYEE.KSDS.CLUSTER)                             -
       FROMKEY(117)
/*
//
```

Figure 10.4 Use of the ALTER command to change the freespace within a KSDS at the time of the initial load. It is assumed that the data set was defined with FREESPACE(5,5) to begin with.

Example 4—Write-protect data set: For our next example, let's imagine that you would like to prevent the users from updating a VSAM data set temporarily. Circumstances that would require such an action might include the following.

1. Logically related data sets are being backed up one after the other. The update of one of them will cause them to be out of synchronization.
2. A system is being converted or upgraded. You would like to freeze the contents of the VSAM files to avoid problems later.
3. Damage to portions of a VSAM data set has been detected. To avoid further damage while you are looking into the problem, you want to prevent the users from continuing with the updates.

Under all the above circumstances, your intention is to protect the data set from any changes. However, you do not want to deny the users read-only access to the files at the same time. If the data set we're working on is EMPLOYEE.KSDS.CLUSTER, the following command will prevent any access to the data set except for read-only operations.

```
ALTER                   -
EMPLOYEE.KSDS.DATA  -
INHIBIT
ALTER                   -
EMPLOYEE.KSDS.INDEX -
INHIBIT
```

Note that the syntax requires the entry names to be those of the data and index components, *not* that of the cluster. The read-only restriction set by an ALTER command can be removed by

```
ALTER                   -
EMPLOYEE.KSDS.DATA  -
UNINHIBIT
ALTER                   -
EMPLOYEE.KSDS.INDEX -
UNINHIBIT
```

Example 5—Changing a password: It's usually wise to change passwords when an employee who knows them doesn't work for you any more. Since a cluster, an alternate index, and a path can each have a password, it may be necessary to consider each one of them individually. It is also common practice to alter passwords on a regular basis. The following command illustrates how the master password can be changed for a KSDS and its related data and index components.

```
ALTER                     -
EMPLOYEE.KSDS.CLUSTER -
MASTERPW(NEWPASS1)
```

```
ALTER                        -
EMPLOYEE.KSDS.DATA           -
MASTERPW(NEWPASS2)
ALTER                        -
EMPLOYEE.KSDS.INDEX          -
MASTERPW(NEWPASS3)
```

Even if the data set was not password-protected at the time of its allocation, protection can be added later with this command. Other password levels can also be altered by using the appropriate parameter names, namely, UPDATEPW, CONTROLPW, and READPW.

Example 6—Changing an entry name: ALTER enables you to change the data set name of a VSAM or a non-VSAM file. Since a VSAM cluster consists of a data component and possibly an index component, their individual name changes must also be considered. The following command changes the name of EMPLOYEE.ESDS.CLUSTER and of its data component.

```
ALTER                                     -
EMPLOYEE.ESDS.CLUSTER                     -
NEWNAME(EMPLOYEE.ESDSNEW.CLUSTER)
ALTER                                     -
EMPLOYEE.ESDS.DATA                        -
NEWNAME(EMPLOYEE.ESDSNEW.DATA)
```

Example 7—Generic change: The names of multiple data sets can be changed with one command by using the generic change capability. Both the entry name and the new name should be expressed as generic names. Remember, the first qualifier cannot be made generic. However, more than one contiguous qualifier can be expressed as generic

```
ALTER                          -
EMPLOYEE.*.CLUSTER             -
NEWNAME(EMPLOYEE.*.CLSTR)
```

The above command will change all data set names in the catalog where the first qualifier is EMPLOYEE and third qualifier is CLUSTER. The third qualifier will be changed to CLSTR. Any data set having other than three qualifiers will *not* be considered at all.

Now, consider the following command.

```
ALTER                -
AB.CD.*.XYZ          -
NEWNAME(RR.*.XYZ)
```

Note the effect that would be achieved on the data set names given in the following example.

Old names	New names
AB.CD.EF.XYZ	RR.EF.XYZ
AB.CD.GH.XYZ	RR.GH.XYZ
AB.CD.IJ.XYZ	RR.IJ.XYZ

The first two qualifiers have been changed and consolidated into one qualifier.

Example 8—Changing SHAREOPTIONS: A company's master file for the general ledger system has been defined with the SHAREOPTIONS of (2,3). This is because, while one system (say, CICS) is doing updates, another batch program can generate reports through read-only access. Although such a SHAREOPTION does not ensure read integrity, it is acceptable to the users. At the end of the month, a trial balance report program is run to see whether the total debits and credits tally. For such a purpose, any read integrity problem will not tally the correct trial balance. In order to obtain exclusive control of the data set, the following procedures are used.

1. SHAREOPTIONS are changed:

```
ALTER                      -
GENERAL.LEDGER.DATA  -
SHAREOPTIONS(1,3)
ALTER                      -
GENERAL.LEDGER.INDEX -
SHAREOPTIONS(1,3)
```

   This will prevent other programs running in the same CPU from updating the cluster once it is open for read-only. Please note that the names used are those of the DATA and the INDEX components and not the cluster.
2. Execute the trial balance check program.
3. Change SHAREOPTIONS back to the previous value:

```
ALTER                      -
GENERAL.LEDGER.DATA  -
SHAREOPTIONS(2,3)
ALTER                      -
GENERAL.LEDGER.INDEX -
SHAREOPTIONS(2,3)
```

   You may wonder why we don't use a DISPOSITION of OLD

in the JCL to take exclusive control of the data set. It is possible to do so and have perfect read integrity, but this will prevent other read-only jobs (if any) from running concurrently with the trial balance check program.

10.3 VERIFY COMMAND

The VERIFY command of Access Method Services is used to check and correct the end-of-data (EOD) and end-of-key-range (EOKR) catalog information for a VSAM data set. End-of-data is the ending RBA of the highest used control area of the data component. The end-of-key range is the ending RBA of the highest used control area of the index component of a KSDS. If this command determines that the cataloged information is incorrect, it will update it with the correct values. The validity of these two values is important in VSAM files because they indicate where the physical endings of the different components of the data set are. If the system doesn't know these values, it might start to write new records over previously written ones.

Consider the following scenario. A KSDS data file is being used to collect transaction records entered through an on-line (e.g., CICS/VS) system. At the beginning of the day it has only a few records, all contained in the first CA [Fig. 10.5(*a*)]. The data set gradually grows as more and more records are added to it and will undoubtedly have CA splits as it increases. If it is allocated on an IBM 3380 disk and has a CI size of 4096 bytes, it will have 150 CI's per CA (a cylinder in this case) provided IMBED was not specified. If 150 CI's are multiplied by 4096 bytes (the size of each one of them), we will get a value of 614,400 bytes for the size of each CA. Hence, in the beginning the high used RBA (HURBA) information of the data component in the catalog will be 614,400 bytes. As users keep adding records to the file, the first CA split will take place. This CA split will increase the value of the high used RBA in the VSAM control blocks to 1,228,800 bytes, although the catalog will still have the value 614,400 bytes [Fig. 10.5(*b*)]. Catalog information is updated from the control blocks only when the data set is closed. If the on-line system goes down before the data set is closed, the catalog will have erroneous information about the HURBA [Fig. 10.5(*c*)]. The next time the on-line system opens the file, it will take the HURBA of the data component, which will still be 614,400 bytes as per the catalog [Fig. 10.5(*d*)]. Any records in the second CA will be inaccessible. The worst part of this is that the next CA split will overlay the existing records in the second CA and you will lose these records forever [Fig. 10.5(*e*)].

So far, only the data component of a data set has been taken into account. The index component also has CA splits and has its HURBA information stored in the catalog. If this information is erroneous, it should be as much of a concern as for the data component.

1. Before First CA split:

First CA has records	Second CA is empty

HURBA in catalog = 614,400 bytes
HURBA in control blocks = 614,400 bytes

2. After First CA split:

First CA has fewer records	Second CA has remaining records

HURBA in catalog = 614,400 bytes
HURBA in control blocks = 1,228,800 bytes

3. After CICS goes down abnormally:

First CA has fewer records	Second CA has records but catalog unaware

HURBA in catalog = 614,400 bytes
HURBA in control blocks—not applicable

4. After CICS is brought up again:

First CA has fewer records	Second CA has records but they're inaccessible

HURBA in catalog = 614,400 bytes
HURBA in control blocks = 614,400 bytes

5. After second CA split:

First CA has fewer records	Old records overlaid by second CA split

HURBA in catalog = 614,400 bytes
HURBA in control blocks = 1,228,800 bytes

Figure 10.5 Sequence of events resulting in a loss of records in a VSAM data set.

Such a catastrophe does not strike without warning, however. When a data set is first opened after a system failure, VSAM gives an "improperly closed file" return code. This return code can be checked *immediately* after opening a file to find out if the last system failure closed the file properly. In batch Cobol programs, you will get a file status of non-zero on opening the data set. This can be tested in the program. However, such a return code cannot be tested in CICS applications. This is because it is CICS which opens the files, not the application program.

There is a simple solution to these problems. You should always execute the VERIFY command on a file before letting an application program process the data in it. This command does three things:

1. It opens the file, thus forming the control blocks of VSAM.
2. It issues a VERIFY macro which compares EOD and EOKR values from the catalog with the true EOD and EOKR values from the file. If there is a discrepancy, it will update these values in the control blocks of the file.
3. It closes the file, thus updating the catalog information from the corrected control blocks.

Figure 10.6 gives an example of the format of this command.

Just as with other commands, you can perform a dynamic allocation of the data set and skip the file allocation in the JCL. For example, the same command could be coded as follows.

```
VERIFY                                    -
DATASET(EMPLOYEE.KSDS.CLUSTER)
```

A base cluster or an alternate index cluster can be the object of this command, but not the path of an alternate index. The cluster name should be used with this command. If data or index component names are used

```
//AMSJOB    JOB (ACCTNO),'JAY RANADE'
//VERIFY    EXEC PGM=IDCAMS
//SYSPRINT  DD SYSOUT=A
//DD1       DD DSN=EMPLOYEE.KSDS.CLUSTER,
//             DISP=SHR
//SYSIN     DD *
  VERIFY                               -
    FILE(DD1)
/*
//
```

Figure 10.6 An example of coding the VERIFY command.

in VERIFY, you may not be able to open the file properly later. Verifying a base cluster does not VERIFY its alternate indexes, so each one of them must be treated separately.

When opening a VSAM file after a system failure, application programmers often make a very common mistake. It can best be explained in the context of a Cobol program. Suppose an application program issues an OPEN for a VSAM file. Since the file was improperly closed because of an earlier system failure, the file status is set to a non-zero value. As the program detects this problem, it issues a CLOSE to the file before ending the processing. This CLOSE causes a major data integrity problem for the data set. It closes the previously improperly closed file while it *silll has* erroneous EOD and EOKR values. The next time an OPEN is issued by an application program (CICS system or batch program), it will not know that the cataloged information is incorrect and the file status will be set to zero. Everything will seem all right, but in the future, records that are missing because they were overlaid may cause data integrity problems that are difficult to trace. The only way to avoid this situation is not to issue a CLOSE if an OPEN was not successful.

If successive VERIFY commands executed on a KSDS give you a non-zero condition code, make sure that the KSDS is loaded. This is a little known fact and is often irritating. Issuing a VERIFY command on a KSDS that does not have any records (newly defined) gives a nonzero condition code, thus making you think the data set is damaged.

VERIFY should be used on all VSAM data sets before CICS is initialized. If a previous CICS termination was not normal, any problems will be resolved through this command. If it gives a return code of zero, it means that the data set was perfect before the command was issued. A non-zero return code means that the data set information was erroneous and that the EOD and EOKR have been corrected. Depending on the circumstances, a non-zero return code given by this command may be taken as an informative message only. Figure 10.7(*a*) and (*b*) shows the output messages of this command when executed on a properly closed and on an improperly closed data set, respectively.

10.3.1 DF/EF Considerations for Using VERIFY

If Data Facility/Extended Function (DF/EF) software is installed, things will be slightly different. Suppose an improperly closed data set is opened in such an environment. When the system detects an *improperly closed file* status, it issues an *implicit* VERIFY macro without any intervention from the program. This macro will correct the EOD and EOKR information in the control blocks, and processing will be correct thereafter. Under normal circumstances the implicit VERIFY function of DF/EF can be trusted to alleviate data integrity problems caused by an improper OPEN.

(a)

```
  VERIFY                                    -
    FILE(DD1)

IDC0001I FUNCTION COMPLETED, HIGHEST CONDITION CODE WAS 0


IDC0002I IDCAMS PROCESSING COMPLETE. MAXIMUM CONDITION CODE WAS 0
```

(b)

```
  VERIFY                                    -
    FILE(DD1)

IDC3300I  ERROR OPENING EMPLOYEE.KSDS.CLUSTER
IDC3351I ** VSAM OPEN RETURN CODE IS 118

IDC0001I FUNCTION COMPLETED, HIGHEST CONDITION CODE WAS 0


IDC0002I IDCAMS PROCESSING COMPLETE. MAXIMUM CONDITION CODE WAS 0
```

Figure 10.7 Output messages when VERIFY command is issued on (*a*) a good data set and (*b*) a data set after a system failure.

However, there is one word of caution. The implicit VERIFY function of DF/EF is a *macro*. It is not the full VERIFY *command* but only a subset of the command. The VERIFY macro does not issue a CLOSE, but the command does. Unless a CLOSE is issued, EOD and EOKR information is not transferred from control blocks to the cataloged values. If another system failure takes place afterward, the control blocks will vanish and the cataloged information may still be erroneous. It is recommended that the VERIFY command still be used in a DF/EF environment. The implicit VERIFY is excellent as a second line of defense.

chapter 11

Listing Catalog Entries

The AMS functional command we will use in this chapter is LISTCAT, which stands for *LIST*ing a *CAT*alog entry. It is useful for listing attributes and characteristics of all VSAM and non-VSAM objects cataloged in a VSAM or ICF catalog. Such objects can be the catalog itself, its aliases, the volumes it owns, clusters, alternate indexes, paths, GDG's, non-VSAM files, etc. The listing also provides statistics about a VSAM object from the time of its allocation, including the number of CI and CA splits, the number of I/O's on index and data components, the number of records added, deleted, and retrieved, and much more useful information. These statistics can help you decide when a KSDS data set requires reorganization. This command can help you determine which data sets were defined before a particular period of time and which data sets will expire within a specified period.

If you have forgotten or do not know the command parameters that were used to define an existing VSAM data set, this command can be helpful in determining what they were. You can list all the data sets beginning with a specific qualifier. For example, in our case it is possible to find all data sets beginning with EMPLOYEE. If need be, you can also list every data set cataloged in a particular VSAM or ICF catalog. You can find all the volumes owned by a VSAM catalog and the aliases that have been defined for it. A listing obtained for a particular volume using

IEHLIST or option 3.7 of SPF[1] will not tell you the space utilization for a VSAM data set. You have to use LISTCAT to find it. Also, option 3.2 of SPF cannot be used to find a VSAM data set's space characteristics. Only LISTCAT can give you that information.

This command will come in handy for all the items mentioned above and many more. An effort has been made not only to familiarize you with the command syntax, but also to teach you to interpret the meaning of different items in the listing. Let's begin with the syntax.

11.1 LISTCAT COMMAND SYNTAX

To use this command, you have to implicitly or explicitly supply AMS with the following three levels of requirements:

1. The name of the VSAM or ICF catalog that contains the information, e.g., 'VSAM.USERCAT.TWO'
2. The name of the entry or entries in the catalog whose information is required, e.g., 'EMPLOYEE.KSDS.CLUSTER'
3. The type of information needed for the entry or entries, e.g., VOLUME, ALLOCATION, NAME, HISTORY, and ALL

Consider the command

```
LISTCAT                               -
CATALOG(VSAM.USERCAT.TWO)             -
ENTRIES(EMPLOYEE.ESDS.CLUSTER) -
ALL
```

Here you are requesting all the characteristics for the entry EMPLOYEE.ESDS.CLUSTER, which exists in a catalog named VSAM.USERCAT.TWO. Since in our case EMPLOYEE is an alias of user catalog VSAM.USERCAT.TWO, it may not be necessary to code the CATALOG parameter at all. AMS can find the required catalog from the first qualifier of the requested entry name. Therefore, the following will give the same results as the previous LISTCAT command.

```
LISTCAT                               -
ENTRIES(EMPLOYEE.ESDS.CLUSTER) -
ALL
```

If the CATALOG parameter is not coded and the first qualifier of the entry name is not the alias of a catalog, the default is to search the master catalog of the system for the particular entry.

[1]Option 3.7 of TSO/SPF can be used to obtain a listing of the volume table of contents (VTOC) for a particular DASD.

11.1.1 Difference Between ENTRIES and LEVEL

The ENTRIES parameter (abbreviated ENT) requires that all the qualifiers of the data set name be given. However, you may replace one of the qualifiers with an asterisk, in which case it becomes the wild card character.

The LEVEL parameter assumes that one or more leading qualifiers of the data set are being given and that all the trailing qualifiers can be anything. Even one of the leading qualifiers can be replaced with an asterisk, in which case it will become the wild card character.

As an example, suppose that VSAM.USERCAT.TWO contains the following names.

```
(Entry 1)   EMPLOYEE.KSDS.CLUSTER
(Entry 2)   EMPLOYEE.KSDS.AIX1.CLUSTER
(Entry 3)   EMPLOYEE.KSDS.AIX2.CLUSTER
(Entry 4)   EMPLOYEE.KSDS.PATH1
(Entry 5)   EMPLOYEE.KSDS.PATH2
(Entry 6)   EMPLOYEE.ESDS.CLUSTER
(Entry 7)   EMPLOYEE.RRDS.CLUSTER
```

If ENTRIES(EMPLOYEE.*) is specified, no entry will be listed, because there is no name with two qualifiers. If ENTRIES-(EMPLOYEE.KSDS.*) is specified, entries 1, 4, and 5 will be listed. If ENTRIES(EMPLOYEE.*.CLUSTER) is specified, entries 1, 6, and 7 will be listed. If LEVEL(EMPLOYEE) is specified, all the entries will be listed. If LEVEL(EMPLOYEE.KSDS) is specified, entries 1 to 5 will be listed.

11.2 LISTING A CLUSTER ENTRY

In order to become more familiar with the information supplied by LISTCAT, we will study one listing in complete detail. Suppose the following command is executed.

```
LISTCAT                        -
ENT(EMPLOYEE.KSDS.CLUSTER) -
ALL
```

This will list all the information about the ENTRIES parameter data set name, which is EMPLOYEE.KSDS.CLUSTER. By coding the ALLOCATION, HISTORY, NAME, or VOLUME parameter, you obtain only the specific information each name suggests. When you code ALL, everything is included. Figure 11.1 gives the output listing produced by executing the above command.

The information is divided into three major sections, the cluster, the data, and the index components. In the case of an ESDS and an RRDS, there will be no information regarding the index component.

11.2.1 Cluster Characteristics

Information about the cluster is split into three groups: HISTORY, PROTECTION, and ASSOCIATIONS.

HISTORY OWNER-IDENT gives the identification if the OWNER parameter was coded while allocating the data set. If the data set was allocated interactively under TSO/SPF (see Chap. 17), this field will contain your TSO ID.

The value of RELEASE will be 2 if the 1976 version of VSAM was used. An earlier version will have a value of 1. CREATION gives the year and the Julian date on which the data set was defined. EXPIRATION gives the year and the Julian date when the data set will expire. Its value will be zero if the TO or FOR parameter was not used during allocation. If the data set is to be deleted before the date listed, the PURGE parameter must be used in the DELETE command.

RCVY-VOL gives the volume serial number of the DASD that contains the catalog recovery area (CRA) for a recoverable VSAM catalog. Since VSAM.USERCAT.TWO was defined using the RECOVERABLE parameter, its value, VSAM02, is given. CRA helps in the restoration of a damaged catalog using the RESETCAT command. This field is not applicable if your data set is cataloged in an ICF catalog.

RCVY-DEVT gives the device type of the DASD which contains the CRA. The value X'3010200E' indicates that the device is an IBM 3380. Some of the commonly used devices and their codes are as follows.

Code	Device
30502009	3330
3050200D	3330-1
30582009	3330V
3050200B	3350
3050200C	3375
3010200E	3380

RCVY-CI provides the CI number within the CRA that contains the duplicate information about the catalog entry. In our case, it is the thirty-sixth CI (X'000024'). This information has no practical use to application programmers.

The PROTECTION-PSWD field contains NULL, indicating that

```
                    LISTING FROM CATALOG -- VSAM.USERCAT.TWO

CLUSTER ------- EMPLOYEE.KSDS.CLUSTER
     HISTORY
       OWNER-IDENT-------(NULL)     CREATION----------84.280     RCVY-VOL----------VSAM02     RCVY-CI--------X'000024'
       RELEASE-----------------2    EXPIRATION--------00.000     RCVY-DEVT----X'3010200E'
     PROTECTION-PSWD-----(NULL)     RACF----------------(NO)
     ASSOCIATIONS
       DATA-----EMPLOYEE.KSDS.DATA
       INDEX----EMPLOYEE.KSDS.INDEX
       AIX------EMPLOYEE.KSDS.AIX1.CLUSTER
       AIX------EMPLOYEE.KSDS.AIX2.CLUSTER

   DATA ------- EMPLOYEE.KSDS.DATA
     HISTORY
       OWNER-IDENT-------(NULL)     CREATION----------84.280     RCVY-VOL----------VSAM02     RCVY-CI--------X'000023'
       RELEASE-----------------2    EXPIRATION--------00.000     RCVY-DEVT----X'3010200E'
     PROTECTION-PSWD-----(NULL)     RACF----------------(NO)
     ASSOCIATIONS
       CLUSTER--EMPLOYEE.KSDS.CLUSTER
     ATTRIBUTES
       KEYLEN------------------9    AVGLRECL--------------50     BUFSPACE-----------10240     CISIZE--------------4096
       RKP---------------------0    MAXLRECL--------------50     EXCPEXIT----------(NULL)     CI/CA----------------150
       SHROPTNS(1,3)    RECOVERY    SUBALLOC         NOERASE     INDEXED        NOWRITECHK    NOIMBED       NOREPLICAT
       UNORDERED         NOREUSE    NONSPANNED
     STATISTICS
       REC-TOTAL--------------10    SPLITS-CI--------------0     EXCPS-------------------35
       REC-DELETED-------------1    SPLITS-CA--------------0     EXTENTS------------------1
       REC-INSERTED------------2    FREESPACE-%CI---------10     SYSTEM-TIMESTAMP:
       REC-UPDATED------------12    FREESPACE-%CA---------20          X'980D50BFAF590000'
       REC-RETRIEVED----------40    FREESPC-BYTES----1224704
     ALLOCATION
       SPACE-TYPE------CYLINDER     HI-ALLOC-RBA-----1228800
       SPACE-PRI---------------2    HI-USED-RBA-------614400
       SPACE-SEC---------------1
     VOLUME
       VOLSER------------VSAM02     PHYREC-SIZE---------4096     HI-ALLOC-RBA-----1228800     EXTENT-NUMBER----------1
       DEVTYPE------X'3010200E'     PHYRECS/TRK-----------10     HI-USED-RBA-------614400     EXTENT-TYPE--------X'40'
       VOLFLAG------------PRIME     TRACKS/CA-------------15
       EXTENTS:
       LOW-CCHH-----X'00080000'     LOW-RBA----------------0     TRACKS-----------------30
       HIGH-CCHH----X'000C000E'     HIGH-RBA---------1228799
```

```
INDEX ------ EMPLOYEE.KSDS.INDEX
  HISTORY
    OWNER-IDENT-------(NULL)      CREATION----------84.280     RCVY-VOL----------VSAM02      RCVY-CI--------X'000010'
    RELEASE-----------------2     EXPIRATION--------00.000     RCVY-DEVT----X'3010200E'
  PROTECTION-PSWD-----(NULL)      RACF----------------(NO)
  ASSOCIATIONS
    CLUSTER--EMPLOYEE.KSDS.CLUSTER
  ATTRIBUTES
    KEYLEN------------------9     AVGLRECL---------------0     BUFSPACE---------------0     CISIZE--------------2048
    RKP---------------------0     MAXLRECL------------2041     EXCPEXIT----------(NULL)     CI/CA-----------------18
    SHROPTNS(1,3)    RECOVERY     SUBALLOC         NOERASE     NOWRITECHK       NOIMBED     NOREPLICAT     UNORDERED
    NOREUSE
  STATISTICS
    REC-TOTAL---------------1     SPLITS-CI--------------0     EXCPS------------------8     INDEX:
    REC-DELETED-------------0     SPLITS-CA--------------0     EXTENTS----------------1     LEVELS-----------------1
    REC-INSERTED------------0     FREESPACE-%CI----------0     SYSTEM-TIMESTAMP:            ENTRIES/SECT----------12
    REC-UPDATED-------------0     FREESPACE-%CA----------0          X'980D50BFAF590000'     SEQ-SET-RBA------------0
    REC-RETRIEVED-----------0     FREESPC-BYTES------34816                                  HI-LEVEL-RBA-----------0
  ALLOCATION
    SPACE-TYPE----------TRACK     HI-ALLOC-RBA-------36864
    SPACE-PRI---------------1     HI-USED-RBA---------2048
    SPACE-SEC---------------1
  VOLUME
    VOLSER-------------VSAM02     PHYREC-SIZE---------2048     HI-ALLOC-RBA-------36864     EXTENT-NUMBER----------1
    DEVTYPE------X'3010200E'      PHYRECS/TRK-----------18     HI-USED-RBA---------2048     EXTENT-TYPE--------X'00'
    VOLFLAG-------------PRIME     TRACKS/CA--------------1
    EXTENTS:
    LOW-CCHH-----X'000D0000'      LOW-RBA----------------0     TRACKS-----------------1
    HIGH-CCHH----X'000D0000'      HIGH-RBA-----------36863
```

Figure 11.1 Catalog listing of entry name EMPLOYEE.KSDS.CLUSTER. ALL was specified to indicate the type of information.

the data set is not password-protected. If its value is SUPP, it means that the object is password-protected but the passwords are being suppressed for security reasons. If the LISTCAT command contains the master password for the object or the catalog, all the passwords will be printed.

ASSOCIATIONS This gives the names of the data and index components associated with the cluster. It also gives the names of alternate index clusters related to the data set.

11.2.2 Data Component

Information about the data component is provided in seven different groups. The HISTORY, PROTECTION, and ASSOCIATIONS groups were explained in Sec. 11.2.1. However, keep in mind that they also pertain to the data component of the cluster. Notice that the recovery control interval is X'000023', which is different from that of the cluster.

ATTRIBUTES This describes the fixed characteristics of the component, most of which were explicitly or implicity specified at the time of allocation.

KEYLEN gives the length of the key as 9 bytes. RKP gives the relative key position of the beginning of the prime key, which is zero in this case. AVGLRECL and MAXLRECL give the average and maximum record lengths of the record as specified in the RECORDSIZE parameter.

BUFSPACE gives the buffer space in bytes. If this parameter is not coded at the time of allocation, the default is to allocate two data CI buffers and one index CI buffer. In our case, the CI sizes for the data and index components are 4096 and 2048, respectively. So the default buffer space is calculated

$$\begin{aligned}\text{BUFSPACE} &= 2 \times 4096 + 2048 \\ &= 10{,}240\end{aligned}$$

EXCPEXIT gives the name of a user-written routine that receives control when an I/O error occurs during data transfer between the buffers and a DASD. Its value is NULL because we do not have any such routine. If such a program does exist, it must be in an authorized library and specified at the time of DEFINE CLUSTER in the EXCEPTIONEXIT parameter. CISIZE gives the data CI size, which in our case is 4096.

CI/CA gives the number of data control intervals in one control area. It is calculated by multiplying the number of tracks per CA by the number of CI's per track. Since the space allocation was made in cylinders, our CA size is 1 cylinder, i.e., 15 tracks for an IBM 3380 device. If we had specified IMBED, the first track of the CA would have been used for the sequence set of the index component and the CA would be 14 tracks in size. One track of an IBM 3380 disk can have 10 CI's of 4096 bytes each. Therefore, there are 15 × 10, or 150, CI's per CA. IBM 3380's are the most widely used DASD today. Figure 11.2 may be used as a quick reference to determine the number of CI's each track can hold for different CI sizes for IBM 3380's and IBM 3350's.

The other attributes listed were implicity or explicity used at the time of the DEFINE CLUSTER. SHROPTNS (1,3) specifies a cross-region shareoption of 1 and a cross-system shareoption of 3. RECOVERY indicates that, on the initial loading, the CA's will be formatted for easy recovery in case of a system or application failure. SUBALLOC indicates that the data set is defined in previously allocated VSAM space. NOERASE specifies that the data component will not be overwritten with binary zeros when deleted. INDEXED indicates that the data component belongs to a KSDS. If NOWRITECHK is used, the CI's will not be reread and compared with buffers. NOIMBED indicates that the first track of the data CA does not have imbedded sequence set CI's. NOREPLICAT means that the index set CI's of the index component will not be replicated. UNORDERED specifies that the volumes will not necessarily be used in the sequence given in the VOLUMES parameter. It does not apply to this particular data set because only one volume, VSAM02, was given at the time of allocation. The NOREUSE parameter will prevent us from setting the high used RBA to zero, thus logically deleting the existing records if the data set is opened as OUTPUT. NONSPANNED indicates that the records will not span CI boundaries.

STATISTICS This group gives the current status of the different statistics of the data set since it was allocated. They cannot be trusted completely if the data set was not closed properly after processing. Improper closing could be due to application failure or system failure. For example, let's suppose that a data set has 1 record to start with. It is opened for updates in CICS, and 1000 records are added to it. In the meantime, CICS comes down. You issue a VERIFY command to properly close it. The data set will have 1001 records in it, but the statistics will show only 1 record because only the normal shutdown of CICS would have updated

	Number of CI's per track	
CI size	**IBM 3380**	**IBM 3350**
512	46	27
1024	31	15
2048	18	8
4096	10	4
6144	6	3
8192	5	2

Figure 11.2 Number of CI's per track for some commonly used CI sizes for IBM 3380 and IBM 3350 DASD's. Each track has 47,968 bytes and 19,254 bytes, respectively.

the information in the catalog. However, incorrect statistical data does not affect the integrity of the data in any way.

REC-TOTAL gives the total number of records in the file, REC-DELETED gives the number of records deleted, and REC-INSERTED gives the number of new record additions. REC-UPDATED refers only to the updating of existing records. REC-RETRIEVED includes retrievals for read-only, deletes, and retrievals for updates.

SPLITS-CI and SPLITS-CA give the number of CI and CA splits caused by record additions and updates. Excessive CI and CA splits, especially the latter, can result in increased I/O's at the time of their occurrence. This is one of the causes of poor response time in CICS systems. These splits can also increase processing time for sequential browses, because the records get out of physical sequence. However, random retrievals are not affected much. FREESPACE-%CI and FREESPACE-%CA show the values of the FREESPACE parameters at the time of data set allocation. Although these values are applicable only for a sequential loading or a resume load of the KSDS, excessive CI and CA splits can be correlated with them to see if more free space should be allocated in the future to minimize the splits. FREESPC-BYTES gives the total number of bytes available in *completely empty* CI's only. This does *not* include the free space in partially filled CI's. In our case, its value is 1,224,704 bytes. This translates into 299 free CI's, each 4096 bytes in size. The primary space allocation was two cylinders, which is 300 CI's. Since one is partially used, containing 10 records, there are 299 available as free CI's.

EXCPS, which stands for *EX*ecute *C*hannel *P*rogram, indicates the number of physical I/O's executed on this component since its allocation. EXTENTS provides the number of physical extents of the data set, which in this case is 1. The maximum number of extents for a suballocated VSAM data set is 123.

SYSTEM-TIMESTAMP is a double-word (16 hex digits) binary number that refers to the date and time the data set was last closed after being opened for updates. It may also be the last time VERIFY was issued on the data set. The value given (X'980D50BFAF590000') represents the time, in microseconds, that has elapsed since January 1, 1900. Only bits 0 to 51 (52 bits) are significant. Bit 51 is increased by 1 every microsecond, and bit 31 changes every 1.048576 seconds. The calendar covers approximately 143 years. The time stamps on the index and data components are verified to be equal before VSAM opens the file. Unequal values indicate that the components were closed at different times, which might indicate a problem.

ALLOCATION SPACE-TYPE will be either CYLINDERS or TRACKS, depending on the allocation parameters used at the time of the DEFINE CLUSTER. SPACE-PRI, which is two cylinders in our case, specifies the primary space allocated initially, while SPACE-SEC refers to the secondary allocation of one cylinder. If the data set must be extended, space will be allocated in increments of the secondary allocation parameter, up to a maximum of 122 times.

HI-ALLOC-RBA is the RBA of the last byte of the last CA in the data set. It indicates the size of the total space allocated in bytes. HI-USED-RBA is the RBA of the *last byte of the highest used CA* in the KSDS. It is an important field, and its value indicates the last CA that contains data records. One of the major functions of the VERIFY command is to verify and correct this value. An incorrect value in this field would make some data records inaccessible.

VOLUME A VOLFLAG value of PRIME indicates that the VOLSER indicated (VSAM02) is the first volume on which data records are stored. If its value is OVERFLOW, it points to the other overflow volumes on which additional data is stored. It can also have a value of CANDIDATE, which indicates a volume reserved for future allocations if needed.

PHYREC-SIZE is the physical record size of the data component, which is 4096 in our case. *Each CI may consist of one or more physical records.* The only physical record sizes supported by VSAM are 512, 1024, 2048, and 4096. The smaller the physical record size, the greater the space being wasted for interblock gaps on the DASD. Any CI size that is a multiple of 4096 gives the optimum DASD space utilization, because the physical record size will also be 4096. If it is not 4096, AMS will determine if it is a multiple of 2048, 1024, or 512, in that order. Whichever is found to be a complete multiple first is selcted by AMS to be the physical record size for the CI. It can be controlled by what you specify in the CISZ parameter of DEFINE CLUSTER. Remember, CI size or physical record size does not influence the processing logic of the program; they are quite transparent to you. However, they do affect the DASD space utilization efficiency.

PHYRECS/TRK gives the number of physical records per track. In this case, since the CI size and physical record size are the same, we have 10 physical records (or CI's) per track. TRACKS/CA is the number of tracks per control area. With a CA size of 1 cylinder, we have 15 tracks per CA.

HI-ALLOC-RBA and HI-USED-RBA have the same meaning as mentioned previously. In the present context, they pertain to the primary allocation on VSAM02.

An EXTENT-NUMBER of 1 specifies that VSAM02 has only one extent allocated for the data set. EXTENT-TYPE value X'40' indicates that this extent is not preformatted. Other extent types can be X'00', which indicates extents contiguous to existing ones. These extents have less processing overhead when converting RBA's to physical disk addresses for performing I/O's. Extent type X'80' is indicative of an embedded sequence set.

LOW-CCHH and HIGH-CCHH gives you the physical location of the data set on the disk pack. CC, which is the first four hex digits, stands for the cylinder number, and HH, the last 4 bytes, stands for the track number. In the listing, the data set starts at the X'0000' track of the X'000B' cylinder. That is, from the first track of cylinder 11 (the first track on a cylinder is considered the zeroth track). It extends up to track 14 of cylinder 12. This adds up to 30 tracks of total data space, which is given under the title TRACKS in the same row of the listing. Knowing the physical location of the data set helps you to find its position relative to others. Thus, you can find out if two parallel processed files are causing performance problems because of excessive movement of the read-write arm between them.

LOW-RBA and HIGH-RBA give the beginning and ending RBA of a particular extent allocation.

11.2.3 Index Component

Most of the fields discussed in reference to the data component have the same meaning when mentioned in this section, but here they will apply to the index component of the cluster. The HISTORY and ASSOCIATIONS groups have fields that you are already familiar with.

In the ATTRIBUTES group, the CI size of the index component is 2048 bytes, which is different from that of the data component. There are 18 CI's per CA, because the CA size for this index component is one track of an IBM 3380. The TRACKS/CA is given in the VOLUME group in the same listing. Note that the CA size of the index component does not have to be, and usually is not, the same as the CA size of the data component.

The AVGLRECL and MAXLRECL for the index records are 0 and 2041, respectively. The maximum logical record length is 7 less than the CI size because 7 bytes are used for the control fields in the CI (RDF and CIDF).

In the STATISTICS group, the total number of index records is given as 1 in the REC-TOTAL field. A FREESPC-BYTES value of 34816 means that there are 17 free index CI's (34,816 divided by 2048) which can be used to contain 17 more index records when the file grows. An EXCPS count of 8 indicates that 8 I/O's have been performed on the index component since its allocation.

LEVELS provides some very important information. It indicates the number of index levels for the index component, including the sequence set as the lowermost level. If there is only one level, which is true in our case, the sequence set and the index set are the same. An ENTRIES/SECT value of 12 is the number of entries per section. It is a technique used by VSAM to divide an index record into sections to improve performance. The value is obtained by calculating the square root of the number of data CI's per CA. Since we have 150 CI's in a CA for the data component, the index record will be divided into 12 sections. SEQ-SET-RBA gives the RBA of the sequence set of the index component. HI-LEVEL-RBA is an important field; it gives the RBA of the highest-level index record. It is from this index record that all the paths are traversed down to the data component.

In the VOLUMES group, LOW-CCHH and HIGH-CCHH point to track zero of cylinder 13. Recall that the data component was on cylinders 11 and 12. Since this allocation is contiguous with the previous one, its EXTENT-TYPE has a value of X'00'. HI-ALLOC-RBA and HI-USED-RBA have the same meanings as for the data component.

LISTCAT listings produce a treasure of information that can be helpful in understanding data set internal architecture. You can also take a quick glance at the parameters that were implicitly and explicitly used for allocation. You will obtain information regarding CI and CA splits that will help you make decisions as to when to reorganize a KSDS or whether or not to leave more free space to minimize these splits. You can see the physical extents of the components and check if they are contiguous or not. This might help you in deciding if the secondary extents can be minimized by allocating a larger primary extent. The difference between HI-USED-RBA and HI-ALLOC-RBA can give you the exact number of unutilized CA's at the end of the data set, which might be indicative of overallocated space. You will find numerous ways to use this information for making efficient use of different data set organizations and VSAM.

11.3 LISTING QUALIFIED ENTRY NAMES

You may use the LEVEL option of the LISTCAT command to list all the data sets beginning with a particular qualifier. If VSAM.USERCAT.TWO is being used by two application projects and each has its unique alias as the first qualifier of the data set name, this feature can be used to obtain file names for each one of them separately. If the aliases are EMPLOYEE and PAYROLL, the following commands will give the data set names for each one of them.

```
LISTCAT LEVEL(EMPLOYEE)
LISTCAT LEVEL(PAYROLL)
```

You can further narrow down your choice by specifying more qualifiers. The following command will list the data set names whose first two qualifiers are EMPLOYEE.KSDS.

```
LISTCAT LEVEL(EMPLOYEE.KSDS)
```

```
                              LISTING FROM CATALOG -- VSAM.USERCAT.TWO
CLUSTER ------- EMPLOYEE.ESDS.CLUSTER
DATA ---------- EMPLOYEE.ESDS.DATA
CLUSTER ------- EMPLOYEE.ESDSTEST.CLUSTER
DATA ---------- EMPLOYEE.ESDSTEST.DATA
AIX ----------- EMPLOYEE.KSDS.AIX1.CLUSTER
DATA ---------- EMPLOYEE.KSDS.AIX1.DATA
INDEX --------- EMPLOYEE.KSDS.AIX1.INDEX
AIX ----------- EMPLOYEE.KSDS.AIX2.CLUSTER
DATA ---------- EMPLOYEE.KSDS.AIX2.DATA
INDEX --------- EMPLOYEE.KSDS.AIX2.INDEX
CLUSTER ------- EMPLOYEE.KSDS.CLUSTER
DATA ---------- EMPLOYEE.KSDS.DATA
INDEX --------- EMPLOYEE.KSDS.INDEX
PATH ---------- EMPLOYEE.KSDS.PATH1
PATH ---------- EMPLOYEE.KSDS.PATH2
CLUSTER ------- EMPLOYEE.RRDS.CLUSTER
DATA ---------- EMPLOYEE.RRDS.DATA
```

Figure 11.3 List of data set names in VSAM.USERCAT.TWO which begin with EMPLOYEE alias.

Notice that we are *not* coding the CATALOG parameter, because the first qualifier is its alias. Figure 11.3 gives the listing produced by executing the following command.

```
LISTCAT LEVEL(EMPLOYEE)
```

Notice that, since we have not used a parameter to qualify the type of information desired, NAME becomes the default. If ALL were coded, we would get every bit of information for each entry listed.

11.4 LISTING ALL ENTRY NAMES

There may be instances when you need the data set names of every VSAM and non-VSAM entry in a particular VSAM or ICF catalog. If you do not code the ENTRIES or LEVEL parameters, the default is to list all the entries in the catalog specified. The following command may be used to obtain such a list for VSAM.USERCAT.TWO.

```
LISTCAT CATALOG(VSAM.USERCAT.TWO)
```

The listing produced for our catalog upon execution appears in Fig. 11.4. It lists all the entries beginning with the aliases EMPLOYEE and SAMPLE. As a convention, we used SAMPLE as the high-end qualifier for non-VSAM files. Technically, you may use an alias as the first qualifier for VSAM as well as non-VSAM files; there are no restrictions.

```
                              LISTING FROM CATALOG -- VSAM.USERCAT.TWO
CLUSTER ------- EMPLOYEE.ESDS.CLUSTER
   DATA ------- EMPLOYEE.ESDS.DATA
CLUSTER ------- EMPLOYEE.ESDSTEST.CLUSTER
   DATA ------- EMPLOYEE.ESDSTEST.DATA
AIX ----------- EMPLOYEE.KSDS.AIX1.CLUSTER
   DATA ------- EMPLOYEE.KSDS.AIX1.DATA
   INDEX ------ EMPLOYEE.KSDS.AIX1.INDEX
   PATH ------- EMPLOYEE.KSDS.PATH1
AIX ----------- EMPLOYEE.KSDS.AIX2.CLUSTER
   DATA ------- EMPLOYEE.KSDS.AIX2.DATA
   INDEX ------ EMPLOYEE.KSDS.AIX2.INDEX
   PATH ------- EMPLOYEE.KSDS.PATH2
CLUSTER ------- EMPLOYEE.KSDS.CLUSTER
   DATA ------- EMPLOYEE.KSDS.DATA
   INDEX ------ EMPLOYEE.KSDS.INDEX
CLUSTER ------- EMPLOYEE.RRDS.CLUSTER
   DATA ------- EMPLOYEE.RRDS.DATA
NONVSAM ------- SAMPLE.AIXUPDT.DATA
NONVSAM ------- SAMPLE.ESDSUPDT.DATA
NONVSAM ------- SAMPLE.INPUT.DATA
NONVSAM ------- SAMPLE.LOAD.DATA
NONVSAM ------- SAMPLE.PROGRAM.LOAD
NONVSAM ------- SAMPLE.RRDSUPDT.DATA
NONVSAM ------- SAMPLE.TRANS.DATA
NONVSAM ------- SAMPLE.TRANS1.DATA
CLUSTER ------- VSAM.USERCAT.TWO
   DATA ------- VSAM.CATALOG.BASE.DATA.RECORD
   INDEX ------ VSAM.CATALOG.BASE.INDEX.RECORD
VOLUME -------- VSAM02
```

Figure 11.4 Listing of all the entries in the catalog VSAM.USERCAT.TWO.

The data and index components of the cluster entry in VSAM.USERCAT.TWO have unfamiliar names which are never used when defining a catalog. These names are generated by AMS. Finally, the volume serial number (VSAM02) gives the DASD containing the VSAM space. If more DASD's were owned by the VSAM catalog, they would also appear in the printout.

11.5 ALIASES AND VOLUME OWNERSHIP OF CATALOGS

Working at a typical MVS installation, you may use various VSAM and ICF catalogs. There may be many unique aliases defined for each one of these catalogs. Knowing the volume ownership of VSAM catalogs is important, because you may use only these volumes in defining data sets. It is not unusual to mix and match catalogs with volumes they don't own and aliases that do not belong to them. This leads to errors in allocating data sets. The following command can be used to list these attributes for our VSAM catalog.

```
LISTCAT                       -
ENTRIES(VSAM.USERCAT.TWO) -
ALL
```

The listing produced appears in Fig. 11.5.

The IN-CAT field refers to the master catalog in which our user catalog has an entry. Notice that the VSAM catalog is considered an entry rather than a catalog in this example.

11.6 CATALOG ASSOCIATION OF AN ALIAS

Sometimes you may know an alias name and use it, but not know the VSAM catalog it belongs to. The following command can be used to find it as shown in the listing produced by it in Fig. 11.6.

```
LISTCAT                  -
ENTRIES(EMPLOYEE) -
ALL
```

```
LISTCAT                                            -                                   00070001
  ENTRIES(VSAM.USERCAT.TWO)                        -                                   00080002
  ALL                                                                                  00090001

USERCATALOG --- VSAM.USERCAT.TWO
     IN-CAT --- CATALOG.VSP3CAT
     HISTORY
       RELEASE----------------2
     VOLUMES
       VOLSER------------VSAM02       DEVTYPE------X'3010200E'     VOLFLAG------------PRIME
     ASSOCIATIONS
       ALIAS----SAMPLE
       ALIAS----EMPLOYEE
```

Figure 11.5 List of aliases and volume ownerships for a VSAM catalog.

```
LISTCAT                                    -          00070001
  ENTRIES(EMPLOYEE)                        -          00080002
  ALL                                                 00090001

ALIAS --------- EMPLOYEE
     IN-CAT --- CATALOG.VSP3CAT
     HISTORY
       RELEASE----------------2
     ASSOCIATIONS
       USERCAT--VSAM.USERCAT.TWO
```

Figure 11.6 Listing giving the catalog name with which an alias is associated.

11.7 AGING OF CATALOG ENTRIES

At an installation of any size you may find many VSAM data sets that were created months, maybe years, ago and that have never been used since then. They take up a lot of expensive DASD space without serving any purpose. Let's suppose you want to find all the VSAM and non-VSAM data sets cataloged in VSAM.USERCAT.TWO that were created more than a year ago. The following command may be used.

```
LISTCAT                       -
CATALOG(VSAM.USERCAT.TWO) -
CREATION(365)
```

The CREATION parameter may have a value in days only. In this particular example, all files that are 365 days old or older will be listed. Thereafter, you may make a decision as to which ones to delete or archive (using EXPORT).

11.8 EXPIRATION OF CATALOG ENTRIES

This feature of the LISTCAT command is used to find entries that might expire in a specified number of days. The TO and FOR parameters must have been used at the time of data set allocation or altered later in order to have a date with which to find such entries. All the entries will continue to exist past the expiration of the time limit, but they might be deleted inadvertently with the DELETE command. If you wish to ensure the retention of data sets past their expiration date, use ALTER to extend the date.

The following command may be used to obtain a list of data sets that will expire in 30 days.

```
LISTCAT                       -
CATALOG(VSAM.USERCAT.TWO) -
EXPIRATION(30)
```

If a data set is defined without giving a TO or FOR parameter, it will show up in every listing. In our case, since we did not give an expiration date at the time of DEFINE CLUSTER, executing this command will list every single entry in the catalog.

11.9 DAMAGED CATALOG ENTRIES

A data or index component is marked unusable in the catalog if a system failure that damages the catalog information of the entry occurs. This is applicable only to VSAM catalogs and not ICF catalogs. The following command may be used to list such entries, if any, in the catalog VSAM.USERCAT.TWO.

```
LISTCAT                       -
CATALOG(VSAM.USERCAT.TWO) -
NOTUSABLE
```

In summary, LISTCAT is a powerful command that provides you with a window into the catalog and its entries. Since the volume of information produced is quite large, it may take you some time before you feel comfortable looking at the abbreviations of different attributes. This chapter does not discuss all the different formats in which you may use this command. Access to appropriate DF/EF or AMS manuals is necessary to become familiar with the other types of information you may extract using this command.

chapter 12

Additional Topics on AMS

The commands discussed in this chapter are among the less frequently used AMS commands. While some will primarily be used by systems programmers, a basic knowledge of all of them is important in order to better understand the functions of Access Method Services. It will also help application programmers to communicate more effectively with systems programmers. IBM's *OS/VS2 Access Method Services* manual will be needed to fully understand all aspects of these commands, because an in-depth discussion is beyond the scope of this book.

12.1 DEFINING A VSAM USER CATALOG

VSAM objects such as clusters, alternate indexes, and paths must be cataloged in a VSAM or ICF catalog. The commands in previous chapters assumed the existence of a VSAM catalog, VSAM.USERCAT.TWO, which owned a disk pack with the volume id VSAM02. It is essential for a catalog to be defined successfully before any VSAM or non-VSAM objects may be cataloged in it. The JCL that was used to define our catalog is in Fig. 12.1

The NAME parameter gives a name to the user catalog entry.

The space allocation parameter indicates that 10 cylinders of space are to be allocated to the catalog. When this space is used up, additional

```
//AMSJOB    JOB (ACCTNO),'JAY RANADE'
//DEFUCAT   EXEC PGM=IDCAMS
//SYSPRINT  DD SYSOUT=A
//SYSIN     DD *
 DEFINE USERCATALOG                                 -
     (NAME(VSAM.USERCAT.TWO)                        -
     CYLINDERS(10,2)                                -
     VOLUME(VSAM02)                                 -
     RECOVERABLE              )                     -
     CATALOG(VSAM.MASTER.CATALOG/GUESS)
/*
//
```

Figure 12.1 JCL used to define VSAM user catalog VSAM.USERCAT.TWO.

allocations will be made in increments of 2 cylinders each. A maximum of 13 secondary allocations are allowed for a user catalog.

The VOLUME parameter gives the volume identification of the disk pack on which the catalog will be defined. This disk pack must not be owned by any other VSAM user catalog either through a DEFINE USERCATALOG or DEFINE SPACE command. Otherwise, the define will fail, because only one VSAM user catalog may have ownership of a volume.

The RECOVERABLE parameter allocates one cylinder for a catalog recovery area for this catalog. The CRA keeps duplicate information about cataloged entries. If the VSAM user catalog becomes damaged somehow, an AMS command called RESETCAT can be used to correct the cataloged information from the CRA.

Last, the CATALOG parameter points to the name of the installation's master catalog in which the user catalog will be defined.

GUESS is the update or master-level password of the master catalog. It will be needed if the master catalog is password-protected (which it usually is).

A user catalog is the first VSAM object defined in VSAM space. When the command in Fig. 12.1 is executed, VSAM space of 10 cylinders will be allocated and the catalog will be defined within it. Therefore, a VSAM catalog is a self-defining object. After successful execution of this command, if you look at the VTOC listing for volume VSAM02 (through the IEHLIST utility or option 3.7 of TSO/ISPF), you will *not* find the name VSAM.USERCAT.TWO. Instead, you will find an entry name for the VSAM space.

The same command can be used to allocate a master catalog. There is no difference between a VSAM user and a VSAM master catalog. A user catalog can be made the master catalog at the time of the initial program loading (IPL) of the system. If you are a systems programmer, you should review the other optional parameters of this command in the IBM *OS/VS2 Access Method Services* manual.

12.2 DEFINING AN ICF USER CATALOG

If your installation has DF/EF software, you have the option of allocating VSAM user catalogs, ICF user catalogs, or both. As discussed in Part 1, ICF catalogs are new and improved VSAM catalogs. More and more users at MVS installations are converting to ICF catalogs. ICF and VSAM catalogs may coexist in the same system.

The structure of an ICF catalog is radically different from that of a VSAM catalog. It consists of two different catalog components: (1) a basic catalog structure (BCS) and (2) a VSAM volume data set (VVDS).

A basic catalog structure has the organization of a KSDS and is allocated through the DEFINE USERCATALOG command. Multiple basic catalog structures can be defined on one disk pack. Up to 36 BCS's can own a volume, whereas a volume can be owned by only one VSAM catalog. The catalog name referred to when defining VSAM objects is the name of the BCS, and application programmers normally use the BCS name.

A VSAM volume data set, which is the second-level structure of an ICF catalog, must be defined on each disk pack that is to contain VSAM data sets. A VVDS is, in fact, an entry-sequenced data set. There is only one VVDS on a disk pack, and it must be defined on the pack before any VSAM data sets can be allocated on that volume. A VVDS is defined using the DEFINE CLUSTER command, but its existence is transparent to application programmers. Its name cannot be arbitrary as in the case of a BCS, it must be named

```
SYS1.VVDS.Vvolser
```

where "volser" is the volume ID of the disk pack on which the VVDS is being defined.

As an example, let's say that we have three disk packs with volume serial numbers VOLID1, VOLID2, and VOLID3. In order to make each one of them eligible for VSAM data set allocation, three DEFINE CLUSTER commands will be used to allocate three VVDS's on them. Their names will be

```
SYS1.VVDS.VVOLID1
SYS1.VVDS.VVOLID2
SYS1.VVDS.VVOLID3
```

We also want to define two BCS's, one on volume VOLID1 and the other on VOLID2. Their names can be your choice. For our example, we'll use

ICF.USERCAT.ONE

and

ICF.USERCAT.TWO

They can be defined using the DEFINE USERCATALOG command for each one. After all the allocations are complete, the whole configuration will resemble Fig. 12.2

We could have allocated both of the BCS's on one volume, because there is no concept of volume ownership in ICF catalogs. Now, we can define VSAM objects in *either* of the two catalogs (BCS), and they can exist on any of the three volumes. Figure 12.3 gives sample JCL for allocating ICF.USERCAT.ONE.

Since the BCS part of the ICF catalog is a KSDS, you will find that some familiar parameters have been coded. The keyword ICF-CATALOG indicates that the command defines an ICF catalog, not a VSAM catalog. Note the use of the FREESPACE parameter. It has been coded so that CI and CA splits can be minimized when VSAM ob-

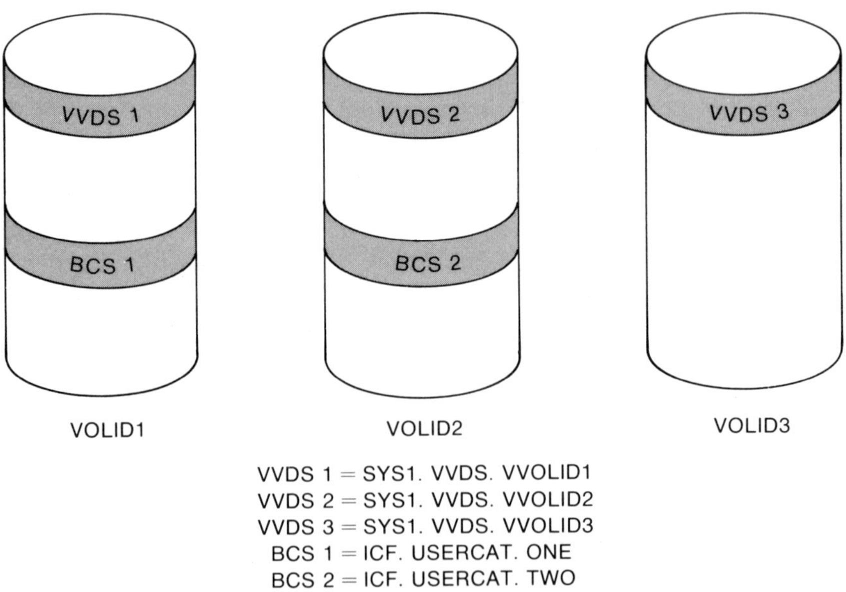

Figure 12.2 An example of BCS and VVDS structures in an ICF catalog environment. Unshaded portions of the volumes indicate usable space where VSAM or non-VSAM objects can be allocated.

```
//AMSJOB    JOB (ACCTNO),'JAY RANADE'
//DEFICF    EXEC PGM=IDCAMS
//SYSPRINT DD SYSOUT=A
//SYSIN     DD *
 DEFINE USERCATALOG                                    -
     (NAME(ICF.USERCAT.ONE)                            -
     VOLUME(VOLID1)                                    -
     CYLINDERS(5,2)                                    -
     ICFCATALOG                                        -
     FREESPACE(20,20)                                  -
     RECORDSIZE(4086,4086))                            -
     DATA                                              -
     (CONTROLINTERVALSIZE(4096))                       -
     INDEX                                             -
     (CONTROLINTERVALSIZE(2048))                       -
     CATALOG(VSAM.MASTER.CATALOG/GUESS)
/*
//
```

Figure 12.3 JCL for defining an ICF catalog named ICF.USERCAT.ONE.

jects are defined in an ICF catalog. Data and index components have been assigned different control interval sizes. Finally, the name of the master catalog and its update (or master) password has been given. Remember that an ICF catalog cannot be defined with the RECOVERABLE attribute.

Figure 12.4 gives sample JCL for defining a VVDS on volume VOLID3. Note that the naming convention for the VVDS must be strictly adhered to. The NONINDEXED parameter indicates that the

```
//AMSJOB    JOB (ACCTNO),'JAY RANADE'
//DEFVVDS   EXEC PGM=IDCAMS
//SYSPRINT DD SYSOUT=A
//SYSIN     DD *
 DEFINE CLUSTER                                        -
     (NAME(SYS1.VVDS.VVOLID3)                          -
     VOLUMES(VOLID3)                                   -
     NONINDEXED                                        -
     CYLINDERS(1,1)            )                       -
     CATALOG(ICF.USERCAT.ONE)
/*
//
```

Figure 12.4 Sample JCL for defining VVDS on volume VOLID3.

```
//AMSJOB    JOB (ACCTNO),'JAY RANADE'
//DEFSPACE EXEC PGM=IDCAMS
//SYSPRINT DD SYSOUT=A
//SYSIN     DD *
 DEFINE SPACE                                          -
     (CYLINDERS(200,50)                                -
     VOLUMES(VSAM02)   )                               -
     CATALOG(VSAM.USERCAT.TWO)
/*
//
```

Figure 12.5 JCL for defining VSAM space on volume VSAM02.

underlying structure is an ESDS. The space allocation parameter will allocate one cylinder initially. As the VVDS grows, secondary extents will be allocated in increments of one cylinder each. Last, the name of the catalog in which the VVDS will be cataloged is given.

Note that, if a BCS is allocated on a volume that does not have a VVDS on it yet, it will be *implicitly* defined by Access Method Services.

12.3 DEFINE SPACE

This command is used to allocate VSAM space on a volume. It is used only for VSAM user catalogs and *not* for ICF user catalogs. ICF catalogs have no concept of SUBALLOCATED VSAM space because all their objects are UNIQUE.

In one of the previous examples in this chapter, a VSAM catalog named VSAM.USERCAT.TWO was allocated on volume VSAM02. In order to define SUBALLOCATED VSAM data sets on this volume, VSAM space must be defined. The JCL given in Fig. 12.5 can be used.

Upon successful execution of the JCL, a primary allocation of 200 cylinders will be earmarked as VSAM space, provided it is available on the pack. An entry will also be made in the VTOC, which can be verified through the IEHLIST utility or option 3.7 of TSO/ISPF. Once the space is used up, secondary allocations will be made in increments of 50 cylinders each.

VSAM space can also be allocated on volumes other than the one on which the catalog exists. For example, if VSAM space is required on a volume with the volume serial number VSAM03, under the ownership of the same catalog, it can be done with the following command.

```
DEFINE SPACE                    -
(CYLINDERS(50,20)               -
VOLUMES(VSAM03))                -
CATALOG(VSAM.USERCAT.TWO)
```

In this case, VSAM03 *must not* be owned by any other VSAM catalog, or the allocation will fail. Once a VSAM catalog allocates VSAM space on a disk pack, it becomes the owner of that volume.

Sometimes there is a requirement to mark a volume as owned by a particular VSAM catalog without allocating any VSAM space on it. This is done to reserve a volume for future use by VSAM. The following command will reserve VSAM04 as a candidate volume.

```
DEFINE SPACE                   -
( CANDIDATE                    -
VOLUMES(VSAM04))               -
CATALOG(VSAM.USERCAT.TWO)
```

Note that the keyword parameter CANDIDATE and other space allocation parameters are mutually exclusive.

12.4 DEFINE ALIAS

This command is used to define an alias for a user catalog (VSAM or ICF) or a non-VSAM data set. An alias can be from 1 to 44 characters long and has the same restrictions as a data set name. Very often this command is used to define a user catalog's alias that is 8 or fewer characters in length. This alias can be used as the leftmost (first) qualifier of a data set name. When so used, it is not necessary to know the name of the catalog in which the data set is to be defined, and the CATALOG parameter or STEPCAT or JOBCAT cards are not needed.

Throughout the text, we have been using EMPLOYEE as the first qualifier of cluster, alternate index, and path names. In fact, EMPLOYEE is the alias of our user catalog VSAM.USERCAT.TWO. The JCL used to define it is in Fig. 12.6.

The RELATE parameter gives the name of the catalog with which the alias is associated. The CATALOG parameter has the name of the

```
//AMSJOB    JOB (ACCTNO),'JAY RANADE'
//DEFALIAS EXEC PGM=IDCAMS
//SYSPRINT DD SYSOUT=A
//SYSIN     DD *
 DEFINE ALIAS                                  -
    (NAME(EMPLOYEE)                            -
    RELATE(VSAM.USERCAT.TWO) )                 -
    CATALOG(VSAM.MASTER.CATALOG/GUESS)
/*
//
```

Figure 12.6 JCL for defining EMPLOYEE as an alias for user catalog VSAM.USERCAT.TWO.

master catalog and its update/master password. After successful execution, the alias EMPLOYEE will be defined as the user catalog's connector in the master catalog.

You can define as many alias entries for a particular user catalog as you like. Each alias can be used as the high-end qualifier for different VSAM or non-VSAM objects. At one installation, it is usual to have multiple user catalogs, each with multiple alias entries. The same alias name cannot be associated with more than one catalog. In an MVS system, your TSO ID is an alias for an ICF or VSAM catalog or an OS catalog (CVOL). That's why, when the TSO ID is used as the first qualifier of a data set name, it is automatically cataloged in the appropriate catalog.

12.5 DEFINE GENERATIONDATAGROUP

Generation data sets are used in an OS environment for maintaining different generations of physical sequential data sets. One of their major purposes is to keep multiple generations of backups of master files for various data sets. When a current generation becomes unusable, jobs can be rerun from previous generations to facilitate easy recovery.

An OS utility, IEHPROGM, or the AMS command DEFINE GDG can be used to define a generation data group. In the latter case, it can be cataloged in either a VSAM or an ICF catalog. For example, let's suppose that there is a need to back up EMPLOYEE.KSDS.CLUSTER every day. In addition, we must keep five generations of the backup data set so that we can recover from week-old data if necessary. Let the generation data group be named EMPLOYEE.KSDS.BACKUP. The JCL in Fig. 12.7 can be used to define it.

After successful execution, a GDG entry will be created in VSAM.USERCAT.TWO. The LIMIT parameter will limit the number

```
//AMSJOB    JOB (ACCTNO),'JAY RANADE'
//DEFGDG    EXEC PGM=IDCAMS
//SYSPRINT DD SYSOUT=A
//SYSIN     DD *
 DEFINE GDG                                        -
     (NAME(EMPLOYEE.KSDS.BACKUP)                   -
     LIMIT(5)                                      -
     NOEMPTY                                       -
     SCRATCH                          )            -
     CATALOG(VSAM.USERCAT.TWO)
/*
//
```

Figure 12.7 JCL for defining a generation data group named EMPLOYEE.KSDS.BACKUP.

```
//AMSJOB    JOB (ACCTNO),'JAY RANADE'
//GDGBACK   EXEC PGM=IDCAMS
//SYSPRINT  DD SYSOUT=A
//BACKUP    DD DSN=EMPLOYEE.KSDS.BACKUP(+1),
//             DISP=(NEW,CATLG,DELETE),UNIT=SYSDA,
//             VOL=SER=VSAM02,
//             SPACE=(CYL,(1,1)),
//             DCB=(GDG.MODEL,RECFM=FB,LRECL=50,BLKSIZE=5000)
//SYSIN     DD *
   REPRO                                        -
     INDATASET(EMPLOYEE.KSDS.CLUSTER)           -
     OUTFILE(BACKUP)
/*
//
```

Figure 12.8 JCL for creating a backup generation data set for EMPLOYEE.KSDS.CLUSTER.

of generation data sets that can be associated with this GDG to 5. Otherwise, this number may be anywhere from 1 to 255.

NOEMPTY, the default parameter, indicates that only the oldest generation data set is to be uncataloged when the limit of 5 is exceeded. Its opposite, the EMPTY parameter, specifies that *all* generations of this data set are to be uncataloged when the limit (5 in this case) is reached.

SCRATCH specifies that the generation data set's entry is to be deleted from the volume's VTOC when a data set is uncataloged. Thus, the space released on the volume will be available for other users. If this parameter is not coded, the default is NOSCRATCH. It specifies that an entry uncataloged as a result of EMPTY/NOEMPTY is not to be deleted. This means that, although the entries are removed from the catalog, they still exist physically and are on the volume's VTOC.

Before you can use the GDG, a model data set control block (DSCB) must be defined on its catalog volume (which is VSAM02 in this case). In most MVS installations, a model DSCB is defined in the master catalog so that it is accessible to everyone. Let's suppose that our model DSCB is named GDG.MODEL. The JCL in Fig. 12.8 can be used to create the first backup generation data set for this GDG.
After successful execution, the first generation data set will be created as

EMPLOYEE.KSDS.BACKUP.G0001V00

If the same JCL is executed five more times, five more generation data sets will be created:

EMPLOYEE.KSDS.BACKUP.G0002V00
EMPLOYEE.KSDS.BACKUP.G0003V00
EMPLOYEE.KSDS.BACKUP.G0004V00
EMPLOYEE.KSDS.BACKUP.G0005V00
EMPLOYEE.KSDS.BACKUP.G0006V00

Bear in mind that, when the sixth generation is created, the first one (with the last qualifier G0001V00) will be uncataloged and deleted because the LIMIT parameter was given a value of 5 when the GDG was defined.

12.6 EXPORT AND IMPORT

These commands are used for the following purposes:

1. To transport a user catalog, a cluster, or an alternate index from one system to another. This can be helpful when making a conversion from DOS/VSE or OS/VS1 to an OS/MVS system.
2. To create backup copies of clusters or alternate indexes using EXPORT and to use them for recovery, restore, and reorganization purposes later using IMPORT.

A discussion of the transportation of user catalogs is beyond the scope of this book. We will concentrate only on using these commands for clusters and alternate indexes.

It might seem as if these commands have the same function as REPRO, but there are some subtle differences in their use for backup and restore purposes. REPRO can be used for VSAM as well as non-VSAM data sets, however, EXPORT and IMPORT can be used *only* for VSAM data sets. Using REPRO, you back up only the logical records of a data set. When the data set is to be restored, it is deleted (if present), defined again, and restored with the records from the backup copy. Using EXPORT, you not only back up the records of the data set but also extract its attributes from the cataloged information. The first few records written in the backup copy are, in fact, the attributes of the data set followed by the actual data records. IMPORT automatically deletes the data set and then defines it from the attribute information contained at the beginning of the backup copy. Then the records are restored to the cluster. *Both REPRO and IMPORT reorganize a KSDS.*

There are two variations of the EXPORT command. A TEMPORARY export does not delete the source object after the backup has been performed, while a PERMANENT export deletes the source after the backup. When using PERMANENT, make sure to export alternate indexes first, because deleting a base cluster will delete the associated alternate indexes as well. Also, when performing a restore, import the base cluster before the alternate indexes. Paths are automatically exported when you export alternate indexes and are redefined upon import. The largest VSAM record size that may be exported is 32,752 bytes for an RRDS and 32,756 bytes for a KSDS or an ESDS.

Figure 12.9 gives the JCL used to export our RRDS EMPLOYEE.RRDS.CLUSTER.

```
//AMSJOB    JOB (ACCTNO),'JAY RANADE'
//RRDSEXPD EXEC PGM=IDCAMS
//SYSPRINT DD SYSOUT=A
//BACKUP    DD DSN=EMPLOYEE.RRDS.BACKUP,
//             DISP=(NEW,CATLG),LABEL=(1,SL),
//             UNIT=TAPE,DCB=(BLKSIZE=6000)
//SYSIN     DD *
   EXPORT                                       -
     EMPLOYEE.RRDS.CLUSTER                      -
     OUTFILE(BACKUP)                            -
     TEMPORARY                                  -
     INHIBITSOURCE                              -
     INHIBITTARGET
/*
//
```

Figure 12.9 JCL for exporting an RRDS named EMPLOYEE.RRDS.CLUSTER.

The OUTFILE parameter points to the DD name of the data set that will receive the exported records. Note that only the BLKSIZE subparameter of the DCB parameter has been coded in the BACKUP DD statement. You are not allowed to code any other DCB subparameters related to the data set characteristics. If BLKSIZE is also omitted, the default is 2048 which, for performance reasons, may be too small. TEMPORARY specifies that the source data set will not be deleted after export. If you code PERMANENT instead, which is also the default parameter, the cluster will be deleted after export. Any alternate indexes on the cluster will also be deleted at that time. NOINHIBITSOURCE indicates that the source data set will be available for updates after export. It is also the default parameter. If INHIBITSOURCE is coded, the source data set will not be available for any operation other than retrieval. This prevents users from performing any updates in between the EXPORT and IMPORT steps. NOINHIBITTARGET specifies that, after the data set has been restored by the IMPORT command, it will be available for any operation including updates. It is also the default parameter. INHIBITTARGET will prevent users from performing any updates on the restored data set after IMPORT. INHIBITSOURCE and INHIBITTARGET can be altered at any time by using the ALTER command.

To restore a data set from a backup copy created by the EXPORT command, you must use the IMPORT command of AMS. Figure 12.10 gives the JCL used to restore EMPLOYEE.RRDS.CLUSTER.

The INFILE parameter specifies the DD name that refers to the backup copy created by the EXPORT command. Since we are using standard label tapes, you don't need to code the DCB parameter. OUT-

```
//AMSJOB    JOB (ACCTNO),'JAY RANADE'
//RRDSIMPO  EXEC PGM=IDCAMS
//SYSPRINT  DD SYSOUT=A
//BACKUP    DD DSN=EMPLOYEE.RRDS.BACKUP,
//             DISP=(OLD,KEEP),LABEL=(1,SL),
//             UNIT=TAPE
//SYSIN     DD *
    IMPORT                                   -
      INFILE(BACKUP)                         -
      OUTDATASET(EMPLOYEE.RRDS.CLUSTER)
/*
//
```

Figure 12.10 JCL for restoring EMPLOYEE.RRDS.CLUSTER from the backup copy created by the EXPORT command.

DATASET refers to the data set being restored. Execution of the JCL will result in the following steps performed in the order given.

1. EMPLOYEE.RRDS.CLUSTER will be deleted.
2. EMPLOYEE.RRDS.CLUSTER will be redefined by AMS. The necessary define attributes will be extracted from the records written at the beginning of the backup data set.
3. The data records will be read from the backup data set and loaded into the newly defined cluster.

12.7 MODAL COMMANDS

Every time an Access Method Services command is executed, it issues a condition code. If multiple commands are executed within one job step, it is possible that you will want a particular command to be executed or bypassed depending on the success or failure of a previous command. This is determined by testing a condition code through the modal commands of AMS.

The condition code generated by AMS may be 0, 4, 8, 12, or 16. These codes, as explained in the *OS/VS2 Access Method Services* manual, are defined as follows:

0: The function was executed as desired.

4: A problem was encountered in executing the function. For example, the system was unable to locate an entry in a LISTCAT command.

8: The requested function was executed, but major specifics were unavoidably bypassed. For example, an entry to be deleted or altered could not be found, or a duplicate name was found when defining an entry.

12: The requested function could not be performed because of a logical error. For example, a value specified for the key length or record size was too large, or certain required parameters were missing.

16: A severe error occurred, causing the remainder of the command stream to be flushed. For example, a SYSPRINT DD statement was missing, an unrecoverable error occurred in a system data set, or an improper modal command sequence was encountered.

As you can see, it is difficult to say which non-zero condition code should be taken seriously enough to become alarmed about. Depending on your requirements, even a condition code of 4 may be cause for some concern. As a general rule, a condition code of zero is desirable in the majority of cases.

You may use IF-THEN-ELSE statements to control the command sequence execution. LASTCC contains the condition code from the most recent command execution, while MAXCC is used to test the highest condition code from any of the previous commands within the *same* job step. The relational operators for comparing LASTCC and MAXCC are

= or EQ for equal

¬= or NE for not equal

> or GT for greater than

< or LT for less than

> = or GE for greater than or equal

< = or LE for less than or equal

The JCL in Fig. 12.11 gives an example of execution control through modal commands.

In this example, the REPRO command loads records from a physical sequential data set into a KSDS. The condition code is tested to make sure that it is zero, which indicates successful completion. If the comparison is equal, the cataloged information is listed through the LISTCAT command. If the condition code from REPRO is not zero, we will delete the KSDS. A non-zero code may be due to out-of-sequence input records, duplicate records, etc. If no action is to be taken on a non-zero condition code, the ELSE clause can be omitted or made a null command. Proper use of the continuation sign should be carefully observed in modal commands.

If the THEN and ELSE commands are not followed by a continua-

```
//AMSJOB    JOB (ACCTNO),'JAY RANADE'
//MODAL     EXEC PGM=IDCAMS
//SYSPRINT DD SYSOUT=A
//SYSIN     DD *
   REPRO                                              -
     IDS(SAMPLE.INPUT.DATA)                           -
     ODS(EMPLOYEE.KSDS.CLUSTER)
   IF  LASTCC = 0                                     -
       THEN                                           -
       LISTCAT                                        -
       ENTRIES(EMPLOYEE.KSDS.CLUSTER) ALL             -
   ELSE                                               -
       DELETE EMPLOYEE.KSDS.CLUSTER
/*
//
```

Figure 12.11 An example of the functional commands' execution control through modal commands (IF-THEN-ELSE).

tion character, a null command will result, which means that no action will be taken. For example, the following variation of the command sequence is valid.

```
IF LASTCC = 0 THEN
ELSE                                    -
    DELETE EMPLOYEE.KSDS.CLUSTER
```

In this case, no action will be taken if the value of LASTCC is 0. Deletion will be performed only if the condition is not true.

When an IF command is used within a THEN-ELSE clause, a *nested* IF command results. Assess Method Services permits 10 levels of depth in nesting. The following is an example of nested IF statements.

```
IF LASTCC = 0          -
THEN IF MAXCC > 4      -
    THEN VERIFY . . .
    ELSE DELETE . . .
ELSE IF LASTCC NE 0 -
    THEN
    ELSE LISTCAT . . .
```

The innermost ELSE clause within the nested IF statements is associated with the innermost THEN clause. The next innermost ELSE goes with the next innermost THEN, and so on, up to a maximum of 10 such combinations.

The SET command is used to reset a previously generated LASTCC or MAXCC. By setting a MAXCC or LASTCC to 16, all processing can be terminated. Consider the following example.

```
VERIFY DS(EMPLOYEE.RRDS.CLUSTER)
IF LASTCC = 0                              -
THEN
ELSE                                       -
   SET MAXCC = 16
```

Here the LASTCC is tested for a condition code of zero. A non-zero code identifies a failure in the execution of a previous program, possibly causing a file to be closed improperly. Since it is desirable to do more research, we want to terminate processing by setting the condition code to 16. Remember that, if a value greater than 16 is assigned to either LASTCC or MAXCC, it will be automatically changed to 16.

If in a single IF command more than one functional command is to be executed as a single unit, they must be delimited by a DO-END sequence.

```
IF LASTCC EQ 0         -
THEN DO
          LISTCAT . . .
          PRINT . . .
     END
ELSE DO
          VERIFY . . .
          REPRO . . .
     END
```

In the above example, LISTCAT and PRINT are treated as one unit and are executed if LASTCC has a value of zero. Otherwise, VERIFY and REPRO are executed as a single unit. *Note that continuation characters should not be used in a DO-END sequence* but may be required for the imbedded commands themselves, e.g., LISTCAT, PRINT, VERIFY, and REPRO. Also, the END command must be on a line by itself.

three

COBOL CODING FOR VSAM FILES

Part 3 addresses the essentials of using Cobol to access VSAM files. It assumes that the reader already has a basic knowledge of Cobol coding and feels comfortable with it. Our purpose is not to learn the language but to find out how its various elements apply to VSAM files. Those who already have experience in coding for indexed sequential files will find both similarities and differences in handling these two different file organizations. Error handling procedures will be found to be of particular interest and are quite different for VSAM files.

KSDS processing is discussed in Chaps. 13 and 14. The latter chapter also enumerates the use of alternate indexes in the Cobol language. Chapter 15 analyzes the uses of ESDS files, while Chap. 16 discusses RRDS files. The numerous examples should make the learning experience easier and more interesting.

chapter **13**

Processing KSDS without Alternate Index(es)

This chapter is devoted to KSDS files without alternate indexes, but most of the language syntax applies to the other file organizations that will be discussed in subsequent chapters. Throughout the book we have been using a KSDS named EMPLOYEE.KSDS.CLUSTER. For this chapter, we will use just the base cluster, on which there are no alternate indexes. All the examples will be developed in the context of this data set. It is worthwhile to restate that VSAM files must exist before you can process them with a program.

13.1 SELECT STATEMENT

Figure 13.1 provides the syntax of the SELECT statement for a KSDS without alternate indexes.

```
SELECT       file-name
             ASSIGN TO assignment-name
             ORGANIZATION IS INDEXED
                                 ⎧SEQUENTIAL⎫
             ACCESS MODE IS      ⎨RANDOM    ⎬
                                 ⎩DYNAMIC   ⎭
             RECORD KEY IS  data-name-1
             PASSWORD IS    data-name-2
             FILE STATUS IS data-name-3
```

Figure 13.1 Syntax of the SELECT statement for a KSDS without alternate index(es).

The assignment name for a KSDS is simply the DD name of the data set in the JCL. It is not necessary to use a prefix before the DD name as you do for other file organizations (such as PS and indexed sequential). Anything used as a prefix will be treated as a comment. The following is valid for the assignment name:

```
SELECT EMPLOYEE-MASTER
    ASSIGN TO EMPMSTR
          •
          •
          •
```

The ORGANIZATION IS INDEXED clause identifies the data set as a KSDS. It must be coded this way for a key-sequenced file.

ACCESS MODE IS specifies the way you want to process the file. If your intent is to process the records sequentially, you can specify SEQUENTIAL, which is also the default clause. If you do, all the operations, such as loading, retrieval, and update, may only be performed sequentially. Selecting the RANDOM option will let you perform random access only, and you will not be able to process the records sequentially. The RANDOM and SEQUENTIAL options are also used for indexed sequential files, but VSAM provides a third alternative, DYNAMIC. It lets you process the records both randomly and sequentially by switching the mode of processing within the program. There is no equivalent option for indexed sequential files.

The RECORD KEY clause gives the data name of the prime key field of the KSDS as coded in the file description (FD) clause. It should have the same key length and offset within the record as specified at the time of the DEFINE CLUSTER. Note that there is *no* NOMINAL KEY clause for a VSAM file. Under ISAM, NOMINAL KEY is a data field, defined in working storage, whose value is used to access a record in the file. Under VSAM, this value is moved directly to the RECORD KEY field that is embedded within the record itself. Remember that the RECORD KEY data field should *not* have an implied decimal point within it.

The PASSWORD clause identifies an alphanumeric field in working storage, defined as X(8), which contains the password of the KSDS cluster. If you are performing read-only processing on the data set, this password can be the READPW. Otherwise, it must be the UPDATEPW or a higher-level password. If the data set is not password-protected, this clause can be omitted.

FILE STATUS is an optional clause, but a very important one. It points to a data name within working storage defined as X(2). Whenever you do any processing on this data set, a 2-character code is *automatically* moved to this field. The value of the code can be tested to verify the success or failure of the operation. The significance of FILE STATUS is

```
IDENTIFICATION DIVISION.
    .
    .
ENVIRONMENT DIVISION.
    .
    .
INPUT-OUTPUT SECTION.
FILE-CONTROL.
       SELECT  EMPLOYEE-MASTER
               ASSIGN TO  EMPMSTR
               ORGANIZATION IS INDEXED
               ACCESS MODE IS RANDOM
               RECORD KEY IS EMPLOYEE-SSN-KEY
               FILE STATUS IS EMPLOYEE-FILE-STATUS.
    .
    .
DATA DIVISION.
FILE SECTION.
FD   EMPLOYEE-MASTER
     LABEL RECORDS ARE STANDARD.
01   EMPLOYEE-RECORD.
     05  EMPLOYEE-SSN-KEY            PIC X(9).
     05  EMPLOYEE-REST               PIC X(41).
    .
    .
WORKING-STORAGE SECTION.
01   EMPLOYEE-FILE-STATUS            PIC X(2).
    .
    .
    .
```

Figure 13.2 Sample coding of the SELECT clause, FD clause, and FILE STATUS for EMPLOYEE.KSDS.CLUSTER for RANDOM processing.

discussed separately in the next section. Figure 13.2 gives a sample of the coding of the SELECT clause for EMPLOYEE.KSDS.CLUSTER, assuming that the data set is not password-protected.

13.2 FILE STATUS

Although optional, FILE STATUS is one of the most important clauses. If specified, it will contain a 2-character code that can be tested to determine the results of the execution of the most recent VSAM file operation in the program logic. It is advisable to have different FILE STATUS data names for each VSAM file processed in a program. It may *not* be defined as the object of an OCCURS DEPENDING ON clause in the working storage section. Figure 13.3 lists the status key values and their meanings.

You don't have to memorize the status keys and their meanings. Most of the status codes are generated only for a particular function. For example, status code 23 indicates that the requested record was not found during a random read request; a status of 10 means that an end-of-file con-

Status key value	Meaning
00	Successful completion of function
02	Duplicate key condition found for nonunique key alternate index
10	End-of-file condition or an optional ESDS file not available
20	No further information
21	Sequence error for sequential load in a KSDS
22	Duplicate key found on a WRITE
23	Record not found
24	No space found to add records for a KSDS or an RRDS
30	No further information
34	No space found to add record for an ESDS
90	No further information
91	Password failure
92	Logic error
93	Resource (enough virtual storage) not available
94	No current record pointer for sequential request
95	Invalid or incomplete file information
96	No DD card
97	Data set was improperly closed; implicit verify issued and file successfully opened (only DF/EF)

Figure 13.3 FILE STATUS key values and their meanings.

dition has been reached while performing a sequential read function. The meanings of the status codes will become more clear when we discuss them as they apply individually to various function requests.

13.3 RESTRICTIONS ON FD STATEMENTS

The FD statement for a VSAM file is almost the same as the one for a non-VSAM file. However, there are some differences:

1. RECORDING MODE IS F may not be specified for VSAM files.
2. BLOCK CONTAINS is optional and is treated as documentation. It is usually omitted.
3. LABEL RECORDS ARE is *always required,* but the STANDARD or OMITTED options do not make any difference.

If you are familiar with ISAM file processing, you will recall that the first byte in a record indicates its active or inactive status. High values (hexadecimal FF) mark it as logically deleted. There is no equivalent byte in VSAM records. Sample coding for an FD entry of a VSAM file appears in Fig. 13.2

13.4 PROCESSING IN PROCEDURE DIVISION

The processing logic for VSAM files is different from that for non-VSAM files. There are direct relationships among the SELECT clause options (SEQUENTIAL, RANDOM, DYNAMIC), different OPEN modes, and the format of Cobol processing statements. This will become more clear as we go further.

13.4.1 Unloaded vs Empty Files

An unloaded VSAM file is one that currently does not and never did have any records in it. Technically speaking, its high used RBA is 0. This can be checked on the catalog listing (the LISTCAT command with an ENTRIES parameter), where it is shown as the HURBA value. An empty VSAM file is one that had records in it at one time which were subsequently deleted (using the DELETE verb in Cobol). Its HURBA will be non-zero. Although both file types have no records in them, they are processed in different ways, so remember the difference between them.

13.4.2 OPEN and CLOSE

OPEN A KSDS can be opened as INPUT, OUTPUT, I-O, or EXTEND. The syntax is

```
                  ⎧INPUT ⎫
OPEN file-name    ⎨OUTPUT⎬
                  ⎪EXTEND⎪
                  ⎩I-O   ⎭
```

If a file is opened as INPUT, you can perform only a read or a browse operation on it. OUTPUT is used *only* when a file is to be loaded sequentially. Either it must be unloaded (i.e., its high used RBA must be zero) or it must have been defined with the REUSE option (even though it might have records in it and a non-zero HURBA). If it is a file defined with REUSE, all the existing records in the data set will be deleted logically before the loading takes place. We learned that the records to be loaded into a KSDS must be in the collating sequence of the prime key. If not, you will get a status code of 21 during the load. Remember, an *empty* file (HURBA non-zero) cannot be opened as OUTPUT or you will get status code 95.

A KSDS can be opened as EXTEND if loading is to resumed after its highest key record. It simulates the MOD option of JCL for physical sequential data sets. The records to be loaded must be in the collating sequence of the prime key, and the first record to be loaded must have a higher key than the highest key record in the KSDS.

A KSDS can be opened as I-O (both input and output) if it has a non-zero high used RBA, meaning that it must contain at least one record or its status must be empty (otherwise status code 90 is returned). A file opened as I-O allows record adds, record deletes, and rewriting of changed records.

Before a file can be successfully opened, the password given in the SELECT statement must be correct for the kind of processing you intend to do. For example, it you use a READPW and the file is opened as I-O, the open will fail with status code 91.

If the OPEN is successful, you will get a status code of 00. In a DF/EF environment, you may also get a status code of 97. This means that the file was not properly closed in a previous run and that an implicit VERIFY has been successfully issued. Depending on the cause of the previous improper close, the program can either safely continue processing or terminate execution (see Sec. 10.3.1 for a discussion of this). Figure 13.4 gives the most common status codes on OPEN and their possible causes.

Status code	Possible reasons
00	Successful open.
90	KSDS is opened for OUTPUT and the access mode is either RANDOM or DYNAMIC. File to be opened I-O is unloaded.
91	Password failure.
92	Logic error. File to be opened is already open.
93	Sufficient virtual storage unavailable. Retry after increasing value of REGION parameter. Resource not available because it is in use elsewhere and the shareoptions do not allow the requested processing option.
95	HURBA of file to be opened OUTPUT is not zero. Length and/or offset of record key in FD does not match the catalog. An attempt was made to open a KSDS as an ESDS.
96	Missing DD card.
97	OPEN successful after an implicit VERIFY.

Figure 13.4 Status key values and their possible causes resulting from OPEN requests.

```
       OPEN  I-O  EMPLOYEE-MASTER.
       IF   EMPLOYEE-FILE-STATUS = '00'
            NEXT SENTENCE
       ELSE
            DISPLAY 'OPEN UNSUCCESSFUL FOR EMPMSTR'
            DISPLAY 'STATUS CODE IS ' EMPLOYEE-FILE-STATUS
            PERFORM  ABNORMAL-TERMINATION.
            .
            .
```

Figure 13.5 Checking successful open of a VSAM file through the status code.

The status code must always be checked after the OPEN. If the OPEN is not successful, processing must be terminated without issuing a CLOSE statement, as the example in Fig. 13.5 illustrates.

An unsuccessfully opened file can lead to complications in program execution which may be difficult to isolate. This is because the execution of Cobol I/O statements presupposes a successfully opened file.

CLOSE The syntax of the CLOSE statement is

```
CLOSE file-name
```

To confirm the successful closing of a file, always check the file status for a value of 00. If the file status is not zero, it may mean that the end-of-data and end-of-key-range values have not been transferred from the control blocks to the cataloged information. It may also indicate that destaging has not been successful if you are using a mass storage system (MSS). Under these circumstances, you might want to restart the processing using the recovery/restart procedures for the system.

13.4.3 READ, WRITE, REWRITE, and DELETE

These are the Cobol verbs used to move VSAM records between buffers and the direct access storage device. We will be using various examples as they pertain to data records in the file EMPLOYEE.KSDS.CLUSTER. Figure 13.6 gives the contents of this file. There are nine records in it, and the prime key for this KSDS is the EMPLOYEE-SSN-KEY, which is in the first 9 bytes.

READ A file must be opened as INPUT or I-O in order to read its records. The READ statement has two formats. The first, which is for *sequential retrievals,* is

```
READ file-name [INTO identifier]
    [AT END imperative statement]
```

111111111	WORLD PLAZA, N.Y., N.Y.	10	M	092150	RANADE
222222222	25 OAKWOODS, N.Y.	19	M	022536	TANAKA
333333333	18 MARSH AVE, S.I., N.Y.	16	F	030942	KRANTZ
444444444	2-52 FOREST HILLS, QUEENS	05	M	090252	BUTLER
555555555	7 PARK AVE, JERSEY CITY	17	M	092057	RANADE
666666666	15 GREENWICH, CT	12	M	030511	ADLER
777777777	8 BROAD ST., S.I., N.Y.	07	F	082913	JOSHI
888888888	KENNER TOWERS, N.Y., N.Y.	04	F	111855	LEHN
999999999	23 SOUTH ST., BRONX. N.Y.	13	F	100846	RAMSEY

EMPLOYEE-SSN-KEY
(Prime Key)

Figure 13.6 Data records in the KSDS EMPLOYEE.KSDS.CLUSTER.

Note that the INTO and AT END clauses are optional. The above format is valid if ACCESS MODE IS SEQUENTIAL was specified in the SELECT statement. It is recommended that you check for a status code of 10 immediately after the read, instead of using the AT END clause. This code signifies that end of file has been reached.

Let's suppose that our KSDS (in Fig. 13.6) was opened as INPUT as in Fig. 13.7. The first READ will return the record with the key 111111111, and any subsequent read will return records in the key sequence. After the record with the key 999999999 is read, a status code of 10 will be generated. In the above example, you would normally expect a status code of 00 or 10. Any other code would indicate an unexpected

```
       OPEN   INPUT   EMPLOYEE-MASTER.
               .
               .
       READ   EMPLOYEE-MASTER.
       IF     EMPLOYEE-FILE-STATUS  =  '00'
              PERFORM   PROCESS-RECORD
       ELSE
              IF     EMPLOYEE-FILE-STATUS  =  '10'
                     PERFORM   END-OF-FILE-ROUTINE
              ELSE
                     PERFORM   ERROR-ROUTINE.
               .
               .
```

Figure 13.7 Sample code for sequential retrievals in a KSDS.

condition and should be handled in the logic. If you continue to use READ after an end-of-file situation, you will get a status code of 94.

The format for the *random* retrievals of KSDS records is

```
READ file-name[INTO identifier]
    [INVALID KEY imperative statement]
```

ACCESS MODE must be RANDOM or DYNAMIC for this. As shown, the INTO and INVALID KEY clauses are optional. Before executing the above statement, you must move the value of the prime key of the record you want into the RECORD KEY area in the FD statement. Consider the example in Fig. 13.8.

A status code of 00 indicates a successful read, while 23 indicates a record-not-found condition. Any other status code signifies an unexpected abnormal situation. If the INVALID KEY clause is also coded with the READ, the imperative statement will be performed on the record-not-found condition as though the program had found a status code of 23.

WRITE WRITE is used to add new records to a file. Records can be added either sequentially or randomly. The format is the same in both cases:

```
WRITE record-name [FROM identifier]
    [INVALID KEY imperative statement]
```

```
           .
           .
    OPEN   INPUT   EMPLOYEE-MASTER.
           .
           .
    MOVE   '444444444'   TO   EMPLOYEE-SSN-KEY.
    READ   EMPLOYEE-MASTER.
    IF     EMPLOYEE-FILE-STATUS = '00'
           PERFORM  PROCESS-RECORD
    ELSE
           IF    EMPLOYEE-FILE-STATUS = '23'
                 PERFORM  RECORD-NOT-FOUND
           ELSE
                 PERFORM  ERROR-ROUTINE.
           .
           .

```

Figure 13.8 Sample code for random retrievals in a KSDS.

Before using the WRITE statement for a KSDS, the RECORD KEY must be set to a desired value. After a successful WRITE, the logical record is no longer available in the FD area.

The first loading of records into an unloaded KSDS should normally be performed in the sequential mode. To do this, the ACCESS MODE must be SEQUENTIAL and the file must be opened as OUTPUT. Incoming records to be loaded must be in the collating sequence of the prime key. Consider the example in Fig. 13.9.

A status code of 21 indicates that the record to be written had a key equal to or less than the one written before. Any code other than 00 or 21 indicates a serious error that must be handled separately.

Records can also be loaded into a KSDS in the resume-load mode by using an ACCESS MODE of SEQUENTIAL and opening the file as EXTEND. Incoming records must be in the collating sequence of the prime key. The first record to be loaded must have a key that is greater than the highest key record in the KSDS.

For purely random additions, records don't have to be in any particular order in the input file. The ACCESS MODE must be RANDOM or DYNAMIC, and the file must be opened as I-O. You should be aware of the possibility that there may already be a record in the KSDS file with the same key as the new record to be added. Consider the example in Fig. 13.10. It checks for a status code of 22, which means that the record to be added already exists in the KSDS. For example, if you try to add a record with the key 555555555 to the KSDS in Fig. 13.6, you will get a status code of 22 because there already is a record in the file with that key value. You might then want to display the contents of the record and resume processing. Remember, status code 21 is generated on a sequential add, while on a random add the status code is 22.

```
          .
          .
     OPEN   OUTPUT   EMPLOYEE-MASTER.
          .
          .
     MOVE   INPUT-RECORD TO EMPLOYEE-RECORD.
     WRITE EMPLOYEE-RECORD.
     IF    EMPLOYEE-FILE-STATUS  =  '00'
           GO TO READ-NEXT-RECORD
     ELSE
           IF    EMPLOYEE-FILE-STATUS  =  '21'
                 PERFORM  OUT-OF-SEQUENCE-RECORD
           ELSE
                 PERFORM  ERROR-ROUTINE.
          .
          .
```

Figure 13.9 Sample coding for sequential loading of a KSDS.

```
       .
       .
       OPEN   I-O   EMPLOYEE-MASTER.
       .
       .
       MOVE   INPUT-REST TO EMPLOYEE-REST.
       MOVE   INPUT-KEY  TO EMPLOYEE-SSN-KEY.
       WRITE EMPLOYEE-RECORD.
       IF    EMPLOYEE-FILE-STATUS = '00'
             GO TO WRITE-NEXT
       ELSE
             IF    EMPLOYEE-FILE-STATUS = '22'
                   PERFORM   DUPLICATE-RECORD-FOUND
             ELSE
                   PERFORM   ERROR-ROUTINE.
       .
       .
```

Figure 13.10 Sample coding for a random add of records in a KSDS.

REWRITE The REWRITE statement enables you to change the contents of an existing record. Normally, such a record is read using a READ statement, its contents are modified as desired, and it is then written back using the REWRITE statement. The only restriction is that you *cannot* change the prime key of the record. After a successful REWRITE, the record is no longer available in the FD area. The syntax is

```
REWRITE record-name [FROM identifier]
    [INVALID KEY imperative statement]
```

ACCESS MODE can be SEQUENTIAL, RANDOM, or DYNAMIC, and the file must be opened as I-O. If the ACCESS MODE is SEQUENTIAL or the file contains spanned records, the REWRITE must be preceded by a successful READ, otherwise the status code will be set to 92. In the other access modes, there is no need to read a record before replacing it. In a KSDS, the record length may be changed before the record is replaced. However, a changed record length should not exceed the maximum record size value specified at the time of DEFINE CLUSTER. As an illustration of the use of this statement, consider the example in Fig. 13.11.

The importance of testing status codes must be emphasized. Normally, the only non-zero status code you should get is a 23, which indicates record-not-found.

DELETE Unlike other statements, DELETE may be used only for VSAM files. It cannot be used for indexed sequential files. It physically deletes a record from the data set, and the space occupied by it is

```
          .
          .
     OPEN  I-O  EMPLOYEE-MASTER.
          .
          .
     MOVE  INPUT-KEY  TO  EMPLOYEE-SSN-KEY.
     READ  EMPLOYEE-MASTER.
     IF    EMPLOYEE-FILE-STATUS = '00'
           NEXT SENTENCE
     ELSE
           GO TO RECORD-NOT-FOUND.
     MOVE INPUT-REST TO EMPLOYEE-REST.
     REWRITE  EMPLOYEE-RECORD.
     IF    EMPLOYEE-FILE-STATUS = '00'
           NEXT SENTENCE
     ELSE
           GO TO RECORD-NOT-REPLACED.
          .
          .
```

Figure 13.11 Sample code showing use of the REWRITE statement.

reclaimed for use by other records. DELETE *does not* change the contents of a record in the FD area. The syntax of this statement is as follows:

```
DELETE file-name
    [INVALID KEY imperative statement]
```

The ACCESS MODE can be SEQUENTIAL, RANDOM, or DYNAMIC, and the file must be opened as I-O. If ACCESS MODE IS SEQUENTIAL is being used, a DELETE statement must be preceded by a successful READ. In other modes, a read is not necessary and the contents of the prime key data item are used to specify the record to be deleted. Consider the example in Fig. 13.12. In this example we will assume that ACCESS MODE is *not* SEQUENTIAL; thus the DELETE statement is not preceded by a READ statement. A status code of 23 indicates that the record to be deleted was not found.

13.4.4 START and READ NEXT

Both these statements are used in the context of a sequential browse operation. So far, we have learned how to read a KSDS sequentially from start to finish with an ACCESS MODE of SEQUENTIAL. There are often applications where the browse operation must be started at a particular key value. We will have to use a combination of START, READ, and READ NEXT to accomplish this.

START The following is the syntax of the START statement:

```
                              { EQUAL TO         }
                              { =                }
START file-name [KEY IS       { GREATER THAN     }  data-name]
                              { >                }
                              { NOT LESS THAN    }
                              { NOT<             }
    [INVALID KEY imperative statement]
```

With this statement, we can indicate where in the data set the record pos-tion should be established by using a relational operator and the key value. The data-name contains the value of the key to be tested. Consider the following examples as they pertain to the data in Fig. 13.6.

MOVE '333333333' TO KEY-VALUE.
START EMPLOYEE-MASTER <u>KEY IS EQUAL TO</u> KEY-VALUE.

Upon successful completion, position will be established at the record with key 333333333.

MOVE '666666666' TO KEY-VALUE.
START EMPLOYEE-MASTER <u>KEY IS GREATER THAN</u> KEY-VALUE.

```
           .
           .
       OPEN  I-O  EMPLOYEE-MASTER.
           .
           .
       MOVE  INPUT-KEY TO EMPLOYEE-SSN-KEY.
       DELETE  EMPLOYEE-MASTER.
       IF   EMPLOYEE-FILE-STATUS = '00'
            NEXT SENTENCE
       ELSE
            IF   EMPLOYEE-FILE-STATUS = '23'
                 PERFORM  RECORD-NOT-FOUND
            ELSE
                 PERFORM  ERROR-ROUTINE.
           .
           .
```

Figure 13.12 Sample coding for use of the DELETE statement.

Upon successful completion, the position will be established at the record with key 777777777, the next record with a key greater than 666666666.

```
MOVE '123456789' TO KEY-VALUE.
START EMPLOYEE-MASTER KEY IS NOT LESS THAN KEY-
  VALUE.
```

Upon successful completion, the position will be established at the record with key 222222222, *which is equal to or greater than 123456789.*

```
MOVE '345678912' TO KEY-VALUE.
START EMPLOYEE-MASTER KEY IS EQUAL TO KEY-VALUE.
```

At completion, the status code returned will be 23 because there is no record in the file that satisfies the relational criteria. The position in the file will be undefined.

If the KEY IS option is not specified, the relational operator implied is EQUAL TO and the data-name is assumed to be the prime key in the FD area. ACCESS MODE in the SELECT clause must be SEQUENTIAL or DYNAMIC. The file must be opened as INPUT or I-O. Upon successful execution of the START statement, the position will be established on the logical record that satisfies the comparison. If the comparison is not satisfied, a status code of 23 will be returned and the position will be undefined. Remember, this statement only establishes the *position* on a record; it does not read the record. The record is read with the READ or READ NEXT statement.

READ NEXT Once a position has been successfully established on a record using the START statement, records can be sequentially retrieved using READ or READ NEXT. READ is used if ACCESS MODE IS SEQUENTIAL was specified. When ACCESS MODE IS DYNAMIC is specified, allowing both sequential and random retrievals, we must use READ NEXT for sequential reads and READ for random reads. *The first record retrieved by* READ NEXT *is the one on which the position has been established using the* START *command.*The syntax of this statement is

```
READ file-name NEXT [INTO identifier]
    [AT END imperative statement]
```

You must check for the end-of-file condition by using either the AT END clause or by testing for a status code of 10. Figure 13.13 gives sample code for the use of START and READ NEXT.

```
                  .
                  .
       OPEN   INPUT   EMPLOYEE-MASTER.
                  .
                  .
       MOVE   '123456789' TO EMPLOYEE-SSN-KEY.
       START    EMPLOYEE-MASTER
                KEY IS   >   EMPLOYEE-SSN-KEY.
       IF     EMPLOYEE-FILE-STATUS  =  '00'
              NEXT SENTENCE
       ELSE
              IF     EMPLOYEE-FILE-STATUS  =  '23'
                     GO TO  POSITION-NOT-ESTABLISHED
              ELSE
                     PERFORM   ABNORMAL-TERMINATION.
*****************************************************************
***** SUCCESSFUL  START ESTABLISHES POSITION         *********
*****                AT   RECORD   '222222222'       *********
*****************************************************************
       READ   EMPLOYEE-MASTER NEXT.
       IF     EMPLOYEE-FILE-STATUS  =  '00'
              PERFORM   PROCESS-RECORD
       ELSE
              IF     EMPLOYEE-FILE-STATUS  =  '10'
                     PERFORM   END-OF-FILE-PARA
              ELSE
                     PERFORM   ABNORMAL-TERMINATION.
                        .
                        .
```

Figure 13.13 Sample code for using START and READ NEXT. Data used is described in Fig. 13.6. ACCESS MODE IS DYNAMIC was specified in the SELECT statement.

13.4.5 Current Record Pointer

In the previous section, we discussed establishing a position within the file by using the START statement. This position, technically speaking, is called the *current record pointer* (CRP). The CRP is a conceptual pointer which applies to sequential requests only and has no meaning for random requests. It indicates the next record to be accessed by a READ (sequential mode) or READ NEXT (dynamic mode) statement.

A CRP can be established through successful execution of an OPEN, READ, READ NEXT, or START command. An OPEN establishes it on the first record in the data set, a READ or READ NEXT sets it on the record immediately following the one just read, and a START sets it on the first record that satisfies the comparison specified in the statement. Whenever you issue a sequential input request, it reads the record the CRP points to and moves the CRP to the next logical record. Each file has its own separate CRP. You don't need any coding to define it, and even its existence is transparent to you. An unsuccessful OPEN, START, READ, or READ NEXT renders the CRP undefined. Any sequential retrieval after this will give a status code of 94, meaning that

Statement number	Cobol statement	Record read/ deleted/written, rewritten	CRP	Status code
1	ACCESS MODE DYNAMIC;OPEN I-O	—	111111111	00
2	READ NEXT	111111111	222222222	00
3	MOVE '666666666' TO KEY; READ random.	666666666	777777777	00
4	DELETE	666666666	777777777	00
5	READ NEXT	777777777	888888888	00
6	MOVE '999999999' TO KEY; START with EQUAL operator	—	999999999	00
7	READ NEXT	999999999	End-of-file	00
8	Change record contents; REWRITE	999999999	End-of-file	00
9	READ NEXT	—	Undefined	10
10	READ NEXT	—	Undefined	94
11	MOVE '123456789' TO KEY; START with GREATER THAN oper.	—	222222222	00
12	Format and WRITE a record with key '789123456'	789123456	222222222	00
13	READ NEXT	222222222	333333333	00
14	CLOSE and OPEN the file	—	111111111	00

Figure 13.14 Effect of various statements on CRP as it applies to records in Fig. 13.6 loaded into EMPLOYEE.KSDS.CLUSTER.

the CRP is undefined. The CRP is also undefined when you hit an end-of-file condition (status code 10). Under these circumstances, the CRP should be reestablished before any input request is made. This can be done by any one of the following: (1) closing and reopening the file, (2) successfully executing the START statement, or (3) successfully executing a random READ request. *The* CRP *is totally unaffected by* DELETE, WRITE, *or* REWRITE. Any execution of these statements will not disturb it, and any subsequent sequential READ or READ NEXT will be executed from the position left by the previously established CRP. Figure 13.14 shows a sequence of events affecting the CRP when various statements are executed on EMPLOYEE.KSDS.CLUSTER with data records as in Fig. 13.6.

13.4.6 Generic Search

In order to set the CRP in a KSDS, you can use a generic key instead of the full key in a START statement. Consider the following example.

```
05  EMPLOYEE-SSN-KEY.
    10  GEN-1-TO-5.
        15  GEN-1-TO-3          PIC X (3).
        15  GEN-4-TO-5          PIC X (2).
    10  GEN-6-TO-9              PIC X (4).
```

In this case, GEN-1-TO-5 or GEN-1-TO-3 can be used as a generic key. GEN-4-TO-5 and GEN-6-TO-9 cannot be used as generic keys because they don't start with the leftmost byte of the full key. This will become clearer if you review the examples given in Fig. 13.15 as they apply to EMPLOYEE.KSDS.CLUSTER.

13.5 ERROR HANDLING

Error checking for VSAM files is more important than for any other file organization. In other file organizations, if there is a fatal error, the operating system takes control and causes a system abend. You notice the abend, trace the reason for it, correct the problem, and restart processing. For VSAM files, the operating system *does not* take over when a fatal error occurs. Control is passed back to your program. If the program does not notice the abnormal condition, the error will go undetected. Consider the following scenario.

There are two programs—one loads records into a physical sequential file and the other loads records into a KSDS data set. Suppose the capacity of both files is a maximum of 1000 records each but there are 1500

Statement number	Cobol statement	CRP
1	MOVE '222' TO GEN-1-TO-3. START EMPLOYEE-MASTER KEY IS EQUAL TO GEN-1-TO-3	222222222
2	MOVE '22234' TO GEN-1-TO-5. START EMPLOYEE-MASTER KEY IS GREATER THAN GEN-1-TO-5	333333333
3	MOVE '776' TO GEN-1-TO-3. START EMPLOYEE-MASTER KEY NOT LESS THAN GEN-1-TO-3	777777777
4	MOVE '9999' TO GEN-6-TO-9. START EMPLOYEE-MASTER KEY IS EQUAL TO GEN-6-TO-9	Possible compilation error because GEN-6-TO-9 is not in the leftmost part of the key

Data set is EMPLOYEE.KSDS.CLUSTER loaded with records as in Fig. 13.6.

Figure 13.15 Use of generic keys in the START statement and its effect on CRP.

records to be loaded. When the program for the physical sequential file is executed, it will start loading records and will be successful up to number 1000. Thereafter, when it tries to load an additional record, it will detect a no-space condition. Control will be given to the operating system, which will cause a system abend with an appropriate abend code. The subsequent steps in the job, if any, will not be executed. Since operators are often trained to look for program abends, they may try to resolve the problem as per documented recovery/restart procedures, or you may get a telephone call in the middle of the night. When the program for the KSDS is executed, it will also successfully load the first 1000 records. At record 1001, it will set the status code to 24 and send an error message. The operating system *will not* take control, and processing will continue. If your program does not check the status codes, you will lose the next 500 records and you will find 500 messages in the log. Operators are not usually trained to read error messages, so you may not know about the problem for the next few days, even for months. This could be a disaster if the file were for example, an accounts receivable master file.

Proper coding should take care of such situations. One possible solution could be to generate a user abend whenever a status code of 24 is encountered in the KSDS program. Cobol has a built-in routine named ILBOABN0 that can be called to cause a user abend. Figure 13.16 gives the sample coding. An appropriate value (of your choice) must be moved to the ABEND-CODE data-name before calling the ABEND-

```
               .
               .
WORKING-STORAGE SECTION.
01   EMPLOYEE-FILE-STATUS            PIC X(2).
01   ABEND-PROGRAM                   PIC X(8)
                          VALUE 'ILBOABNO'.
01   ABEND-CODE                      PIC S9(3)
                                     COMP.
               .
               .
PROCEDURE DIVISION.
               .
               .
       IF    EMPLOYEE-FILE-STATUS = '24'
             DISPLAY 'NO SPACE CONDITION'
             DISPLAY 'FILE STATUS IS ' EMPLOYEE-FILE-STATUS
             MOVE +999 TO ABEND-CODE
             CALL ABEND-PROGRAM USING ABEND-CODE.
               .
               .
```

Figure 13.16 Sample code for causing a user abend based on a status code leading to an unrecoverable situation.

PROGRAM. In our case, the program will be abnormally terminated with the user abend of U999.

In general, most of the status codes whose values are 23 or less are expected situations. Based on program logic, you can easily recover and continue with processing. Status codes of 24 or more indicate serious errors (except status code 97) that are usually difficult to recover from. It is wise to terminate the processing rather than to continue with a serious error condition.

In previous sections, we noticed that some Cobol statements have INVALID KEY and AT END clauses. Since these clauses are optional, it is not necessary to use them. Checking status codes will take care not only of situations handled by these optional clauses but also situations that are *not* handled by them. Depending on your coding techniques, you may use them or totally omit them in writting your program. For example, suppose you are reading a record randomly in a KSDS. If the record is not found, the imperative statement of the INVALID KEY clause will be executed if coded in the program. A status code of 23 will also be moved to the FILE STATUS data-name. If the record is not read because of some other error, the INVALID KEY clause will not be activated. However, the status code can still be checked to determine the nature of the error. Figure 13.17 gives two sample codes, one that uses the INVALID KEY clause and one that does not. Both accomplish the same thing.

Similarly, you can also omit the AT END clause and check for a status code of 10 instead. The status codes in Figs. 13.3 and 13.4 should be reviewed thoroughly to get a feel for the possible situations that must be taken care of in the program logic.

```
READ-NEXT-PARA.
               .
               .
        MOVE  INPUT-KEY  TO  EMPLOYEE-SSN-KEY.
        READ   EMPLOYEE-MASTER
                INVALID KEY PERFORM RECORD-NOT-FOUND
                GO  TO  READ-NEXT-PARA.
        IF     EMPLOYEE-FILE-STATUS  NOT  =  '00'
               PERFORM   SERIOUS-ERROR-PARA.
        PERFORM   PROCESS-RECORD-PARA.
        GO  TO  READ-NEXT-PARA.
               .
               .
```

(*a*)

```
READ-NEXT-PARA.
               .
               .
        MOVE  INPUT-KEY  TO  EMPLOYEE-SSN-KEY.
        READ  EMPLOYEE-MASTER.
        IF    EMPLOYEE-FILE-STATUS  =  '00'
              PERFORM   PROCESS-RECORD-PARA
              GO  TO  READ-NEXT-PARA
        ELSE
              IF    EMPLOYEE-FILE-STATUS  =  '23'
                    PERFORM   RECORD-NOT-FOUND
                    GO  TO  READ-NEXT-PARA
              ELSE
                    PERFORM   SERIOUS-ERROR-PARA.
               .
               .
```

(*b*)

Figure 13.17 (*a*) Error handling using an INVALID KEY clause. (*b*) Error handling without using an INVALID KEY clause.

13.6 PROGRAM EXAMPLE 1: LOADING AN UNLOADED KSDS

In Chap. 7, we used the REPRO command to load records into an unloaded KSDS. Although it is simple to use, REPRO does not provide any capabilities for editing the input data. A program is needed if the input must be built, scanned, or rearranged.

In this example, we will load records into EMPLOYEE.KSDS.CLUSTER using a Cobol program. The file's status is UNLOADED (HURBA = 0). We will assume that the incoming records from SAMPLE.INPUT.DATA are already sorted on the prime key.

Since this is a sequential load, ACCESS MODE IS SEQUENTIAL will be used and the file will be opened as OUTPUT. Figure 13.18 gives the code for a complete program for accomplishing this.

The logic of the code is fairly self-explanatory, since we have discussed and used all the features in previous sections. However, some additional comments are required. When writing the records to our KSDS, we check for a status code of 21. This status code indicates whether or not the records are out of sequence. Since the input file is sorted on the prime key, why do we look for an out-of-sequence situation? The answer is that we may get two input records with the same key. Since this would result in status code 21, it must be checked. Also note that any status code other than 00 or 21 is a serious matter in a sequential load. It might be 24, which means that the VSAM file ran out of space. So, our program causes a user abend after displaying such a status code.

```
 IDENTIFICATION DIVISION.
 PROGRAM-ID.   KSDSLOAD.
 AUTHOR.       RANADE.
*****************************************************
*** THIS PROGRAM READS A PHYSICAL SEQUENTIAL ****
*** FILE SORTED ON PRIME KEY AND LOADS       ****
*** RECORDS INTO KSDS (EMPLOYEE MASTER)      ****
*****************************************************

 ENVIRONMENT DIVISION.
 CONFIGURATION SECTION.
 INPUT-OUTPUT SECTION.
 FILE-CONTROL.
     SELECT  INPUT-FILE
             ASSIGN TO UT-S-INPUT.

     SELECT  EMPLOYEE-MASTER
             ASSIGN TO  EMPMSTR
             ORGANIZATION IS INDEXED
             ACCESS MODE IS SEQUENTIAL
             RECORD KEY IS EMPLOYEE-SSN-KEY
             FILE STATUS IS EMPLOYEE-FILE-STATUS.

 DATA DIVISION.
 FILE SECTION.
 FD  INPUT-FILE
     LABEL RECORDS ARE STANDARD
     RECORD CONTAINS 50 CHARACTERS
     BLOCK CONTAINS 0 RECORDS.
 01  INPUT-RECORD.
     05  INPUT-KEY                   PIC X(9).
     05  INPUT-REST.
         10  INPUT-EMPADD            PIC X(26).
```

Figure 13.18 Program listing for the sequential loading of EMPLOYEE.KSDS. CLUSTER from sorted SAMPLE.INPUT.DATA.

```
                10  INPUT-EMPNUM          PIC X(2).
                10  INPUT-EMPSEX          PIC X.
                10  INPUT-EMPDOB          PIC X(6).
                10  INPUT-EMPNAME         PIC X(6).

       FD  EMPLOYEE-MASTER
           LABEL RECORDS ARE STANDARD.
       01  EMPLOYEE-RECORD.
           05  EMPLOYEE-SSN-KEY          PIC X(9).
           05  EMPLOYEE-REST             PIC X(41).

       WORKING-STORAGE SECTION.
       01  EMPLOYEE-FILE-STATUS          PIC X(2).
       01  ABEND-PROGRAM                 PIC X(8)
                                   VALUE 'ILBOABNO'.
       01  ABEND-CODE                    PIC S999 COMP
                                   VALUE +999.

       PROCEDURE DIVISION.
       100-MAIN-PARA.
           OPEN OUTPUT EMPLOYEE-MASTER.
      ****************************************************************
      ***  TEST FOR SUCESSFUL OPEN OF VSAM DATASET ****
      ****************************************************************
           IF   EMPLOYEE-FILE-STATUS = '00'
                NEXT SENTENCE
           ELSE
                DISPLAY 'OPEN ERROR ON EMPMSTR'
                DISPLAY 'STATUS CODE IS  '
                        EMPLOYEE-FILE-STATUS
                CALL ABEND-PROGRAM USING ABEND-CODE.
           OPEN INPUT INPUT-FILE.
           PERFORM  200-LOAD-EMPMSTR THRU 200-EXIT.
           CLOSE INPUT-FILE
                 EMPLOYEE-MASTER.
      ****************************************************************
      ***  TEST FOR SUCESSFUL CLOSE OF VSAM DATASET ***
      ****************************************************************
           IF   EMPLOYEE-FILE-STATUS = '00'
                NEXT SENTENCE
           ELSE
                DISPLAY 'CLOSE ERROR ON EMPMSTR'
                DISPLAY 'STATUS CODE IS  '
                        EMPLOYEE-FILE-STATUS
                CALL ABEND-PROGRAM USING ABEND-CODE.
           GOBACK.

       200-LOAD-EMPMSTR.
           READ  INPUT-FILE
                 AT END GO TO 200-EXIT.
           IF   (INPUT-KEY IS NUMERIC)          AND
                (INPUT-EMPADD NOT = SPACES)     AND
                (INPUT-EMPNUM IS NUMERIC)       AND
                (INPUT-EMPSEX = 'M' OR 'F')     AND
                (INPUT-EMPDOB IS NUMERIC)       AND
                (INPUT-EMPNAME NOT = SPACES)
                NEXT SENTENCE
```

```
           ELSE
                   DISPLAY 'BAD INPUT RECORD   '
                               INPUT-RECORD
                   GO TO 200-LOAD-EMPMSTR.
           MOVE INPUT-RECORD TO EMPLOYEE-RECORD.
           WRITE EMPLOYEE-RECORD.
      ******************************************************
      ***  TEST FOR SUCESSFUL WRITE TO VSAM DATASET ***
      ******************************************************
           IF      EMPLOYEE-FILE-STATUS = '00'
                   GO TO 200-LOAD-EMPMSTR
           ELSE
                   IF     EMPLOYEE-FILE-STATUS = '21'
                          DISPLAY 'OUT OF SEQUENCE RECORD '
                                  INPUT-RECORD
                          GO TO 200-LOAD-EMPMSTR
                   ELSE
                          DISPLAY 'SEVERE VSAM ERROR'
                          DISPLAY 'STATUS CODE IS  '
                                  EMPLOYEE-FILE-STATUS
                          CALL ABEND-PROGRAM USING ABEND-CODE.
       200-EXIT.
           EXIT.
```

Figure 13.18 (*continued*)

13.6.1 Execution JCL

Coding execution JCL for VSAM files is a simple matter. In most cases, you need to code only the DSN and DISPOSITION parameters. The rest of the file attributes are drawn by the system from the cataloged information. Figure 13.19 gives the JCL for executing the load program. SYSOUT has been coded for the display messages, if any, and SYSUDUMP is for the dumps produced by user abends or system abends.

```
//LOADJOB   JOB (ACCTNO),'JAY RANADE'
//LOADSTEP  EXEC PGM=KSDSLOAD
//STEPLIB   DD DSN=SAMPLE.PROGRAM.LOAD,DISP=SHR
//          DD DSN=SYS1.COBLIB,DISP=SHR
//INPUT     DD DSN=SAMPLE.INPUT.DATA,
//             DISP=OLD
//EMPMSTR   DD DSN=EMPLOYEE.KSDS.CLUSTER,
//             DISP=OLD
//SYSOUT    DD SYSOUT=A
//DISPLAY   DD SYSOUT=A
//SYSUDUMP  DD SYSOUT=A
//
```

Figure 13.19 JCL for executing a load program for KSDS.

```
OPEN ERROR ON EMPMSTR
STATUS CODE IS  95
```

(a)

```
IAT6140 JOB ORIGIN FROM GROUP=ANYLOCAL, DSP=IR , DEVICE=INTRDR    , 000
02:05:39 IAT2000 JOB 0071 LOADJOB  SELECTED SYSR       GRP=CLASSF
02:05:39  IEF403I LOADJOB - STARTED - TIME=02.05.39
02:05:58  IEF450I LOADJOB LOADSTEP - ABEND S000 U0999 - TIME=02.05.58
02:05:58 *
02:05:58  ****************************************
02:05:58  ****************************************
02:05:58  ***  LOADJOB ,KSDSLOAD,LOADSTEP ABEND U0999  ***
02:05:58  ****************************************
02:05:58  ****************************************
02:06:18  IEF404I LOADJOB - ENDED - TIME=02.06.18
IEF236I ALLOC. FOR LOADJOB LOADSTEP
IEF237I 179   ALLOCATED TO STEPLIB
IEF237I 344   ALLOCATED TO
IEF237I 179   ALLOCATED TO SYS00002
IEF237I 179   ALLOCATED TO INPUT
IEF237I 179   ALLOCATED TO EMPMSTR
IEF237I JES3 ALLOCATED TO SYSOUT
IEF237I JES3 ALLOCATED TO DISPLAY
IEF237I JES3 ALLOCATED TO SYSUDUMP
IEC161I 084(048,016,IGGOCLB7)-003,LOADJOB,LOADSTEP,EMPMSTR,,,
IEC161I EMPLOYEE.KSDS.CLUSTER,,VSAM.USERCAT.TWO
IEF472I LOADJOB LOADSTEP - COMPLETION CODE - SYSTEM=000 USER=0999
IEF285I    SAMPLE.PROGRAM.LOAD                              KEPT
IEF285I    VOL SER NOS= VSAM02.
IEF285I    SYS1.COBLIB                                      KEPT
IEF285I    VOL SER NOS= SYSLNK.
IEF285I    VSAM.USERCAT.TWO                                 KEPT
IEF285I    VOL SER NOS= VSAM02.
IEF285I    SAMPLE.INPUT.DATA                                KEPT
IEF285I    VOL SER NOS= VSAM02.
IEF285I    EMPLOYEE.KSDS.CLUSTER                            KEPT
IEF285I    VOL SER NOS= VSAM02.
IEF285I    LOADSTEP.SYSOUT                                  SYSOUT
IEF285I    LOADSTEP.DISPLAY                                 SYSOUT
IEF285I    LOADSTEP.SYSUDUMP                                SYSOUT
```

(b)

Figure 13.20 (*a*) Display message caused by an unsuccessful open. (*b*) User abend message in a job log.

Execution of this JCL will load the KSDS successfully. To get a feel for some of the status codes and user abends, let's execute this program a second time on the same file. You know that a loaded file cannot be opened as OUTPUT. Therefore, you expect the OPEN to fail and cause execution of the user abend routine. Figure 13.20 gives the display message and the user abend printout on the second run.

13.7 PROGRAM EXAMPLE 2: RANDOM UPDATE OF A KSDS

We will expand the example from the previous section to explain random updates. A random update involves the addition of new records, the deletion of old records, and the changing of existing records. The file must be opened as I-O. The ACCESS MODE may be RANDOM or DYNAMIC.

Record 1	A	333000000	22 ESSEX ESTATES, L.I., N.Y.	18	F	102148	ROMANO
Record 2	D	444444444					
Record 3	A	888888888	18 9th ST, SCARSDALE, N.Y.	11	M	052962	CHENG
Record 4	C	666000000				010159	
Record 5	D	777000000					
Record 6	C	555555555	780 5th AVE, N.Y., N.Y.				

Figure 13.21 Record contents of SAMPLE.TRANS.DATA which will be used as input to update EMPLOYEE.KSDS.CLUSTER.

In this example, our KSDS will again be EMPLOYEE.KSDS.CLUSTER. It contains the same records that were sequentially loaded in the previous section (Fig. 13.6). They are each 50 bytes long. Our transaction file will be SAMPLE.TRANS.DATA. It has records of 51 bytes each. The first byte will have the character A, D, or C to indicate which of the ADD, DELETE, or CHANGE functions is needed. The rest of the 50 bytes (positions 2 through 51) will have other key and nonkey fields of the record. The transaction file has the records given in Fig. 13.21.

As you can see, the records with the update code A have data in all the fields because new records are to be created. Records with the update code D have key information only because that is all that is needed to delete a record. Records with the update code C contain data only in the field that is to be changed in the master file. Records do not have to be in sorted order for random updates.

Now, let's get down to coding. The program should be able to take care of all unexpected situations: a record to be added may already exist in the KSDS; a record to be changed or deleted may not exist at all. If the status codes are not checked properly for these situations, errors will go undetected. For simplicity, our program will not edit the transaction records. In a program used in production, you should edit the input records thoroughly before processing. Figure 13.22 gives the code for the update program.

When adding a new record, we check for a status code of 22. This indicates a duplicate record condition. For deletes, we check for a status code of 23, which means the record was not found. Note that we are *not* reading a record before the delete. This is because the ACCESS MODE specified was DYNAMIC. For a record change, we read the record, change its contents, and rewrite it. We anticipate the possibility of record-not-found condition on a read by checking for a status code of 23. Other abnormal conditions that will cause a user abend may not occur at all during the life of the system. But for the rare instance when it does, we want to be ready to trace it and take appropriate action.

```
 IDENTIFICATION DIVISION.
 PROGRAM-ID.  KSDSUPDT.
 AUTHOR.      RANADE.
*************************************************************
*************************************************************
*** THIS PROGRAM READS A PHYSICAL SEQUENTIAL ****
*** FILE. BASED ON UPDATE CODE A,D OR C, IT  ****
*** ADDS,DELETES OR CHANGES RECORDS IN KSDS. ****
*************************************************************
*************************************************************

 ENVIRONMENT DIVISION.
 CONFIGURATION SECTION.
 INPUT-OUTPUT SECTION.
 FILE-CONTROL.

      SELECT  TRANS-FILE
              ASSIGN TO UT-S-TRANS.

      SELECT  EMPLOYEE-MASTER
              ASSIGN TO  EMPMSTR
              ORGANIZATION IS INDEXED
              ACCESS MODE  IS DYNAMIC
              RECORD KEY IS EMPLOYEE-SSN-KEY
              FILE STATUS IS EMPLOYEE-FILE-STATUS.

 DATA DIVISION.
 FILE SECTION.

 FD   TRANS-FILE
      LABEL RECORDS ARE STANDARD
      RECORD CONTAINS 51 CHARACTERS
      BLOCK CONTAINS 0 RECORDS.
 01   TRANS-RECORD.
      05   TRANS-CODE                    PIC X.
      05   TRANS-KEY                     PIC X(9).
      05   TRANS-REST.
           10   TRANS-EMPADD             PIC X(26).
           10   TRANS-EMPNUM             PIC X(2).
           10   TRANS-EMPSEX             PIC X.
           10   TRANS-EMPDOB             PIC X(6).
           10   TRANS-EMPNAME            PIC X(6).


 FD   EMPLOYEE-MASTER
      LABEL RECORDS ARE STANDARD.
 01   EMPLOYEE-RECORD.
      05   EMPLOYEE-SSN-KEY              PIC X(9).
      05   EMPLOYEE-REST.
           10   EMPLOYEE-EMPADD          PIC X(26).
           10   EMPLOYEE-EMPNUM          PIC X(2).
           10   EMPLOYEE-EMPSEX          PIC X.
           10   EMPLOYEE-EMPDOB          PIC X(6).
           10   EMPLOYEE-EMPNAME         PIC X(6).

```

Figure 13.22 Program listing for the random update of EMPLOYEE.KSDS.CLUSTER from SAMPLE.TRANS.DATA. The program takes care of adds, changes, and deletes.

```
 WORKING-STORAGE SECTION.
 01  EMPLOYEE-FILE-STATUS              PIC X(2).
 01  ABEND-PROGRAM                     PIC X(8)
                                 VALUE 'ILBOABNO'.
 01  ABEND-CODE                        PIC S999 COMP
                                 VALUE +999.
 PROCEDURE DIVISION.
 100-MAIN-PARA.
     OPEN  I-O   EMPLOYEE-MASTER.
*************************************************
***  TEST FOR SUCESSFUL OPEN OF VSAM DATASET ****
*************************************************
     IF   EMPLOYEE-FILE-STATUS = '00'
          NEXT SENTENCE
     ELSE
          DISPLAY 'OPEN ERROR ON EMPMSTR'
          DISPLAY 'STATUS CODE IS  '
                  EMPLOYEE-FILE-STATUS
          CALL ABEND-PROGRAM USING ABEND-CODE.
     OPEN INPUT TRANS-FILE.
     PERFORM  200-UPDATE-EMPMSTR THRU 200-EXIT.
     CLOSE TRANS-FILE
           EMPLOYEE-MASTER.
*************************************************
***  TEST FOR SUCESSFUL CLOSE OF VSAM DATASET ***
*************************************************
     IF   EMPLOYEE-FILE-STATUS = '00'
          NEXT SENTENCE
     ELSE
          DISPLAY 'CLOSE ERROR ON EMPMSTR'
          DISPLAY 'STATUS CODE IS  '
                  EMPLOYEE-FILE-STATUS
          CALL ABEND-PROGRAM USING ABEND-CODE.
     GOBACK.

 200-UPDATE-EMPMSTR.
     READ  TRANS-FILE
           AT END GO TO 200-EXIT.
     IF   TRANS-CODE = 'A'
          PERFORM 300-ADD-RECORD
                  THRU 300-EXIT
     ELSE
          IF   TRANS-CODE = 'D'
               PERFORM 400-DELETE-RECORD
                       THRU 400-EXIT
          ELSE
               IF   TRANS-CODE = 'C'
                    PERFORM 500-CHANGE-RECORD
                            THRU 500-EXIT
               ELSE
                    DISPLAY 'ILLEGAL TRANS CODE FOR'
                    DISPLAY 'RECORD ' TRANS-RECORD.
          GO TO 200-UPDATE-EMPMSTR.
 200-EXIT.
     EXIT.
```

```
 300-ADD-RECORD.
     MOVE TRANS-KEY TO EMPLOYEE-SSN-KEY.
     MOVE TRANS-REST TO EMPLOYEE-REST.
     WRITE  EMPLOYEE-RECORD.
*************************************************************
***  TEST FOR SUCESSFUL  ADD TO  VSAM DATASET ***
*************************************************************
     IF   EMPLOYEE-FILE-STATUS = '00'
          GO TO 300-EXIT
     ELSE
          IF   EMPLOYEE-FILE-STATUS = '22'
               DISPLAY 'DUPLICATE RECORD ON ADD '
               DISPLAY  TRANS-RECORD
               GO TO 300-EXIT
          ELSE
               DISPLAY 'SERIOUS ERROR ON ADD '
               DISPLAY 'STATUS CODE IS  '
                        EMPLOYEE-FILE-STATUS
               CALL ABEND-PROGRAM USING ABEND-CODE.
 300-EXIT.
     EXIT.
 400-DELETE-RECORD.
     MOVE TRANS-KEY TO EMPLOYEE-SSN-KEY.
     DELETE EMPLOYEE-MASTER.
*************************************************************
***  TEST FOR SUCESSFUL DELETE IN VSAM DATASET***
*************************************************************
     IF   EMPLOYEE-FILE-STATUS = '00'
          GO TO 400-EXIT
     ELSE
          IF   EMPLOYEE-FILE-STATUS = '23'
               DISPLAY 'RECORD NOT FOUND ON DELETE '
               DISPLAY  TRANS-RECORD
               GO TO 400-EXIT
          ELSE
               DISPLAY 'SERIOUS ERROR ON DELETE'
               DISPLAY 'STATUS CODE IS  '
                        EMPLOYEE-FILE-STATUS
               CALL ABEND-PROGRAM USING ABEND-CODE.
 400-EXIT.
     EXIT.


 500-CHANGE-RECORD.
     MOVE TRANS-KEY TO EMPLOYEE-SSN-KEY.
     READ EMPLOYEE-MASTER.
*************************************************************
***  TEST FOR SUCESSFUL READ  OF VSAM RECORD  ***
*************************************************************
     IF   EMPLOYEE-FILE-STATUS = '00'
          NEXT SENTENCE
     ELSE
          IF   EMPLOYEE-FILE-STATUS = '23'
               DISPLAY 'RECORD NOT FOUND ON READ'
               DISPLAY  TRANS-RECORD
               GO TO 500-EXIT
```

```
            ELSE
                DISPLAY 'SERIOUS ERROR ON READ '
                DISPLAY 'STATUS CODE IS  '
                        EMPLOYEE-FILE-STATUS
                CALL ABEND-PROGRAM USING ABEND-CODE.
        IF    TRANS-EMPADD   NOT = SPACES
              MOVE TRANS-EMPADD   TO EMPLOYEE-EMPADD.
        IF    TRANS-EMPNUM   NOT = SPACES
              MOVE TRANS-EMPNUM   TO EMPLOYEE-EMPNUM.
        IF    TRANS-EMPSEX   NOT = SPACES
              MOVE TRANS-EMPSEX   TO EMPLOYEE-EMPSEX.
        IF    TRANS-EMPDOB   NOT = SPACES
              MOVE TRANS-EMPDOB   TO EMPLOYEE-EMPDOB.
        IF    TRANS-EMPNAME NOT = SPACES
              MOVE TRANS-EMPNAME TO EMPLOYEE-EMPNAME.
        REWRITE  EMPLOYEE-RECORD.
*************************************************************
***   TEST FOR SUCESSFUL  REWRITE TO VSAM FILE ***
*************************************************************
        IF    EMPLOYEE-FILE-STATUS = '00'
              GO TO 500-EXIT
        ELSE
              DISPLAY 'SERIOUS ERROR ON REWRITE '
              DISPLAY 'STATUS CODE IS  '
                      EMPLOYEE-FILE-STATUS
              CALL ABEND-PROGRAM USING ABEND-CODE.
 500-EXIT.
        EXIT.
```

Figure 13.22 (*continued*)

You may also find a lot of redundant code in the program. This was added to keep the logic for our example simple. Coding is a matter of personal style. As you become more comfortable, you may code a program differently. But, you should never sacrifice error checking to reduce redundancy.

The JCL for VSAM files for update programs is the same as the one for load programs. Figure 13.23 gives the JCL for running this program.

If you thoroughly scrutinize the transaction records in Fig. 13.21, you will find that records 3, 4, and 5 should generate error conditions. This was done purposely to give you a feel for duplicate records and record-not-found conditions. Figure 13.24 gives the display messages that resulted when the program was run with the data in Fig. 13.21.

We have not discussed a form of update that involves changing the prime key itself. Since REWRITE does not permit us to change the prime key of the record, it is accomplished using the following technique.

1. READ a record with the old key.

```
//UPDTJOB   JOB (ACCTNO),'JAY RANADE'
//UPDTSTEP  EXEC PGM=KSDSUPDT
//STEPLIB   DD DSN=SAMPLE.PROGRAM.LOAD,DISP=SHR
//          DD DSN=SYS1.COBLIB,DISP=SHR
//TRANS     DD DSN=SAMPLE.TRANS.DATA,
//             DISP=OLD
//EMPMSTR   DD DSN=EMPLOYEE.KSDS.CLUSTER,
//             DISP=OLD
//SYSOUT    DD SYSOUT=A
//DISPLAY   DD SYSOUT=A
//SYSUDUMP  DD SYSOUT=A
//
```

Figure 13.23 JCL for running update program KSDSUPDT.

```
DUPLICATE RECORD ON ADD
A888888888 18,9TH ST,SCARSDALE,N.Y  11M052962CHENG
RECORD NOT FOUND ON READ
C666000000                                 010159
RECORD NOT FOUND ON DELETE
D777000000
```

Figure 13.24 Display of error messages when KSDSUPDT program was run to update EMPLOYEE.KSDS.CLUSTER. Transaction records used were as in Fig. 13.21.

2. Change the prime key and issue a WRITE. This will create a new record with the new key.
3. DELETE the record with the old key.

If a status code of 22 is received in step 2, you can display the new key and the error message and continue with processing. But if you receive a status code of 23 in step 3 (which is very rare because you just read the record a moment ago), a serious condition is indicated. You might want to terminate processing in such a case. Although we could have incorporated the above logic into our update program, it is preferable to have a separate program perform this function.

Last, the use of status codes for error handling cannot be emphasized enough. If you don't use them, systems using VSAM files will be unreliable. In the following chapters, we will make ample use of these codes.

chapter 14

Processing a KSDS with Alternate Index(es)

In the last chapter, we discussed a KSDS without alternate indexes. Almost all the concepts we learned will be valid for this chapter as well. It is important that they be understood properly before proceeding further. The approach used will be to discuss the add-ons to what we have already learned. Comparisons and contrasts will be made wherever applicable. The procedure for error handling will focus on status codes.

Throughout the book, we have used a KSDS named EMPLOYEE.KSDS.CLUSTER. In Chap. 13, we assumed that it had no alternate indexes or paths defined over it. Now, we will consider it with two alternate indexes and the two corresponding paths. The first alternate index, on EMPLOYEE-NUMBER, has a unique key, while the other, on EMPLOYEE-NAME, has a nonunique key. Their names are

```
EMPLOYEE.KSDS.AIX1.CLUSTER
EMPLOYEE.KSDS.PATH1
EMPLOYEE.KSDS.AIX2.CLUSTER
EMPLOYEE.KSDS.PATH2
```

They were defined with the parameters in the examples in Chaps. 6 and 9.

14.1 SELECT STATEMENT

Figure 14.1 gives the syntax of the SELECT statement for a KSDS with alternate index(es).

We'll skip the clauses that were discussed in the last chapter and start with the ALTERNATE RECORD KEY clause. There may be as many of these clauses as there are alternate index paths defined over the base cluster. If the alternate index path is password-protected, you must code its PASSWORD clause and give the appropriate password through the data-name in the working storage section. If the path's alternate index was defined with the NONUNIQUEKEY parameter (e.g., Employee-Name), you must also code the WITH DUPLICATES option. FILE STATUS will hold the status code for the base cluster as well as the alternate index path processing.

If a Cobol program processes a KSDS with only the prime key, the processing logic will be the same whether or not it has alternate indexes. No specification of ALTERNATE RECORD KEY is required. Its upgrade set will still be maintained by VSAM.

Although the base cluster and its associated alternate indexes are physically different data sets, they are all coded in the *same* SELECT statement. Alternate indexes do not have separate assignment names. Figure 14.2 provides the sample coding for the SELECT clause for EMPLOYEE.KSDS.CLUSTER and its corresponding alternate indexes. We will assume that none of them are password-protected.

```
SELECT     file-name
           ASSIGN TO assignment-name
           ORGANIZATION IS INDEXED
                                 (SEQUENTIAL)
           ACCESS MODE IS        {RANDOM    }
                                 (DYNAMIC   )
           RECORD KEY IS data-name-1
           PASSWORD IS   data-name-2
           ALTERNATE RECORD KEY IS data-name-3
           PASSWORD IS   data-name-4
           ALTERNATE RECORD KEY IS data-name-5
           PASSWORD IS   data-name-6
           WITH DUPLICATES
           .
           .
           .
           .
           FILE STATUS IS data-name-n.
```

Figure 14.1 Syntax of a SELECT statement for a KSDS with alternate index(es).

```
             .
             .
FILE-CONTROL.
     SELECT  EMPLOYEE-MASTER
             ASSIGN TO EMPMSTR
             ORGANIZATION IS INDEXED
             ACCESS MODE IS RANDOM
             RECORD KEY IS EMPLOYEE-SSN-KEY
             ALTERNATE RECORD KEY IS EMPLOYEE-NUM-KEY
             ALTERNATE RECORD KEY IS EMPLOYEE-NAME-KEY
                       WITH DUPLICATES
             FILE STATUS IS EMPLOYEE-FILE-STATUS.
             .
             .
DATA DIVISION.
FILE SECTION.
FD   EMPLOYEE-MASTER
     LABEL RECORDS ARE STANDARD.
01   EMPLOYEE-RECORD.
     05   EMPLOYEE-SSN-KEY                       PIC X(9).
     05   EMPLOYEE-ADDRESS                       PIC X(26).
     05   EMPLOYEE-NUM-KEY                       PIC X(2).
     05   EMPLOYEE-SEX                           PIC X.
     05   EMPLOYEE-DOB                           PIC X(6).
     05   EMPLOYEE-NAME-KEY                      PIC X(6).
             .
             .
WORKING-STORAGE SECTION.
01   EMPLOYEE-FILE-STATUS                        PIC X(2).
             .
             .
```

Figure 14.2 Sample coding of a SELECT clause for EMPLOYEE.KSDS.CLUSTER and its alternate indexes for RANDOM processing.

14.2 FILE STATUS

All the status codes applicable to a data set without alternate indexes are also applicable when alternate indexes exist. However, there is one status code that applies only to an alternate index. The value 02 is returned for nonunique key alternate indexes if they were allocated with the WITH DUPLICATES option. This means that, while processing records, an *expected* nonunique key situation has occurred. The situation is normal because it is expected and, under most circumstances, this informative status code can be ignored. In the case of the Employee-Master file, you may expect this code if you add an employee record where the name field matches the name of an existing employee.

14.3 PROCESSING IN PROCEDURE DIVISION

All the statements for processing in the PROCEDURE DIVISION that we learned in the last chapter are also applicable in this one. There are some necessary changes in syntax and several concepts unique to alternate indexes that we must discuss.

14.3.1 Upgrade Set

All alternate indexes that were defined with the UPGRADE option become members of the upgrade set of the base cluster. When a base cluster is opened for write operations, its upgrade set is also opened for processing. Any adds, changes, or deletes on the base cluster are *automatically* reflected in its upgrade set. A base cluster and its upgrade set are kept in synchronization at all times.

An alternate index defined with the NOUPGRADE option does not become a member of the upgrade set. Any updates on the base cluster are not reflected in it. It becomes the user's responsibility to keep it in synchronization with the base cluster.

In our case, both of the alternate indexes of EMPLOYEE.KSDS.CLUSTER were defined with the UPGRADE option.

14.3.2 OPEN and CLOSE

When a base cluster is opened for processing, its alternate index paths are also opened. You don't have to code separate statements for this purpose. Likewise, when a base cluster is closed, the corresponding alternate index paths are also closed. A successful OPEN or CLOSE of the base cluster and all its alternate index paths will result in a status code of 00.

14.3.3 Building an AIX at Base Cluster Load Time

In this section we will discuss two different methods of loading alternate indexes. Let's suppose you have defined a base cluster named EMPLOYEE.KSDS.CLUSTER. You have also defined two alternate indexes and the two corresponding paths over them. The status of the base cluster and both the alternate indexes will be *unloaded* at this time because neither one of them contains any records yet. To load records into the base cluster, the file will be opened as OUTPUT in the Cobol program. You might expect that key-pointer records in alternate indexes will automatically be built, since both of them were defined with the UPGRADE option. This will not happen, because the UPGRADE attribute is not effective for an alternate index unless it is built using BLDINDEX. So, the normal procedure under these circumstances would be as follows.

1. Load the base cluster with records, opening it as OUTPUT.
2. Build an alternate index on both members of the UPGRADE

set using the BLDINDEX command separately for each one of them.

After both these functions have been completed, the status of the alternate indexes will be changed from unloaded to loaded. After this, any time the base cluster is opened for updates, all changes will be reflected in the upgrade set.

Let's look at some of the problems that might result from the above approach. Upon execution of BLDINDEX for the Employee-Number AIX, you might find that there is a duplicate key condition on one of the Employee-Numbers. Since they are supposed to be unique, what will you do? Will you delete one of the two records in the base cluster? If so, how? If there had been a procedure for loading alternate indexes at the same time the base cluster was loaded, you could have rejected and displayed such a record and continued with the processing. You could easily test for a status code of 22, which would be generated by this condition.

There is a way to accomplish this with an execution time option of the PARM parameter of the JCL. It is coded as follows.

```
//LOADSTEP  EXEC PGM=YOURPGM,PARM='/AIXBLD'
```

AIXBLD accomplishes the automatic building of all the alternate index key-pointer records while the data records are sequentially loaded into the base cluster. The main advantage of using this method is that your program will detect duplicate key values in unique key alternate indexes and can decide how to handle them at the time of the loading of the base cluster itself. The disadvantage is that, when a Cobol program is being run with this feature, the huge Access Method Services program must also be present. This requires a lot of extra virtual storage.

If you also need to pass application-related information through the PARM parameter, it must be listed before the "/". The slash acts as a delimiter between application-related and system-related values. For example, if you wish to pass the characters ABC to the program, the PARM parameter will be coded as follows.

```
PARM='ABC/AIXBLD'
```

You *must* provide a SYSPRINT DD card in the JCL for Access Method Services messages. Failure to do so will result in a status value of 95 during OPEN processing.

Using BLDINDEX is still the better and more efficient way to load an alternate index, and it should be used whenever possible. For example, if an alternate index cluster itself has multiple CI and CA splits and must be reorganized, the BLDINDEX command would be the appropriate choice. Moreover, while performing a reorganization, you would not expect to find duplicate keys on a unique key alternate index. The run-time option of AIXBLD is handy for loading data sets for the first time, such as when performing a system conversion from non-VSAM to VSAM file organization.

14.3.4 Key of Reference

The key of reference is the key in the base cluster which is currently being used to retrieve records. It may be the prime key or one of the alternate keys. Your program looks at the base cluster records as if they are sequenced on the key of reference. In Chap. 13, we dealt only with the prime key, so the key of reference was always the prime key. In this chapter, we will use the prime key as well as alternate keys to retrieve records. If we are using one of the alternate keys at a particular moment, this key will remain our key of reference until we start to use a different key to access the records. You cannot have more than one key of reference at a time.

14.3.5 READ, READ NEXT, WRITE, REWRITE, and DELETE

The syntax and effect of some of these verbs is slightly different when used in the context of alternate indexes. We will use examples that refer to the data records in the file EMPLOYEE.KSDS.CLUSTER. Figure 14.3(a) gives the contents of this file. There are nine records in it, and the prime key is Employee-SSN in the first nine byte positions.

We will assume that our two alternate indexes were built using the BLDINDEX command. Their contents are shown in Fig. 14.3 (*b*) and (*c*), respectively. (Remember that the first 5 characters, appearing as dots, contain the record control information for alternate indexes.)

READ and READ NEXT To use these statements, the file must be opened as INPUT or I-O. There are two formats, the first being for sequential retrievals:

```
READ file-name [NEXT] [INTO identifier]
    [AT END imperative statement]
```

Note that the INTO and AT END clauses are optional. If ACCESS MODE IS SEQUENTIAL is specified in the SELECT statement, the NEXT clause will also be optional. It has no effect on the sequential retrieval order because retrievals are made in the collating sequence of the key of reference. If ACCESS MODE IS DYNAMIC is specified, the NEXT clause *will* be used for sequential retrievals. Its omission indicates a random retrieval.

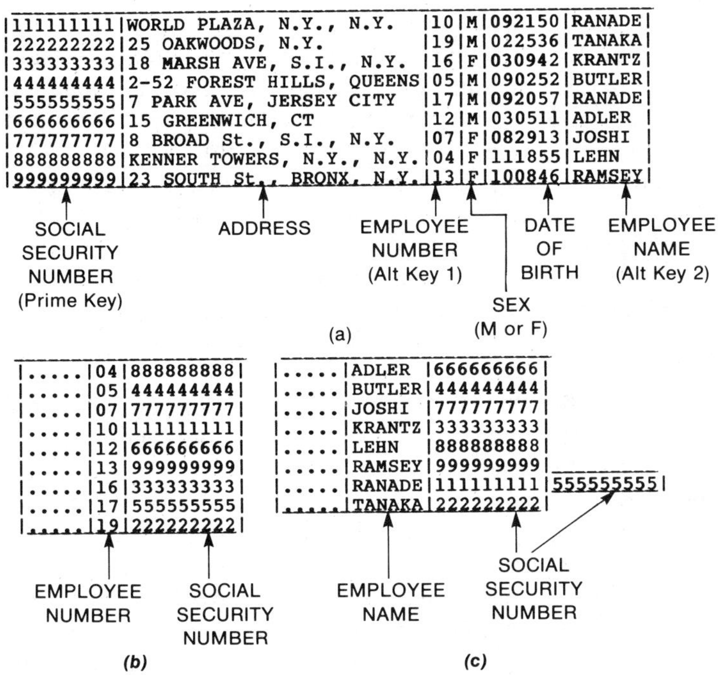

Figure 14.3 (*a*) Data records in the KSDS EMPLOYEE.KSDS.CLUSTER. (*b*) Contents of alternate index on Employee-Number. (*c*) Contents of alternate index on Employee-Name.

Records can be retrieved sequentially using either the prime key or the alternate key sequence. The key of reference identifies which of the keys will be used for retrievals.

When performing sequential reads on the alternate key, a status code of 10 signifies an end-of-file condition on the alternate key sequence. For example, if sequential retrievals are made using the Employee-Number as the key of reference, status code 10 will be returned when a sequential READ or READ NEXT is executed after the record with Employee-Number 19 is returned [Fig. 14.3 (*b*)].

The format for the *random* retrieval of KSDS records is

```
READ  file-name [INTO identifier]
      [KEY is data-name]
    [INVALID KEY imperative statement]
```

ACCESS MODE must be RANDOM or DYNAMIC, and the INTO and INVALID KEY clauses are optional. The KEY IS clause is also optional if retrievals will be sequenced on the prime key alone, because the data-name of the prime key field is the default option. However, if the retrievals must be sequenced on any of the alternate keys, the data-name in the KEY IS clause must be that of the particular alternate key you wish to use. Consider Fig. 14.4 to grasp this concept better. We will assume that ACCESS MODE IS DYNAMIC has been specified and that the data records are those in Fig. 14.3 (*a*), (*b*), and (*c*).

Note that, when accessing data with an alternate key, a status code of 23 indicates a record-not-found condition for that particular alternate key value. Also, the key of reference can be switched between the prime key and any of the alternate keys by using a START or a random READ statement. The OPEN statement always makes the prime key the key of reference.

WRITE The syntax of the WRITE statement was described in the last chapter. The use of alternate indexes does not affect it, but you should be aware of some additional factors.

Before the WRITE statement can be executed for a KSDS, its RECORD KEY must be set to the desired value. After a successful WRITE, the logical record is no longer available in the FD area.

When a record is added to the base cluster with a WRITE, the corresponding entries are automatically applied to each member of the UPGRADE set. This process is transparent, and no additional programming is required. For example, suppose the following record is added to EMPLOYEE.KSDS.CLUSTER.

400000000	Trump Castle, N.Y., N.Y.	01	M	081848	DECKER

In addition to adding a record to the base cluster, the following records will be added to the Employee-Number and Employee-Name alternate indexes, respectively.

. . . . .	01	400000000

. . . . .	DECKER	400000000

Any subsequent retrievals on alternate keys will reflect the corresponding changes. Alternate indexes that are not members of the upgrade set (defined with the NOUPGRADE option of DEFINE AIX) are not updated automatically.

You may wonder what happens if VSAM detects an abnormal situation while performing updates on the members of an upgrade set. For example, let's suppose that a KSDS has 10 alternate indexes in its upgrade set—5 of which are nonunique key and the other 5 are unique key alternate indexes. When a record is being added to the base cluster, an add will also be performed on each member of the upgrade set, one by one. On the

Cobol statement	Key of reference	Record in base cluster retrieved	CRP
OPEN INPUT EMPLOYEE-MASTER.	EMPLOYEE-SSN-KEY	—	111111111
READ EMPLOYEE-MASTER NEXT.	EMPLOYEE-SSN-KEY	111111111	222222222
MOVE '13' TO EMPLOYEE-NUM-KEY. READ EMPLOYEE-MASTER KEY IS EQUAL TO EMPLOYEE-NUM-KEY.	EMPLOYEE-NUM-KEY	999999999	16
READ EMPLOYEE-MASTER NEXT.	EMPLOYEE-NUM-KEY	333333333	17
MOVE 'SMITH' TO EMPLOYEE-NAME-KEY. READ EMPLOYEE-MASTER KEY IS EQUAL TO EMPLOYEE-NAME-KEY.	Record not found. Status code returned is 23		
MOVE 'TANAKA' TO EMPLOYEE-NAME-KEY. READ EMPLOYEE-MASTER KEY IS EQUAL TO EMPLOYEE-NAME-KEY.	EMPLOYEE-NAME-KEY	222222222	End-of-file
READ EMPLOYEE-MASTER NEXT.	Note: status code returned = 10	None	Undefined
READ EMPLOYEE-MASTER NEXT.	Note: status code returned = 94	None	Undefined

Figure 14.4 Example showing the effect of different Cobol statements on the CRP, key of reference, and records retrieved. ACCESS MODE IS DYNAMIC is assumed.

tenth record add to a unique key alternate index, VSAM might detect that it *already* has a record with that alternate key. Will it delete the records added to the base cluster and the other nine alternate indexes? The answer is yes. Although you will get a status code of 22, you can rest assured that the base cluster and the members of the upgrade set are not out of synchronization. Imagine yourself writing code to back out in-flight partial updates on alternate indexes. It's a relief to know that VSAM is responsible for maintaining the data integrity of incomplete updates on alternate indexes in the upgrade set.

REWRITE The syntax of REWRITE is

```
REWRITE record-name [ FROM identifier ]
     [INVALID KEY imperative statement]
```

It is no different than that used without alternate indexes. Normally, a record is read using the READ statement, its contents are changed, and then it is written back using the REWRITE statement. You cannot change the contents of the prime key before REWRITE, otherwise you will get a non-zero status code. The file must be opened as I-O, and ACCESS MODE can be SEQUENTIAL, RANDOM, or DYNAMIC.

One of the best features of REWRITE is that you can change the values of the alternate key fields before rewriting the record. VSAM takes complete responsibility for making the necessary adds and deletes on the alternate indexes of the upgrade set to effect the changes. This feature can best be demonstrated with an example. We will assume that the KSDS involved is that in Fig. 14.3 (*a*) and that its alternate indexes exist as in Fig. 14.3 (*b*) and (*c*).

```
MOVE '444444444' TO EMPLOYEE-SSN-KEY.
READ EMPLOYEE-MASTER.
```

The record returned in the FD area is

444444444	2-52, Forest Hills, Queens	05	M	090252	BUTLER

During processing, the contents of the record are changed to

444444444	2-52, Forest Hills, Queens	11	M	090252	CUTLER

Note that EMPLOYEE-NUM-KEY has been changed from 05 to 11 and that EMPLOYEE-NAME-KEY has been changed from BUTLER to CUTLER.

```
REWRITE EMPLOYEE-RECORD.
```

Upon successful execution of the REWRITE, the following two records will have been deleted from the Employee-Number and Employee-Name alternate indexes.

.....	05	444444444

.....	BUTLER	444444444

Also, the following two records will have been added to the Employee-Number and Employee-Name alternate indexes, respectively.

.....	11	444444444

.....	CUTLER	444444444

The final outcome will be that the base cluster and the alternate indexes in the upgrade set will be in synchronization. No programming effort is required for this. It is done automatically by VSAM and is completely transparent to you. If during any of the adds to the upgrade set VSAM detects an abnormal condition such as a duplicate key for a unique key alternate index, it backs out *all* the changes. In this case, it would nullify all the deletes by performing the corresponding adds for the deleted records. Again, it is transparent to you. However, you will get a non-zero status code signifying failure of completion of the event. Data integrity, the most important factor, is maintained at all times.

Alternate key fields that are not modified before REWRITE are not touched at all. Any changes made in the alternate keys of alternate indexes that are *not* members of the upgrade set are not handled by VSAM.

DELETE The syntax of this statement is the same whether or not you use alternate indexes:

```
DELETE file-name
    [INVALID KEY imperative statement]
```

Deleting records from the base cluster also involves the automatic deletion of records from the alternate indexes in the upgrade set. This function is performed automatically by VSAM. The ACCESS MODE can be SEQUENTIAL, RANDOM, or DYNAMIC, but the file must be opened as I-O.

To elaborate further on the deletion process, let's discuss an example in the context of EMPLOYEE.KSDS.CLUSTER as shown in Fig. 14.3(*a*) and the associated alternate indexes shown in Fig. 14.3(*b*) and (*c*). The following sequence of events explains how the deletion process works.

```
MOVE '999999999' TO EMPLOYEE-SSN-KEY.
READ EMPLOYEE-MASTER.
```

The record returned in the FD area is

999999999	23 South St., Bronx, N.Y.	13	F	100846	RAMSEY

```
DELETE EMPLOYEE-MASTER.
```

The record with SSN = 999999999 will be deleted from the base cluster.

Since Employee-Number and Employee-Name alternate indexes are members of the upgrade set, the following records from these alternate index clusters will also be deleted.

.....	13	999999999	(Employee-Number alternate index)

.....	RAMSEY	999999999	(Employee-Name alternate index)

14.3.6 START Statement

START is used to position the current record pointer and is another way to establish the key of reference. In the previous chapter, our key of reference was always the prime key, and therefore the CRP was always positioned on it. We can also establish an alternate key as the key of reference and establish the CRP on it using the START statement. The syntax of this statement is the same for alternate keys as it is for the prime key:

```
                                ⎧ EQUAL TO        ⎫
                                ⎪ =               ⎪
START file-name [KEY IS         ⎨ GREATER THAN    ⎬ data-name]
                                ⎪ >               ⎪
                                ⎪ NOT LESS THAN   ⎪
                                ⎩ NOT <           ⎭
      [INVALID KEY imperative statement]
```

If the CRP is to be positioned on the prime key, the data-name will refer to the name of the prime key field, which is also the default in this statement. However, if the CRP is to be established on an alternate key, the data-name will refer to the name of the alternate key as given in the record description. In the latter case, the alternate key will also become the key of reference. Subsequent sequential retrievals from this point onward will be in the order of the collating sequence of the key of reference. The key of reference may be changed at any time by executing the START statement again. Note that the START statement only establishes a CRP and a key of reference; it *does not* return any records to the FD area. Retrieval is accomplished only through a READ or READ NEXT statement.

The examples in Fig. 14.5 will make it more clear. We still refer to the records in EMPLOYEE.KSDS.CLUSTER as given in Fig. 14.3(*a*) and its associated alternate indexes as given in Fig. 14.3(*b*) and (*c*).

In these examples, sequential retrievals using READ NEXT (ACCESS MODE IS DYNAMIC) return records in the sequence of the key of reference. We could have used READ if ACCESS CODE IS SEQUENTIAL had been given in the SELECT statement.

14.3.7 CRP AND KEY OF REFERENCE

We have already discussed this topic in the context of the OPEN, READ, READ NEXT, and START verbs. To tie it all together, read the following summary carefully.

1. A successful OPEN always establishes the prime key as the key of reference. The CRP is set on the first logical record in the base cluster.
2. A successfully executed START establishes the key referred to in the data-name as the key of reference. The CRP is set on the logical record that meets the criteria set by the logical operators in the comparison.
3. If the CRP becomes undefined because of an end-of-file condition, a CLOSE statement, an unsuccessful START, or an unsuccessful READ, it must be reestablished. If it is not reestablished, all subsequent sequential READ statements will return a status code of 94.
4. The CRP has no meaning if ACCESS MODE is RANDOM.
5. The CRP is not affected by DELETE, WRITE, or REWRITE.
6. The CRP can be changed or reestablished any number of times during the execution of a program.

The examples in Fig. 14.6 should be reviewed to fully understand the concepts stated above. Note that the interspersed WRITE, REWRITE, and DELETE statements have no effect on the CRP. Refer to Fig. 14.3 for data records.

14.3.8 Generic Search

In order to set the CRP in a KSDS, you can use a generic key instead of the full prime key or full alternate key in the START statement. Consider Fig. 14.7.

In this case, NUM-1 or NAME-1 can be used as a generic key. NUM-2 or NAME-2-TO-6 cannot be used as a generic key because they don't start with the leftmost byte of the full key. This will be clear if you

Cobol statement	Key of reference	Record in base cluster retrieved	CRP
MOVE '222222222' TO EMPLOYEE-SSN-KEY. START EMPLOYEE-MASTER KEY IS GREATER THAN EMPLOYEE-SSN-KEY.	EMPLOYEE-SSN-KEY	—	333333333
READ EMPLOYEE-MASTER NEXT.	EMPLOYEE-SSN-KEY	333333333	444444444
MOVE '18' TO EMPLOYEE-NUM-KEY. START EMPLOYEE-MASTER KEY NOT LESS THAN EMPLOYEE-NUM-KEY.	EMPLOYEE-NUM-KEY	—	19
READ EMPLOYEE-MASTER NEXT.	EMPLOYEE-NUM-KEY	222222222	End-of-file
MOVE 'RANADE' TO EMPLOYEE-NAME-KEY. START EMPLOYEE-MASTER KEY IS EQUAL TO EMPLOYEE-NAME-KEY.	EMPLOYEE-NAME-KEY	—	RANADE 111111111
READ EMPLOYEE-MASTER NEXT.	EMPLOYEE-NAME-KEY	111111111	RANADE 555555555
READ EMPLOYEE-MASTER NEXT.	EMPLOYEE-NAME-KEY	555555555	TANAKA

Figure 14.5 Examples showing use of the START statement and its effect on the CRP and the key of reference. READ NEXT is being used to retrieve records thereafter. ACCESS MODE IS DYNAMIC is assumed.

Statement number	Cobol statement*	Key of reference*	Record in base cluster read, written, or deleted	CRP
1	ACCESS MODE DYNAMIC; OPEN I-O.	SSN-KEY	—	111111111
2	MOVE '555555555' TO SSN-KEY. READ KEY IS EQUAL TO SSN-KEY.	SSN-KEY	555555555	666666666
3	Change address field REWRITE	SSN-KEY	555555555	666666666
4	READ NEXT	SSN-KEY	666666666	777777777
5	MOVE '10' TO NUM-KEY. START KEY IS EQUAL TO NUM-KEY.	NUM-KEY	—	10
6	MOVE '123456789' TO SSN-KEY. MOVE '15' TO NUM-KEY. MOVE 'RETTON' TO NAME-KEY. WRITE.	NUM-KEY	123456789	10
7	READ NEXT.	NUM-KEY	111111111	12
8	MOVE 'TAAAAA' TO NAME-KEY. START KEY IS GREATER THAN NAME-KEY.	NAME-KEY	—	TANAKA
9	MOVE '999999999' TO SSN-KEY. DELETE	NAME-KEY	999999999	TANAKA
10	READ NEXT	NAME-KEY	222222222	End-of-file
11	READ NEXT	—	Status code = 10	No CRP
12	READ NEXT	—	Status code = 94	No CRP
13	CLOSE	—	—	—
14	OPEN INPUT	SSN-KEY	—	111111111

*SSN-KEY = EMPLOYEE-SSN-KEY, NUM-KEY = EMPLOYEE-NUM-KEY, NAME-KEY = EMPLOYEE-NAME-KEY.

Figure 14.6 Examples showing that the CRP and the key of reference are not affected by WRITE, REWRITE, or DELETE.

```
                .
                .
        05  EMPLOYEE-NUM-KEY.
            10  NUM-1-TO-2.
                15  NUM-1              PIC X.
                15  NUM-2              PIC X.
                .
                .
        05  EMPLOYEE-NAME-KEY.
            10  NAME-1-TO-6.
                15  NAME-1             PIC X.
                15  NAME-2-TO-6        PIC X(5).
                .
                .
```

Figure 14.7 Split of alternate keys into their generic components.

review the examples given in Fig. 14.8 as they apply to EMPLOYEE.KSDS.CLUSTER and its alternate indexes containing records as in Fig. 14.3 (*a*), (*b*), and (*c*).

14.3.9 Summary of Permissible Combinations

We already know that KSDS files can have an ACCESS MODE of SEQUENTIAL, RANDOM, or DYNAMIC and that they can be opened as INPUT, OUTPUT, I-O, or EXTEND. The different I/O verbs we can use are OPEN, READ, WRITE, REWRITE, START, DELETE, and CLOSE. Certain combinations of access modes, open modes, and I/O verbs (except CLOSE) are permitted, while others are not. Figure 14.9 provides the permissible combinations in tabular form. This table can be used as a quick reference when needed.

14.4 RETRIEVAL SEQUENCE FOR NONUNIQUE KEY ALTERNATE INDEXES

Sequential retrieval processing through an alternate key defined WITH DUPLICATES permits you to read multiple base cluster records with different prime keys but equal alternate key values. The most important point to remember is that these records are retrieved in the same order in which they were written to the alternate index cluster. If the alternate index cluster was just loaded or reorganized using BLDINDEX, you will get the records in prime key sequence within an alternate key sequence. But, if adds are made to the file later, the prime key storage sequence within an alternate key may not be in ascending order.

Cobol statement	Key of reference	CRP
MOVE '1' TO NUM-1. START EMPLOYEE-MASTER KEY IS EQUAL TO NUM-1.	EMPLOYEE-NUM-KEY	10
MOVE 'R' TO NAME-1. START EMPLOYEE-MASTER KEY IS EQUAL TO NAME-1.	EMPLOYEE-NAME-KEY	RAMSEY
MOVE '1' TO NUM-1. START EMPLOYEE-MASTER KEY IS GREATER THAN NUM-1.	—	Undefined
MOVE 'ANAKA' TO NAME-2-TO-6. START EMPLOYEE-MASTER KEY IS EQUAL TO NAME-2-TO-6.	Probable compilation error. Generic key must start from left most byte of full key	—

The data set is EMPLOYEE.KSDS.CLUSTER with its associated alternate indexes.

Figure 14.8 Use of generic keys in a START statement and its effect on the CRP for a particular key of reference.

ACCESS MODE	OPEN mode: INPUT	OUTPUT	I-O	EXTEND
SEQUENTIAL	OPEN READ START	OPEN WRITE	OPEN READ START REWRITE DELETE	OPEN WRITE
RANDOM	OPEN READ	OPEN WRITE	OPEN READ WRITE REWRITE DELETE	
DYNAMIC	OPEN READ START	OPEN WRITE	OPEN READ START WRITE REWRITE DELETE	

Figure 14.9 I/O verbs allowed with particular ACCESS MODEs and OPEN modes.

Let's consider an example. Suppose one of the records in the Employee-Name alternate index is as follows.

.....	LEHN	888888888

Now let's add the following two records to the base cluster in the order shown.

666000000	25 Greenwich Vill, N.Y.	11	F	080857	LEHN
555000000	3rd Ave, Suffolk, N.Y.	18	M	070552	LEHN

Since the Employee-Name alternate index is a member of the upgrade set, it will also be updated. Successful updates will result in the following record:

.....	LEHN	888888888	666000000	555000000

As you can see, VSAM does not store the prime keys in ascending sequence. It adds them in the order that they are processed. When you retrieve records with the alternate key 'LEHN ', they will be returned as follows.

888888888	Kenner Towers, N.Y., N.Y.	04	F	111855	LEHN
666000000	25 Greenwich Vill, N.Y.	11	F	080857	LEHN
555000000	3rd Ave, Suffolk, N.Y.	18	M	070552	LEHN

If the alternate index file is reorganized using the BLDINDEX command, the same record will look like

.....	LEHN	555000000	666000000	888888888

As you can see, the records can now be retrieved in the ascending sequence of the prime key within the alternate key. This often ignored fact must be kept in mind when developing program logic involving nonunique key alternate index(es). You will recall that to reorganize an alternate index you must delete it (DELETE), redefine it (DEFINE AIX), and rebuild it (BLDINDEX).

14.5 LOGIC OF DUPLICATE KEY CONDITION

If you are processing a KSDS *without* alternate indexes, a duplicate key condition indicates that you are trying to add a record with a key value that the base cluster already has. You will receive a status code of 22. If you are processing a KSDS *with* alternate indexes, a duplicate key condition is the result of one of three possible situations.

14.5.1 Permissible Duplicate Key during READ

If a status code of 02 is returned following a READ, it indicates that a permissible duplicate key follows. It is an expected situation. Consider the Cobol statements in Fig. 14.10 as they pertain to the data in Fig. 14.3.

The first READ returns a status code of 02 to the program to indicate that at least one record with the same nonunique alternate key

```
           MOVE 'RANADE'  TO  EMPLOYEE-NAME-KEY.
           START  EMPLOYEE-MASTER
                  KEY = EMPLOYEE-NAME-KEY.
*******************************************************
***    NOTE: STATUS CODE = '00';NO RECORD READ ***
*******************************************************
           READ  EMPLOYEE-MASTER  NEXT.
*******************************************************
***    NOTE: RECORD READ IS WITH KEY 111111111  ***
***      STATUS CODE IS '02' BECAUSE ANOTHER    ***
***       RECORD WITH THE SAME NAME FOLLOWS.    ***
*******************************************************
           READ  EMPLOYEE-MASTER NEXT.
*******************************************************
***    NOTE: RECORD READ IS WITH KEY 555555555  ***
***      STATUS CODE IS '00' BECAUSE NO OTHER   ***
***       RECORD WITH THE SAME KEY EXISTS.      ***
*******************************************************
```

Figure 14.10 Example of a duplicate key condition (status code 02) on a READ through a nonunique key alternate index.

follows. Your program logic should probably perform READ NEXT operations until the status code becomes 00. A status code of 00 indicates that the last record following the ones with the same nonunique key has been read. No status key testing is shown in this example, but you should never ignore it in your own program.

14.5.2 Permissible Duplicate Key during WRITE or REWRITE

If a status code of 02 is returned on a WRITE or REWRITE, it indicates that a permissible duplicate key has been created on one or more alternate indexes. Needless to say, these alternate indexes must be defined as nonunique key. Consider the Cobol statements in Fig. 14.11 as they pertain to the data in Fig. 14.3.

Note that a status code of 02 on a WRITE or REWRITE indicates only an expected situation. It does not indicate an error, because at the time of DEFINE AIX you specified the NONUNIQUEKEY parameter to indicate the characteristics of the key involved. However, when more than one nonunique key alternate index is involved, a status code of 02 *does not* indicate which alternate key or keys triggered this situation.

14.5.3 Nonpermissible Duplicate Key during WRITE or REWRITE

If a status code of 22 is returned on a WRITE or REWRITE, it can mean that you are trying to add a record with an existing prime key and/or an existing unique key alternate index key. You cannot determine which one

```
           MOVE '555000000'   TO   EMPLOYEE-SSN-KEY.
           MOVE '01'          TO   EMPLOYEE-NUM-KEY.
           MOVE 'ADLER '      TO   EMPLOYEE-NAME-KEY.
           WRITE  EMPLOYEE-RECORD.
      *****************************************************
      ***          RECORD ADD IS SUCCESSFUL             ***
      *** STATUS CODE IS '02' BECAUSE A RECORD WITH     ***
      *** ALTERNATE KEY 'ADLER ' ALREADY EXISTS         ***
      *****************************************************
           MOVE '999999999'   TO   EMPLOYEE-SSN-KEY.
           READ EMPLOYEE-MASTER.
           MOVE 'BUTLER'      TO   EMPLOYEE-NAME-KEY.
           REWRITE  EMPLOYEE-RECORD.
      *****************************************************
      ***        RECORD REWRITE IS SUCCESSFUL           ***
      *** STATUS CODE IS '02' BECAUSE A RECORD WITH     ***
      *** ALTERNATE KEY 'BUTLER' ALREADY EXISTS.        ***
      *** NOTE THAT ALTERNATE KEY RECORD 'RAMSEY'       ***
      *** WILL BE DELETED.                              ***
      *****************************************************
```

Figure 14.11 Example of a duplicate key condition (status code 02) on a WRITE and a REWRITE.

```
     MOVE  '444444444'  TO EMPLOYEE-SSN-KEY.
     MOVE  '02'         TO EMPLOYEE-NUM-KEY.
     MOVE  'CHENG '     TO EMPLOYEE-NAME-KEY.
     WRITE EMPLOYEE-RECORD.
*****************************************************
***           RECORD ADD IS UNSUCCESSFUL          ***
*** STATUS CODE IS '22' BECAUSE A RECORD WITH     ***
*** PRIME KEY '444444444' ALREADY EXISTS.         ***
*****************************************************
     MOVE  '333333333'  TO EMPLOYEE-SSN-KEY.
     READ  EMPLOYEE-MASTER.
     MOVE  '19'         TO EMPLOYEE-NUM-KEY.
     REWRITE  EMPLOYEE-RECORD.
*****************************************************
***         RECORD REWRITE IS UNSUCCESSFUL        ***
*** STATUS CODE IS '22' BECAUSE A RECORD WITH     ***
*** ALTERNATE KEY '19' ALREADY EXISTS IN THE      ***
*** EMPLOYEE-NUMBER ALTERNATE INDEX.              ***
*****************************************************
```

Figure 14.12 Example of a duplicate key condition (status code 22) on a WRITE and a REWRITE.

of the above situations caused it or if it was a combination of both. If you have multiple unique key alternate indexes, it also does not tell you which one or ones of those caused this status code. The best thing to do in such circumstances is to display the record that caused the status code and continue processing. Later on, you may use other techniques (AMS commands such as PRINT, etc.) to determine the cause of the condition. The Cobol statements in Fig. 14.12, as they refer to data in Fig. 14.3, may be reviewed to familiarize yourself with this situation.

14.6 JCL FOR ALTERNATE INDEXES

When using alternate indexes in a Cobol program, you must specify a DD statement for the base cluster and for each alternate index path. The DD name for the base cluster is part of the assignment name in the SELECT statement. For the SELECT statement coded in Fig. 14.2 the DD name for the base cluster is EMPMSTR. However, Cobol does not have a language mechanism for explicitly declaring DD names for the alternate paths. The convention that has developed for assigning DD names for the alternate key paths is to take the base cluster DD name and append a 1 to it for the first alternate index path. The suffix is incremented by 1 for each successive path associated with an alternate index.

In our case, the DD name for the base cluster is EMPMSTR and, according to convention, the DD names for both paths are EMPMSTR1 and EMPMSTR2. The JCL for the SELECT clause in Fig. 14.2 appears in Fig. 14.13.

```
//VSAMJOB   JOB (ACCTNO),'JAY RANADE'
//AIXSTEP   EXEC PGM=AIXPGM
//EMPMSTR   DD DSN=EMPLOYEE.KSDS.CLUSTER,
//             DISP=SHR
//EMPMSTR1  DD DSN=EMPLOYEE.KSDS.PATH1,
//             DISP=SHR
//EMPMSTR2  DD DSN=EMPLOYEE.KSDS.PATH2,
//             DISP=SHR
//
```

Figure 14.13 JCL for the SELECT clause given in Fig. 14.2.

Note that the data set names for EMPMSTR1 and EMPMSTR2 are the PATH names and *not* the alternate index cluster names.

If the DD name for the base cluster is 8 characters long, you cannot append another digit to it. Again according to convention, you must truncate the rightmost character of the DD name and then append the suffix. If you have more than 9 alternate indexes on the base cluster, you might have to drop the rightmost 2 characters from the DD name. Similarly, if you have more than 99 alternate indexes, you might have to drop the rightmost 3 characters from the DD name. Let's take an extreme example. Suppose a base cluster has 100 alternate indexes and its assignment name (DD name) is BASECLST:

DD name for the 1st path will be BASECLS1

DD name for the 9th path will be BASECLS9

DD name for the 10th path will be BASECL10

DD name for the 99th path will be BASECL99

DD name for the 100th path will be BASEC100

In our example, the only assignment name in the SELECT statement will be BASECLST. The other DD names for the paths are derived from this name. Make sure that the sequence of ALTERNATE KEY IS clauses has one-to-one correspondence with the sequence of DD names for the paths.

14.7 PROGRAM EXAMPLE 1: SEQUENTIAL LOAD OF AN UNLOADED KSDS WITH ALTERNATE INDEXES USING THE AIXBLD FEATURE

In the last chapter, we reviewed a program that loaded records into an unloaded KSDS assuming that the base cluster did not have any alternate indexes. Now, we will write a program that not only will load the base cluster but will also build the alternate index clusters concurrently using the object time AIXBLD option. The program logic will be more or less the same as in the last chapter. The SELECT statement must include the ALTERNATE RECORD KEY IS clause for each alternate index to be built. In addition to the status code of 21 (incoming records out of sequence), we will also test for a status code of 22 (duplicate records). As we already know, the advantage of building alternate indexes at object time is to reject duplicate records on unique key alternate indexes. The status code of 02 will be ignored, because the Employee-Name alternate index permits nonunique keys. Any status code other than 00, 02, 21, or 22 will be indicative of a serious error, and the program will cause a user abend. To keep the logic simple, no editing will be done to check the validity of the input data. Figure 14.14 gives the code for the complete program.

Note that the SELECT statement includes ALTERNATE RECORD KEY IS clauses, which are a must if the AIXBLD option is to be used. In addition, all the rejected records are displayed using a DISPLAY statement.

```
IDENTIFICATION DIVISION.
PROGRAM-ID.    AIXBLDPG.
AUTHOR.        RANADE.
**************************************************
*** THIS PROGRAM READS A PHYSICAL SEQUENTIAL ****
***    FILE SORTED ON PRIME KEY AND LOADS     ****
***      RECORDS INTO KSDS (EMPMSTR).         ****
***   OBJECT TIME OPTION OF AIXBLD WILL BE    ****
***     USED TO BUILD ALTERNATE INDEXES.      ****
**************************************************

ENVIRONMENT DIVISION.
CONFIGURATION SECTION.
INPUT-OUTPUT SECTION.
FILE-CONTROL.
    SELECT  INPUT-FILE
            ASSIGN TO UT-S-INPUT.
    SELECT  EMPLOYEE-MASTER
            ASSIGN TO  EMPMSTR
            ORGANIZATION IS INDEXED
            ACCESS MODE IS SEQUENTIAL
            RECORD KEY IS EMPLOYEE-SSN-KEY
            ALTERNATE RECORD KEY IS EMPLOYEE-NUM-KEY
            ALTERNATE RECORD KEY IS EMPLOYEE-NAME-KEY
                      WITH DUPLICATES
            FILE STATUS IS EMPLOYEE-FILE-STATUS.

DATA DIVISION.
FILE SECTION.
FD  INPUT-FILE
    LABEL RECORDS ARE STANDARD
    RECORD CONTAINS 50 CHARACTERS
    BLOCK CONTAINS 0 RECORDS.
01  INPUT-RECORD                      PIC X(50).
```

Figure 14.14 Program listing for the sequential loading of EMPLOYEE.KSDS. CLUSTER and building its associated alternate indexes at object time.

```
 FD  EMPLOYEE-MASTER
     LABEL RECORDS ARE STANDARD.
 01  EMPLOYEE-RECORD.
     05  EMPLOYEE-SSN-KEY          PIC X(9).
     05  EMPLOYEE-ADDRESS          PIC X(26).
     05  EMPLOYEE-NUM-KEY          PIC X(2).
     05  EMPLOYEE-SEX              PIC X.
     05  EMPLOYEE-DOB              PIC X(6).
     05  EMPLOYEE-NAME-KEY         PIC X(6).

 WORKING-STORAGE SECTION.
 01  EMPLOYEE-FILE-STATUS          PIC X(2).
 01  ABEND-PROGRAM                 PIC X(8)
                              VALUE 'ILBOABNO'.
 01  ABEND-CODE                    PIC S999 COMP
                              VALUE +999.

 PROCEDURE DIVISION.
 100-MAIN-PARA.
     OPEN OUTPUT EMPLOYEE-MASTER.
*******************************************************
***  TEST FOR SUCESSFUL OPEN OF VSAM DATASET ****
*******************************************************
     IF   EMPLOYEE-FILE-STATUS = '00'
          NEXT SENTENCE
     ELSE
          DISPLAY 'OPEN ERROR ON EMPMSTR'
          DISPLAY 'STATUS CODE IS  '
                   EMPLOYEE-FILE-STATUS
          CALL ABEND-PROGRAM USING ABEND-CODE.

     OPEN INPUT INPUT-FILE.
     PERFORM  200-LOAD-EMPMSTR THRU 200-EXIT.

     CLOSE INPUT-FILE
           EMPLOYEE-MASTER.
*******************************************************
***  TEST FOR SUCESSFUL CLOSE OF VSAM DATASET ***
*******************************************************
     IF   EMPLOYEE-FILE-STATUS = '00'
          NEXT SENTENCE
     ELSE
          DISPLAY 'CLOSE ERROR ON EMPMSTR'
          DISPLAY 'STATUS CODE IS  '
                   EMPLOYEE-FILE-STATUS
          CALL ABEND-PROGRAM USING ABEND-CODE.
     GOBACK.

 200-LOAD-EMPMSTR.
     READ  INPUT-FILE
           AT END GO TO 200-EXIT.
     MOVE INPUT-RECORD TO EMPLOYEE-RECORD.
     WRITE EMPLOYEE-RECORD.
*******************************************************
***  TEST FOR SUCESSFUL WRITE TO VSAM DATASET ***
*******************************************************
     IF   EMPLOYEE-FILE-STATUS = '00' OR '02'
          GO TO 200-LOAD-EMPMSTR
```

```
           ELSE
                IF    EMPLOYEE-FILE-STATUS = '21'
                      DISPLAY 'OUT OF SEQUENCE RECORD '
                              INPUT-RECORD
                      GO TO 200-LOAD-EMPMSTR
                ELSE
                      IF    EMPLOYEE-FILE-STATUS = '22'
                            DISPLAY 'DUPLICATE RECORD
                                    INPUT-RECORD
                            GO TO 200-LOAD-EMPMSTR
                      ELSE
                            DISPLAY 'SEVERE VSAM ERROR'
                            DISPLAY 'STATUS CODE IS   '
                                    EMPLOYEE-FILE-STATUS
                            CALL ABEND-PROGRAM USING ABEND-CODE.
       200-EXIT.
           EXIT.
```

Figure 14.14 *(continued)*

The JCL in Fig. 14.15 can be used to run this program.

Note the use of AIXBLD in the PARM parameter. The SYSPRINT DD statement is a must for AMS messages; otherwise you will get an open error with a file status of 95. Remember that the path names *must* be used instead of the alternate index cluster names.

Now let's run this program by executing the JCL in Fig. 14.15. The data records in the input file are sorted on the prime key. Their contents appear in Fig. 14.16.

```
//AIXBLD    JOB (ACCTNO),'JAY RANADE'
//LOADSTEP  EXEC PGM=AIXBLDPG,PARM='/AIXBLD'
//STEPLIB   DD DSN=SAMPLE.PROGRAM.LOAD,DISP=SHR
//          DD DSN=SYS1.COBLIB,DISP=SHR
//SYSPRINT  DD SYSOUT=A
//INPUT     DD DSN=SAMPLE.LOAD.DATA,
//             DISP=OLD
//EMPMSTR   DD DSN=EMPLOYEE.KSDS.CLUSTER,
//             DISP=SHR
//EMPMSTR1  DD DSN=EMPLOYEE.KSDS.PATH1,
//             DISP=SHR
//EMPMSTR2  DD DSN=EMPLOYEE.KSDS.PATH2,
//             DISP=SHR
//SYSOUT    DD SYSOUT=A
//DISPLAY   DD SYSOUT=A
//SYSUDUMP  DD SYSOUT=A
//
```

Figure 14.15 JCL for executing the AIXBLDPG program for building alternate indexes at object time.

```
Record  1   |111111111|WORLD PLAZA, N.Y., N.Y.   |10|M|092150|RANADE|
Record  2   |222222222|25 OAKWOODS, N.Y.         |19|M|022536|TANAKA|
Record  3   |222233333|CHELSEA AVE, N.Y., N.Y.   |10|F|010159|ORTEGA|
Record  4   |333333333|18 MARSH AVE, S.I., N.Y.  |16|F|030942|KRANTZ|
Record  5   |444444444|2-52 FOREST HILLS, QUEENS|05|M|090252|BUTLER|
Record  6   |444455555|52 MURRAY HILLS, N.Y.     |11|M|091854|RANADE|
Record  7   |555555555|7 PARK AVE, JERSEY CITY   |17|M|092057|RANADE|
Record  8   |555566666|23 PEACE TOWER. N.Y.      |19|F|020852|CHOU  |
Record  9   |666666666|15 GREENWICH, CT          |12|M|030511|ADLER |
Record 10   |666677777|85 RICHARD LANE, N.Y.     |02|M|081860|RANADE|
Record 11   |777777777|8 BROAD ST., S.I., NY     |07|F|082913|JOSHI |
Record 12   |777788888|NICHOLAS TERRACE. NY      |01|F|120349|RANADE|
Record 13   |888888888|KENNER TOWERS, N.Y., NY   |04|F|111855|LEHN  |
Record 14   |888899999|10 DOWNING ST, N.Y.       |08|F|060553|RANADE|
Record 15   |999999999|23 SOUTH St, BRONX, N.Y.  |13|F|100846|RAMSEY|
```

UNIQUE KEY (Prime) — UNIQUE KEY (Alternate) — NONUNIQUE KEY (Alternate)

Figure 14.16 Data records in SAMPLE.LOAD.DATA for executing the AIXBLDPG program.

You will notice that there are 15 records in the file. Nine of them are the same as those in Fig 14.3 (*a*). The other six have been added to cause permissible and nonpermissible duplicate record conditions. Let's look at the expected results of each add in Fig. 14.17.

Record numbers 3 and 8 cause a duplicate record condition (status code 22) because we are trying to add a second record with a key identical

Record number	Status code	Explanation
1	00	Add successful
2	00	Add successful
3	22	Duplicate record condition on Employee-Num-Key = 10
4	00	Add successful
5	00	Add successful
6	02	Permissible duplicate record; ignored
7	02	Permissible duplicate record; ignored
8	22	Duplicate record condition on Employee-Num-Key = 19
9	00	Add successful
10	02	Permissible duplicate record; ignored
11	00	Add successful
12	02	Permissible duplicate record; ignored
13	00	Add successful
14	02	Permissible duplicate record; ignored
15	00	Add successful

Figure 14.17 Analysis of the effect of each record in program AIXBLDPG.

to one already in the unique key alternate index. Record numbers 6, 7, 10, 12, and 14 cause permissible duplicate record conditions (status code 02) because we are trying to add records with a key identical to one in the nonunique key alternate index. After adding record number 14, the alternate index record with the key RANADE will look like

.....	RANADE	111111111	444455555	555555555
		666677777	777788888	888899999

14.7.1 Automatic ALTER with AIXBLD

The AIXBLD feature, when invoked, issues an ALTER command to modify the RECORDSIZE and KEYS parameters of the base cluster. It also issues multiple ALTER commands to change the KEYS parameter of the alternate indexes. It gets these values from the record description and SELECT statement of the Cobol program. So, no matter what values you specified at the time the base cluster and the alternate indexes were allocated, they will be overridden (if incorrect) when our load program is executed. This feature of AIXBLD has been provided to correct any specification errors you may have made in the DEFINE parameters.

In our example, the RECORDSIZE and KEYS parameters were omitted completely at the time of the DEFINE CLUSTER and DEFINE AIX. The default values given to them by AMS were

```
RECORDSIZE(4086,32600)
KEYS(64,0)
```

When our program was executed and the AIXBLD feature was invoked by AMS, it did the following.

1. ALTER these values in the base cluster and alternate indexes to the correct values.
2. Load the base cluster with dummy records.
3. Issue BLDINDEX to update the alternate indexes with the dummy records.
4. Delete the dummy records from the base cluster and alternate indexes.
5. Proceed with the regular loading of the base cluster and its upgrade set.

Note that items 1 to 4 are completely transparent to you. When reading the program source listings, you probably noticed that there is no code or logic given to provide these features explicitly. Figure 14.18 shows the AMS and display messages produced by executing the program.

```
 ALTER EMPLOYEE.KSDS.CLUSTER                                          -
 RECORDSIZE( 00050 00050 ) KEYS( 009 00000)

IDC0531I ENTRY EMPLOYEE.KSDS.CLUSTER ALTERED

IDC0001I FUNCTION COMPLETED, HIGHEST CONDITION CODE WAS 0



 ALTER EMPLOYEE.KSDS.PATH1                                            -
                              KEYS( 002 00035)

IDC0531I ENTRY EMPLOYEE.KSDS.PATH1 ALTERED

IDC0001I FUNCTION COMPLETED, HIGHEST CONDITION CODE WAS 0



 ALTER EMPLOYEE.KSDS.PATH2                                            -
                              KEYS( 006 00044)

IDC0531I ENTRY EMPLOYEE.KSDS.PATH2 ALTERED

IDC0001I FUNCTION COMPLETED, HIGHEST CONDITION CODE WAS 0



 BLDINDEX INFILE( EMPMSTR           ) OUTFILE( EMPMSTR1          )

IDC0652I EMPLOYEE.KSDS.PATH1 SUCCESSFULLY BUILT

IDC0001I FUNCTION COMPLETED, HIGHEST CONDITION CODE WAS 0

 BLDINDEX INFILE( EMPMSTR           ) OUTFILE( EMPMSTR2          )

IDC0652I EMPLOYEE.KSDS.PATH2 SUCCESSFULLY BUILT

IDC0001I FUNCTION COMPLETED, HIGHEST CONDITION CODE WAS 0
```

(a)

```
DUPLICATE RECORD       222233333 CHELSEA AV,N.Y,N.Y       10F010159ORTEGA
DUPLICATE RECORD       555566666 23,PEACE TOWER,N.Y       19F020852CHOU
```

(b)

Figure 14.18 Access Method Services and display messages produced by executing the AIXBLDPG program on the data in Fig. 14.16. (*a*) SYSPRINT messages from AIXBLD. (*b*) SYSOUT messages from the program.

14.8 PROGRAM EXAMPLE 2: RANDOM UPDATE OF A KSDS WITH AN UPGRADE SET

For this example, we will use the base cluster EMPLOYEE.KSDS.CLUSTER. It has the alternate indexes and paths defined in Chap. 9. Their names are

EMPLOYEE.KSDS.AIX1.CLUSTER
EMPLOYEE.KSDS.PATH1
EMPLOYEE.KSDS.AIX2.CLUSTER
EMPLOYEE.KSDS.PATH2

The base cluster is loaded with records, and the alternate indexes have already been built using BLDINDEX.

In this program, we will use a transaction file similar in structure to the one used for the KSDSUPDT program in the last chapter. Its record length is 51 bytes. The first byte contains A, C, or D to indicate whether the transaction is to be used for adding, changing, or deleting a record in the KSDS. The rest of the fields have a one-to-one correspondence with the fields of the KSDS record.

We already know that the upgrade set of the base cluster is automatically updated by VSAM when a change is made in the base cluster. There is no specific processing logic in the program to take care of this feature. However, the program must have the logic to anticipate and take care of status codes of 02 and 22, indicating permissible duplicate record and nonpermissible duplicate record conditions, respectively. To keep the code simple, we will not edit the input data. Since the access mode used is RANDOM, the records in the input transaction file don't have to be sorted. Figure 14.19 shows a sample listing for this program.

```
IDENTIFICATION DIVISION.
PROGRAM-ID.  KSAIXUPD.
AUTHOR.      RANADE.
**************************************************
*** THIS PROGRAM READS A PS FILE AND BASED    ****
*** ON UPDATE CODE A,C OR D, IT ADDS,DELETES  ****
***        OR CHANGES RECORDS IN  EMPMSTR.    ****
**************************************************

ENVIRONMENT DIVISION.
CONFIGURATION SECTION.
INPUT-OUTPUT SECTION.
FILE-CONTROL.

        SELECT  TRANS-FILE
                ASSIGN TO UT-S-TRANS.

        SELECT  EMPLOYEE-MASTER
                ASSIGN TO  EMPMSTR
                ORGANIZATION IS INDEXED
                ACCESS MODE  IS RANDOM
                RECORD KEY IS EMPLOYEE-SSN-KEY
                ALTERNATE RECORD KEY IS EMPLOYEE-EMPNUM
                ALTERNATE RECORD KEY IS EMPLOYEE-EMPNAME
                          WITH DUPLICATES
                FILE STATUS IS EMPLOYEE-FILE-STATUS.

DATA DIVISION.
FILE SECTION.
FD   TRANS-FILE
        LABEL RECORDS ARE STANDARD
        RECORD CONTAINS 51 CHARACTERS
        BLOCK CONTAINS 0 RECORDS.
```

Figure 14.19 Program listing for the random update of EMPLOYEE.KSDS.CLUSTER and its upgrade set. The transaction file is SAMPLE.AIXUPDT.DATA. The program takes care of adds, changes, and deletes.

```
 01   TRANS-RECORD.
      05   TRANS-CODE                 PIC X.
      05   TRANS-KEY                  PIC X(9).
      05   TRANS-REST.
           10   TRANS-EMPADD          PIC X(26).
           10   TRANS-EMPNUM          PIC X(2).
           10   TRANS-EMPSEX          PIC X.
           10   TRANS-EMPDOB          PIC X(6).
           10   TRANS-EMPNAME         PIC X(6).


 FD   EMPLOYEE-MASTER
      LABEL RECORDS ARE STANDARD.
 01   EMPLOYEE-RECORD.
      05   EMPLOYEE-SSN-KEY           PIC X(9).
      05   EMPLOYEE-REST.
           10   EMPLOYEE-EMPADD       PIC X(26).
           10   EMPLOYEE-EMPNUM       PIC X(2).
           10   EMPLOYEE-EMPSEX       PIC X.
           10   EMPLOYEE-EMPDOB       PIC X(6).
           10   EMPLOYEE-EMPNAME      PIC X(6).
 WORKING-STORAGE SECTION.
 01   EMPLOYEE-FILE-STATU             PIC X(2).
 01   ABEND-PROGRAM                   PIC X(8)
                               VALUE 'ILBOABNO'.
 01   ABEND-CODE                      PIC S999 COMP
                               VALUE +999.
 PROCEDURE DIVISION.
 100-MAIN-PARA.
      OPEN  I-O   EMPLOYEE-MASTER.
*****************************************************
***  TEST FOR SUCESSFUL OPEN OF VSAM DATASET ****
*****************************************************
      IF   EMPLOYEE-FILE-STATUS = '00'
           NEXT SENTENCE
      ELSE
           DISPLAY 'OPEN ERROR ON EMPMSTR'
           DISPLAY 'STATUS CODE IS  '
                   EMPLOYEE-FILE-STATUS
           CALL ABEND-PROGRAM USING ABEND-CODE.
      OPEN INPUT TRANS-FILE.
      PERFORM  200-UPDATE-EMPMSTR THRU 200-EXIT.
      CLOSE TRANS-FILE
            EMPLOYEE-MASTER.
*****************************************************
***  TEST FOR SUCESSFUL CLOSE OF VSAM DATASET ***
*****************************************************
      IF   EMPLOYEE-FILE-STATUS = '00'
           NEXT SENTENCE
      ELSE
           DISPLAY 'CLOSE ERROR ON EMPMSTR'
           DISPLAY 'STATUS CODE IS  '
                   EMPLOYEE-FILE-STATUS
           CALL ABEND-PROGRAM USING ABEND-CODE.
      GOBACK.
 200-UPDATE-EMPMSTR.
      READ  TRANS-FILE
            AT END GO TO 200-EXIT.
      IF   TRANS-CODE = 'A'
           PERFORM 300-ADD-RECORD
                   THRU 300-EXIT
      ELSE
           IF   TRANS-CODE = 'D'
                PERFORM 400-DELETE-RECORD
                        THRU 400-EXIT
```

```
                ELSE
                     IF    TRANS-CODE = 'C'
                           PERFORM 500-CHANGE-RECORD
                                   THRU 500-EXIT
                     ELSE
                           DISPLAY 'ILLEGAL TRANS CODE FOR'
                           DISPLAY 'RECORD ' TRANS-RECORD.
                GO TO 200-UPDATE-EMPMSTR.
       200-EXIT.
           EXIT.

       300-ADD-RECORD.
           MOVE TRANS-KEY TO EMPLOYEE-SSN-KEY.
           MOVE TRANS-REST TO EMPLOYEE-REST.
           WRITE  EMPLOYEE-RECORD.
      *****************************************************
      ***  TEST FOR SUCESSFUL  ADD TO  VSAM DATASET ***
      *****************************************************
           IF    EMPLOYEE-FILE-STATUS = '00' OR '02'
                DISPLAY 'ADD SUCCESSFUL,STATUS CODE IS   '
                        EMPLOYEE-FILE-STATUS
                DISPLAY 'RECORD IS   ' TRANS-RECORD
                GO TO 300-EXIT
           ELSE
                IF    EMPLOYEE-FILE-STATUS = '22'
                      DISPLAY 'DUPLICATE RECORD ON ADD '
                      DISPLAY 'RECORD IS   ' TRANS-RECORD
                      GO TO 300-EXIT
                ELSE
                      DISPLAY 'SERIOUS ERROR ON ADD '
                      DISPLAY 'STATUS CODE IS  '
                              EMPLOYEE-FILE-STATUS
                      DISPLAY 'RECORD IS   ' TRANS-RECORD
                      CALL ABEND-PROGRAM USING ABEND-CODE.
       300-EXIT.
           EXIT.
       400-DELETE-RECORD.
           MOVE TRANS-KEY TO EMPLOYEE-SSN-KEY.
           DELETE EMPLOYEE-MASTER.
      *****************************************************
      ***  TEST FOR SUCESSFUL DELETE IN VSAM DATASET***
      *****************************************************
           IF    EMPLOYEE-FILE-STATUS = '00'
                DISPLAY 'DELETE SUCCESSFUL   '
                DISPLAY 'RECORD IS   ' TRANS-RECORD
                GO TO 400-EXIT
           ELSE
                IF    EMPLOYEE-FILE-STATUS = '23'
                      DISPLAY 'RECORD NOT FOUND ON DELETE '
                      DISPLAY  'RECORD IS   ' TRANS-RECORD
                      GO TO 400-EXIT
                ELSE
                      DISPLAY 'SERIOUS ERROR ON DELETE'
                      DISPLAY 'STATUS CODE IS  '
                              EMPLOYEE-FILE-STATUS
                      DISPLAY 'RECORD IS   ' TRANS-RECORD
                      CALL ABEND-PROGRAM USING ABEND-CODE.
       400-EXIT.
           EXIT.
       500-CHANGE-RECORD.
           MOVE TRANS-KEY TO EMPLOYEE-SSN-KEY.
           READ EMPLOYEE-MASTER.
```

Figure 14.19 (*continued*)

```
*************************************************************
***   TEST FOR SUCESSFUL READ  OF VSAM RECORD   ***
*************************************************************
       IF    EMPLOYEE-FILE-STATUS = '00'
             NEXT SENTENCE
       ELSE
             IF    EMPLOYEE-FILE-STATUS = '23'
                   DISPLAY 'RECORD NOT FOUND ON READ'
                   DISPLAY 'RECORD IS   ' TRANS-RECORD
                   GO TO 500-EXIT
             ELSE
                   DISPLAY 'SERIOUS ERROR ON READ '
                   DISPLAY 'STATUS CODE IS   '
                              EMPLOYEE-FILE-STATUS
                   DISPLAY 'RECORD IS   ' TRANS-RECORD
                   CALL ABEND-PROGRAM USING ABEND-CODE.
       IF    TRANS-EMPADD   NOT = SPACES
             MOVE TRANS-EMPADD   TO EMPLOYEE-EMPADD.
       IF    TRANS-EMPNUM   NOT = SPACES
             MOVE TRANS-EMPNUM   TO EMPLOYEE-EMPNUM.
       IF    TRANS-EMPSEX   NOT = SPACES
             MOVE TRANS-EMPSEX   TO EMPLOYEE-EMPSEX.
       IF    TRANS-EMPDOB   NOT = SPACES
             MOVE TRANS-EMPDOB   TO EMPLOYEE-EMPDOB.
       IF    TRANS-EMPNAME NOT = SPACES
             MOVE TRANS-EMPNAME TO EMPLOYEE-EMPNAME.
       REWRITE  EMPLOYEE-RECORD.
*************************************************************
***   TEST FOR SUCESSFUL  REWRITE TO VSAM FILE ***
*************************************************************
       IF    EMPLOYEE-FILE-STATUS = '00' OR '02'
             DISPLAY 'REWRITE SUCCESSFUL   '
             DISPLAY 'STATUS CODE IS   '
                        EMPLOYEE-FILE-STATUS
             DISPLAY 'RECORD IS   ' TRANS-RECORD
             GO TO 500-EXIT
       ELSE
                   IF    EMPLOYEE-FILE-STATUS = '22'
                         DISPLAY 'DUPLICATE RECORD ON REWRITE '
                         DISPLAY 'RECORD IS   ' TRANS-RECORD
                         GO TO 500-EXIT
                   ELSE
                         DISPLAY 'SERIOUS ERROR ON REWRITE '
                         DISPLAY 'STATUS CODE IS   '
                                    EMPLOYEE-FILE-STATUS
                         DISPLAY 'RECORD IS   ' TRANS-RECORD
                         CALL ABEND-PROGRAM USING ABEND-CODE.
 500-EXIT.
       EXIT.
```

Figure 14.19 *(continued)*

According to this program, one of the major differences between updating a simple KSDS and a KSDS with an upgrade set is the occurrence of status code 02. It is returned in this program when you add or change a record that results in the creation of a permissible duplicate key condition on a nonunique key alternate index. You might wonder why this program is issuing display messages for successful adds and changes. This is done intentionally to make you more familiar with status code 02.

In the REWRITE logic, we are also testing for status code 22, which indicates a nonpermissible duplicate key condition. This status code will be returned if you try to change a unique alternate key value that results in a duplicate key condition on its alternate index. In this program, you will get these results when you make changes that create a second record with the same EMPLOYEE-EMPNUM.

Now let's execute this program on a real transaction file. Figure 14.20 shows the records within the base cluster and alternate indexes as

```
KEY OF RECORD - 111111111
111111111 WORLD PLAZA,N.Y,N.Y        10M092150RANADE

KEY OF RECORD - 222222222
222222222 25,OAKWOODS,N.Y            19M022536TANAKA

KEY OF RECORD - 333333333
333333333 18,MARSH AV,S.I,N.Y        16F030942KRANTZ

KEY OF RECORD - 444444444
444444444 2-52,FOREST HILLS,QUEENS 05M090252BUTLER

KEY OF RECORD - 555555555
555555555 7,PARK AV,JERSEY CITY      17M092057RANADE

KEY OF RECORD - 666666666
666666666 15,GREENWICH ,CT           12M030511ADLER

KEY OF RECORD - 777777777
777777777 8,BROAD ST,S.I,N.Y         07F082913JOSHI

KEY OF RECORD - 888888888
888888888 KENNER TOWERS,N.Y,N.Y      04F111855LEHN

KEY OF RECORD - 999999999
999999999 23,SOUTH ST,BRONX,N.Y      13F100846RAMSEY
```

(*a*)

```
KEY OF RECORD - 04
.....04888888888

KEY OF RECORD - 05
.....05444444444

KEY OF RECORD - 07
.....07777777777

KEY OF RECORD - 10
.....10111111111

KEY OF RECORD - 12
.....12666666666

KEY OF RECORD - 13
.....13999999999

KEY OF RECORD - 16
.....16333333333

KEY OF RECORD - 17
.....17555555555

KEY OF RECORD - 19
.....19222222222
```

(*b*)

```
KEY OF RECORD - ADLER
.....ADLER 666666666

KEY OF RECORD - BUTLER
.....BUTLER444444444

KEY OF RECORD - JOSHI
.....JOSHI 777777777

KEY OF RECORD - KRANTZ
.....KRANTZ333333333

KEY OF RECORD - LEHN
.....LEHN  888888888

KEY OF RECORD - RAMSEY
.....RAMSEY999999999

KEY OF RECORD - RANADE
.....RANADE111111111555555555

KEY OF RECORD - TANAKA
.....TANAKA222222222
```

(*c*)

Figure 14.20 Contents of base cluster and its alternate indexes before executing the KSAIXUPD program. (*a*) Base cluster. (*b*) Employee-Num AIX. (*c*) Employee-Name AIX.

	TRANS-CODE						
Record 1	A	111122222	28 DEBBIE ST, S.I., N.Y.	01	M	062164	SMITH
Record 2	A	222233333	25 OZONE PARK, QUEENS	07	F	081846	MCNEAL
Record 3	A	333344444	JOURNAL SQUARE, JERSEY,NJ	03	M	121250	JOSHI
Record 4	D	444444444					
Record 5	D	123456789					
Record 6	C	888888888	KANNER PLAZA, N.Y., N.Y.			121855	
Record 7	C	666666666		11			
Record 8	C	222222222					OSAKA

Figure 14.21 Contents of SAMPLE.AIXUPDT.DATA.

they existed *before* the updates. Figure 14.21 gives the transaction file records that are to be used to update the KSDS file.

Upon successful execution of the program, the display messages produced are those in Fig. 14.22. Note that for each transaction record, there is one output message. The status codes are self-explanatory for the kind of processing done on a transaction record. Status codes 00 and 02 are informational messages only. Any other status code indicates an unsuccessful attempt. Figure 14.23 gives the character dump of the base cluster and its alternate indexes after the update program was executed.

As discussed in the previous chapter, we may have situations where the update involves changing the prime key itself. While REWRITE up-

```
ADD SUCCESSFUL,STATUS CODE IS  00
RECORD IS  A111122222 28,DEBBIE ST,S.I,N.Y        01M062164SMITH
DUPLICATE RECORD ON ADD
RECORD IS  A222233333 25,OZONE PARK,QUEENS       07F081846MCNEAL
ADD SUCCESSFUL,STATUS CODE IS  02
RECORD IS  A333344444 JOURNAL SQUARE,JERSEY,N.J03M121250JOSHI
DELETE SUCCESSFUL
RECORD IS  D444444444
RECORD NOT FOUND ON DELETE
RECORD IS  D123456789
REWRITE SUCCESSFUL
STATUS CODE IS  00
RECORD IS  C888888888 KANNER PLAZA,N.Y,N.Y           121855
REWRITE SUCCESSFUL
STATUS CODE IS  00
RECORD IS  C666666666                        11
REWRITE SUCCESSFUL
STATUS CODE IS  00
RECORD IS  C222222222                                       OSAKA
```

Figure 14.22 Display messages generated upon execution of the KSAIXUPD program.

```
KEY OF RECORD - 111111111
111111111 WORLD PLAZA,N.Y,N.Y       10M092150RANADE

KEY OF RECORD - 111122222
111122222 28,DEBBIE ST,S.I,N.Y      01M062164SMITH

KEY OF RECORD - 222222222
222222222 25,OAKWOODS,N.Y           19M022536OSAKA

KEY OF RECORD - 333333333
333333333 18,MARSH AV,S.I,N.Y       16F030942KRANTZ

KEY OF RECORD - 333344444
333344444 JOURNAL SQUARE,JERSEY,N.J03M121250JOSHI

KEY OF RECORD - 555555555
555555555 7,PARK AV,JERSEY CITY     17M092057RANADE

KEY OF RECORD - 666666666
666666666 15,GREENWICH ,CT          11M030511ADLER

KEY OF RECORD - 777777777
777777777 8,BROAD ST,S.I,N.Y        07F082913JOSHI

KEY OF RECORD - 888888888
888888888 KANNER PLAZA,N.Y,N.Y      04F121855LEHN

KEY OF RECORD - 999999999
999999999 23,SOUTH ST,BRONX,N.Y     13F100846RAMSEY
```

(*a*)

```
KEY OF RECORD - 01
.....01111122222

KEY OF RECORD - 03
.....03333344444

KEY OF RECORD - 04
.....04888888888

KEY OF RECORD - 07
.....07777777777

KEY OF RECORD - 10
.....10111111111

KEY OF RECORD - 11
.....11666666666

KEY OF RECORD - 13
.....13999999999

KEY OF RECORD - 16
.....16333333333

KEY OF RECORD - 17
.....17555555555

KEY OF RECORD - 19
.....19222222222
```

(*b*)

```
KEY OF RECORD - ADLER
.....ADLER 666666666

KEY OF RECORD - JOSHI
.....JOSHI 777777777333344444

KEY OF RECORD - KRANTZ
.....KRANTZ333333333

KEY OF RECORD - LEHN
.....LEHN  888888888

KEY OF RECORD - OSAKA
.....OSAKA 222222222

KEY OF RECORD - RAMSEY
.....RAMSEY999999999

KEY OF RECORD - RANADE
.....RANADE111111111555555555

KEY OF RECORD - SMITH
.....SMITH 111122222
```

(*c*)

Figure 14.23 Character dump of a KSDS and its upgrade set after execution of the KSAIXUPD program. (*a*) Base cluster. (*b*) Employee-Num AIX. (*c*) Employee-Name AIX.

dates the upgrade set for any changes made in alternate keys, it gives an illogical error if the prime key is modified. However, the prime key can be changed using the following technique.

1. Try to READ a record with the *new* key. If you are successful, display the error message and skip processing steps 2, 3, and 4.
2. READ the record with the old key *and* save it in the working storage area.
3. DELETE the record with the old key.
4. Change the prime key in the working storage and WRITE the record with the new key.

The reason we want to read the record with the new key in step 1 is to find out whether there is an existing record with the new key. If there is, we have no need to go any further. Also, we cannot switch the processing in steps 3 and 4 because the unique alternate keys must be deleted before issuing a WRITE. If we don't do this, step 4 will always give a status code of 22 even if a single unique key alternate index is present in the upgrade set. All this processing can either be incorporated into the program KSAIXUPD or can be handled by a separate program.

A final word of caution is in order. Alternate indexes provide the ability to view base cluster records on a field other than the prime key. Their indiscriminate use, especially when they are part of the upgrade set, will affect performance adversely. So, don't use them unless they are absolutely necessary for the application.

In the next chapter (Chap. 15), Program Example 1 (Sec. 15.4) makes use of the Employee-Name alternate key to illustrate the use of a nonunique key on a KSDS.

chapter 15

Processing an ESDS

Entry-sequenced data sets are also called *sequential VSAM files*. They are in many ways used like physical sequential files, but they have several processing characteristics that are lacking in plain physical sequential data sets. One of the main advantages is that you can have alternate indexes on an ESDS when used in CICS. You don't have the same capability with a PS data set.

The use of an ESDS may be appropriate in certain CICS applications where sequential processing is desirable. For example, an ESDS is frequently used as an on-line data collection transaction file so that transactions can be used later to update master files in the batch mode. An ESDS can also be used as an audit-trail file of on-line transactions when a master file is updated in real time. Such audit-trail files are maintained as a historical record of on-line changes both for recovery purposes and to generate batch reports on daily on-line activity. PS data sets are not a viable alternative because CICS doesn't support them in the same way.

When designing your system, it is important to remember that, while alternate indexes on an ESDS are supported by CICS, they are *not* supported in a batch Cobol environment. When choosing between a KSDS and an ESDS with an alternate index, keep in mind that certain types of on-line applications perform better when an ESDS with an alternate index is used. While both function similarly, there are no CI or CA split problems in an ESDS base cluster. A batch Cobol environment also does not support random access by RBA on an ESDS, while CICS does provide this facility.

ESDS data sets have not gained much popularity because of some of the limitations on their use in a batch environment. In addition to the items mentioned above, they also cannot be used as generation data sets of a generation data group. After reading the rest of this chapter, you will be in a better position to decide whether an ESDS or a PS data set is more suitable for a specific application.

In Program Example 2 of this chapter (Sec. 15.5), we will refer to an ESDS named EMPLOYEE.TRANS.CLUSTER. Its record length is 52 bytes. We will assume that it is a data collection file under a CICS application called the personnel/payroll system. Data collected in this file will be used as transactions to update EMPLOYEE.KSDS.CLUSTER.

15.1 SELECT STATEMENT

Figure 15.1 provides the syntax of the SELECT statement for an ESDS.

The Cobol reserved word OPTIONAL may be specified only for files that are opened as INPUT. It is used to indicate that a file may *not* always be present when the program is executed.

The assignment name for an ESDS differs from that of a KSDS. The DD name for an ESDS file *must* be prefixed with AS-. For example, if the DD name is TRANS, the assignment-name must be AS-TRANS. Omission of the prefix AS- will result in execution time error messages related to data set control blocks that are difficult to interpret.

ORGANIZATION is always SEQUENTIAL for an ESDS. The only ACCESS MODE you can specify for an ESDS in batch Cobol programs is SEQUENTIAL. Since both specifications are also the default statements, they may be omitted from the code. You should be familiar with the rest of the clauses, since they were discussed in previous chapters.

Figure 15.2 gives sample coding of the SELECT statement for EMPLOYEE.TRANS.CLUSTER, assuming that the data set is not password-protected.

```
SELECT    [OPTIONAL] file-name
          ASSIGN TO  assignment-name
          ORGANIZATION IS SEQUENTIAL
          ACCESS MODE IS SEQUENTIAL
          PASSWORD IS data-name-1
          FILE STATUS IS data-name-2
```

Figure 15.1 Syntax of a SELECT statement for an ESDS.

```
IDENTIFICATION DIVISION.
    .
    .
ENVIRONMENT DIVISION.
    .
    .
INPUT-OUTPUT SECTION.
FILE-CONTROL.
       SELECT  TRANS-FILE
               ASSIGN TO  AS-TRANS
               ORGANIZATION IS SEQUENTIAL
               ACCESS MODE IS SEQUENTIAL
               FILE STATUS IS TRANS-FILE-STATUS.
    .
    .
DATA DIVISION.
FILE SECTION.
FD  TRANS-FILE
       LABEL RECORDS ARE STANDARD.
01  TRANS-RECORD                          PIC X(52).
    .
    .
WORKING-STORAGE SECTION.
01  TRANS-FILE-STATUS                     PIC X(2).
    .
    .
    .
```

Figure 15.2 Sample coding of a SELECT statement for EMPLOYEE.TRANS. CLUSTER.

15.2 FILE STATUS

Most of the status codes that we have learned so far are not applicable to an ESDS. Since ESDS does not have any keys, status codes 02 and 20 through 24 will never be returned. A no-space condition on a WRITE returns a status code of 34, unlike the situation with a KSDS or RRDS, where it is 24.

15.3 PROCESSING IN THE PROCEDURE DIVISION

Since ESDS files are accessed and processed in almost the same way as PS files, the processing logic is similar. The file status must be checked after every I/O operation to verify its outcome.

15.3.1 Restrictions for ESDS

Since records in an ESDS cannot be deleted, you may not use the Cobol DELETE statement. To simulate the delete function, you may use your own indicators within the record to identify a deletion. For example, you may choose the convention of moving high values to the first byte of the record and rewriting it to signify that it has been logically deleted. However, all programs accessing the data set must follow the same convention for logical deletions.

An ESDS file can only be read sequentially. In order to read a particular record, you must read all the preceding ones. The use of the START verb is not supported, so you cannot begin browsing anywhere other than at the beginning of the file.

15.3.2 OPEN

An ESDS can be opened in the same ways as a KSDS. The syntax of the OPEN statement is

```
                 ⎧INPUT ⎫
OPEN file-name   ⎨OUTPUT⎬
                 ⎨EXTEND⎬
                 ⎩I-O   ⎭
```

A file opened as OUTPUT must not have any records in it. If you want to resume loading an already loaded ESDS, it must be opened as EXTEND. A file can be opened as I-O if the REWRITE statement is to be used for modifying the records.

When SELECT OPTIONAL is specified in the FILE-CONTROL, OPEN verifies the presence of an optional file. If the file doesn't exist, the first READ will result in a status code of 10. An optional file may be opened *only* as INPUT.

15.3.3 READ, WRITE, and REWRITE

These are the only verbs of Cobol that may be used for record I/O to an ESDS.

READ This statement will retrieve records sequentially from the beginning of the file to the end. The first READ statement after OPEN will retrieve the first record in the data set. You may not start browsing randomly from within the file. If the records were originally defined and loaded as variable-length records, you must take this into consideration during READ operations by providing the OCCURS DEPENDING ON clause.

WRITE When the file is opened as OUTPUT, the first WRITE will write the record at the beginning of the data set. All subsequent WRITE commands will place records in the file one after the other in entry sequence. If the file is opened as EXTEND, the first WRITE will begin after the last loaded record. EXTEND functions just like the MOD option of the DISPOSITION parameter in JCL for physical sequential files. You can write fixed-length as well as variable-length ESDS records.

REWRITE You may REWRITE a record after reading and changing its contents. *The record length may not be changed.* The only way to accomplish a record-length change in an ESDS file is by reading the old file as input, changing the record contents, and creating a new one as output. Note that the file must be opened as I-O to use the REWRITE statement.

15.4 PROGRAM EXAMPLE 1: LOADING AN ESDS

In this example, we will use an ESDS as a backup for the KSDS named EMPLOYEE.KSDS.CLUSTER. In order to do this, the ESDS must already be defined. We will read the KSDS on the Employee-Name alternate index and load the records into the ESDS one by one. This example will demonstrate not only how to load an ESDS but also how to read a KSDS on a non-unique key alternate index. We will make ample use of FILE STATUS checking as we have in the past. Figure 15.3 gives the sample code for the program.

```
 IDENTIFICATION DIVISION.
 PROGRAM-ID.  ESDSLOAD.
 AUTHOR.      RANADE.
*****************************************************
*** THIS PROGRAM READS EMPLOYEE.KADS.CLUSTER ****
*** ON EMPLOYEE-NAME ALTERNATE INDEX AND     ****
*** LOADS RECORDS INTO AN ESDS.              ****
*****************************************************
 ENVIRONMENT DIVISION.
 CONFIGURATION SECTION.
 INPUT-OUTPUT SECTION.
 FILE-CONTROL.
        SELECT  EMPLOYEE-MASTER
                ASSIGN TO  EMPMSTR
                ORGANIZATION IS INDEXED
                ACCESS MODE IS SEQUENTIAL
                RECORD KEY IS EMPLOYEE-SSN-KEY
                ALTERNATE RECORD KEY IS EMPLOYEE-NAME-KEY
                         WITH DUPLICATES
                FILE STATUS IS EMPLOYEE-FILE-STATUS.
        SELECT  BACKUP-MASTER
                ASSIGN TO  AS-BACKUP
                ORGANIZATION IS SEQUENTIAL
                ACCESS MODE IS SEQUENTIAL
                FILE STATUS IS BACKUP-FILE-STATUS.
```

Figure 15.3 Program listing for loading records into an ESDS after reading them on an Employee-Name alternate index from EMPLOYEE.KSDS.CLUSTER.

```
 DATA DIVISION.
 FILE SECTION.
 FD  EMPLOYEE-MASTER
     LABEL RECORDS ARE STANDARD.
 01  EMPLOYEE-RECORD.
     05  EMPLOYEE-SSN-KEY          PIC X(9).
     05  FILLER                    PIC X(35).
     05  EMPLOYEE-NAME-KEY         PIC X(6).
 FD  BACKUP-MASTER
     LABEL RECORDS ARE STANDARD.
 01  BACKUP-RECORD                 PIC X(50).

 WORKING-STORAGE SECTION.
 01  EMPLOYEE-FILE-STATUS          PIC X(2).
 01  BACKUP-FILE-STATUS            PIC X(2).
 01  ABEND-PROGRAM                 PIC X(8)
                           VALUE 'ILBOABNO'.
 01  ABEND-CODE                    PIC S999 COMP
                           VALUE +999.

 PROCEDURE DIVISION.
 100-MAIN-PARA.
     OPEN INPUT  EMPLOYEE-MASTER.
*****************************************************
***  TEST FOR SUCESSFUL OPEN OF EMPMSTR          ****
*****************************************************

     IF   EMPLOYEE-FILE-STATUS = '00'
          NEXT SENTENCE
     ELSE
          DISPLAY 'OPEN ERROR ON EMPMSTR'
          DISPLAY 'STATUS CODE IS  '
                  EMPLOYEE-FILE-STATUS
          CALL ABEND-PROGRAM USING ABEND-CODE.
     OPEN OUTPUT  BACKUP-MASTER.
*****************************************************
***  TEST FOR SUCESSFUL OPEN OF BACKUP           ****
*****************************************************

     IF   BACKUP-FILE-STATUS = '00'
          NEXT SENTENCE
     ELSE
          DISPLAY 'OPEN ERROR ON BACKUP'
          DISPLAY 'STATUS CODE IS  '
                  BACKUP-FILE-STATUS
          CALL ABEND-PROGRAM USING ABEND-CODE.
     PERFORM  200-PROCES ING-PARA  THRU  200-EXIT.
     CLOSE EMPLOYEE-MASTER.
*****************************************************
***  TEST FOR SUCESSFUL CLOSE OF EMPMSTR          ***
*****************************************************

     IF   EMPLOYEE-FILE-STATUS = '00'
          NEXT SENTENCE
     ELSE
          DISPLAY 'CLOSE ERROR ON EMPMSTR'
          DISPLAY 'STATUS CODE IS  '
                  EMPLOYEE-FILE-STATUS
          CALL ABEND-PROGRAM USING ABEND-CODE.
     CLOSE BACKUP-MASTER.
```

```
******************************************************
***   TEST FOR SUCESSFUL CLOSE OF BACKUP          ***
******************************************************
           IF    BACKUP-FILE-STATUS = '00'
                 NEXT SENTENCE
           ELSE
                 DISPLAY 'CLOSE ERROR ON BACKUP'
                 DISPLAY 'STATUS CODE IS   '
                         BACKUP-FILE-STATUS
                 CALL ABEND-PROGRAM USING ABEND-CODE.
           GOBACK.

       200-PROCESSING-PARA.
           MOVE LOW-VALUES TO EMPLOYEE-NAME-KEY.
           START  EMPLOYEE-MASTER
                   KEY IS > EMPLOYEE-NAME-KEY.
******************************************************
***   TEST FOR SUCESSFUL EXECUTION OF START       ***
******************************************************
           IF    EMPLOYEE-FILE-STATUS = '00'
                 NEXT SENTENCE
           ELSE
                 DISPLAY 'UNEXPECTED CONDITION ON START'
                 DISPLAY 'STATUS CODE IS '
                         EMPLOYEE-FILE-STATUS
                 CALL ABEND-PROGRAM USING ABEND-CODE.
           PERFORM 300-READ-AND-WRITE THRU 300-EXIT.
       200-EXIT.
           EXIT.

       300-READ-AND-WRITE.
           READ  EMPLOYEE-MASTER.
******************************************************
***   TEST FOR SUCESSFUL READ OF EMPMSTR          ***
******************************************************
           IF    EMPLOYEE-FILE-STATUS = '00' OR '02'
                 NEXT SENTENCE
           ELSE
                 IF    EMPLOYEE-FILE-STATUS = '10'
                       GO TO 300-EXIT
                 ELSE
                       DISPLAY  'READ ERROR ON EMPMSTR'
                       DISPLAY  'STATUS CODE IS '
                                EMPLOYEE-FILE-STATUS
                       CALL  ABEND-PROGRAM USING ABEND-CODE.
           MOVE EMPLOYEE-RECORD TO BACKUP-RECORD.
           WRITE BACKUP-RECORD.
******************************************************
***   TEST FOR SUCESSFUL WRITE TO BACKUP          ***
******************************************************
           IF    BACKUP-FILE-STATUS = '00'
                 NEXT SENTENCE
           ELSE
                 DISPLAY 'WRITE ERROR ON BACKUP'
                 DISPLAY 'STATUS CODE IS   '
                         BACKUP-FILE-STATUS
                 CALL ABEND-PROGRAM USING ABEND-CODE.
           GO TO 300-READ-AND-WRITE.
       300-EXIT.
           EXIT.
```

Figure 15.3 *(continued)*

Notice the assignment name for the backup file. The prefix AS- indicates that this file is an ESDS. Although EMPLOYEE-MASTER has two alternate indexes, we are coding only the one used in the SELECT statement. We have provided different data-names for the status codes of each of the files. Although we could have used only one name, it is good practice to use different names for each VSAM file.

Since serious errors could go undetected, the use of status code testing in the PROCEDURE DIVISION is extensive. In order to begin reading the KSDS file from the beginning of the Employee-Name alternate index, the START verb has been used in 200-PROCESSING-PARA. Any status code other than 00 generated by START is being considered a fatal error. We are causing a user abend on status code 23, which means that no Employee-Name key greater than low values has been found. Since Employee-Name should always be greater than low-values, status code 23 would indicate that the file is empty. For other applications, you might prefer to take a different action for an empty file. Depending on the nature of the application, this may be an expected situation and not an error. Also notice the testing for the occurrence of status code 02 on reading through EMPLOYEE-NAME-KEY. This indicates that an expected duplicate record condition has occurred. This is normal for a nonunique key alternate index.

In the 300-READ-AND-WRITE paragraph, status code 10, indicating an end-of-file on the EMPLOYEE-MASTER file, transfers control to 300-EXIT. When writing a record to the ESDS we accept only a status code of 00 to indicate successful completion of the add. Any other value indicates an error condition. For example, status code 34 in this case means lack of enough space at the end of the file to perform a successful add.

The JCL for an ESDS file is the same as that for a KSDS file. Normally, you would only require the DSN and DISP parameter. The rest of the attributes of the data set are taken from its cataloged entry. Figure 15.4 gives the sample JCL for executing our ESDSLOAD program.

Note that the first alternate index path in the Cobol select statement is given the DD name EMPMSTR1. Don't confuse this with the DSN, which includes the qualifier PATH2 as we defined it earlier.

15.5 PROGRAM EXAMPLE 2: IN-PLACE UPDATE OF ESDS RECORDS

In this example, we will use the feature of ESDS that makes it possible to perform an in-place update on existing records. Let's consider a personnel/payroll system whose master file is a KSDS named EMPLOYEE.KSDS.CLUSTER. By now you are quite familiar with its record format, which has been discussed many times previously (see Fig. 6.1).

```
//ESDSLOAD JOB (ACCTNO),'JAY RANADE'
//LOADSTEP EXEC PGM=ESDSLOAD
//STEPLIB  DD DSN=SAMPLE.PROGRAM.LOAD,DISP=SHR
//         DD DSN=SYS1.COBLIB,DISP=SHR
//EMPMSTR  DD DSN=EMPLOYEE.KSDS.CLUSTER,
//            DISP=SHR
//EMPMSTR1 DD DSN=EMPLOYEE.KSDS.PATH2,
//            DISP=SHR
//BACKUP   DD DSN=EMPLOYEE.ESDS.CLUSTER,
//            DISP=OLD
//SYSOUT   DD SYSOUT=A
//DISPLAY  DD SYSOUT=A
//SYSUDUMP DD SYSOUT=A
//
```

Figure 15.4 Sample JCL for executing the ESDSLOAD program for loading an ESDS file. Source code for the program is given in Fig. 15.3.

In this system, updates to the master file are done from EMPLOYEE.TRANS.CLUSTER, a transaction file which is an ESDS. Transaction records are added on-line to this ESDS through a CICS transaction. The record length of the transaction file is 52 bytes, and it has the following format.

1. First byte: Transaction code (A, D, or C)
2. Second byte: Transaction status (P or R)
3. Next 50 bytes: Same as the master file record layout

The first byte, whose value can be A, D, or C, indicates whether a record is to be added, deleted, or changed in the master file. The second byte will have a value of spaces when the transaction record is created by CICS. After CICS is shut down and batch programs start processing, the value of this byte will be set to P if the record is accepted and processed for the master file update. If for any reason the record is rejected, the value of the byte will be set to R. In either case, a record will be written back to the ESDS file after moving either P or R to the second byte. The next time CICS comes up, new transaction records will be added to the end of the file. In addition, the rejected transactions may be modified to correct errors, and the transaction status will be changed back to spaces. At the end of the week, the processed transaction records will be eliminated from the ESDS by transferring them to an archive data set. This is done so that only records still needed for update activity are retained in the transaction file.

The batch program sequentially reads from the ESDS and processes only records for which the transaction status is spaces. Depending on the transaction code, it adds, deletes, or changes records in the master file. A transaction may be rejected in processing for one of the following reasons.

1. Duplicate key condition on add
2. Record-not-found condition on delete
3. Duplicate key condition on change (Employee-Number alternate key) or record-not-found condition on READ before change (prime key)
4. Record rejection on editing (e.g., date-of-birth field is not numeric or transaction code is invalid)

To keep the processing logic simple, we will not perform any data editing in this sample program. As usual, we will carry out extensive checking for the status codes returned. Figure 15.5 gives the sample code for this program.

```
IDENTIFICATION DIVISION.
PROGRAM-ID.  ESDSUPDT.
AUTHOR.      RANADE.
*****************************************************************
*** THIS PROGRAM READS AN ESDS TRANSACTION    ****
*** FILE AND BASED ON TRANSACTION CODE OF     ****
*** A,D OR C, IT ADDS,DELETES OR CHANGES      ****
*** RECORDS IN EMPMSTR.                       ****
*****************************************************************

ENVIRONMENT DIVISION.
CONFIGURATION SECTION.
INPUT-OUTPUT SECTION.
FILE-CONTROL.
    SELECT  TRANS-FILE
            ASSIGN TO  AS-TRANS
            ORGANIZATION IS SEQUENTIAL
            ACCESS MODE IS SEQUENTIAL
            FILE STATUS IS TRANS-FILE-STATUS.
    SELECT  EMPLOYEE-MASTER
            ASSIGN TO  EMPMSTR
            ORGANIZATION IS INDEXED
            ACCESS MODE  IS RANDOM
            RECORD KEY IS EMPLOYEE-SSN-KEY
            ALTERNATE RECORD KEY IS EMPLOYEE-EMPNUM
            ALTERNATE RECORD KEY IS EMPLOYEE-EMPNAME
                      WITH DUPLICATES
            FILE STATUS IS EMPLOYEE-FILE-STATUS.

DATA DIVISION.
FILE SECTION.
```

Figure 15.5 Program listing for the random update of EMPLOYEE.KSDS.CLUSTER and its upgrade set. The transaction file is EMPLOYEE.TRANS.CLUSTER. The program takes care of adds, deletes, and changes.

```
 FD  TRANS-FILE
     LABEL RECORDS ARE STANDARD.
 01  TRANS-RECORD.
     05  TRANS-CODE                   PIC X.
     05  TRANS-STATUS                 PIC X.
     05  TRANS-REST.
         10  TRANS-SSN                PIC X(9).
         10  TRANS-ADDR               PIC X(26).
         10  TRANS-NUM                PIC X(2).
         10  TRANS-SEX                PIC X.
         10  TRANS-DOB                PIC X(6).
         10  TRANS-NAME               PIC X(6).

 FD  EMPLOYEE-MASTER
     LABEL RECORDS ARE STANDARD.
 01  EMPLOYEE-RECORD.
     05  EMPLOYEE-SSN-KEY             PIC X(9).
     05  EMPLOYEE-REST.
         10  EMPLOYEE-EMPADD          PIC X(26).
         10  EMPLOYEE-EMPNUM          PIC X(2).
         10  EMPLOYEE-EMPSEX          PIC X.
         10  EMPLOYEE-EMPDOB          PIC X(6).
         10  EMPLOYEE-EMPNAME         PIC X(6).

 WORKING-STORAGE SECTION.
 01  TRANS-FILE-STATUS                PIC X(2).
 01  EMPLOYEE-FILE-STATUS             PIC X(2).
 01  ABEND-PROGRAM                    PIC X(8)
                              VALUE 'ILBOABNO'.
 01  ABEND-CODE                       PIC S999 COMP
                              VALUE +999.

 PROCEDURE DIVISION.
 100-MAIN-PARA.
     OPEN  I-O   TRANS-FILE.
***********************************************************
***  TEST FOR SUCESSFUL OPEN OF TRANS-FILE            ****
***********************************************************

     IF    TRANS-FILE-STATUS = '00'
           NEXT SENTENCE
     ELSE
           DISPLAY 'OPEN ERROR ON TRANS'
           DISPLAY 'STATUS CODE IS   '
                   TRANS-FILE-STATUS
           CALL ABEND-PROGRAM USING ABEND-CODE.
     OPEN  I-O   EMPLOYEE-MASTER.
***********************************************************
***  TEST FOR SUCESSFUL OPEN OF EMPMSTR               ****
***********************************************************
     IF    EMPLOYEE-FILE-STATUS = '00'
           NEXT SENTENCE
     ELSE
           DISPLAY 'OPEN ERROR ON EMPMSTR'
           DISPLAY 'STATUS CODE IS   '
                   EMPLOYEE-FILE-STATUS
           CALL ABEND-PROGRAM USING ABEND-CODE.
     PERFORM  200-UPDATE-EMPMSTR THRU 200-EXIT.
     CLOSE TRANS-FILE.
```

```
*****************************************************
***  TEST FOR SUCESSFUL CLOSE OF TRANS-FILE       ***
*****************************************************

         IF    TRANS-FILE-STATUS = '00'
               NEXT SENTENCE
         ELSE
               DISPLAY 'CLOSE ERROR ON TRANS'
               DISPLAY 'STATUS CODE IS  '
                       TRANS-FILE-STATUS
               CALL ABEND-PROGRAM USING ABEND-CODE.
         CLOSE EMPLOYEE-MASTER.
*****************************************************
***  TEST FOR SUCESSFUL CLOSE OF EMPMSTR          ***
*****************************************************

         IF    EMPLOYEE-FILE-STATUS = '00'
               NEXT SENTENCE
         ELSE
               DISPLAY 'CLOSE ERROR ON EMPMSTR'
               DISPLAY 'STATUS CODE IS  '
                       EMPLOYEE-FILE-STATUS
               CALL ABEND-PROGRAM USING ABEND-CODE.
         GOBACK.

     200-UPDATE-EMPMSTR.
         READ  TRANS-FILE.
         IF    TRANS-FILE-STATUS = '00'
               NEXT SENTENCE
         ELSE
               IF    TRANS-FILE-STATUS = '10'
                     GO TO 200-EXIT
               ELSE
                     DISPLAY 'READ ERROR ON TRANS'
                     DISPLAY 'STATUS CODE IS  '
                             TRANS-FILE-STATUS
                     CALL ABEND-PROGRAM USING ABEND-CODE.

         IF    TRANS-STATUS = ' '
               NEXT SENTENCE
         ELSE
               GO TO 200-UPDATE-EMPMSTR.
         IF    TRANS-CODE = 'A'
               PERFORM 300-ADD-RECORD
                       THRU 300-EXIT
         ELSE
               IF    TRANS-CODE = 'D'
                     PERFORM 400-DELETE-RECORD
                             THRU 400-EXIT
               ELSE
                     IF    TRANS-CODE = 'C'
                           PERFORM 500-CHANGE-RECORD
                                   THRU 500-EXIT
                     ELSE
                           DISPLAY 'ILLEGAL TRANS CODE FOR'
                           DISPLAY 'RECORD ' TRANS-RECORD
                           PERFORM 700-UPDATE-TRANS-REJECT
                                   THRU 700-EXIT.
               GO TO 200-UPDATE-EMPMSTR.
```

```
 200-EXIT.
     EXIT.

 300-ADD-RECORD.
     MOVE TRANS-REST TO EMPLOYEE-RECORD.
     WRITE  EMPLOYEE-RECCRD.
***********************************************************
***  TEST FOR SUCESSFUL  ADD TO  EMPMSTR       ***
***********************************************************

     IF   EMPLOYEE-FILE-STATUS = '00' OR '02'
          PERFORM 600-UPDATE-TRANS-PROCESS
                  THRU 600-EXIT
     ELSE
          IF   EMPLOYEE-FILE-STATUS = '22'
               DISPLAY 'DUPLICATE RECORD ON ADD '
               DISPLAY 'RECORD IS  ' TRANS-RECORD
               PERFORM 700-UPDATE-TRANS-REJECT
                       THRU 700-EXIT
          ELSE
               DISPLAY 'SEVERE  ERROR ON ADD '
               DISPLAY 'STATUS CODE IS  '
                       EMPLOYEE-FILE-STATUS
               CALL ABEND-PROGRAM USING ABEND-CODE.
 300-EXIT.
     EXIT.

 400-DELETE-RECORD.
     MOVE TRANS-SSN TO EMPLOYEE-SSN-KEY.
     DELETE EMPLOYEE-MASTER.
***********************************************************
***  TEST FOR SUCESSFUL DELETE IN EMPMSTR      ***
***********************************************************
     IF   EMPLOYEE-FILE-STATUS = '00'
          PERFORM 600-UPDATE-TRANS-PROCESS
                  THRU 600-EXIT
     ELSE
          IF   EMPLOYEE-FILE-STATUS = '23'
               DISPLAY ' RECORD NOT FOUND ON DELETE '
               DISPLAY 'RECORD IS  ' TRANS-RECORD
               PERFORM 700-UPDATE-TRANS-REJECT
                       THRU 700-EXIT
          ELSE
               DISPLAY 'SERIOUS ERROR ON DELETE'
               DISPLAY 'STATUS CODE IS  '
                       EMPLOYEE-FILE-STATUS
               DISPLAY 'RECORD IS  ' TRANS-RECORD
               CALL ABEND-PROGRAM USING ABEND-CODE.
 400-EXIT.
     EXIT.
 500-CHANGE-RECORD.
     MOVE TRANS-SSN TO EMPLOYEE-SSN-KEY.
     READ EMPLOYEE-MASTER.
***********************************************************
***  TEST FOR SUCESSFUL READ  OF VSAM RECORD   ***
***********************************************************
     IF   EMPLOYEE-FILE-STATUS = '00'
          NEXT SENTENCE
```

Figure 15.5 *(continued)*

```
     ELSE
          IF   EMPLOYEE-FILE-STATUS = '23'
               DISPLAY 'RECORD NOT FOUND ON READ'
               DISPLAY 'RECORD IS  ' TRANS-RECORD
               PERFORM 700-UPDATE-TRANS-REJECT
                       THRU 700-EXIT
               GO TO 500-EXIT
          ELSE
               DISPLAY 'SERIOUS ERROR ON READ '
               DISPLAY 'STATUS CODE IS  '
                       EMPLOYEE-FILE-STATUS
               DISPLAY 'RECORD IS  ' TRANS-RECORD
               CALL ABEND-PROGRAM USING ABEND-CODE.
     IF   TRANS-ADDR  NOT = SPACES
          MOVE TRANS-ADDR    TO EMPLOYEE-EMPADD.
     IF   TRANS-NUM   NOT = SPACES
          MOVE TRANS-NUM     TO EMPLOYEE-EMPNUM.
     IF   TRANS-SEX  NOT = SPACES
          MOVE TRANS-SEX     TO EMPLOYEE-EMPSEX.
     IF   TRANS-DOB  NOT = SPACES
          MOVE TRANS-DOB     TO EMPLOYEE-EMPDOB.
     IF   TRANS-NAME NOT = SPACES
          MOVE TRANS-NAME    TO EMPLOYEE-EMPNAME.
     REWRITE  EMPLOYEE-RECORD.
*****************************************************
***  TEST FOR SUCESSFUL  REWRITE TO EMPMSTR     ***
*****************************************************
     IF   EMPLOYEE-FILE-STATUS = '00' OR '02'
          PERFORM 600-UPDATE-TRANS-PROCESS
                  THRU 600-EXIT
     ELSE
          IF   EMPLOYEE-FILE-STATUS = '22'
               DISPLAY 'DUPLICATE RECORD ON REWRITE'
               DISPLAY 'RECORD IS  ' TRANS-RECORD
               PERFORM 700-UPDATE-TRANS-REJECT
                       THRU 700-EXIT
          ELSE
               DISPLAY 'SEVERE ERROR ON REWRITE'
               DISPLAY 'STATUS CODE IS  '
                       EMPLOYEE-FILE-STATUS
               DISPLAY 'RECORD IS  ' TRANS-RECORD
               CALL ABEND-PROGRAM USING ABEND-CODE.
 500-EXIT.
     EXIT.

 600-UPDATE-TRANS-PROCESS.
     MOVE 'P' TO TRANS-STATUS.
     REWRITE TRANS-RECORD.
*****************************************************
***  TEST FOR SUCESSFUL REWRITE TO TRANS-FILE ***
*****************************************************
     IF   TRANS-FILE-STATUS NOT = '00'
          DISPLAY 'REWRITE ERROR ON TRANS'
          DISPLAY 'STATUS CODE IS '
                  TRANS-FILE-STATUS
          DISPLAY 'RECORD IS  ' TRANS-RECORD
          CALL ABEND-PROGRAM USING ABEND-CODE.
```

```
 600-EXIT.
        EXIT.

 700-UPDATE-TRANS-REJECT.
        MOVE 'R' TO TRANS-STATUS.
        REWRITE TRANS-RECORD.
***********************************************************
***   TEST FOR SUCESSFUL REWRITE TO TRANS-FILE ***
***********************************************************
        IF    TRANS-FILE-STATUS NOT = '00'
              DISPLAY 'REWRITE ERROR ON TRANS'
              DISPLAY 'STATUS CODE IS '
                      TRANS-FILE-STATUS
              DISPLAY 'RECORD IS  ' TRANS-RECORD
              CALL ABEND-PROGRAM USING ABEND-CODE.
 700-EXIT.
        EXIT.
```

Figure 15.5 *(continued)*

The ESDS file is being opened as I-O in order to make use of the REWRITE statement. After executing a READ on the transaction file, we test for a status code of 10 to detect an end-of-file condition. We could also have used the AT END clause. On a record add or change to the Employee-Master file, we accept status codes of 00 and 02 as normal. Status code 02 could be due to the addition of a permissible duplicate key on the Employee-Name alternate index. Status code 22 on an add or change indicates a duplicate record on a prime key or unique key alternate index. In either case, no update is made. Status code 23 on delete denotes a record-not-found condition. Notice the use of REWRITE on the transaction file in the 600-UPDATE-TRANS-PROCESS and 700-UPDATE-TRANS-REJECT paragraphs.

If you find that the use of DISPLAY and CALL statements is too extensive in these examples, remember that the purpose is to keep the program logic simple even at the cost of writing redundant code. Our intention here is to understand the processing complexity of VSAM files, not to write efficient programs. You may, of course, write more precise and efficient code depending on the program logic.

In a nutshell, ESDS files can be more useful than PS files in certain applications. Their use as data collection or audit-trail files should be a top consideration in CICS. Their usefulness will be further enhanced if batch Cobol compilers support the use of alternate indexes on them. Nevertheless, the ability to update records in place is a useful feature which may meet the design requirements of certain unique applications.

chapter 16

Processing an RRDS

The architecture of an RRDS was discussed in Chap. 2. To recap briefly, an RRDS may be considered a chain of fixed-length slots. Each slot is identified by its position relative to the first slot of the file, beginning with one, and may contain only one record. This slot number is known as the relative record number. Records can be processed sequentially or randomly by their RRN's. VSAM views an empty slot as one that contains no data record. Before a record is inserted in one of the slots, VSAM makes certain that it is empty. An RRDS cluster has no index component, so you can retrieve a record randomly *only* if you know the RRN of the slot it is in. Similarly, when adding records to the file, you must also know the RRN of the empty slot to which the record can be written. An RRN is *not* part of the data record, unlike the key of a KSDS, which is imbedded in the record itself.

Since an RRN is the axle around which the whole retrieval/update process of an RRDS revolves, there should be a way to develop a relationship between some unique field of a record and the RRN of the slot in which it will be written and from which it will be retrieved. A *hashing algorithm* (or a randomizing routine) can be used for this purpose. The algorithm ideally should give a unique RRN when supplied with a unique field value for a record. In real life, it is difficult to develop such an algorithm. What happens if the algorithm results in the same RRN for two or more different input field values? This is the major reason why RRDS is the least popular of the three VSAM data set architectures. On the other hand, if such an algorithm can be developed, RRDS guarantees one I/O per random retrieval or write operation. This makes it the *most* efficient of the three VSAM data set organizations for random processing.

We will develop a simple hashing algorithm for the update/retrieval process for EMPLOYEE.RRDS.CLUSTER, which was defined in Chap. 6. We will use this cluster as the master file for the personnel/payroll system instead of using the KSDS as we have done so far. Our file has the same record format as EMPLOYEE.KSDS.CLUSTER. The records are of fixed length, with 50 bytes each. We have to map a unique field of this record to a unique RRN within the data set. There are only two unique fields in the record layout, EMPLOYEE-SSN and EMPLOYEE-NUM. For this example, we will use EMPLOYEE-NUM as the unique identification field for a particular record. The hashing algorithm will simply use this number as the RRN itself.[1] Before we make such a decision, we must ensure that the application system requires and will use EMPLOYEE-NUM as the *only* identification field for record retrievals/updates. Since this field is only two numeric digits in size, there cannot be more than 99 employees (hence relative record number slots) in the data set. This may sound like an impractical application, but it will serve our purpose, which is to learn RRDS processing. The records of the personnel/payroll system, when loaded into EMPLOYEE.RRDS.CLUSTER using EMPLOYEE-NUM as the RRN itself, are shown in Fig 16.1.

Note that 20 slots are shown in the figure, but only 9 are being used for the records. The other 11 slots are empty. They will be used only when a record with the corresponding EMPLOYEE-NUM is added to this file.

16.1 SELECT STATEMENT

Figure 16.2 gives the syntax of the SELECT statement for an RRDS.

Assignment name is the DD name of the data set in the JCL. It is not necessary to use a prefix before the DD name. If one is used, it is treated as a comment. The following is valid for the assignment name.

```
SELECT EMPLOYEE-MASTER
    ASSIGN TO EMPMSTR
       •
       •
       •
```

[1]James Martin, *Computer Data Base Organization,* 2d ed. Prentice-Hall, Englewood Cliffs, NJ, 1977, chap. 21.

```
RRN=1  |_________|______________________________|__|_|______|______|
RRN=2  |_________|______________________________|__|_|______|______|
RRN=3  |_________|______________________________|__|_|______|______|
RRN=4  |888888888|KENNER TOWERS, N.Y., N.Y.     |04|F|111855|LEHN  |
RRN=5  |444444444|2-52, FOREST HILLS, QUEENS    |05|M|090252|BUTLER|
RRN=6  |_________|______________________________|__|_|______|______|
RRN=7  |777777777|8 BROAD ST, S.I., N.Y.        |07|F|082913|JOSHI |
RRN=8  |_________|______________________________|__|_|______|______|
RRN=9  |_________|______________________________|__|_|______|______|
RRN=10 |111111111|WORLD PLAZA, N.Y., N.Y.       |10|M|092150|RANADE|
RRN=11 |_________|______________________________|__|_|______|______|
RRN=12 |666666666|15 GREENWICH, CT              |12|M|030511|ADLER |
RRN=13 |999999999|23 SOUTH ST, BRONX, N.Y.      |13|F|100846|RAMSEY|
RRN=14 |_________|______________________________|__|_|______|______|
RRN=15 |_________|______________________________|__|_|______|______|
RRN=16 |333333333|18 MARSH AVE, S.I., N.Y.      |16|F|030942|KRANTZ|
RRN=17 |555555555|7 PARK AVE, JERSEY CITY       |17|M|092057|RANADE|
RRN=18 |_________|______________________________|__|_|______|______|
RRN=19 |222222222|25 OAKWOODS, N.Y.             |19|M|022536|TANAKA|
RRN=20 |_________|______________________________|__|_|______|______|
                                                 ^
                                                 |
                                            EMPLOYEE-NUM
```

Figure 16.1 Record contents of EMPLOYEE.RRDS.CLUSTER including empty slots. EMPLOYEE-NUM has been used as the RRN itself.

The ORGANIZATION IS RELATIVE clause identifies the data set to be an RRDS. This clause must not be omitted and should be coded this way for a relative record file.

The three access modes are the same as those already discussed in previous chapters. In the ACCESS MODE IS clause, SEQUENTIAL is the default. Hence it can be omitted if sequential processing is desired.

The RELATIVE KEY IS clause specifies the data item that will contain the RRN for a particular logical record. Data-name-1 is *not* part of the logical record. It must be defined in the WORKING-STORAGE SECTION as an *unsigned integer* data item. It must be large enough to contain the largest possible RRN for the data set. If the access mode is

```
SELECT     file-name
           ASSIGN TO   assignment-name
           ORGANIZATION IS RELATIVE
                           { SEQUENTIAL }
           ACCESS MODE IS  { RANDOM     }
                           { DYNAMIC    }
           RELATIVE KEY IS data-name-1
           PASSWORD IS     data-name-2
           FILE STATUS IS  data-name-3.
```

Figure 16.2 Syntax of a SELECT statement for an RRDS.

```
IDENTIFICATION DIVISION.
   .
   .
ENVIRONMENT DIVISION.
   .
   .
INPUT-OUTPUT SECTION.
FILE-CONTROL.
    SELECT  EMPLOYEE-MASTER
            ASSIGN TO  EMPMSTR
            ORGANIZATION IS RELATIVE
            ACCESS MODE IS RANDOM
            RELATIVE KEY IS EMPLOYEE-RRN
            FILE STATUS IS EMPLOYEE-FILE-STATUS.
   .
   .
DATA DIVISION.
FILE SECTION.
FD  EMPLOYEE-MASTER
    LABEL RECORDS ARE STANDARD.
01  EMPLOYEE-RECORD                     PIC X(50).
   .
   .
WORKING-STORAGE SECTION.
01  EMPLOYEE-FILE-STATUS                PIC X(2).
01  EMPLOYEE-RRN                        PIC 9(2).
   .
   .
   .
```

Figure 16.3 Sample coding of a SELECT statement for EMPLOYEE.RRDS.CLUSTER for RANDOM processing.

sequential and the START verb is not to be used to begin browsing at a particular record, this clause can be omitted.

The PASSWORD and the FILE STATUS clauses have already been discussed in previous chapters. Figure 16.3 gives sample coding of the SELECT statement for EMPLOYEE.RRDS.CLUSTER, assuming that the data set is not password-protected.

Notice that EMPLOYEE-RRN has been defined as 9(2), which can contain a maximum value of 99. This is because, in our example, the employee number cannot exceed two digits. In other applications, the size should be large enough to contain the largest RRN possible for the data set.

16.2 FILE STATUS

The status codes for an RRDS are the same as for a KSDS. Their meanings are similar, except that in an RRDS reference is made to the RRN

Status key value	Meaning
00	Successful completion of function
10	End-of-file condition on a READ
20	No further information
22	Slot with specific RRN not empty on WRITE
23	Record not found for a particular RRN
24	No space to add record
30	No further information
90	No further information
91	Password failure
92	Logic error
93	Resource (data set or enough virtual storage) not available
94	No current record pointer for sequential request
95	Invalid or incomplete file information
96	No DD card
97	Data set was improperly closed; implicit VERIFY issued and file successfully opened (only DF/EF)

Figure 16.4 FILE STATUS key values and their meanings for an RRDS.

for status codes between 22 and 24. Figure 16.4 gives the status key values and their meanings.

As with the other file organizations, the significance of status codes cannot be overemphasized. Testing of the status code is recommended after each data set operation.

16.3 PROCESSING IN PROCEDURE DIVISION

You will find many similarities between processing a KSDS and an RRDS. One of the major differences in the processing logic is that instead of using a record key we make use of the RRN for record processing.

16.3.1 Limitations of RRDS

Before we learn the syntax and the working logic of various Cobol statements, let's look at some major limitations of an RRDS. An RRDS does not support alternate indexes. So, if you require more than one view of the file on different record fields, an RRDS is not suitable for this particular application. For example, in EMPLOYEE.RRDS.CLUSTER, you cannot randomly access a record on the EMPLOYEE-SSN field. A KSDS with alternate indexes will probably be the only choice in such a case.

An RRDS also *does not* support variable-length records. You can have *only* fixed-length records. If you do require a variable-length record, the fixed length must be equal to the maximum record size possible.

Although an RRN acts like a pseudo-key, you *cannot* use the generic search capability for an RRDS.

16.3.2 OPEN

An RRDS can be opened as INPUT, OUTPUT, or I-O. The syntax is

```
              ⎧INPUT ⎫
OPEN file-name⎨OUTPUT⎬
              ⎩I-O   ⎭
```

An RRDS *cannot* be opened as EXTEND. Successful execution of an OPEN INPUT or OPEN I-O sets the CRP to the first *existing record* in the data set after bypassing all the empty slots before such a record. For the data records shown in Fig. 16.1, such an OPEN will set the CRP to RRN = 4. Thus the record with the smallest RRN is considered the first record. If the file is unloaded, the first sequential READ after a successful OPEN will set the status code to 10.

An RRDS already having records in it cannot be opened as OUTPUT. It must be opened as I-O for record additions.

16.3.3 READ, WRITE, REWRITE, and DELETE

These are the same Cobol verbs that are used to move records between buffers and the direct access storage device for other VSAM file organizations. We will use various examples as they pertain to data records in the file EMPLOYEE.RRDS.CLUSTER. Figure 16.1 gives the contents of this file.

READ An RRDS must be opened as INPUT or I-O in order to read its records. The format for sequential retrievals is

```
READ file-name [INTO identifier]
    [AT END imperative statement]
```

This format is valid if ACCESS MODE IS SEQUENTIAL was specified in the SELECT statement. If the AT END clause is not used, check for a status code of 10 immediately after the READ.

Let's suppose that our RRDS (in Fig 16.1) was opened as INPUT as in Fig. 16.5. The first READ will return the record with RRN 4, thus skipping the first three empty slots.

Any subsequent READ will read the next nonempty slots in RRN

```
       OPEN   INPUT   EMPLOYEE-MASTER.
            .
            .
       READ   EMPLOYEE-MASTER.
       IF     EMPLOYEE-FILE-STATUS = '00'
              PERFORM PROCESS-RECORD
       ELSE
              IF    EMPLOYEE-FILE-STATUS = '10'
                    PERFORM   END-OF-FILE-ROUTINE
              ELSE
                    PERFORM   ERROR-ROUTINE.
            .
            .
            .
```

Figure 16.5 Sample code for sequential retrievals in an RRDS.

sequence. After the record with an RRN of 19 is read, a status code of 10 will be generated. The RELATIVE KEY clause, if specified for this file, will contain the value of the RRN of the record that has most recently been retrieved. This value can be checked and used in any way that you like.

The format for *random* retrievals of RRDS records is

```
READ file-name [INTO identifier]
     [INVALID KEY imperative statement]
```

ACCESS MODE must be RANDOM or DYNAMIC for this. Before executing the above statement, you must move the value of the RRN of the record to be retrieved to the RELATIVE KEY data item. If no record is found in the slot identified by the RRN, the status code will be set to 23. Consider the example in Fig. 16.6.

The READ statement will retrieve the record with an RRN value of 5, i.e., the record in the fifth slot of the data set, and the status key will be set to 00. If a value of 15 had been moved to EMPLOYEE-RRN, the READ would have failed, thus setting the status code to 23. This is because the slot with an RRN of 15 is empty.

WRITE WRITE is used to add new records to a file. The syntax of this statement is

```
WRITE record-name [FROM identifier]
     [INVALID KEY imperative statement]
```

The file must be opened as OUTPUT or I-O. If the file is opened as OUTPUT and ACCESS MODE IS SEQUENTIAL is specified,

```
                .
                .
       OPEN   INPUT   EMPLOYEE-MASTER.
                .
                .
       MOVE   5   TO   EMPLOYEE-RRN.
       READ   EMPLOYEE-MASTER.
       IF     EMPLOYEE-FILE-STATUS = '00'
              PERFORM   PROCESS-RECORD
       ELSE
              IF     EMPLOYEE-FILE-STATUS = '23'
                     PERFORM   RECORD-NOT-FOUND
              ELSE
                     PERFORM   ERROR-ROUTINE.
                .
                .
```

Figure 16.6 Sample code for random retrievals in an RRDS.

records are written in consecutive slots starting with an RRN of 1 and incrementing by 1 for each successive WRITE. This kind of processing may not find much use in real-life applications unless incoming records are in consecutive RRN order without any missing RRN's. But, if the file is opened as OUTPUT and ACCESS MODE IS RANDOM or ACCESS MODE IS DYNAMIC is specified, the RELATIVE KEY data item must contain the desired RRN before the WRITE is executed. Thus the record will be written into the slot specified in the RELATIVE KEY data item.

If the file is to be opened as I-O, ACCESS IS RANDOM or ACCESS IS DYNAMIC must be specified. You cannot have ACCESS IS SEQUENTIAL. Again, the RELATIVE KEY data item must contain the desired RRN before a WRITE is executed. The record will be written into the slot specified in the RELATIVE KEY data item. Consider the example in Fig 16.7. We check for a status code of 22, which means that the WRITE was unsuccessful because it did not find an empty slot as specified in the RELATIVE KEY data item. Any code other than 00 or 22 indicates a serious error. For example, status code 24 would mean that the RRN is outside the file boundaries and thus the WRITE is unsuccessful because of lack of file space.

REWRITE The REWRITE statement enables you to change the contents of an existing record. The file must be opened in the I-O mode. The syntax is

```
REWRITE record-name [FROM identifier]
    [INVALID KEY imperative statement]
```

```
             .
             .
             ACCESS  MODE IS RANDOM.
             .
             .
         OPEN I-O EMPLOYEE-MASTER.
             .
             .
         MOVE   INPUT-EMPNUM   TO   EMPLOYEE-RRN.
         MOVE   INPUT-RECORD   TO   EMPLOYEE-RECORD.
         WRITE   EMPLOYEE-RECORD.
         IF    EMPLOYEE-FILE-STATUS = '00'
               GO TO WRITE-NEXT
         ELSE
               IF    EMPLOYEE-FILE-STATUS = '22'
                     PERFORM DUPLICATE-RECORD-FOUND
               ELSE
                     PERFORM ERROR-ROUTINE.
             .
             .
```

Figure 16.7 Sample coding for the use of a WRITE statement.

If the file is in the SEQUENTIAL access mode, REWRITE must be preceded by a successful READ statement. Thus the REWRITE will replace the record read by the previous READ. In RANDOM or DYNAMIC access modes, there is no need to read a record before replacing it. In this case, the RRN of the record to be replaced is specified in the RELATIVE KEY data item. Since an RRDS does not have a key, you can change any field in the record before using REWRITE. This feature can cause some problems. The sequence of events leading to this could be one of the following.

1. You read a record, change its fields (including the one that determines the RRN), and rewrite it. The correspondence between the unique field and the RRN may be lost. However, the record will be written back into the same slot from which it was read.
2. If, in the course of changing a record, you change the RELATIVE KEY data item, there are two potential problems that you must be sure to catch. First, if you rewrite with the new relative key, you may overlay an existing record that you hadn't intended to; and second, the record that you intended to overlay will still exist in the old slot.

In any of the above cases, the status code will not be indicative of the potential problem.

DELETE DELETE logically removes a record from a particular slot. The relative position of the slot does not change after the deletion. However, the space occupied by the empty slot can be reused only if you write a record in the same slot position with the same RRN. The syntax of DELETE is

```
DELETE file-name
    [INVALID KEY imperative statement]
```

The file must be opened in the I-O mode. If ACCESS MODE IS SEQUENTIAL is specified, the previous I/O statement must have been a successfully executed READ. In the other access modes, there are no such restrictions, but the RELATIVE KEY data item must contain the RRN of the record to be deleted before issuance of this statement.

Suppose we have an application where records of employees who were born before January 1, 1920, have to be deleted because they retired after the age of 65. Figure 16.8 gives sample coding for this. After successful execution of the program, records with an RRN of 7 and 9 will be deleted from EMPLOYEE.RRDS.CLUSTER.

```
                   .
                   .
                   ACCESS MODE IS SEQUENTIAL.
                   .
                   .
           OPEN  I-O  EMPLOYEE-MASTER.
                   .
                   .
       READ-NEXT.
           READ  EMPLOYEE-MASTER.
           IF    EMPLOYEE-FILE-STATUS = '00'
                 NEXT SENTENCE
           ELSE
                 IF    EMPLOYEE-FILE-STATUS = '10'
                       GO TO END-OF-FILE-PARA
                 ELSE
                       GO TO SEVERE-ERROR-READ.
           IF    EMPLOYEE-DOB-YEAR > '19'
                 GO TO READ-NEXT
           ELSE
                 DELETE EMPLOYEE-MASTER.
           IF    EMPLOYEE-FILE-STATUS = '00'
                 GO TO READ-NEXT
           ELSE
                 GO TO SEVERE-ERROR-DELETE.
                   .
                   .
```

Figure 16.8 Sample code showing the use of a DELETE statement.

16.3.4 START and READ NEXT

Both these statements can be used in the context of a sequential browse operation.

START The following is the syntax of the START statement.

```
                              ⎧EQUAL TO        ⎫
                              ⎪=               ⎪
START file-name [KEY IS       ⎨GREATER THAN    ⎬ data-name]
                              ⎪>               ⎪
                              ⎪NOT LESS THAN   ⎪
                              ⎩NOT <           ⎭
     [INVALID KEY imperative-statement]
```

With this statement, we can indicate where in the data set the record position should be established by using a relational operator and the RELATIVE KEY value. Consider the following examples as they pertain to the data in Fig. 16.1.

```
MOVE 07 TO EMPLOYEE-RRN.
START EMPLOYEE-MASTER KEY IS EQUAL TO
   EMPLOYEE-RRN.
```

Upon successful execution, the position will be established at the record with an RRN of 7.

```
MOVE 08 TO EMPLOYEE-RRN.
START EMPLOYEE-MASTER KEY IS GREATER THAN
   EMPLOYEE-RRN.
```

Upon successful execution, the position will be established at the record with an RRN of 10.

```
MOVE 13 TO EMPLOYEE-RRN.
START EMPLOYEE-MASTER KEY IS NOT LESS THAN
   EMPLOYEE-RRN.
```

Upon successful execution, the position will be established at the record with an RRN of 13.

```
MOVE 02 TO EMPLOYEE-RRN.
START EMPLOYEE-MASTER KEY IS EQUAL TO
   EMPLOYEE-RRN.
```

After completion, the status code returned will be 23 because the slot with an RRN of 02 is empty and the relational criterion is not satisfied.

When the KEY IS option is not specified, the equal-to relational operator is implied. The data set item used in the comparison is *always* the RELATIVE KEY data item as specified in the SELECT statement.

READ NEXT Once a position is successfully established on a record using the START statement, records can be sequentially retrieved using READ (for ACCESS MODE IS SEQUENTIAL) or READ NEXT (for ACCESS MODE IS DYNAMIC). The syntax of this statement is

```
READ file-name NEXT [INTO identifier ]
    [AT END imperative statement]
```

Each execution of this statement will read the record pointed to by the current record pointer and will move the CRP to the next slot containing a record. If there are any empty slots, they will be skipped while the CRP is being advanced. Figure 16.9 gives sample code for the use of START and READ NEXT for an RRDS.

16.3.5 Current Record Pointer

A CRP for an RRDS is similar to a CRP for a KSDS. It is a conceptual pointer that applies only to sequential requests and has no meaning for random retrievals. A CRP indicates the next record to be accessed by a READ (sequential mode) or READ NEXT (dynamic mode).

A CRP can be established through a successful OPEN, READ, READ NEXT, or START. An OPEN establishes it on the first nonempty RRDS slot, skipping all the empty slots before it. A READ or READ NEXT sets it on the nonempty slot immediately following the one just read. A START sets it on the first slot that satisfies the comparison in the statement.

A *sequential* retrieval request always reads the slot that the CRP points to and moves the CRP to the next nonempty slot. A CRP that has been rendered undefined because of an unsuccessful OPEN, START, READ, or READ NEXT must be reestablished before issuing another sequential browse request. This can be done with a CLOSE followed by a successful OPEN, successful execution of a START statement, or successful execution of a random READ.

A CRP is *unaffected* by DELETE, WRITE, or REWRITE. Execution of these statements will leave the CRP pointing to the same RRN as before, and any subsequent sequential READ or READ NEXT will be executed from the position left by the previously established CRP. Figure 16.10 shows a sequence of events affecting the CRP when various state-

```
                 .
                 .
       OPEN  INPUT  EMPLOYEE-MASTER.
                 .
                 .
       MOVE    6  TO EMPLOYEE-RRN.
       START EMPLOYEE-MASTER
                KEY IS > EMPLOYEE-RRN.
       IF    EMPLOYEE-FILE-STATUS = '00'
             NEXT SENTENCE
       ELSE
             IF    EMPLOYEE-FILE-STATUS = '23'
                   GO TO POSITION-NOT-ESTABLISHED
             ELSE
                   PERFORM ABNORMAL-TERMINATION.
*****************************************************************
**** SUCCESSFUL START ESTABLISHES POSITION   ****
****           AT RRN '07'                   ****
*****************************************************************
       READ EMPLOYEE-MASTER NEXT.
       IF    EMPLOYEE-FILE-STATUS = '00'
             PERFORM PROCESS-RECORD
       ELSE
             IF    EMPLOYEE-FILE-STATUS = '10'
                   PERFORM END-OF-FILE-PARA
             ELSE
                   PERFORM ABNORMAL-TERMINATION.
*****************************************************************
**** SUCCESSFUL READ WILL RETRIEVE RECORD    ****
**** WITH RRN '07' AND CRP IS MOVED TO RRN   ****
**** '10', THUS SKIPPING EMPTY SLOTS WITH    ****
**** RRN '08' AND '09'                       ****
*****************************************************************
                 .
                 .
```

Figure 16.9 Sample code for using START and READ NEXT. The data used is described in Fig. 16.1. ACCESS MODE IS DYNAMIC was specified in the SELECT statement.

ments are executed on EMPLOYEE.RRDS.CLUSTER with data records as in Fig. 16.1.

16.3.6 Summary of Possible Combinations

We already know that RRDS files can have an access mode of SEQUENTIAL, RANDOM, or DYNAMIC and that they can be opened as INPUT, OUTPUT, or I-O. The different I-O verbs we can use are OPEN, READ, WRITE, REWRITE, START, DELETE, and CLOSE. Certain combinations of access modes, OPEN modes, and I/O verbs (except CLOSE) are permitted, while others are not. Figure 16.11 provides

Statement number	Cobol statement	RRN of record read/deleted/ written/rewritten	RRN of CRP	Status code
1	ACCESS MODE DYNAMIC; OPEN I-O	—	04	00
2	READ NEXT	04	05	00
3	MOVE 07 TO RELATIVE KEY; READ random	07	10	00
4	DELETE	07	10	00
5	READ NEXT	10	12	00
6	MOVE 19 TO RELATIVE KEY; START with EQUAL operator	—	19	00
7	READ NEXT	19	End-of-file	00
8	Change record contents; REWRITE	19	End-of-file	00
9	READ NEXT	—	Undefined	10
10	READ NEXT	—	Undefined	94
11	MOVE 01 TO RELATIVE KEY; START with > operator	—	04	00
12	Format and WRITE a record with RRN = 15	15	04	00
13	READ NEXT	04	05	00
14	CLOSE and then OPEN the file	—	04	00

Figure 16.10 Effect of various statements on CRP as it applies to the records in Fig. 16.1 loaded into EMPLOYEE.RRDS.CLUSTER.

ACCESS MODE	OPEN mode: INPUT	OUTPUT	I-O
SEQUENTIAL	OPEN READ START	OPEN WRITE	OPEN READ START REWRITE DELETE
RANDOM	OPEN READ	OPEN WRITE	OPEN READ WRITE REWRITE DELETE
DYNAMIC	OPEN READ START	OPEN WRITE	OPEN READ START WRITE REWRITE DELETE

Figure 16.11 Tabular representation of I/O verbs allowed for an RRDS with particular ACCESS MODEs and OPEN modes.

the permissible combinations in tabular form. This table can be used as a quick reference when needed.

16.4 PROGRAM EXAMPLE 1: LOADING AN RRDS

Loading an RRDS is quite different from loading a KSDS or an ESDS. While you can sort records on the prime key and load a file straight into a KSDS, there is no similar straightforward technique for an RRDS. The reason for this is that you have to use a hashing algorithm to determine the RRN for a record. The RRN generated could be a purely random number. So, the logic for loading an RRDS for the first time is almost the same as for updating it later on.

We will write a program that reads a PS data set and loads EMPLOYEE.RRDS.CLUSTER from scratch. The input records are the same as those we have used in previous chapters. Figure 16.12 gives the contents of the input file SAMPLE.INPUT.DATA.

We will use Employee-Number, which is a unique field, as the RRN itself for loading the records. The program should take care of duplicate record conditions if two or more records with the same Employee-Number (hence the same RRN) happen to be in the input file. As you can see, the records in SAMPLE.INPUT.DATA are not sorted on the Employee-Number field. It would be more efficient if they were sorted in this particular case because there would be less movement of the read-

111111111	WORLD PLAZA, N.Y., N.Y.	10	M	092150	RANADE
222222222	25 OAKWOODS, N.Y.	19	M	022536	TANAKA
333333333	18 MARSH AVE, S.I., N.Y.	16	F	030942	KRANTZ
444444444	2-52 FOREST HILLS, QUEENS	05	M	090252	BUTLER
555555555	7 PARK AVE, JERSEY CITY	17	M	092057	RANADE
666666666	15 GREENWICH, CT	12	M	030511	ADLER
777777777	8 BROAD ST., S.I., N.Y.	07	F	082913	JOSHI
888888888	KENNER TOWERS, N.Y., N.Y.	04	F	111855	LEHN
999999999	23 SOUTH ST.. BRONX. N.Y.	13	F	100846	RAMSEY

Employee-Number

Figure 16.12 Record contents of file SAMPLE.INPUT.DATA which are being used to load EMPLOYEE.RRDS.CLUSTER.

write head on the disk. However, the program logic will not be affected, even though records will be processed out of sequence. After the program has successfully loaded the RRDS, the contents of the data set should look exactly as shown in Fig. 16.1. In order to keep the logic simple, we will not do any editing. Figure 16.13 gives the sample code for such a program.

```
 IDENTIFICATION DIVISION.
 PROGRAM-ID.   RRDSLOAD.
 AUTHOR.       RANADE.
*************************************************************
*** THIS PROGRAM READS A PHYSICAL SEQUENTIAL ****
*** FILE AND LOADS RECORDS INTO EMPLOYEE      ****
*** MASTER, AN RRDS.EMPLOYEE-NUMBER AS SUCH   ****
*** IS BEING USED AS THE RRN FOR THE DATASET.****
*************************************************************

 ENVIRONMENT DIVISION.
 CONFIGURATION SECTION.
 INPUT-OUTPUT SECTION.
 FILE-CONTROL.
      SELECT  INPUT-FILE
              ASSIGN TO UT-S-INPUT.
      SELECT  EMPLOYEE-MASTER
              ASSIGN TO  EMPMSTR
              ORGANIZATION IS RELATIVE
              ACCESS MODE IS RANDOM
              RELATIVE KEY IS EMPLOYEE-RRN
              FILE STATUS IS EMPLOYEE-FILE-STATUS.
```

Figure 16.13 Program listing for the initial load of EMPLOYEE.RRDS.CLUSTER from SAMPLE.INPUT.DATA. EMPLOYEE-NUM is being used as the RRN for the RRDS.

```

 DATA DIVISION.
 FILE SECTION.
 FD  INPUT-FILE
     LABEL RECORDS ARE STANDARD
     RECORD CONTAINS 50 CHARACTERS
     BLOCK CONTAINS 0 RECORDS.
 01  INPUT-RECORD.
     05  FILLER                          PIC X(35).
     05  INPUT-EMPNUM                    PIC 9(2).
     05  FILLER                          PIC X(13).
 FD  EMPLOYEE-MASTER
     LABEL RECORDS ARE STANDARD.
 01  EMPLOYEE-RECORD                     PIC X(50).

 WORKING-STORAGE SECTION.
 01  EMPLOYEE-FILE-STATUS                PIC X(2).
 01  EMPLOYEE-RRN                        PIC 9(2).
 01  ABEND-PROGRAM                       PIC X(8)
                                   VALUE 'ILBOABN0'.
 01  ABEND-CODE                          PIC S999 COMP
                                   VALUE +999.
 PROCEDURE DIVISION.
 100-MAIN-PARA.
     OPEN OUTPUT EMPLOYEE-MASTER.
*****************************************************************
*****************************************************************
***  TEST FOR SUCESSFUL OPEN OF RRDS                        ****
*****************************************************************
*****************************************************************
     IF    EMPLOYEE-FILE-STATUS = '00'
           NEXT SENTENCE
     ELSE
           DISPLAY 'OPEN ERROR ON EMPMSTR'
           DISPLAY 'STATUS CODE IS  '
                   EMPLOYEE-FILE-STATUS
           CALL ABEND-PROGRAM USING ABEND-CODE.
     OPEN INPUT INPUT-FILE.
     PERFORM  200-LOAD-EMPMSTR THRU 200-EXIT.
     CLOSE INPUT-FILE
           EMPLOYEE-MASTER.
*****************************************************************
*****************************************************************
***  TEST FOR SUCESSFUL CLOSE OF RRDS                        ***
*****************************************************************
*****************************************************************
     IF    EMPLOYEE-FILE-STATUS = '00'
           NEXT SENTENCE
     ELSE
           DISPLAY 'CLOSE ERROR ON EMPMSTR'
           DISPLAY 'STATUS CODE IS  '
                   EMPLOYEE-FILE-STATUS
           CALL ABEND-PROGRAM USING ABEND-CODE.
     GOBACK.

 200-LOAD-EMPMSTR.
     READ  INPUT-FILE
           AT END GO TO 200-EXIT.
```

```
           MOVE INPUT-RECORD TO EMPLOYEE-RECORD.
           MOVE INPUT-EMPNUM TO EMPLOYEE-RRN.
           WRITE EMPLOYEE-RECORD.
      ***********************************************************
      ***********************************************************
      ***  TEST FOR SUCESSFUL WRITE TO RRDS                   ***
      ***********************************************************
      ***********************************************************
           IF    EMPLOYEE-FILE-STATUS = '00'
                 GO TO 200-LOAD-EMPMSTR
           ELSE
                 IF    EMPLOYEE-FILE-STATUS = '22'
                       DISPLAY 'DUPLICATE RECORD'
                               INPUT-RECORD
                       GO TO 200-LOAD-EMPMSTR
                 ELSE
                       DISPLAY 'SEVERE VSAM ERROR ON WRITE'
                       DISPLAY 'STATUS CODE IS  '
                               EMPLOYEE-FILE-STATUS
                       DISPLAY 'RECORD IS  ' INPUT-RECORD
                       CALL ABEND-PROGRAM USING ABEND-CODE.
       200-EXIT.
           EXIT.
```

Figure 16.13 (*continued*)

In writing the initial load programs for the other data set organizations (KSDS and ESDS), we used ACCESS MODE IS SEQUENTIAL. For an RRDS, this would have written records beginning with an RRN of 1 and incrementing it by 1 for each subsequent add. This is not what we want for this application. We want the RRN to be the Employee-Number. So, we have used ACCESS MODE IS RANDOM. In the PROCEDURE DIVISION, the record is written to the EMPLOYEE-MASTER after setting the RELATIVE KEY to the value of the Employee-Number for the particular record. This ensures that the record is being written in the right slot. We check for status code 22 to detect any duplicate record conditions.

The execution JCL for an RRDS is the same as that for a KSDS or an ESDS. Figure 16.14 gives the sample JCL for the execution of program RRDSLOAD.

16.5 PROGRAM EXAMPLE 2: RANDOM UPDATE OF AN RRDS

In the previous example we learned how to load an unloaded RRDS in the random access mode. Now, we will update the *same* RRDS with record additions, changes, and deletions. We will use a physical sequential file as input for the various transactions. Its record length is 51 bytes, the first byte containing A, C, or D to indicate whether the transaction is to be used for adding, changing, or deleting a record of the RRDS. The

```
//LOADJOB   JOB (ACCTNO),'JAY RANADE'
//LOADSTEP  EXEC PGM=RRDSLOAD
//STEPLIB   DD DSN=SAMPLE.PROGRAM.LOAD,DISP=SHR
//          DD DSN=SYS1.COBLIB,DISP=SHR
//INPUT     DD DSN=SAMPLE.INPUT.DATA,
//             DISP=OLD
//EMPMSTR   DD DSN=EMPLOYEE.RRDS.CLUSTER,
//             DISP=OLD
//SYSOUT    DD SYSOUT=A
//DISPLAY   DD SYSOUT=A
//SYSUSUMP  DD SYSOUT=A
//
```

Figure 16.14 JCL for executing the load program for an RRDS.

rest of the fields have a one-to-one correspondence with the fields of the RRDS record. Employee-Number, of course, is the RRN for the records. ACCESS MODE IS RANDOM will be used, and the file will be opened as I-O. No editing will be done on the input data. Figure 16.15 has a sample listing for this program.

```
 IDENTIFICATION DIVISION.
 PROGRAM-ID.   RRDSUPDT.
 AUTHOR.       RANADE.
*****************************************************************
*** THIS PROGRAM READS A PS FILE. BASED ON       ****
*** TRANSACTION CODE A,D OR C ,IT ADDS,          ****
*** DELETES OR CHANGES RECORDS IN RRDS.          ****
*****************************************************************
 ENVIRONMENT DIVISION.
 CONFIGURATION SECTION.
 INPUT-OUTPUT SECTION.
 FILE-CONTROL.
     SELECT  TRANS-FILE
             ASSIGN TO UT-S-TRANS.
     SELECT  EMPLOYEE-MASTER
             ASSIGN TO  EMPMSTR
             ORGANIZATION IS RELATIVE
             ACCESS MODE  IS RANDOM
             RELATIVE KEY IS EMPLOYEE-RRN
             FILE STATUS IS EMPLOYEE-FILE-STATUS.
 DATA DIVISION.
 FILE SECTION.
 FD  TRANS-FILE
     LABEL RECORDS ARE STANDARD
     RECORD CONTAINS 51 CHARACTERS
     BLOCK CONTAINS 0 RECORDS.
```

Figure 16.15 Program listing for a random update of EMPLOYEE.RRDS.CLUSTER. The transaction file is SAMPLE.RRDSUPDT.DATA. The program takes care of adds, changes, and deletes.

```
 01   TRANS-RECORD.
          05  TRANS-CODE                          PIC X.
          05  TRANS-REST.
              10  TRANS-SSN                       PIC X(9).
              10  TRANS-ADD                       PIC X(26).
              10  TRANS-NUM                       PIC 9(2).
              10  TRANS-SEX                       PIC X.
              10  TRANS-DOB                       PIC X(6).
              10  TRANS-NAME                      PIC X(6).
 FD   EMPLOYEE-MASTER
      LABEL RECORDS ARE STANDARD.
 01   EMPLOYEE-RECORD.
      10  EMPLOYEE-SSN                            PIC X(9).
      10  EMPLOYEE-ADD                            PIC X(26).
      10  EMPLOYEE-NUM                            PIC 9(2).
      10  EMPLOYEE-SEX                            PIC X.
      10  EMPLOYEE-DOB                            PIC X(6).
      10  EMPLOYEE-NAME                           PIC X(6).

 WORKING-STORAGE SECTION.
 01   EMPLOYEE-FILE-STATUS                        PIC X(2).
 01   EMPLOYEE-RRN                                PIC 9(2).
 01   ABEND-PROGRAM                               PIC X(8)
                                          VALUE 'ILBOABNO'.
 01   ABEND-CODE                                  PIC S999 COMP
                                          VALUE +999.

 PROCEDURE DIVISION.
 100-MAIN-PARA.
      OPEN  I-O   EMPLOYEE-MASTER.
*****************************************************************
***  TEST FOR SUCESSFUL OPEN OF RRDS                         ****
*****************************************************************

      IF    EMPLOYEE-FILE-STATUS = '00'
            NEXT SENTENCE
      ELSE
            DISPLAY 'OPEN ERROR ON EMPMSTR'
            DISPLAY 'STATUS CODE IS  '
                    EMPLOYEE-FILE-STATUS
            CALL ABEND-PROGRAM USING ABEND-CODE.
      OPEN INPUT TRANS-FILE.
      PERFORM  200-UPDATE-EMPMSTR THRU 200-EXIT.
      CLOSE TRANS-FILE
             EMPLOYEE-MASTER.
*****************************************************************
***  TEST FOR SUCESSFUL CLOSE OF RRDS                         ***
*****************************************************************

      IF    EMPLOYEE-FILE-STATUS = '00'
            NEXT SENTENCE
      ELSE
            DISPLAY 'CLOSE ERROR ON EMPMSTR'
            DISPLAY 'STATUS CODE IS  '
                    EMPLOYEE-FILE-STATUS
            CALL ABEND-PROGRAM USING ABEND-CODE.
      GOBACK.


 200-UPDATE-EMPMSTR.
      READ  TRANS-FILE
             AT END GO TO 200-EXIT.
```

```
           IF    TRANS-CODE = 'A'
                 PERFORM 300-ADD-RECORD
                         THRU 300-EXIT
           ELSE
                 IF    TRANS-CODE = 'D'
                       PERFORM 400-DELETE-RECORD
                               THRU 400-EXIT
                 ELSE
                       IF    TRANS-CODE = 'C'
                             PERFORM 500-CHANGE-RECORD
                                     THRU 500-EXIT
                       ELSE
                             DISPLAY 'ILLEGAL TRANS CODE FOR'
                             DISPLAY 'RECORD ' TRANS-RECORD.
                 GO TO 200-UPDATE-EMPMSTR.
       200-EXIT.
           EXIT.

       300-ADD-RECORD.
           MOVE TRANS-NUM TO EMPLOYEE-RRN.
           MOVE TRANS-REST TO EMPLOYEE-RECORD.
           WRITE  EMPLOYEE-RECORD.
      ***********************************************************
      ***   TEST FOR SUCESSFUL  ADD TO  RRDS                  ***
      ***********************************************************
           IF    EMPLOYEE-FILE-STATUS = '00'
                 GO TO 300-EXIT
           ELSE
                 IF    EMPLOYEE-FILE-STATUS = '22'
                       DISPLAY 'DUPLICATE RECORD ON ADD '
                       DISPLAY 'RECORD IS  ' TRANS-RECORD
                       GO TO 300-EXIT
                 ELSE
                       DISPLAY 'SEVERE ERROR ON ADD '
                       DISPLAY 'STATUS CODE IS  '
                               EMPLOYEE-FILE-STATUS
                       DISPLAY 'RECORD IS  ' TRANS-RECORD
                       CALL ABEND-PROGRAM USING ABEND-CODE.
       300-EXIT.
           EXIT.

       400-DELETE-RECORD.
           MOVE TRANS-NUM TO EMPLOYEE-RRN.
           DELETE EMPLOYEE-MASTER.
      ***********************************************************
      ***   TEST FOR SUCESSFUL DELETE IN RRDS                 ***
      ***********************************************************
           IF    EMPLOYEE-FILE-STATUS = '00'
                 GO TO 400-EXIT
           ELSE
                 IF    EMPLOYEE-FILE-STATUS = '23'
                       DISPLAY 'RECORD NOT FOUND ON DELETE '
                       DISPLAY 'RECORD IS  ' TRANS-RECORD
                       GO TO 400-EXIT
                 ELSE
                       DISPLAY 'SEVERE ERROR ON DELETE'
                       DISPLAY 'STATUS CODE IS  '
                               EMPLOYEE-FILE-STATUS
                       DISPLAY 'RECORD IS  ' TRANS-RECORD
                       CALL ABEND-PROGRAM USING ABEND-CODE.
```

```
 400-EXIT.
        EXIT.

 500-CHANGE-RECORD.
        MOVE TRANS-NUM TO EMPLOYEE-RRN.
        READ EMPLOYEE-MASTER.
*********************************************************
***   TEST FOR SUCESSFUL READ  OF RRDS RECORD       ***
*********************************************************
        IF    EMPLOYEE-FILE-STATUS = '00'
              NEXT SENTENCE
        ELSE
              IF    EMPLOYEE-FILE-STATUS = '23'
                    DISPLAY 'RECORD NOT FOUND ON READ'
                    DISPLAY 'RECORD IS  ' TRANS-RECORD
                    GO TO 500-EXIT
              ELSE
                    DISPLAY 'SEVERE ERROR ON READ '
                    DISPLAY 'STATUS CODE IS  '
                            EMPLOYEE-FILE-STATUS
                    DISPLAY 'RECORD IS  ' TRANS-RECORD
                    CALL ABEND-PROGRAM USING ABEND-CODE.
        IF    TRANS-SSN  NOT = SPACES
              MOVE TRANS-SSN  TO EMPLOYEE-SSN.
        IF    TRANS-ADD  NOT = SPACES
              MOVE TRANS-ADD  TO EMPLOYEE-ADD.
        IF    TRANS-SEX  NOT = SPACES
              MOVE TRANS-SEX  TO EMPLOYEE-SEX.
        IF    TRANS-DOB  NOT = SPACES
              MOVE TRANS-DOB  TO EMPLOYEE-DOB.
        IF    TRANS-NAME NOT = SPACES
              MOVE TRANS-NAME TO EMPLOYEE-NAME.
        REWRITE  EMPLOYEE-RECORD.
*********************************************************
***   TEST FOR SUCESSFUL  REWRITE TO RRDS           ***
*********************************************************
        IF    EMPLOYEE-FILE-STATUS = '00'
              GO TO 500-EXIT
        ELSE
              DISPLAY 'SEVERE ERROR ON REWRITE '
              DISPLAY 'STATUS CODE IS  '
                      EMPLOYEE-FILE-STATUS
              DISPLAY 'RECORD IS  ' TRANS-RECORD
              CALL ABEND-PROGRAM USING ABEND-CODE.
 500-EXIT.
        EXIT.
```

Figure 16.15 *(continued)*

As usual, we are making extensive status code checks in order to determine the outcome of the execution of various statements. We may expect status code 23 on READ or DELETE, which means that the record cannot be found. On a WRITE, the status code could be 22 if there is already a record in the same RRN slot for which the record add is intended.

```
RELATIVE RECORD NUMBER - 4
888888888 KENNER TOWERS,N.Y,N.Y      04F111855LEHN

RELATIVE RECORD NUMBER - 5
444444444 2-52,FOREST HILLS,QUEENS 05M090252BUTLER

RELATIVE RECORD NUMBER - 7
777777777 8,BROAD ST,S.I,N.Y         07F082913JOSHI

RELATIVE RECORD NUMBER - 10
111111111 WORLD PLAZA,N.Y,N.Y        10M092150RANADE

RELATIVE RECORD NUMBER - 12
666666666 15,GREENWICH ,CT           12M030511ADLER

RELATIVE RECORD NUMBER - 13
999999999 23,SOUTH ST,BRONX,N.Y      13F100846RAMSEY

RELATIVE RECORD NUMBER - 16
333333333 18,MARSH AV,S.I,N.Y        16F030942KRANTZ

RELATIVE RECORD NUMBER - 17
555555555 7,PARK AV,JERSEY CITY      17M092057RANADE

RELATIVE RECORD NUMBER - 19
222222222 25,OAKWOODS,N.Y            19M022536TANAKA
```

Figure 16.16 Character dump of EMPLOYEE.RRDS.CLUSTER before executing the RRDSUPDT program.

	Trans-Code			Employee-Number			
Record 1	A	111122222	28 DEBBIE ST., S.I., N.Y.	01	M	062164	SMITH
Record 2	A	222233333	25 OZONE PARK, QUEENS	07	F	081846	MCNEAL
Record 3	D			12			
Record 4	D			15			
Record 5	C		KANNER PLAZA, N.Y., N.Y.	04			
Record 6	C			20			CARSON

Figure 16.17 Contents of SAMPLE.RRDSUPDT.DATA.

```
DUPLICATE RECORD ON ADD
RECORD IS   A222233333 25,OZONE PARK,QUEENS      07F081846MCNEAL
RECORD NOT FOUND ON DELETE
RECORD IS   D                                    15
RECORD NOT FOUND ON READ
RECORD IS   C                                    20          CARSON
```

Figure 16.18 Display messages generated upon execution of the RRDSUPDT program.

Now let's execute the program on a real transaction file. Figure 16.16 gives the character dump of EMPLOYEE.RRDS.CLUSTER as it existed *before* the updates. The contents of this dump are the same as those shown in Fig 16.1. The transaction records contained in SAMPLE.RRDSUPDT.DATA are those given in Fig. 16.17.

As you can see, there are six records in the transaction file. The records have been purposely created so that records 1, 3, and 5 perform a successful add, delete, and change, respectively, but records 2, 4, and 6 produce unsuccessful updates. Upon successful execution of the program, the three display messages for the unsuccessful updates are given in Fig. 16.18.

Status codes and the messages generated are self-explanatory. The master files had nine records to start with. After three updates (one add, one delete, and one change), it will still have nine records. Figure 16.19 shows a character dump after the execution of RRDSUPDT.

Finally, let's consider a typical update problem. How do we handle a case where one of the changes required in the record is the EMPLOYEE-

```
RELATIVE RECORD NUMBER - 1
111122222 28,DEBBIE ST,S.I,N.Y      01M062164SMITH

RELATIVE RECORD NUMBER - 4
888888888 KANNER PLAZA,N.Y,N.Y      04F111855LEHN

RELATIVE RECORD NUMBER - 5
444444444 2-52,FOREST HILLS,QUEENS 05M090252BUTLER

RELATIVE RECORD NUMBER - 7
777777777 8,BROAD ST,S.I,N.Y        07F082913JOSHI

RELATIVE RECORD NUMBER - 10
111111111 WORLD PLAZA,N.Y,N.Y       10M092150RANADE

RELATIVE RECORD NUMBER - 13
999999999 23,SOUTH ST,BRONX,N.Y     13F100846RAMSEY

RELATIVE RECORD NUMBER - 16
333333333 18,MARSH AV,S.I,N.Y       16F030942KRANTZ

RELATIVE RECORD NUMBER - 17
555555555 7,PARK AV,JERSEY CITY     17M092057RANADE

RELATIVE RECORD NUMBER - 19
222222222 25,OAKWOODS,N.Y           19M022536TANAKA
```

Figure 16.19 Character dump of EMPLOYEE.RRDS.CLUSTER after execution of the RRDSUPDT program.

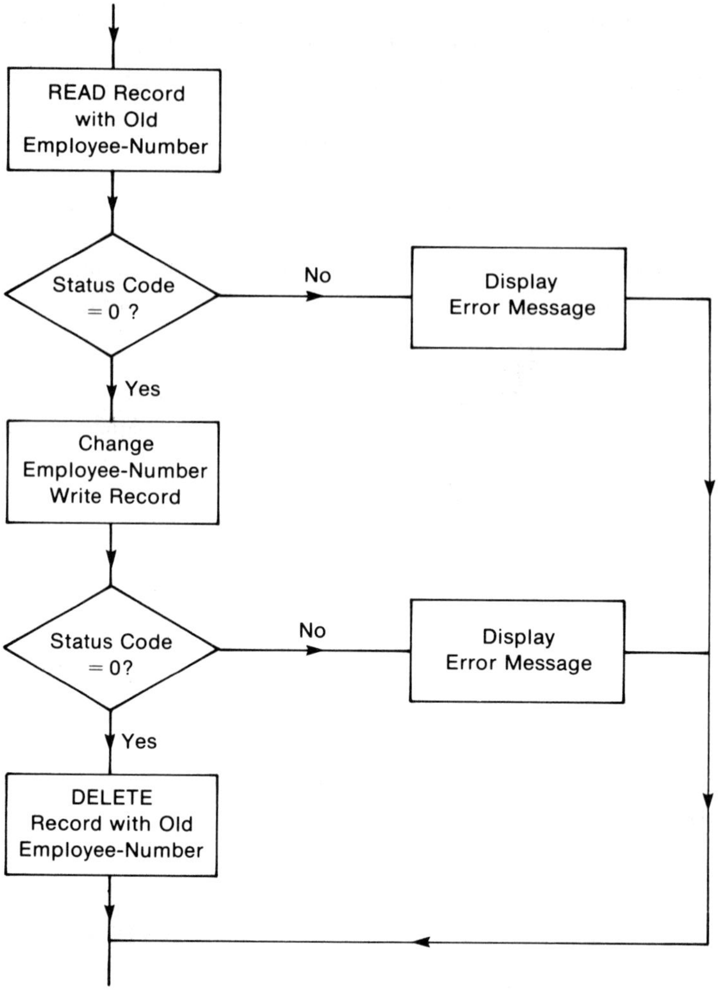

Figure 16.20 Flowchart for a typical problem where the field to be changed is the one that affects the RRN itself.

NUM itself? Since this value is also the RRN of the record, we cannot simply change its value and rewrite the record. It should be done using logic similar to that given in the flowchart in Fig. 16.20.

Although the update program RRDSUPDT does not take care of this aspect of record updating (it is, in fact, an add and a delete), it can easily be incorporated into the program logic. Some designers prefer to have a separate update program for this kind of change.

Now, a final word of caution is in order. RRDS files do not provide a facility for checking whether unique fields occur more than once. For example, in this particular case we cannot verify whether a second record with an existing EMPLOYEE-SSN has also been added. A KSDS with alternate indexes allows the rejection of such updates, but in an RRDS other means have to be provided to take care of such situations. However, depending on our imagination and design skills, we can always find a use for this data set organization. Remember, an RRDS incurs only one I/O for each file-processing statement, while a KSDS may generate anywhere from two to four.

four

MISCELLANEOUS TOPICS

Part 4 will cover VSAM features that do not logically fit into any of the previous chapters. Most of the topics are unrelated to each other. The section on the differences in how VS Cobol II handles VSAM will be useful if your installation is planning to or has already installed this compiler. We will also cover some elementary concepts of performance considerations. This topic could be the subject matter of an entire book. You should study VSAM data set sharing carefully to fully appreciate the problems involved. The use of AMS commands under TSO/SPF will be found to be a useful and powerful tool.

chapter 17

Additional Features of VSAM

This chapter is a mixture of unrelated topics that are quite useful and interesting. Each section can be read independently of the others.

17.1 ISAM-TO-VSAM CONVERSION

You might be working at one of the few installations that are still using ISAM as the access method for random access files. Even installations that have converted to VSAM may still have some production systems using indexed sequential files. You should be aware of the fact that IBM does not support ISAM anymore. The VS Cobol II compiler[1] doesn't even compile a program that has the NOMINAL KEY (for ISAM) clause coded in it. So, if you have any programs using ISAM, you may not be able to modify them and compile them using the VS Cobol II compiler. Also, CICS/VS 1.7 does not support ISAM files at all. If you have been delaying the conversion process, do it now.

Conversion involves two phases. Phase 1 consists of converting data sets from ISAM to VSAM, usually without modifying any Cobol programs. This is normally easy and accomplished quickly. Phase 2 consists of converting the source code of the Cobol programs themselves to

[1]The VS Cobol II compiler is the latest IBM compiler that supports MVS/XA architecture. It will be discussed in Sec. 17.6.

conform to VSAM restrictions and requirements. This is a relatively time-consuming job.

Phase 1: File Conversion This phase involves the use of an IBM program product called ISAM Interface Program (IIP), which eases the process of conversion from ISAM to VSAM. It consists of the following two steps.

1. Convert the files from indexed sequential to KSDS's. This can be accomplished by allocating a KSDS using DEFINE CLUSTER and the REPRO command to transfer all the records from the indexed sequential file into it. When allocating the KSDS, make sure that the record length, key length, and its offset are the same as those of the file being converted.
2. Convert the JCL job streams that are using the related files from indexed sequential to VSAM. This is quite simple. While ISAM files require a long parameter list on the DD card, VSAM files need only the DSN and DISP parameters in most cases. When converting JCL job streams, the recovery and restart procedures, as they specifically apply to VSAM files, must be reconsidered. The programs and procedures that were used to reorganize ISAM files should also be modified. If the file was being deleted and defined using JCL statements, you will have to code the DELETE and DEFINE CLUSTER commands to perform the same function.

Once these two steps are finished, your conversion is complete. You do not have to modify any programs. ISAM Interface Program, which is a standard feature of the system software, takes care of the rest. When a program that was written to process ISAM files tries to open the data set and detects that it is a VSAM file, IIP takes control and becomes an interface between the ISAM-coded program and the KSDS data set. Basically, it traps all the file I/O statements and translates them into equivalent VSAM requests. When the file I/O is complete, it checks the VSAM return codes and translates them back into the ISAM codes. The program thinks it is processing an ISAM file, and the presence of a KSDS becomes transparent to it. Figure 17.1 gives a pictorial view of how IIP interfaces with the program and how the indexed sequential data sets are converted to KSDS's.

With the exception of the application program's VSAM JCL, you don't have to code any JCL to use the IIP. Even its presence is transparent to you. It is invoked automatically.

There are, however, certain considerations you should keep in mind. You must make sure that the existing ISAM programs do not violate any of the restrictions for using the interface. The program must run successfully under ISAM. If the program is ever modified, it must be tested against ISAM data sets. The interface cannot be trusted if the parameters are invalid for ISAM itself. If an ISAM program has two SELECT state-

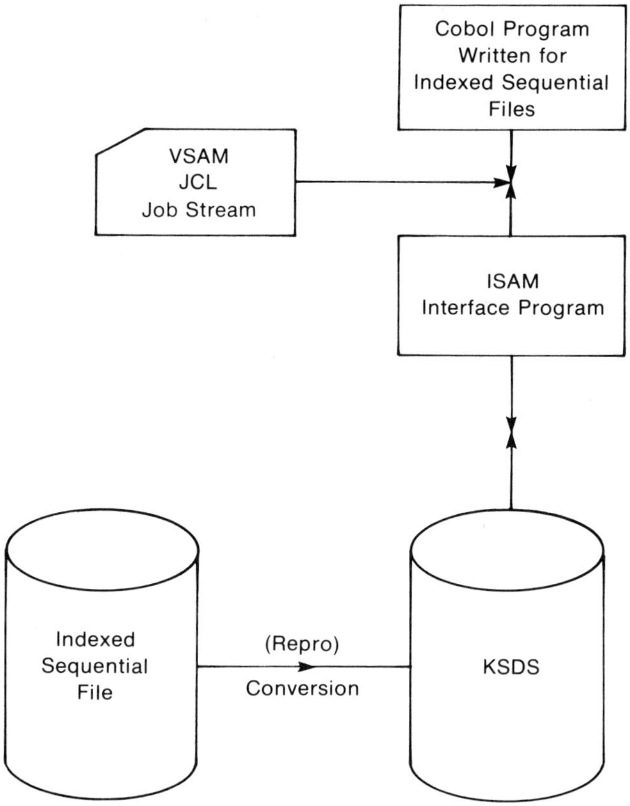

Figure 17.1 IIP as an interface between an ISAM-coded Cobol program and a KSDS converted from an indexed sequential file.

ments for the same indexed sequential file, make sure that they point to the same assignment name, hence DD name. Otherwise, there may be data integrity problems. If a program is reading records into a work area that is smaller than the record size, increase the work area to the size of the record. These are among the most common restrictions when using IIP for a Cobol program.

Phase 2 This phase involves changing the programs themselves to make use of VSAM verbs and statements. This is done to make use of new VSAM features like alternate indexes, the use of DELETE, etc. IIP does not have much overhead on processing cycles or virtual storage, so performance considerations should not be a reason for conversion. If your installation is planning to use the VS Cobol II compiler, you have no choice but to convert ISAM-coded programs to VSAM code.

In a nutshell, converting from ISAM to VSAM for a Cobol environment is not a very difficult task. All it requires is careful planning.

17.2 FEATURES OF VSAM NOT AVAILABLE IN BATCH COBOL

VSAM is a powerful access method. To make full use of its capabilities, you must use assembler language. High-level language compilers like OS/VS Cobol do not support all the features available. *The following are some of the features that are unavailable through Cobol. Some are available through use of the means described.*

1. *Access by RBA:* Accessing an ESDS or a KSDS record by its RBA is available in CICS but not in batch Cobol.
2. *Control interval processing:* Low-level processing, such as accessing a CI as data, is available in assembler. However, you become responsible for maintaining CIDF's, RDF's, and other system-related functions.
3. *Alternate indexes for ESDS's:* CICS will allow you to process alternate indexes on an ESDS but not in batch Cobol.
4. *Multiple-string processing:* Multiple strings let you maintain multiple positions within a data set. CICS lets you maintain such positions in the data set for sequential browse purposes.
5. *Skip sequential processing:* This kind of processing allows you to sequentially browse through a data set by skipping records in between. This processing is much faster because it finds the required data CI by using only the sequence set of the index component. Although CICS supports it batch Cobol does not.
6. *Journaling:* Journaling allows you to keep a log of all of the changes applied to the data set. You may provide for recovery and restoration of a cluster from such journals without running the update application programs again. Batch Cobol does not support it.
7. *Alternate index as a data set:* You may not process an alternate index as an individual data set in batch Cobol.
8. *Read previous processing:* CICS provides for the reading of VSAM records in reverse order.

17.3 JCL RESTRICTIONS FOR VSAM FILES

Under normal circumstances, only two parameters of JCL are coded for VSAM files. They are the DSN and DISP parameters. A third parameter that we haven't discussed before, called AMP, is used only for VSAM files and is helpful for allocating I/O buffers for optimum performance (see Sec 17.4). All other JCL parameters are neither required nor useful. Their use, however, can cause certain problems. To make you aware of their effect, review the following discussion.

1. AFF: This parameter has no meaning in an OS/VS2 environment. However, if coded, and if the components of a KSDS

reside on different device types (e.g., IBM 3350 and 3380), the results will be unpredictable.

2. DCB: VSAM data sets are described by an access method control block and not a data control block. DCB describes only non-VSAM files such as physical sequential, partitioned data sets, and indexed sequential, so it is not applicable to VSAM.
3. DISP: If CATLG or UNCATLG is coded, a message is written but the data set is not affected because VSAM data sets are cataloged and uncataloged through AMS commands. VSAM data sets are deleted with the AMS command of DELETE, so coding DELETE on DISP will not have any affect either. You should always code OLD or SHR for VSAM data sets. If NEW is coded, OS/VS will allocate space, although it will never be used.
4. DSN: Temporary names cannot be used with VSAM data sets (names starting with "&&"). All backward references using *.ddname are permitted unless the data and index components of a KSDS reside on different device types. In the latter case, the results are unpredictable.
5. LABEL: Because all VSAM data sets reside on direct access storage devices, the subparameters of BLP, NL, and NSL have no meaning for VSAM files.
6. SEP: This parameter has no meaning in an OS/VS2 environment, but if used, and the data and index components reside on different device types, the results will be unpredictable.
7. SPACE: Space for VSAM data sets is acquired through AMS commands and not with this parameter. However, if this parameter is specified, the primary extent will be allocated but never used by VSAM.
8. VOLUME: The REF subparameter of this parameter, if coded, must have the referenced volumes as a subset of the data set volumes given in the catalog record. Otherwise, the results will be unpredictable.

For ease of use and simplicity, it is recommended that you avoid the use of parameters other than DSN, DISP, and AMP for VSAM data sets.

17.4 USE OF THE AMP PARAMETER

The access method parameter (AMP) complements information in an access control block. In most cases, its use is not mandatory. It is primarily used to allocate I/O buffers for the index and data components for optimum performance. The most commonly used subparameters are the following.

1. AMORG: This parameter, which stands for *A*ccess *M*ethod *ORG*anization, indicates that the particular DD statement

refers to a VSAM data set. For example, if you are planning to use DUMMY as a VSAM data set for a TRANS file, the DD statement must be coded as

```
//TRANS DD DUMMY, AMP='AMORG'
```

If you have an existing VSAM data set, this parameter need not be coded.

2. BUFND: This parameter gives the number of I/O buffers needed for the data component of the cluster. Each buffer is the size of the data CI. The default value is two data buffers, one of which is used only during CI/CA splits. The number of data buffers left for normal processing is one. One buffer is sufficient for random processing in batch programs, but not for sequential processing. Refer to Sec. 17.5 for more thorough discussion of this topic.
3. BUFNI: This parameter gives the number of I/O buffers needed for the index component of the KSDS. Each buffer is the size of the index CI. This subparameter may be coded only for a KSDS because ESDS's and RRDS's don't have index components. The default value is one index buffer, which is enough for sequential batch processing but is not normally sufficient for random accesses. Refer to Sec. 17.5 for a more thorough discussion of this subject.
4. BUFSP: This parameter indicates the number of bytes required for index and data component buffers. If the value is more than the value given in the BUFFERSPACE parameter of DEFINE CLUSTER, it overrides the BUFFERSPACE. Otherwise, the BUFFERSPACE takes precedence. Its value is calculated as

$$\text{BUFSP} = \text{DATA CISIZE} \times \text{BUFND} + \text{INDEX CISIZE} \times \text{BUFNI}$$

We do not recommend that you use this parameter, but let VSAM perform the calculations from the values given in BUFND and BUFNI instead.

The following is an example of coding for the AMP parameter.

```
//EMPMSTR DD DSN=EMPLOYEE.KSDS.CLUSTER,
//           DISP=SHR,
//           AMP=('BUFNI=5', 'BUFND=12')
```

The BUFNI value will allocate 5 index buffers while the BUFND value will allocate 12 data buffers for the EMPMSTR file. Knowing the CI sizes of these components, VSAM calculates the BUFSP value, which has intentionally been omitted from the JCL.

17.5 PERFORMANCE CONSIDERATIONS FOR BATCH JOBS

Performance is a very important consideration for any computer system. For on-line systems, it means having a good response time. For batch systems, it involves completing the batch function in a shorter run time. While poor response time becomes quite obvious in on-line (e.g., CICS) systems, it is not so obvious if a batch job takes an excessively long time to run. Sometimes a long-running batch job also affects the on-line systems. When processing an increased number of transactions for a night, or when a job has to be restarted because of system failure, the batch job might not be completed in its own normal or scheduled time frame. If you are unable to bring up the on-line system because a batch program is still running, the on-line system is, needless to say, adversely affected. Thus, fine-tuning of batch systems is critical. For systems that have to be up almost around-the-clock, it is vital that you have efficiently running jobs for updates, reorganizations, and backups.

Although it is quite simple to fine-tune a batch system, it has been the author's experience that few installations have ever looked into this aspect of systems management. *The secret of having a better run time is to have fewer and faster I/O's on any data set.* Look at the pictorial representation of a typical KSDS given in Fig. 17.2.

The index has three levels. For performing a random I/O, VSAM

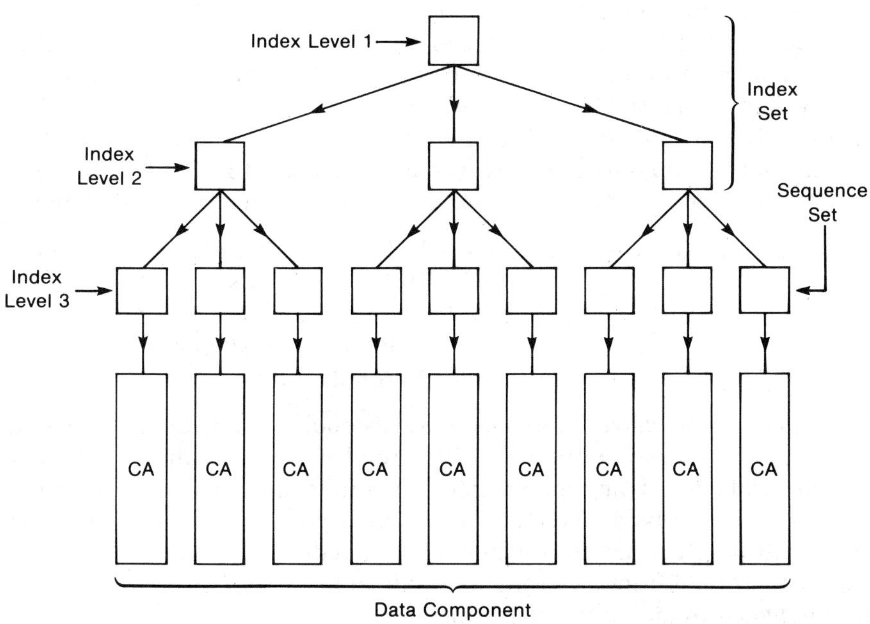

Figure 17.2 Index and data components of a typical KSDS. The index has three levels.

Device	Average seek time, ms	Average rotational delay, ms	Data transfer for 4K CI, ms	Total I/O time, ms
IBM 3350	25	8.4	3.3	36.7
IBM 3375	19	10.1	2.2	31.3
IBM 3380	16	8.4	1.3	25.7

Figure 17.3 Average I/O time for some DASD's under ideal conditions (no queue wait, no channel busy, etc.) assuming the CI size is 4096 bytes.

will have to read the top level of the index, the second level of the index, and finally, the sequence set, which is the third level of the index. This will locate the correct data CI where the record is expected to be. Accessing the data component CI causes another read. If the value of BUFNI (index buffers) is 1, an access to each level of the index will involve one I/O because the old buffer will have to be replaced with a new one. Remember, BUFNI = 1 is also the default if you do not code this parameter. In all, there will be four I/O's (three for the index plus one for the data). Now, let's look at a typical average I/O time for some of the direct access storage devices available as given in Fig. 17.3.

The *average seek time* is the time it takes for the read-write arm of the DASD to get to the desired cylinder. The *average rotational delay* is the average time it takes for the data on a particular track of the cylinder to come under the read-write head. The *transfer rate* is the time it takes for the channel to transfer data from the DASD to memory. As you can see, even for an IBM 3380, the average I/O time is 25.7 milliseconds. Executing four I/O's to read a record randomly will involve 102.8 milliseconds of I/O time *alone*. How many seconds of I/O time will it take to execute 1 million *random* reads? Consider the following calculation.

$$
\begin{aligned}
\text{Total I/O time for 1 million reads} &= 1{,}000{,}000 \times 102.8/1000.0 \text{ seconds} \\
&= 102{,}800 \text{ seconds} \\
&= 102{,}800 \text{ seconds} \\
&\quad \div 3600 \text{ seconds/hour} \\
&= 28.6 \text{ hours}
\end{aligned}
$$

Remember, these calculations are for ideal conditions and do not take into account any processing overhead. We are also assuming that all of the 1 million reads are being performed randomly and that no sequential processing is involved. Wouldn't it be nice if you could reduce this time from 28.6 hours to about 8.6 hours? Just reduce the number of I/O's required per read from an average of four to just over one. This could be accomplished by doing the following.

1. Always keep the first- and second-level indexes in core, which has a much faster access time than the I/O's on electromechanical devices. We will require four index buffers for the first two levels to be in core and one additional buffer for a sequence set record, which is at the third level. So the value of BUFNI = 5 will be coded for the AMP parameter.
2. Use IMBED when allocating the KSDS cluster. This will put the sequence set on the first track of the data CA. If this is done, there will be no seek time involved when going from the third level of the index (sequence set) to the data CI, because the read-write arm will already be positioned at the right cylinder. The DD statement for the file will be coded as follows.

```
//EMPMSTR DD DSN=EMPLOYEE.KSDS.CLUSTER,
//           DISP=SHR,
//           AMP=('BUFNI=5','BUFND=2')
```

For purely random processing, a BUFND value of 2 is sufficient. This is also the default. Without going any further into the theoretical aspects of batch fine-tuning, you may use the cookbook approach that follows.

BUFNI If ACCESS MODE IS RANDOM or DYNAMIC is specified for a KSDS, BUFNI plays a significant role in reducing I/O's for the index component. The optimum value can be determined from the information gathered from the catalog listing of the cluster using the LISTCAT command. There are two different methods for finding BUFNI, depending on whether IMBED or NOIMBED was specified at the time of DEFINE CLUSTER.

If IMBED was specified, the following equation should be used.

$$\text{BUFNI} = \frac{\text{HURBA of index}}{\text{CI size of index}} + 1$$

If NOIMBED was specified or implied, the equation is

$$\text{BUFNI} = \frac{\text{HURBA of index}}{\text{CI size of index}} - \frac{\text{HURBA of data}}{\text{CI size of data} \times \text{number of data CI's per CA}} + 1$$

These calculations should result in a whole number. If not, you are doing something wrong. If the calculated value of BUFNI is used in the AMP parameter, it will put the high-level index in virtual memory and will use one buffer for I/O's on the sequence set. This will ensure that for any random retrieval/update request there will *never* be more than one physical I/O on the index component, and sometimes there will be none.

For ACCESS MODE IS SEQUENTIAL, the value of BUFNI can be 1, which is also the default. So, you do not have to code this parameter at all.

BUFND If ACCESS MODE IS SEQUENTIAL or DYNAMIC is specified, BUFND plays an important part in reducing I/O's for the data component. The optimum value depends on the the kind of device being used for the data component (e.g., IBM 3350 or IBM 3380). Its value can be

$$\text{BUFND} = (N \times \text{number of CI's per track}) + 2$$

where N represents the number of DASD tracks that will be read with each access. Its value can be any integer number, such as 1, 2, or 3. The higher the value, the more buffers you will need. An increased number of data buffers does not always mean better performance. For time-critical systems, different values of N should be tried, beginning with 1. The value where an increasing N does not significantly reduce the processing time is the optimum N value. If your installation is short on virtual storage, the value of N selected may be 1. The number of CI's per track can be determined from the catalog listing values generated by LISTCAT. Its equation is

$$\text{Number of data-component CI's per track} = \frac{\text{CI/CA for data component}}{\text{tracks per CA for data component}}$$

The value of BUFND, if properly coded, can significantly reduce processing time for backups and reorganizations (e.g., using REPRO). Try it. You will be amazed at the results. Using REPRO, some installations have experienced a reduction in backup time from 8 to 2 hours.

If ACCESS MODE IS RANDOM is specified, the default value of 2 for BUFND is sufficient for batch Cobol program processing.

17.6 VS COBOL II COMPILER ENHANCEMENTS

The VS Cobol compiler is the latest IBM compiler that supports MVS/XA architecture. However, it also runs under an OS/VS (non-XA) system. It does not support some of the 1974 Cobol features (Report Writer, Communications Language, etc.), but it does have some new enhancements. The compiler and the programs it produces can be run in either a 24- or a 31-bit addressing mode. Since many of the readers of this book will not yet have this compiler, it is being discussed as a separate topic.

The single largest improvement in the handling of VSAM is in the expanded error-handling capabilities available under VS Cobol II. In the

SELECT statement, the status code has two data areas for getting feedback regarding the outcome of a VSAM data set I/O. The FILE STATUS can now be coded as follows.

```
        •
        •
FILE STATUS IS data-name-1
               data-name-2.
        •
        •
```

Data-name-1 is the same 2-byte field that gives the status code under the 1974 Cobol compiler. Data-name-2 is an *additional 6-byte* field which gives more detailed information regarding the status of each I/O. The 6 bytes consist of three subfields. Each is a binary number and 2 bytes in size. Figure 17.4 gives sample coding for the Employee-Master file for a VS Cobol II-compiled program.

The 6 bytes of additional information are called the VSAM feedback area. If you do not use its contents, your programs can still rely upon the 2-byte status code information. However, the feedback area gives you the status with greater precision and detail.

The three feedback areas of VSAM are called the *return code,* the *function code,* and the *feedback code,* respectively. This VSAM status code information is given to the Cobol program as such without any transformation. Thus, a Cobol program has the same information available for

```
                   .
                   .
           SELECT  EMPLOYEE-MASTER
                   ASSIGN TO EMPMSTR
                   ORGANIZATION IS INDEXED
                   ACCESS MODE IS DYNAMIC
                   RECORD KEY IS EMPLOYEE-SSN-KEY
                   FILE STATUS IS EMPLOYEE-FILE-STATUS
                                  EMPLOYEE-VSAM-FEEDBACK.
                   .
                   .
                   .
 WORKING-STORAGE SECTION.
 01   EMPLOYEE-FILE-STATUS                      PIC X(2).
 01   EMPLOYEE-VSAM-FEEDBACK.
      05  EMP-RETURN-CODE                       PIC 9(4) COMP.
      05  EMP-FUNCTION-CODE                     PIC 9(4) COMP.
      05  EMP-FEEDBACK-CODE                     PIC 9(4) COMP.
                   .
                   .
```

Figure 17.4 SELECT statement showing the new format of FILE STATUS for a VS Cobol II compiler.

Return code	Meaning
0	Request completed successfully
8	Logical error; kind of error is indicated in feedback code
12	Physical error; kind of error is indicated in feedback code

*A return code of 4, which is returned for asynchronous processing, does not apply to Cobol programs.

Figure 17.5 Return codes in decimal values and their meanings.

status verification as an assembler program. The following considerations should be kept in mind while checking the VSAM feedback area.

- If no call has been made to VSAM, its value is zero.
- It is set only when VSAM gives a non-zero return code (the first 2 bytes out of 6 bytes).
- It is undefined if status code is zero (2-byte area).

Each of the three subfields of the VSAM feedback area are discussed separately.

Return Code The return code contains the contents of register 15. Its values and their meanings are given in Fig. 17.5.

Function Code Function code relates to what the status of the upgrade set is as a result of the occurrence of a logical (RC = 8) or physical (RC = 12) error. Obviously, the Cobol statement that issued the request failed because of the error. Figure 17.6 gives the various function codes and their meanings.

Function code	Function being attempted	Upgrade set status
0	Access the base cluster	Correct
1	Access the base cluster	May be incorrect
2	Access alternate index over the base cluster	Correct
3	Access alternate index over the base cluster	May be incorrect
4	Upgrade processing	Correct
5	Upgrade processing	May be incorrect

Figure 17.6 Function codes in decimal values and their meanings.

All the even function codes (0, 2, 4) imply a safe status, while the odd ones (1, 3, 5) indicate a probable error. The program logic can determine if the upgrade set is out of synchronization after a request failure.

Feedback Code There are two types of feedback codes. When the return code has a value of 8, this code has a meaning in the context of logical errors. For a return code of 12, it pertains to physical errors. The value of the logical error feedback code can be from 4 to 208, while for a physical error it may be from 4 to 24. To discuss all the possible feedback codes is beyond the scope of our current discussion. You may refer to OS/VS *VSAM Programmers Guide* to determine their values and corresponding meanings.

17.7 VSAM DATA SET SHARING

Data set sharing means that a data set is processed concurrently by more than one user. Concurrency may involve read and/or write operations. In VSAM, this sharing feature is controlled by the SHAREOPTIONS parameter in different commands of AMS. Although this has already been discussed in Chap. 6, we will go into more detail here. The SHAREOPTIONS parameter can have two values. The first value dictates cross-region sharing, i.e., when different programs are running in different address spaces (regions) of the *same CPU*. The second value indicates cross-system sharing, i.e., when different programs are running in different address spaces of *different CPU's*.

Cross-Region Sharing The value of the cross-region sharing portion can be 1, 2, 3, or 4. The default value is 1. The meaning of these values and their influence on read/write integrity are as follows.

SHAREOPTION 1 The data set can either be opened for update by one region *or* opened for read-only by multiple regions. If one program opened the file for input, many other programs could also open it for input, but you could not have a program open it for I-O. On the other hand, if one program opened the file for I-O, no other program can have access to it at the same time. This shareoption provides perfect read and write integrity. Remember, a CICS region is considered one program, although you may have multiple transactions running under it concurrently. Therefore, if CICS has opened the file for update, any batch programs or TSO sessions running *in the same CPU* would not be able to read any records from that file.

SHAREOPTION 2 This shareoption permits one program to update the data set *and* many programs to read it at the same time. However, until the first program has finished updating and closed the file, no program can open it for update. This provides perfect write integrity, but read integrity is not guaranteed. This feature may be used if CICS is updating master files and you want a quick report produced by running a batch program in the same CPU. Performance considerations must be kept in mind when trying such data set sharing.

SHAREOPTION 3 This option allows multiple programs to update and read concurrently. CI and CA splits caused by one region are not communicated to the other region. So this may cause both write and read integrity problems. Responsibility for maintaining data integrity rests with the programs. Since Cobol does not provide any way to maintain data integrity under these circumstances, use of this shareoption is not recommended.

SHAREOPTION 4 This shareoption provides the same features as shareoption 3. However, each random access causes all the buffers to be invalidated and refreshed. This increases the I/O's on the data set, thus causing performance problems. It also requires programs to issue ENQ and DEQ macros for serializing the updates. Cobol does not provide for using these macros. So, use of this option is also not recommended.

Cross-System Sharing The value of cross-system sharing can be only 3 or 4. They have the meanings as follows:

SHAREOPTION 3 When using this option, any number of programs can update or read a file. Maintaining read and write integrity is the user's responsibility. Cobol does not provide any features for maintaining the integrity. Since this option is also the default value, you have no way to prevent any user from using cross-system sharing. If you run two update programs concurrently from two different CPU's and they update a VSAM file on a shared DASD, you could, in all probability, experience lost and duplicate records in the data set. Since you have no way of preventing such file sharing, installation guidelines must clearly prohibit their use for Cobol programs.

SHAREOPTION 4 This option has the same characteristics as shareoption 3. The only difference is that each random read request results in buffer invalidation and refresh and each random update request results in an immediate write of the buffers. This adds to the I/O's while maintaining some data integrity. Use of the RESERVE and RELEASE macros is required to serialize the update requests at the device (DASD) level. Cobol does not provide any facility to use these macros. Also, VSAM will not allow a CA split under this shareoption in a non-DF/EF environment. So, if record adds and updates are done in such a way that a

CA split is needed, you will get a non-zero file status and the update will not be successful.

In a nutshell, use of cross-system sharing is not recommended for updates. However, if one of the programs in the other CPU is executing read-only requests, you may only have to be concerned with read integrity.

In cross-region sharing, all the values of SHAREOPTIONS are effective only if the data set in each job step executing the program is specified with DISP = SHR. Any program that opens the file with DISP = OLD, will not let any other user share it at all. Also, the SHAREOPTION is not effective when a data set is in the load mode (opened as OUTPUT).

17.8 AMS COMMANDS EXECUTION UNDER TSO/SPF

All the AMS commands discussed in the book (except MODAL commands) can be executed either in the TSO READY mode or in SPF option 6. This feature allows you to execute the commands in an interactive mode without ever having to write any batch JCL. The command syntax is the same as if it were executed as a batch job. If you need any assistance regarding the command syntax, you can access the HELP function under these facilities. For example, the following will give you a description of defining a GDG under option 6 of SPF.

```
===> HELP DEFGDG
```

The total length of the command, including its parameters and their values, cannot be more than 256 characters. In fact, you may not be able to type any additional characters after this limit. For this reason, TSO provides abbreviations for all the commands and their parameters. You may look at all these abbreviations by using HELP. The command may be entered in its entirety without taking into consideration the new lines or the continuation character. The entire string of 256 characters is considered to be one valid line. You are permitted to split a parameter or its value over two lines.

For example, let's suppose that you want a listing of EMPLOYEE.KSDS.CLUSTER displayed under option 6 of SPF. The command will be typed as follows.

```
===> LISTCAT ENT('EMPLOYEE.KSDS.CLUSTER') ALL
```

Upon hitting the Enter key, the display will appear as in Fig. 17.7. Three asterisks (***) on the bottom left of the screen indicate that more display is pending. Hitting the Enter key will display the next screen page, and so on.

```
---------------------------- TSO COMMAND PROCESSOR ------------------------------------
ENTER TSO COMMAND OR CLIST BELOW:

===> LISTCAT ENT('EMPLOYEE.KSDS.CLUSTER') ALL

CLUSTER ------- EMPLOYEE.KSDS.CLUSTER
     IN-CAT --- VSAM.USERCAT.TWO
     HISTORY
       OWNER-IDENT--------(NULL)       CREATION----------84.277        RCVY-VOL-------
----VSAM02       RCVY-CI---------X'00000F'
       RELEASE------------------2      EXPIRATION-------00.000         RCVY-DEVT----X
'3010200E'
     PROTECTION-PSWD------(NULL)       RACF------------------(NO)
     ASSOCIATIONS
       DATA------EMPLOYEE.KSDS.DATA
       INDEX----EMPLOYEE.KSDS.INDEX
       AIX-------EMPLOYEE.KSDS.AIX1.CLUSTER
       AIX-------EMPLOYEE.KSDS.AIX2.CLUSTER
   DATA ------- EMPLOYEE.KSDS.DATA
     IN-CAT --- VSAM.USERCAT.TWO
     HISTORY
***
```

Figure 17.7 Listing of EMPLOYEE.KSDS.CLUSTER produced interactively under option 6 of TSO/SPF.

You may have used the LISTCAT command under TSO/SPF to get a listing of data sets cataloged with your TSO ID as the first qualifier of the data set names. Using LISTCAT without using either ENTRIES (abbreviated ENT) or LEVEL (abbreviated LEV) gives a default of LEVEL ('tsoid'). So, the effect of the following commands will be the same.

===> LISTCAT or ===> LISTCAT LEV('tsoid')

So, in a way, you may have been using LISTCAT without realizing that it is an AMS command.

It is important to enclose the data set names in quotes. If you don't, TSO/SPF will affix your TSO ID in front of the data set name. So, if your TSO ID is ABC, the command

===> LISTCAT ENT(EMPLOYEE.KSDS.CLUSTER) ALL

will be interpreted as

===> LISTCAT ENT('ABC.EMPLOYEE.KSDS.CLUSTER') ALL

The execution of the interpreted version will either give you the contents of the wrong data set, if it exists, or give the message that the data set is not cataloged.

Option 6 of SPF is very handy when using (1) VERIFY to close an improperly closed data set, (2) REPRO to load files, or (3) PRINT to look at the contents of a data set. Figure 17.8 gives examples for the use of these commands on EMPLOYEE.KSDS.CLUSTER.

```
------------------------------ TSO COMMAND PROCESSOR -----
ENTER TSO COMMAND OR CLIST BELOW:

===> VERIFY DS('EMPLOYEE.KSDS.CLUSTER')

 ERROR OPENING EMPLOYEE.KSDS.CLUSTER
** VSAM OPEN RETURN CODE IS 118
***
```

(a)

```
------------------------------ TSO COMMAND PROCESSOR ------------------------------
ENTER TSO COMMAND OR CLIST BELOW:

===> REPRO IDS('SAMPLE.INPUT.DATA') ODS('EMPLOYEE.KSDS.CLUSTER') REPLACE

NUMBER OF RECORDS PROCESSED WAS 9
***
```

(b)

```
------------------------------ TSO COMMAND PROCESSOR ------------------------------
ENTER TSO COMMAND OR CLIST BELOW:

===> TSO PRINT IDS('EMPLOYEE.KSDS.CLUSTER') CHAR

KEY OF RECORD - 111111111
111111111 WORLD PLAZA,N.Y,N.Y        10M092150RANADE
KEY OF RECORD - 222222222
222222222 25,OAKWOODS,N.Y            19M022536TANAKA
KEY OF RECORD - 333333333
333333333 18,MARSH AV,S.I,N.Y        16F030942KRANTZ
KEY OF RECORD - 444444444
444444444 2-52,FOREST HILLS,QUEENS   05M090252BUTLER
KEY OF RECORD - 555555555
555555555 7,PARK AV,JERSEY CITY      17M092057RANADE
KEY OF RECORD - 666666666
666666666 15,GREENWICH ,CT           12M030511ADLER
KEY OF RECORD - 777777777
777777777 8,BROAD ST,S.I,N.Y         07F082913JOSHI
KEY OF RECORD - 888888888
888888888 KENNER TOWERS,N.Y,N.Y      04F111855LEHN
***
```

(c)

Figure 17.8 (*a*) Use of VERIFY under SPF option 6. (*b*) use of REPRO to load a data set. (*c*) use of PRINT to print records on the terminal.

It is important to know the VSAM user catalogs, their aliases, and the volumes they own. If you forgot their relationships, the commands given in Fig. 17.9 can be used to interactively find them out.

17.9 USE OF STEPCAT AND JOBCAT

STEPCAT and JOBCAT refer to the DD statements that identify VSAM user catalogs. STEPCAT is coded at the job step level immediately after the EXEC statement. Different user catalogs can be concatenated under it. All the data sets in this job step are first searched for in these catalogs in the order of concatenation. The following is an example of the use of this statement.

```
//STEPCAT DD DSN=VSAM.USERCAT.TWO,DISP=SHR
```

```
------------------------------ TSO COMMAND PROCESSOR ---------------------------------
ENTER TSO COMMAND OR CLIST BELOW:

===> LISTCAT ENT('VSAM.USERCAT.TWO') ALL

USERCATALOG --- VSAM.USERCAT.TWO
      IN-CAT --- CATALOG.VSP3CAT
      HISTORY
        RELEASE------------------2
      VOLUMES
        VOLSER-------------VSAM02       DEVTYPE-------X'3010200E'       VOLFLAG----------
------PRIME
      ASSOCIATIONS
        ALIAS-----SAMPLE
        ALIAS-----EMPLOYEE
***
```

(a)

```
------------------------------ TSO COMMAND PROCESSOR ---------------------------------
ENTER TSO COMMAND OR CLIST BELOW:

===> LISTCAT ENT('EMPLOYEE') ALL

ALIAS ---------- EMPLOYEE
      IN-CAT --- CATALOG.VSP3CAT
      HISTORY
        RELEASE------------------2
      ASSOCIATIONS
        USERCAT--VSAM.USERCAT.TWO
***
```

(b)

Figure 17.9 (*a*) Command for identifying the aliases and the volumes owned by a catalog. (*b*) command use to identify the catalog name from the given alias.

JOBCAT is coded at the job level immediately after the JOB card. You may also concatenate multiple user catalogs under it. If a data set is not found in the catalogs of STEPCAT, it is searched for in the catalogs specified in the JOBCAT in the order of concatenation. The following is an example of coding this statement.

```
//JOBCAT DD DSN=VSAM.USERCAT.TWO,DISP=SHR
```

In all the examples given in this book, we have not coded either of these DD statements. All the data sets we used had leftmost qualifiers that were the aliases of the VSAM user catalogs (e.g., EMPLOYEE). So, even though STEPCAT and JOBCAT were not given, the system could find the appropriate catalogs from the aliases. It is recommended that, wherever possible, aliases should be used as the first qualifiers of the data set names, rather than using the STEPCAT and JOBCAT statements.

17.10 VSAM UNDER CICS

There are certain VSAM characteristics that must be kept in mind when VSAM files are being accessed in a CICS/VS environment. Since it is beyond the scope of this book to enumerate all such considerations, you should refer to the appropriate CICS/VS manuals for the details. The following are some of the highlights.

1 VSAM files are opened by CICS and not by individual application programs. The SERVREQ parameter of the File Control Table (DFHFCT macro) controls the open mode functions (read-only, update, delete, etc.). Functions not given in this table cannot be performed by CICS applications.

2 CICS region/address space looks like one application program when it comes to the interpretation of SHAREOPTIONS for a VSAM cluster. There can be *multiple tasks* within CICS performing concurrent updates to a VSAM file. The maintenance of file integrity is the joint responsibility of VSAM and CICS in this case. If a SHAREOPTION of 1 is specified for a VSAM cluster and it is open for update under CICS, no other region (CICS or batch) in the same CPU can open the file, even for read-only purposes. SHAREOPTION 2 is recommended if it is necessary for batch jobs to read the file while CICS transactions are making updates on it, although read integrity cannot be guaranteed in this case. Make sure that, in the CICS initialization JCL, a DISPOSITION of SHR is coded for such a VSAM file. If a DISPOSITION of OLD is coded, CICS will obtain exclusive control of the data set no matter what the shareoption is.

A SHAREOPTION of 3 is a dangerous option to code because it allows multiple regions (CICS or batch) to update the file concurrently. Any CA splits (or possibly CI splits also) may create a duplicate record or missing record situation. It may also result in problems in the index component of a KSDS, thus causing CICS tasks to hang.

A SHAREOPTION of 4 ensures some data integrity but causes the buffers to be refreshed on each I/O. High I/O activity may cause response time problems in CICS.

Cross-system sharing of VSAM files for update purposes should never be done in a CICS environment because it requires the use of device RESERVE and RELEASE macros and CICS has no mechanism for issuing them.

3 CI and CA splits (especially the latter), cause excessive I/O's on the data set. In a CICS environment, it may become the cause of poor response time. FREESPACE parameters should be carefully selected to eliminate or minimize such splits. Listings using the LISTCAT command should be reviewed at regular intervals to determine if the data set needs reorganization because of excessive CI/CA splits.

4 A KSDS can be opened for update purposes only if its high used RBA (HURBA) is non-zero. If a data set is newly defined, its HURBA can be made non-zero by opening it for OUTPUT in a batch program, writing a dummy record into it, and then closing it. Later, it you delete the dummy record (even in the same program), the HURBA will still be non-zero, although there are no longer any records in the file. You may also use the REPRO command to load a dummy record into an unloaded KSDS, thus making its HURBA non-zero.

5 When CICS is coming up, all the VSAM files that have been coded in its initialization JCL must exist. The absence of a single file will prevent CICS from coming up. These days, however, VSAM files are not hard-coded in the CICS initialization JCL. They are dynamically allocated later, either using appropriate CICS transactions or through a File Control Program exit routine.

6 Be careful about using a base cluster with a large upgrade set. All the alternate indexes that are part of the upgrade set result in a lot of I/O's when a record is added/updated in the base cluster. Again, excessive I/O's may slow down CICS response time.

7 If you have a base cluster with an upgrade set, it is recommended that record changes be performed by reading the record for UPDATE using only the prime key and not through an alternate index path. Access via the path should be kept for inquiry functions only, not for update purposes. However, this restriction does not exist for CICS/VS 1.7 and subsequent releases.

8 If you have a base cluster with an upgrade set, make sure that all of the alternate index paths are defined in the file control table of CICS by including the optional BASE parameter. Failure to do so may result in the base cluster and the upgrade set not being in synchronization with each other.

9 There are many applications where the data is collected in a transaction file (also called a *data collection file)* through various CICS transactions and the updates are applied to the master files in batch mode after CICS has come down. Such a data collection file, which is usually a KSDS, may start out empty each morning and accumulate transactions during the course of the day. Because of excessive adds, this file may have multiple CI and CA splits, thus causing performance problems. It is recommended that you use an ESDS with an alternate index path instead of a KSDS. Although both perform virtually the same functions, an alternate index will have fewer CI and CA splits because of its smaller size, thus creating fewer performance problems. Bear in mind that in a batch environment you will have to delete the alternate index over an ESDS if you are using Cobol programs, because they are not supported by the Cobol compiler.

10 There are three performance parameters in the file control table, namely, STRNG, BUFNI, and BUFND. The value of STRNG should be adjusted to that there is no significant string wait in the CICS shutdown statistics. The value of BUFNI should be large enough to put all the index set records in virtual storage and, in addition, it should have one additional buffer for each string (STRNG). The value of BUFND should be the number of strings plus one.[2]

11 VSAM files with heavy I/O activity should be put on different DASD's so that I/O service time is not increased by longer seek times, I/O queue waits, device busy waits and rotational position sensing (RPS) misses.

There is more to VSAM under CICS than can be discussed in this section. You should refer to the appropriate CICS manuals for more details about it.

[2]Refer to Jay Ranade, VSAM: Performance, Design, and Fine Tuning.

APPENDIXES

appendix **A**

VSAM Terminology Glossary

Access Method Services (AMS) A multifunction service utility program that helps in performing various functions on VSAM files, non-VSAM files, VSAM catalogs, and ICF catalogs. Such functions include allocations, deletions, loading, printing, alternate indexing, reorganizations, alterations, backups, etc.

AIXBLD feature A run-time PARM parameter option that causes the automatic building of all the alternate index clusters while the data records are being sequentially loaded into an unloaded base cluster.

alias of a catalog Another name for a catalog. It may be used as the first qualifier of a data set name, thus eliminating the need to code STEPCAT and JOBCAT DD statements and the CATALOG parameter within AMS commands.

ALTER command One of the Access Method Services commands that performs the alteration of many of the attributes and characteristics of a VSAM object (e.g., passwords, name, volumes).

alternate index A data set that contains alternate keys and one or more pointers to the data set records of a KSDS or an ESDS.

alternate index cluster A KSDS cluster consisting of an index and a data component, which keeps key-pointer pair records for an alternate index.

alternate key A key that provides access to a base cluster through field(s) other than the prime key.

backup A copy of a data set. It can be used to reconstruct the data set if necessary.

backup process The process of creating a backup copy of the data records in a data set. The REPRO and EXPORT commands of Access Method Services can be used to backup a VSAM data set.

Basic Catalog Structure (BCS) The first level of the two-level catalog structure of an ICF catalog. The second level is the VSAM Volume Data Set.

base cluster A KSDS, an ESDS, or an RRDS.

BCS (See **Basic Catalog Structure**)

CA (See **control area**)

candidate volume A DASD which does not have VSAM data sets or VSAM space on it yet but is owned by a VSAM catalog and may be used for VSAM objects in the future.

catalog (See **master catalog** and **user catalog**)

catalog recovery area (CRA) An ESDS that exists on each volume owned by a recoverable VSAM (not ICF) catalog. It contains duplicates of the catalog entries and can be used to reconstruct a damaged catalog.

CI (See **control interval**)

CIDF (See **control interval description field**)

control area (CA) The building block of a VSAM data set. It consists of a group of control intervals and is used for distributing free space and local reorganizations for a KSDS. The format information it contains (Software End of File) is used to help the VERIFY command correct the high used RBA information. One and only one sequence set record in a KSDS points to one data CA.

control area split The movement of half of the records in an existing control area to a new control area because a record add or update cannot be accommodated in the existing control area. This results in two approximately half-full control areas instead of one full and one empty CA.

control interval (CI) A unit of data that is transferred between auxiliary storage and virtual storage. It contains records, free space, and control information.

control interval access Also called *low-level access*. A whole CI and not a logical record is processed as one logical entity.

control interval description field (CIDF) A field consisting of the last 4 bytes of a control interval. It contains information about the offset and the length of free space in the CI.

control interval split The movement of some records from an existing CI to another free CI in the same CA because a record add or update cannot be accommodated in the existing one. This results in two half-empty CI's instead of one full and one empty CI.

CRA (See **catalog recovery area**)

cylinder An area of data storage on a disk device consisting of multiple concentric tracks. The read-write arm of the disk can access the data on a cylinder with one seek.

DASD (See **direct access storage device**)

data component The part of the cluster or alternate index that contains the data records.

Data Facility/Extended Functions (DF/EF) An IBM program product for MVS environments which has enhanced the capabilities of VSAM. This product is a prerequisite for ICF catalogs.

data integrity Safety of data from unintentional damage or an out-of-synchronization condition.

data security Safety of data from unauthorized access with the intention of use, theft, or destruction.

data set A major unit of the storage of information consisting of one or more data records. This term is synonymous with *file* in this book.

DEFINE command An Access Method Services functional command used to allocate VSAM objects such as catalogs, clusters, alternate indexes, paths, and page data sets.

DELETE command An Access Method Services command used to delete VSAM and non-VSAM objects such as clusters, alternate indexes, and paths.

Destage To transfer data from a DASD to a mass storage system.

direct access Access of data by its location without consideration of its placement relative to other units of data.

direct access storage device (DASD) A magnetic medium for data storage where access to particular data can be made directly without having to read the preceding data. An IBM 3380 is a DASD. Magnetic tapes are not DASD's because data can be accessed only sequentially.

dynamic allocation Allocation of a data set or a volume without the use of information contained in the JCL. Internally, it is done by SVC 99.

entry One or more records in a VSAM or ICF catalog containing information about a cataloged object.

entry name Same as a data set name.

entry sequence The order of storage of data records in an ESDS according to their physical arrival sequence rather than a key value.

entry-sequenced data set (ESDS) A data set whose records are stored and accessed in physical sequence without consideration of a key field.

ESDS (See **entry-sequenced data set)**

exception exit A user-written program that takes control when an exceptional condition (e.g., an I/O error) occurs.

extent Contiguous area on a DASD allocated for VSAM space or a data set.

free space Space left in a KSDS at the time of the initial or resume load to allow for record additions and updates later and to minimize or prevent CI and CA splits.

GDG (See **generation data group entry**)

generation data group (GDG) entry An entry that allows multiple non-VSAM data sets to be related to each other by their relative generation numbers.

generation data set A data set that is a member of a generation data group.

generic key A left-justified set of one or more characters of a key that are a subset of the full key (e.g., for key ABC, generic keys are A and AB.

generic name A qualified data set name in which one qualifier (except the first one) is replaced by an asterisk. The asterisk indicates that *any* value in that position is acceptable.

horizontal pointer A pointer in the sequence set of an index component that points to the next sequence set record so that access to top-level indexes becomes unnecessary for keyed sequential access.

IBM 3350 A disk device with 317 megabytes of storage capacity. It has 555 cylinders. Each cylinder has 30 tracks, each with a capacity of 19,254 bytes.

IBM 3380 A disk device with 630 megabytes of storage capacity per access mechanism (VOLSER). It has 885 cylinders of 15 tracks each. Each track has a capacity of 47,968 bytes.

IBM 3380 (double density) A disk device with 1260 megabytes of storage capacity per access mechanism (VOLSER). It has 1770 cylinders of 15 tracks each. Each track has a capacity of 47,968 bytes. Such DASD's consist of models AE4 and BE4.

ICF (See **Integrated Catalog Facility**)

index component An independent constituent of a KSDS, catalog, or alternate index that helps in establishing the sequence of records in the data component.

index entry Catalog entry for an index component.

index set The set of index records above the sequence set level.

Integrated Catalog Facility (ICF) The name of the catalog associated with the DF/EF program product.

ISAM interface program (IIP) An interface program that makes it possible for a program written to process indexed sequential files to gain access to a KSDS.

job catalog A catalog allocated for a job by means of a JOBCAT DD statement.

key A field within a record that identifies a record or a set of records.

key compression A technique used to reduce storage requirements for an index that involves elimination of characters from the front and back of a key.

key of reference The key (prime or one of the alternates) which is *currently* being used to access records in a base cluster. To the application program, the records in the base cluster seem to be sequenced on the key of reference.

key sequence The order in which records may be accessed in a sequence based on a key value within each record.

key-sequenced data set (KSDS) A data set whose records can be accessed in key sequence.

KSDS (See **key-sequenced data set**)

LISTCAT command An AMS command used to list the attributes and statistics of a VSAM or non-VSAM object (Chap. 11).

master catalog A VSAM or an ICF catalog containing information and connector entries for user catalogs, data sets, volumes, data spaces, etc. There is always one master catalog for an MVS system. It is established at initial program load time.

nonunique key An alternate key that points to one or more data records in a base cluster.

object An entity created by VSAM such as a cluster, an alternate index, their components, a catalog, a path, or VSAM space.

OPTIONAL file A read-only ESDS file which may not *always* be present when the program which requires it is executed. In the Cobol language, such a file is indicated in the SELECT statement by the use of the OPTIONAL clause.

page space An ESDS that acts as a paging data set for OS/VS2 systems.

password A combination of 1 to 8 characters assigned to a VSAM object at the time of its DEFINE to prevent unauthorized access to the object. It may be changed later through the ALTER command.

path A data set name referred to for accessing the records of a base cluster through an alternate index. A path can also be the alias of a data set name.

physical record A set of one or more 512-, 1024-, 2048-, or 4096-byte-long blocks that constitute a control interval. Each block is a physical record.

pointer An address or a key value used to locate a control interval or a record.

primary space allocation Initial allocation of space on a DASD reserved for a data set or VSAM space.

prime key A unique field in a KSDS used for sequencing, storage, and accessing of its data records.

PRINT command An AMS command used to print the records of a data set in character, hex, or dump format.

qualifier Each segment of a data set name separated from other segments by periods.

RBA (See **relative byte address**)

RDF (See **record description field**)

recoverable catalog A VSAM catalog defined with the RECOVERABLE parameter so that each volume maintains a catalog recovery area to contain duplicate information about the entries. The duplicate information is used for recovery upon catalog failure.

relative byte address (RBA) The displacement of a data record or a control interval from the beginning of the data set.

relative record data set (RRDS) A data set whose records are loaded into fixed-length slots and retrieved through the use of a relative record number.

relative record number (RRN) An integer number that identifies the relative position of a slot from the beginning of an RRDS.

reorganization The process of unloading and then reloading the contents of a KSDS in order to put its records into physical sequence.

REPRO command An AMS command used to copy records from one data set to another.

RESTORE The process of recreating a data set from its backup copy after a system or application failure or problem.

reusable data set A VSAM data set whose high used RBA is reset to zero when opened as OUTPUT. Resetting the RBA logically deletes any existing records.

rotational delay The time it takes for the data on a particular track of a cylinder to reach the read-write head.

RRDS (See **relative record data set**)

secondary space allocation Space on a DASD that is allocated when the primary space allocation is used up.

seek time delay The time it takes for the read-write arm of a DASD to reach the desired cylinder.

sequence set The lowest level of the index component of a KSDS or an alternate index cluster which points to the data component CI's. Each record of a sequence set points to a full control area.

shared DASD A direct access storage device (e.g., a disk) which is accessible from more than one system (e.g., MVS) in twin-CPU or multi-CPU configurations.

SHAREOPTIONS Attributes of a VSAM data set which control the concurrent sharing of its data by different programs running in the same CPU or different CPUs. The types of sharing can be at the read and/or update levels.

slot Space in a relative record data set where a record can be placed.

spanned record A logical record whose length is greater than the control interval size, thus requiring it to span over more than one CI.

Stage The movement of data from a mass storage system to a DASD.

step catalog A VSAM or an ICF catalog allocation that lasts for the duration of the job step and is identified by the STEPCAT DD statement.

upgrade set A set of alternate indexes that are automatically updated and kept in synchronization when the base cluster to which they belong is updated.

user catalog A VSAM or ICF catalog that contains information about clusters, alternate indexes, paths, non-VSAM files, etc.

VERIFY command An AMS command used to close an improperly closed VSAM data set after a system or application failure. It sets the end-of-data (EOD) and end-of-key-range (EOKR) pointers in the catalog to the correct values.

vertical pointer A pointer in an index record that points to an index set or sequence set record at the next lower level.

VSAM space A storage area set aside on a DASD for exclusive use and management by VSAM.

VSAM volume data set (VVDS) An ESDS defined on each volume for storing the characteristics of the VSAM data sets residing on that volume. It is the second part of an ICF catalog, the first part being the basic catalog structure.

VVDS (See **VSAM volume data set**)

appendix B

AMS Command Summary for OS/VS2/MVS

Parameters	Abbrev.
ALTER	---
entryname[/password]	---
[ADDVOLUMES(volser [volser...])]	AVOL
[ATTEMPTS(number)]	ATT
[AUTHORIZATION(entrypoint[string])]	AUTH
* [BUFND]	BFND
* [BUFNI]	BFNI
[BUFFERSPACE(size)]	BUFSP, BUFSPC
[CODE(code)]	---
[CONTROLPW(password)]	CTLPW
[DESTAGEWAIT|NODESTAGEWAIT]	DSTGW NDSTGW
[EMPTY|NOEMPTY]	EMP NEMP
[ERASE|NOERASE]	ERAS NERAS
[EXCEPTIONEXIT(entrypoint)]	EEXT
[FILE(dname)]	---
[FREESPACE(CI-percent[CA-percent])]	FSPC
[INHIBIT|UNINHIBIT]	INH UNINH
[KEYS(length offset)]	---
[MASTERPW(password)]	MRPW
[NEWNAME(newname)]	NEWNM
[NULLIFY(	NULL
[AUTHORIZATION(MODULE|STRING)]	AUTH MDLE STRG
[CODE]	--
[CONTROLPW]	CTLPW
[EXCEPTIONEXIT]	EEXT
[MASTERPW]	MRPW
[OWNER]	---
[READPW]	RDPW
[RETENTION]	RETN
[UPDATEPW])]	UPDPW
[OWNER(ownerid)]	---
[READPW(password)]	RDPW
[RECORDSIZE(average maximum)]	RECSZ
[REMOVEVOLUMES(volser[volser...])]	RVOL
[SCRATCH|NOSCRATCH]	SCR NSCR
[SHAREOPTIONS(crossregion [crosssystem])]	SHR
[STAGE|BIND|CYLINDERFAULT]	--- --- CYLF
* [STRNO]	---
[TO(date)|FOR(days)]	--- ---
[UNIQUEKEY|NONUNIQUEKEY]	UNQK NUNQK
[UPDATE|NOUPDATE]	UPD NUPD
[UPDATEPW(password)]	UPDPW
[UPGRADE|NOUPGRADE]	UPG NUPG
[WRITECHECK|NOWRITECHECK]	WCK NWCK
[CATALOG(catname[/password])]	CAT

Parameters	Abbrev.
BLDINDEX	BIX
{INFILE(dname[/password])|	IFILE
INDATASET(entryname[/password])}	IDS
{OUTFILE (dname[/password]	OFILE
[dname[/password]...])|	
OUTDATASET(entryname[/password]	ODS
[entryname[/password]...])}	
[CATALOG(catname[/password])]	CAT
[EXTERNALSORT|<u>INTERNALSORT</u>]	ESORT ISORT
[WORKFILES(dname dname)]	WFILE

* This parameter applies to ICF catalogs only.

Parameters	Abbrev.
DEFINE	DEF
ALIAS	---
(NAME(aliasname)	---
RELATE(entryname))	REL
[CATALOG(catname[/password])]	CAT

Parameters	Abbrev.
DEFINE ALTERNATEINDEX	DEF/AIX
(NAME(entryname)	---
RELATE(entryname[/password])	REL
{CYLINDERS (primary[secondary]) |	CYL
RECORDS(primary[secondary]) |	REC
TRACKS(primary[secondary])}	TRK
VOLUMES(volser[volser...])	VOL
[ATTEMPTS(number|2)]	ATT
[AUTORIZATION(entrypoint[string])]	AUTH
[BUFFERSPACE(size)]	BUFSP, BUFSPC
[CODE(code)]	---
[CONTROLINTERVALSIZE(size)]	CSZ, CNVSZ
[CONTROLPW(password)]	CTLPW
[DESTAGEWAIT|NODESTAGEWAIT]	DSTGW NDSTGW
[ERASE|NOERASE]	ERAS NERAS
[EXCEPTIONEXIT(entrypoint)]	EEXT
[FILE(dname)]	---
[FREESPACE(CI-percent[CA-percent]|0 0)]	FSPC
[IMBED|NOIMBED]	IMBD NIMBD
[KEYRANGES((lowkey highkey) [(lowkey highkey)...])]	KRNG
[KEYS(length offset|64 0)]	---
[MASTERPW(password)]	MRPW
[MODEL(entryname[/password] [catname[/password]])]	---
[ORDERED|UNORDERED]	ORD UNORD
[OWNER(ownerid)]	---
[READPW(password)]	RDPW
* [RECATALOG|NORECATALOG	RCTLG NRCTLG
[RECORDSIZE(average maximum| 4086 32600)]	RECSZ
[REPLICATE|NOREPLICATE]	REPL NREPL
[REUSE|NOREUSE]	RUS NRUS
[SHAREOPTIONS(crossregion [crosssystem]|1 3)]	SHR
[SPEED|RECOVERY]	--- RCVY
[STAGE|BIND|CYLINDERFAULT]	--- --- CYLF
[TO(date)|FOR(days)]	--- ---
[UNIQUE|SUBALLOCATION]	UNQ SUBAL
[UNIQUEKEY|NONUNIQUEKEY]	UNQK NUNQK
[UPDATEPW(password)]	UPDPW
[UPGRADE|NOUPGRADE]	UPG NUPG
[WRITECHECK|NOWRITECHECK])	WCK NWCK

(Continued)

* This parameter applies to ICF catalogs only.

DEFINE ALTERNATEINDEX (continued)

Parameters	Abbrev.
[DATA	---
([ATTEMPTS(number)]	ATT
[AUTHORIZATION(entrypoint[string])]	AUTH
[BUFFERSPACE(size)]	BUFSP, BUFSPC
[CODE(code)]	---
[CONTROLINTERVALSIZE(size)]	CISZ, CNVSZ
[CONTROLPW(password)]	CTLPW
[CYLINDERS(primary[secondary]) |	CYL
RECORDS(primary[secondary]) |	REC
TRACKS(primary[secondary])]	TRK
[DESTAGEWAIT | NODESTAGEWAIT]	DSTGW NDSTGW
[ERASE | NOERASE]	ERAS NERAS
[EXCEPTIONEXIT(entrypoint)]	EEXT
[FILE(dname)]	---
[FREESPACE(CI-percent[CA-percent])]	FSPC
[KEYRANGES(lowkey highkey)	KRNG
[(lowkey highkey)...])]	
[KEYS(length offset)]	---
[MASTERPW(password)]	MRPW
[MODEL(entryname[/password]	---
[catname[/password]])]	
[NAME(entryname)]	---
[ORDERED | UNORDERED]	ORD UNORD
[OWNER(ownerid)]	---
[READPW(password)]	RDPW
[RECORDSIZE(average maximum)]	RECSZ
[REUSE | NOREUSE]	RUS NRUS
[SHAREOPTIONS(crossregion[crosssystem])]	SHR
[SPEED | RECOVERY]	--- RCVY
[STAGE | BIND | CYLINDERFAULT]	--- --- CYLF
[UNIQUE | SUBALLOCATION]	UNQ SUBAL
[UNIQUEKEY | NONUNIQUEKEY]	UNQK NUNQK
[UPDATEPW(password)]	UPDPW
[VOLUMES(volser[volser...])]	VOL
[WRITECHECK | NOWRITECHECK])]	WCK NWCK

Parameters	Abbrev.
[INDEX	IX
([ATTEMPTS(number)]	ATT
[AUTHORIZATION(entrypoint[string])]	AUTH
[CODE(code)]	---
[CONTROLINTERVALSIZE(size)]	CISZ
[CONTROLPW(password)]	CTLPW
[CYLINDERS(primary[secondary]) |	CYL
RECORDS(primary[secondary]) |	REC
TRACKS(primary[secondary])]	TRK
[DESTAGEWAIT | NODESTAGEWAIT]	DSTGW NDSTGW
[EXCEPTIONEXIT(entrypoint)]	EEXT
[FILE(dname)]	---
[IMBED | NOIMBED]	IMBD NIMBD
[MASTERPW(password)]	MRPW
[MODEL(entryname[/password]	---
[catname[/password]])]	
[NAME(entryname)]	---
[ORDERED | UNORDERED]	ORD UNORD
[OWNER(ownerid)]	---
[READPW(password)]	RDPW
[REPLICATE | NOREPLICATE]	REPL NREPL
[REUSE | NOREUSE]	RUS NRUS
[SHAREOPTIONS(crossregion[crosssystem])]	SHR
[STAGE | BIND | CYLINDERFAULT]	--- --- CYLF
[UNIQUE | SUBALLOCATION]	UNQ SUBAL
[UPDATEPW(password)]	UPDPW
[VOLUMES(volser[volser...])]	VOL
[WRITECHECK | NOWRITECHECK])]	WCK NWCK
[CATALOG(catname[/password])]	CAT

Parameters	Abbrev.
DEFINE CLUSTER	DEF CL
(NAME(entryname)	---
{CYLINDERS(primary[secondary])|	CYL
RECORDS(primary[secondary])|	REC
TRACKS(primary[secondary])}	TRK
VOLUMES(volser[volser...])	VOL
[ATTEMPTS(number|2)]	ATT
AUTHORIZATION(entrypoint[string])]	AUTH
[BUFFERSPACE(size)]	BUFSP, BUFSPC
[CODE(code)]	---
[CONTROLINTERVALSIZE(size)]	CISZ, CNVSZ
[CONTROLPW(password)]	CTLPW
[DESTAGEWAIT|NODESTAGEWAIT]	DSTGW NDSTGW
[ERASE|NOERASE]	ERAS NERAS
[EXCEPTIONEXIT(entrypoint)]	EEXT
[FILE(dname)]	---
[FREESPACE(CI-percent [CA-percent]|0 0)]	FSPC
[IMBED|NOIMBED]	IMBD NIMBD
[INDEXED|NOINDEXED|NUMBERED]	IXD NIXD NUMD
[KEYRANGES((lowkey highkey) [(lowkey highkey)...])]	KRNG
[KEYS(length offset|64 0)]	---
[MASTERPW(password)]	MRPW
[MODEL(entryname[/password] [catname[/password]])]	---
[ORDERED|UNORDERED]	ORD UNORD
[OWNER(ownerid)]	---
[READPW(password)]	RDPW
* [RECATALOG|NORECATALOG]	RCTLG NRCTLG
[RECORDSIZE(average maximum)]	RECSG
[REPLICATE|NOREPLICATE]	REPL NREPL
[REUSE|NOREUSE]	RUS NRUS
[SHAREOPTIONS(crossregion [crosssystem]|1 3)]	SHR
[SPANNED|NONSPANNED]	SPND NSPND
[SPEED|RECOVERY]	--- RCVY
[STAGE|BIND|CYLINDERFAULT]	--- --- CYLF
[TO(date)|FOR(days)]	--- ---
[UNIQUE|SUBALLOCATION]	UNQ SUBAL
[UPDATEPW(password)]	UPDPW
[WRITECHECK|NOWRITECHECK])	WCK NWCK

(Continued)

* This parameter applies to ICF catalogs only.

DEFINE CLUSTER (continued)

Parameters	Abbrev.
[DATA	
([ATTEMPTS(number)]	ATT
[AUTHORIZATION(entrypoint[string])]	AUTH
[BUFFERSPACE(size)]	BUFSP, BUFSPC
[CODE(code)]	---
[CONTROLINTERVALSIZE(size)]	CISZ, CNVSZ
[CONTROLPW(password)]	CTLPW
[CYLINDERS(primary[secondary])|	CYL
RECORDS(primary[secondary])|	REC
TRACKS(primary[secondary])]	TRK
[DESTAGEWAIT|NODESTAGEWAIT]	DSTGW NDSTGW
[ERASE|NOERASE]	ERAS NERAS
[EXCEPTIONEXIT(entrypoint)]	EEXT
[FILE(dname)]	---
[FREESPACE(CI-percent[CA-percent])]	FSPC
[KEYRANGES((lowkey highkey)	KRNG
[(lowkey highkey)...])]	
[KEYS(length offset)]	---
[MASTERPW(password)]	MRPW
[MODEL(entryname[/password]	---
[catname[/password]])]	
[NAME(entryname)]	---
[ORDERED|UNORDERED]	ORD UNORD
[OWNER(ownerid)]	---
[READPW(password)]	RDPW
[RECORDSIZE(average maximum)]	RECSG
[REUSE|NOREUSE]	RUS NRUS
[SHAREOPTIONS(crossregion[crosssystem])]	SHR
[SPANNED|NONSPANNED]	SPND NSPND
[SPEED|RECOVERY]	--- RCVY
[STAGE|BIND|CYLINDERFAULT]	--- --- CYLF
[UNIQUE|SUBALLOCATION]	UNQ SUBAL
[UPDATEPW(password)]	UPDPW
[VOLUMES(volser[volser...])]	VOL
[WRITECHECK|NOWRITECHECK]	WCK NWCK

(Continued)

DEFINE CLUSTER (continued)

<table>
<tr><th>Parameters</th><th>Abbrev.</th></tr>
<tr><td>[INDEX</td><td>IX</td></tr>
<tr><td>([ATTEMPTS(number)]</td><td>ATT</td></tr>
<tr><td>[AUTHORIZATION(entrypoint[string])]</td><td>AUTH</td></tr>
<tr><td>[CODE(code)]</td><td>---</td></tr>
<tr><td>[CONTROLINTERVALSIZE(size)]</td><td>CISZ, CNVSZ</td></tr>
<tr><td>[CONTROLPW(password)]</td><td>CTLPW</td></tr>
<tr><td>[CYLINDERS(primary[secondary])|</td><td>CYL</td></tr>
<tr><td>RECORDS(primary[secondary])|</td><td>REC</td></tr>
<tr><td>TRACKS(primary[secondary])]</td><td>TRK</td></tr>
<tr><td>[DESTAGEWAIT|NODESTAGEWAIT]</td><td>DSTGW NDSTGW</td></tr>
<tr><td>[EXCEPTIONEXIT(entrypoint)]</td><td>EEXT</td></tr>
<tr><td>[FILE(dname)]</td><td>---</td></tr>
<tr><td>[IMBED|NOIMBED]</td><td>IMBD NIMBD</td></tr>
<tr><td>[MASTERPW(password)]</td><td>MRPW</td></tr>
<tr><td>[MODEL(entryname[/password]</td><td>---</td></tr>
<tr><td>[catname[/password]])]</td><td></td></tr>
<tr><td>[NAME(entryname)]</td><td>---</td></tr>
<tr><td>[ORDERED|UNORDERED]</td><td>RD UNORD</td></tr>
<tr><td>[OWNER(ownerid)]</td><td>---</td></tr>
<tr><td>[READPW(password)]</td><td>RDPW</td></tr>
<tr><td>[REPLICATE|NOREPLICATE]</td><td>REPL NREPL</td></tr>
<tr><td>[REUSE|NOREUSE]</td><td>RUS NRUS</td></tr>
<tr><td>[SHAREOPTIONS(crossregion[crosssystem])]</td><td>SHR</td></tr>
<tr><td>[STAGE|BIND|CYLINDERFAULT]</td><td>--- --- CYLF</td></tr>
<tr><td>[UNIQUE|SUBALLOCATION]</td><td>UNQ SUBAL</td></tr>
<tr><td>[UPDATEPW(password)]</td><td>UPDPW</td></tr>
<tr><td>[VOLUMES(volser[volser...])]</td><td>VOL</td></tr>
<tr><td>[WRITECHECK|NOWRITECHECK]</td><td>WCK NWCK</td></tr>
<tr><td></td><td></td></tr>
<tr><td>[CATALOG(catname[/password])]</td><td>CAT</td></tr>
</table>

<table>
<tr><th>Parameters</th><th>Abbrev.</th></tr>
<tr><td>DEFINE GENERATIONDATAGROUP</td><td>DEF GDG</td></tr>
<tr><td>(NAME(entryname)</td><td>---</td></tr>
<tr><td>LIMIT(limit)</td><td>LIM</td></tr>
<tr><td>[EMPTY|<u>NOEMPTY</u>]</td><td>EMP NEMP</td></tr>
<tr><td>[OWNER(ownerid)]</td><td>---</td></tr>
<tr><td>[SCRATCH|<u>NOSCRATCH</u>]</td><td>SCR NSCR</td></tr>
<tr><td>[TO(date)|FOR(days)])</td><td>---</td></tr>
<tr><td></td><td></td></tr>
<tr><td>[CATALOG(catname[/password])]</td><td>CAT</td></tr>
</table>

<table>
<tr><th>Parameters</th><th>Abbrev.</th></tr>
<tr><td>DEFINE PATH</td><td>DEF ---</td></tr>
<tr><td>(NAME(entryname)</td><td>---</td></tr>
<tr><td>PATHENTRY(entryname[/password])</td><td>PENT</td></tr>
<tr><td>[ATTEMPTS(number|<u>2</u>)]</td><td>ATT</td></tr>
<tr><td>[AUTHORIZATION(entrypoint[string])]</td><td>AUTH</td></tr>
<tr><td>[CODE(code)]</td><td>---</td></tr>
<tr><td>[CONTROLPW(password)]</td><td>CTLPW</td></tr>
<tr><td>[FILE(dname)]</td><td>---</td></tr>
<tr><td>[MASTERPW(password)]</td><td>MRPW</td></tr>
<tr><td>[MODEL(entryname[/password]</td><td>---</td></tr>
<tr><td>[catname[/password]])]</td><td></td></tr>
<tr><td>[OWNER(ownerid)]</td><td>---</td></tr>
<tr><td>[READPW(password)]</td><td>RDPW</td></tr>
<tr><td>* [RECATALOG|<u>NORECATALOG</u>]</td><td>RCTLG NRCTLG</td></tr>
<tr><td>[TO(date)|FOR(days)]</td><td>--- ---</td></tr>
<tr><td>[<u>UPDATE</u>|NOUPDATE]</td><td>UPD NUPD</td></tr>
<tr><td>[UPDATEPW(password)])</td><td>UPDPW</td></tr>
<tr><td></td><td></td></tr>
<tr><td>[CATALOG(catname[/password])]</td><td>CAT</td></tr>
</table>

* This parameter applies to ICF catalogs only.

<table>
<tr><th>Parameters</th><th>Abbrev.</th></tr>
<tr><td>DEFINE SPACE</td><td>DEF SPC</td></tr>
<tr><td>({CANDIDATE|</td><td>CAN</td></tr>
<tr><td>CYLINDERS(primary[secondary])|</td><td>CYL</td></tr>
<tr><td>RECORDS(primary[secondary])</td><td>REC</td></tr>
<tr><td>RECORDSIZE(average maximum)|</td><td>RECSZ</td></tr>
<tr><td>TRACKS(primary[secondary])}</td><td>TRK</td></tr>
<tr><td>VOLUMES(volser[volser...])</td><td>VOL</td></tr>
<tr><td>[FILE(dname)])</td><td>---</td></tr>
<tr><td></td><td></td></tr>
<tr><td>[CATALOG(catname[/password])]</td><td>CAT</td></tr>
</table>

<table>
<tr><th></th><th>Parameters</th><th>Abbrev.</th></tr>
<tr><td></td><td>DEFINE USERCATALOG|MASTERCATALOG</td><td>DEF UCAT MCAT</td></tr>
<tr><td></td><td>(NAME(entryname)</td><td>---</td></tr>
<tr><td></td><td>{CYLINDERS(primary[secondary])|</td><td>CYL</td></tr>
<tr><td></td><td>RECORDS(primary[secondary])|</td><td>REC</td></tr>
<tr><td></td><td>TRACKS(primary[secondary])}</td><td>TRK</td></tr>
<tr><td></td><td>VOLUME(volser)</td><td>VOL</td></tr>
<tr><td></td><td>[ATTEMPTS(number|2)]</td><td>ATT</td></tr>
<tr><td></td><td>[AUTHORIZATION(entrypoint[string])]</td><td>AUTH</td></tr>
<tr><td></td><td>[BUFFERSPACE(size|3072)]</td><td>BUFSP, BUFSPC</td></tr>
<tr><td>*</td><td>[BUFND(number)]</td><td>BFND</td></tr>
<tr><td>*</td><td>[BUFNI(number)]</td><td>BFNI</td></tr>
<tr><td></td><td>[CODE(code)]</td><td>---</td></tr>
<tr><td>*</td><td>[CONTROLINTERVALSIZE(size)]</td><td>CISZ, CNVSZ</td></tr>
<tr><td></td><td>[CONTROLPW(password)]</td><td>CTLPW</td></tr>
<tr><td></td><td>[DESTAGEWAIT|NODESTAGEWAIT]</td><td>DSTGW NDSTGW</td></tr>
<tr><td></td><td>[FILE(dname)]</td><td>---</td></tr>
<tr><td>*</td><td>[FREESPACE(CI-percent[CA-percent]|0 0)]</td><td>FSPC</td></tr>
<tr><td>*</td><td>[IMBED|NOIMBED]</td><td>IMBD NIMBD</td></tr>
<tr><td></td><td>[MASTERPW(password)]</td><td>MRPW</td></tr>
<tr><td></td><td>[MODEL(entryname[/password]
[catname[/password]])]</td><td>---</td></tr>
<tr><td></td><td>[OWNER(ownerid)]</td><td>---</td></tr>
<tr><td></td><td>[READPW(password)]</td><td>RDPW</td></tr>
<tr><td>*</td><td>[RECORDSIZE(average maximum)]</td><td>RECSZ</td></tr>
<tr><td></td><td>[RECOVERABLE|NOTRECOVERABLE]</td><td>RVBL NRVBL</td></tr>
<tr><td>*</td><td>[REPLICATE|NOREPLICATE]</td><td>REPL NREPL</td></tr>
<tr><td>*</td><td>[SHAREOPTIONS(crossregion[crosssystem]|3 4)]</td><td>SHR</td></tr>
<tr><td>*</td><td>[STRNO(number)]</td><td>---</td></tr>
<tr><td></td><td>[TO(date)|FOR(days)]</td><td>--- ---</td></tr>
<tr><td></td><td>[UPDATEPW(password)]</td><td>UPDPW</td></tr>
<tr><td>*</td><td>[VSAMCATALOG|ICFCATALOG]</td><td>VSAMCAT ICFCAT</td></tr>
<tr><td></td><td>[WRITECHECK|NOWRITECHECK])</td><td>WCK NWCK</td></tr>
</table>

<table>
<tr><th></th><th>Parameters</th><th>Abbrev.</th></tr>
<tr><td></td><td>[DATA</td><td>---</td></tr>
<tr><td></td><td>([BUFFERSPACE(size)]</td><td>BUFSP, BUFSPC</td></tr>
<tr><td></td><td>[CYLINDERS(primary[secondary])|</td><td>CYL</td></tr>
<tr><td></td><td>RECORDS(primary[secondary])|</td><td>REC</td></tr>
<tr><td></td><td>TRACKS(primary[secondary])]</td><td>TRK</td></tr>
<tr><td>*</td><td>[BUFND(number)]</td><td>BFND</td></tr>
<tr><td>*</td><td>[CONTROLINTERVALSIZE(size)]</td><td>CISZ, CNVSZ</td></tr>
<tr><td></td><td>[DESTAGEWAIT|NODESTAGEWAIT]</td><td>DSTGW NDSTGW</td></tr>
<tr><td>*</td><td>[FREESPACE(CI-percent[CA-percent]|0 0)]</td><td>FSPC</td></tr>
<tr><td>*</td><td>[RECORDSIZE(average maximum)]</td><td>RECSZ</td></tr>
<tr><td></td><td>[RECOVERABLE|NOTRECOVERABLE]</td><td>RVBL NRVBL</td></tr>
<tr><td></td><td>[WRITECHECK|NOWRITECHECK])]</td><td>WCK NWCK</td></tr>
</table>

* This parameter applies to ICF catalogs only.

DEFINE USERCATALOG|MASTERCATALOG (continued)

	Parameters	Abbrev.
	[INDEX	IX
	([CYLINDERS(primary)|	CYL
	RECORDS(primary)|	REC
	TRACKS(primary)]	TRK
*	[BUFNI(number)]	BFNI
*	[CONTROLINTERVALSIZE(size)]	CISZ or CNVSZ
	[DESTAGEWAIT|NODESTAGEWAIT]	DSTGW NDSTGW
*	[<u>IMBED</u>|NOIMBED]	IMBD NIMBD
*	[REPLICATE|<u>NOREPLICATE</u>]	REPL NREPL
	[WRITECHECK|NOWRITECHECK])]	WCK NWCK
	[CATALOG(mastercatname[/password])]	CAT

	Parameters	Abbrev.
	DELETE	DEL
	(entryname[/password]	---
	[entryname[/password]...])	
	[ALIAS|	---
	ALTERNATEINDEX|	AIX
	CLUSTER|	CL
	GENERATIONDATAGROUP|	GDG
	NONVSAM|	NVSAM
	PAGESPACE|	PGSPC
	PATH|	---
	SPACE|	SPC
*	TRUENAME|	TNAME
*	VVR|	
	USERCATALOG|	UCAT
	PAGESPACE|]	PGSPC
	[ERASE|NOERASE]	ERAS NERAS
	[FILE(dname)]	---
	[FORCE|<u>NOFORCE</u>]	FRC NFRC
	[PURGE|<u>NOPURGE</u>]	PRG NPRG
*	[RECOVERY|<u>NORECOVERY</u>]	RCVRY NRCVRY
	[<u>SCRATCH</u>|NOSCRATCH]	SCR NSCR
	[CATALOG(catname[/password])]	CAT

Parameters	Abbrev.
EXPORT	EXP
usercatname[/password]	---
DISCONNECT	DCON

Parameters	Abbrev.
EXPORT	EXP
entryname[/password]	---
{OUTFILE(dname)|OUTDATASET(entryname)}	OFILE ODS
[INFILE(dname)]	IFILE
[ERASE|NOERASE]	ERAS NERAS
[INHIBITSOURCE|<u>NOINHIBITSOURCE</u>]	INHS NINHS
[INHIBITTARGET|<u>NOINHIBITTARGET</u>]	INHT NINHT
[PURGE|<u>NOPURGE</u>]	PRG NPRG
[TEMPORARY|<u>PERMANENT</u>]	TEMP PERM

* This parameter applies to ICF catalogs only.

Parameters	Abbrev.
IMPORT	IMP
CONNECT	CON
OBJECTS((usercatname	OBJ
DEVICETYPE(devtype)	DEVT
VOLUMES(volser)))	VOL
[CATALOG(mastercatname[/password])]	CAT

Parameters	Abbrev.
IMPORT	IMP
{INFILE(dname)|INDATASET(entryname)}	IFILE IDS
{OUTFILE(dname[/password])|	OFILE
OUTDATASET(entryname[/password])}	ODS
[ERASE|NOERASE]	ERAS NERAS
[INTOEMPTY]	IEMPTY
[OBJECTS((entryname	OBJ
[FILE(dname)]	---
[KEYRANGES((lowkey highkey)	KRNG
[(lowkey highkey)...])]	
[NEWNAME(newname)]	NEWNM
[ORDERED|UNORDERED]	ORD UNORD
[VOLUMES(volser[volser...])])	VOL
[(entryname...)...])]	
[PURGE|<u>NOPURGE</u>]	PRG NPRG
[SAVRAC|<u>NOSAVRAC</u>]	--- ---
[CATALOG(catname[/password])]	CAT

Parameters	Abbrev.
LISTCAT	LISTC
[CATALOG(catname[/password])]	CAT
[ENTRIES(entryname[/password]	ENT
[entryname[/password]...])|	
LEVEL(level)]	LVL
[ALIAS]	---
[ALTERNATEINDEX]	AIX
[CLUSTER]	CL
[DATA]	---
[GENERATIONDATAGROUP]	GDG
[INDEX]	IX
[NONVSAM]	NVSAM
[PAGESPACE]	PGSPC
[PATH]	---
[SPACE]	SPC
[USERCATALOG]	UCAT
[ALL|	---
ALLOCATION|	ALLOC
HISTORY|	HIST
<u>NAME</u>|	---
VOLUME]	VOL
[CREATION(days)]	CREAT
[EXPIRATION(days)]	EXPIR
* [FILE(dname)]	---
[NOTUSABLE]	NUS
[OUTFILE(dname)]	OFILE
[SPACE]	SPC

* This parameter applies to ICF catalogs only.

```
| Parameters                                          | Abbrev.      |
|                                                     |              |
| PRINT                                               |              |
|    {INFILE(dname[/password])|                       | IFILE        |
|     INDATASET(entryname[/password])}                | IDS          |
|    [OUTFILE(dname)]                                 | OFILE        |
|    [CHARACTER|DUMP|HEX]                             | CHAR --- ---|
|    [FROMKEY(key)|FROMADDRESS(address)|              | FKEY FADDR   |
|     FROMNUMBER(number)|SKIP(count)]                 | FNUM ---     |
|    [TOKEY(key)|TOADDRESS(address)|                  | --- TADDR    |
|     TONUMBER(number)|COUNT(count)]                  | TNUM ---     |
```

```
| Parameters                                          | Abbrev.      |
|                                                     |              |
| REPRO                                               | ---          |
|    {INFILE(dname[/password]                         | IFILE        |
|      [  ENVIRONMENT(DUMMY)])|                        | ENV DUM      |
|    INDATASET(entryname[/password]                   | IDS          |
|       [  ENVIRONMENT(DUMMY)])}                      | ENV DUM      |
|    {OUTFILE(dname[/password])|                      | OFILE        |
|     OUTDATASET(entryname[/password])}               | ODS          |
|*   [ENTRIES(entryname[/password])                   | ENT          |
|       [entryname[/password]...])|                   |              |
|*      LEVEL(level)]                                 | LVL          |
|*   [FILE(dname)]                                    | ---          |
|    [FROMKEY(key)|FROMADDRESS(address)|              | FKEY FADDR   |
|     FROMNUMBER(number)|SKIP(count)]                 | FNUM ---     |
|*   [MERGECAT|NOMERGECAT]                            | MRGC NMRGC   |
|    [REPLACE|NOREPLACE]                              | REP NREP     |
|    [REUSE|NOREUSE]                                  | RUS NRUS     |
|    [TOKEY(key)|TOADDRESS(address)|                  | --- TADDR    |
|     TONUMBER(number)|COUNT(count)]                  | TNUM ---     |
```

```
| Parameters                                          | Abbrev.      |
|                                                     |              |
| VERIFY                                              | VFY          |
|    {FILE(dname[/password])|                         | ---          |
|     DATASET(entryname[/password])}                  | DS           |
```

```
| Parameters                                          | Abbrev.      |
|                                                     |              |
| IF                                                  |              |
|    {LASTCC|MAXCC}{[  comparand][  number]}          |              |
|    THEN[  command|                                  |              |
|      DO                                             |              |
|      command set                                    |              |
|      END]                                           |              |
|    [ELSE[  command|                                 |              |
|      DO                                             |              |
|      command set                                    |              |
|      END]]                                          |              |
```

```
| Parameters                                          | Abbrev.      |
| SET                                                 |              |
|    {MAXCC|LASTCC}{[  ]=[  ]number}                  |              |
```

* This parameter applies to ICF catalogs only.

appendix **C**

Cobol Syntax for VSAM

Format Notation

- Reserved words are printed in uppercase letters.
- Keywords are underlined. Their use is required by the syntax unless the format itself is optional.
- All data-names and paragraph names (programmer-defined) are in lowercase letters.
- One and only one choice is required for the vertically stacked options within braces.
- Items within square brackets may be used or omitted depending on program requirements.
- Ellipses following an item indicate that the item can be repeated any number of times.

SELECT STATEMENT

FORMAT 1--VSAM SEQUENTIAL FILE ENTRIES (ESDS)

FILE-CONTROL

```
     SELECT [OPTIONAL] file-name
     ASSIGN TO assignment-name-1  [assignment-name-2]...

                            ┌AREA ┐
    [RESERVE integer        │     │   ]
                            └AREAS┘
       [ORGANIZATION IS SEQUENTIAL]
       [ACCESS MODE IS SEQUENTIAL]
    [PASSWORD IS data-name-1]
    [FILE STATUS IS data-name-2].
```

FORMAT 2--VSAM INDEXED FILE ENTRIES (KSDS)

FILE-CONTROL.

```
     SELECT file-name
     ASSIGN TO assignment-name  [assignment-name-2]...
                            ┌AREA ┐
    [RESERVE integer        │     │    ]
                            └AREAS┘
     ORGANIZATION IS INDEXED
                         ┌SEQUENTIAL┐
    [ACCESS MODE IS      │RANDOM    │      ]
                         └DYNAMIC   ┘
     RECORD KEY IS data-name-3
         [PASSWORD IS data-name-1]
    [ALTERNATE RECORD KEY IS data-name-4
         [PASSWORD IS data-name-5]
       [WITH DUPLICATES] ]...
    [FILE STATUS IS data-name-2].
```

FORMAT 3--VSAM Relative File Entries (RRDS)

FILE-CONTROL.

```
     SELECT file-name
     ASSIGN TO assignment-name-1  [assignment-name-2]...
                           ┌AREA ┐
    [RESERVE integer       │     │   ]
                           └AREAS┘
     ORGANIZATION IS RELATIVE
                       ┌ SEQUENTIAL [RELATIVE KEY IS data-name-6]  ┐
                       │  ┌RANDOM ┐                                 │ ]
    [ACCESS MODE IS    │  │       │   [RELATIVE KEY IS data-name-7 │
                       └  └DYNAMIC┘                                ┘
    [PASSWORD IS data-name-1]
    [FILE STATUS IS data-name-2].
```

OPEN STATEMENT

FORMAT 1--VSAM Sequential and Indexed Files.

```
            ⎧INPUT ⎫
OPEN        ⎨OUTPUT⎬     file-name-1 [file-name-2]....
            ⎪I-O   ⎪
            ⎩EXTEND⎭
```

FORMAT 2--VSAM Relative Files

```
            ⎧INPUT ⎫
OPEN        ⎨OUTPUT⎬     file-name-1 [file-name-2]....
            ⎩I-O   ⎭
```

WRITE STATEMENT

FORMAT 1--VSAM Sequential Files

```
WRITE record-name  [FROM identifier]
```

FORMAT 2--VSAM Indexed and Relative Files

```
WRITE    record-name  [FROM  identifier ]
     [INVALID KEY   imperative-statement]
```

START STATEMENT

```
START file-name [KEY IS  ⎧EQUAL TO    ⎫
                         ⎪=           ⎪
                         ⎨GREATER THAN⎬      data-name]
                         ⎪>           ⎪
                         ⎪NOT LESS THAN⎪
                         ⎩NOT <       ⎭
     [INVALID KEY   imperative-statement]
```

READ STATEMENT

FORMAT 1--Sequential Retrieval

```
READ file-name  [NEXT]  RECORD  [INTO identifier]
     [AT END  imperative-statement]
```

FORMAT 2--Random Retrieval

```
READ  file-name  RECORD  [INTO identifier]
     [KEY IS data-name]
     [INVALID KEY  imperative-statement]
```

DELETE STATEMENT

```
DELETE  file-name  RECORD
     [INVALID KEY  imperative statement]
```

REWRITE STATEMENT

```
REWRITE  record-name  [FROM identifier]
     [INVALID KEY  imperative statement]
```

CLOSE STATEMENT

```
CLOSE  file-name-1  file-name-2  [WITH LOCK]
```

appendix D

Record-Length Formulas for Alternate Indexes

The following formulas may be used to determine record lengths for alternate index allocations. Values thus calculated are substituted in the RECORDSIZE parameter.

Unique key KSDS

5 + length of alternate key + length of prime key

Nonunique key KSDS

5 + length of alternate key + $n \times$ length of prime key

where n is the number of average and maximum occurrences of the nonunique alternate key.

Unique key ESDS

5 + length of alternate key + 4 (for RBA pointers)

Nonunique key ESDS

5 + length of alternate key + $n \times 4$

where n is the number of average and maximum occurrences of nonunique alternate key.

appendix **E**

Track Capacity for IBM 3380 and IBM 3350 for Different CI Sizes

	Number of CI's per track	
CI size	**IBM 3380***	**IBM 3350†**
512	46	27
1024	31	15
2048	18	8
4096	10	4
6144	6	3
8192	5	2

*Number of bytes per track for IBM 3380 = 47,968.
†Number of bytes per track for IBM 3350 = 19,254.

appendix F

File Status Values and Their Meanings

Status key value	Meaning
00	Successful completion of function
02	Duplicate key condition found for nonunique key alternate index
10	End-of-file condition or an optional ESDS file not available
20	No further information
21	Sequence error for sequential load in a KSDS
22	Duplicate key found on a WRITE
23	Record not found
24	No space found to add records for a KSDS or an RRDS
30	No further information
34	No space found to add record for an ESDS
90	No further information
91	Password failure
92	Logic error
93	Resource (enough virtual storage) not available
94	No current record pointer for sequential request
95	Invalid or incomplete file information
96	No DD card
97	Data set was improperly closed; implicit verify issued and file successfully opened (only DF/EF)

appendix G

File Status Values for OPEN Requests and Their Meanings

Status code	Possible reasons
00	Successful open.
90	KSDS is opened for OUTPUT and the access mode is either RANDOM or DYNAMIC. File to be opened I-O is unloaded.
91	Password failure.
92	Logic error. File to be opened is already open.
93	Sufficient virtual storage unavailable. Retry after increasing value of REGION parameter. Resource not available because it is in use elsewhere and the shareoptions do not allow the requested processing option.
95	HURBA of file to be opened OUTPUT is not zero. Length and/or offset of record key in FD does not match the catalog. An attempt was made to open a KSDS as an ESDS.
96	Missing DD card.
97	OPEN successful after an implicit VERIFY.

appendix H

Valid Combinations of Cobol I/O Verbs, ACCESS MODEs, and OPEN Modes for a KSDS

<table>
<tr><th rowspan="2">ACCESS MODE</th><th colspan="4">OPEN mode</th></tr>
<tr><th>INPUT</th><th>OUTPUT</th><th>I-O</th><th>EXTEND</th></tr>
<tr><td>SEQUENTIAL</td><td>OPEN
READ
START</td><td>OPEN

WRITE</td><td>OPEN
READ
START

REWRITE
DELETE</td><td>OPEN

WRITE</td></tr>
<tr><td>RANDOM</td><td>OPEN
READ</td><td>OPEN

WRITE</td><td>OPEN
READ
WRITE
REWRITE
DELETE</td><td></td></tr>
<tr><td>DYNAMIC</td><td>OPEN
READ
START</td><td>OPEN

WRITE</td><td>OPEN
READ
START
WRITE
REWRITE
DELETE</td><td></td></tr>
</table>

appendix I

Valid Combinations of Cobol I/O Verbs, ACCESS MODEs, and OPEN Modes for an RRDS

ACCESS MODE	OPEN mode		
	INPUT	OUTPUT	I-O
SEQUENTIAL	OPEN READ START	OPEN WRITE	OPEN READ START REWRITE DELETE
RANDOM	OPEN READ	OPEN WRITE	OPEN READ WRITE REWRITE DELETE
DYNAMIC	OPEN READ START	OPEN WRITE	OPEN READ START WRITE REWRITE DELETE

Bibliography of Suggested IBM Manuals

Access Method Services and VSAM

GC26-3838 *OS/VS Virtual Storage Access Method (VSAM) Programmer's Guide.*
GC26-3842 *Planning for Enhanced VSAM under OS/VS.*
GC26-3819 *OS/VS Virtual Storage Access Method (VSAM): Options for Advanced Applications.*
SY26-3825 *OS/VS2 Virtual Storage Access Method (VSAM) Logic.*
SY26-3826 *OS/VS2 Catalog Management Logic.*
SY35-0010 *OS/VS2 Access Method Services Logic.*
GC26-3841 *OS/VS2 Access Method Services.*
GC26-4019 *MVS/XA Access Method Services Reference.*
GC26-4015 *MVS/XA VSAM Programmer's Guide.*

Data Facility/Extended Functions

SC26-3966 *DF/EF: AMS Administration and Services.*
GH20-3960 *Data Facility Extended Function: General Information.*
SY26-3882 *OS/VS2 DF/EF: Catalog Diagnosis Reference.*
SY26-3887 *OS/VS2 Data Facility Extended Function: Diagnosis Guide.*
LY26-3888 *OS/VS2 MVS Data Facility Extended Function: Access Method Services Logic.*

VS COBOL

GC26-3857 *IBM VS COBOL for OS/VS.*
SC28-6483 *IBM OS/VS COBOL Compiler and Library Programmer's Guide.*

VS COBOL II

GC26-4042 *VS Cobol II General Information.*
GC26-4047 *VS Cobol II Application Programming: Language Reference.*
SC26-4045 *VS Cobol II Application Programming Guide.*

Miscellaneous

GC26-3902 *OS/VS2 MVS Utilities.*
GC26-3875 *OS/VS2 MVS Data Management Services Guide.*
GC28-0692 *OS/VS2 JCL.*
GC38-1002 *OS/VS Message Library: VS2 System Messages.*
GC28-1148 *MVS/XA JCL.*
Ranade, Jay VSAM: Performance, Design, and Fine Tuning.

INDEX

A

P

Q

R

S

W